D0504988

000000689247

HELLO, DARLINGS!

www.**transworldbooks**.co.uk

HELLO, DARLINGS!

The Authorized Biography of Kenny Everett

James Hogg and Robert Sellers

BANTAM PRESS

LONDON · TORONTO · SYDNEY · AUCKLAND · JOHANNESBURG

TRANSWORLD PUBLISHERS
61–63 Uxbridge Road, London W5 5SA
A Random House Group Company
www.transworldbooks.co.uk

First published in Great Britain
in 2013 by Bantam Press
an imprint of Transworld Publishers

Copyright © James Hogg and Robert Sellers 2013

James Hogg and Robert Sellers have asserted their right under the Copyright,
Designs and Patents Act 1988 to be identified as the authors of this work.

A CIP catalogue record for this book
is available from the British Library.

ISBNs 9780593072110 (hb)
9780593072127 (tpb)

This book is sold subject to the condition that it shall not,
by way of trade or otherwise, be lent, resold, hired out,
or otherwise circulated without the publisher's prior
consent in any form of binding or cover other than that
in which it is published and without a similar condition,
including this condition, being imposed on the
subsequent purchaser.

Addresses for Random House Group Ltd companies outside the UK
can be found at: www.randomhouse.co.uk
The Random House Group Ltd Reg. No. 954009

The Random House Group Limited supports the Forest Stewardship Council® (FSC®),
the leading international forest-certification organisation. Our books carrying the FSC label are
printed on FSC®-certified paper. FSC is the only forest-certification scheme supported
by the leading environmental organisations, including Greenpeace. Our paper
procurement policy can be found at www.randomhouse.co.uk/environment

Typeset in 11.5/14.5pt Minion by
Falcon Oast Graphic Art Ltd.
Printed and bound in Great Britain by
CPI Group (UK) Ltd, Croydon, CR0 4YY

DUDLEY LIBRARIES	
000000689247	
Askews & Holts	
	£18.99
GL	

For Kenny

Contents

Let's Bomb Russia!

A WEST LONDON RESTAURANT, mid-afternoon, Thursday, 2 June 1983. Film director Michael Winner and Kenny Everett have just finished a rather boozy lunch.

MW: I wonder if you could do me a favour, Kenny?

KE: If I can, Michael. Fire away!

MW: Well, I've been asked to round up a few celebrity guests for the Young Conservative rally on Sunday and I wondered if you'd help me out?

KE: Ooh, I don't know, Michael. I don't do politics. Bores me to tears!

MW: Oh, come on, Kenny. You won't be the only one there.

KE: Who else is going?

MW: Well, there's Steve Davis.

KE: What, the snooker player?

MW: That's the one. And Jimmy Tarbuck.

KE: Steve Davis and Jimmy Tarbuck? Hardly my set, Michael.

MW: Rubbish, Kenny! Look, it's just a bit of fun. All you have to do is come along to Wembley Conference Centre on Sunday. Don't worry, we'll send a car for you. You'll have some champagne, say something funny on stage and that'll be it. I'll even introduce you to the Iron Lady!

KE: Say something funny. At a Young Conservative rally? Like what?

MW: I don't know, we'll think of something.

KE: I suppose it'll have to be something controversial, as it's me . . . OK, how about 'Let's bomb Russia'?

MW: Ah! Perfect! Yes, Kenny. Start off with that.

KE: What? 'Let's bomb Russia'? Won't that upset a few people? Like the Russians, maybe?

MW: Oh, don't worry about them, dear. They'll be safely back in Moscow making homemade vodka. As I said, it's just a bit of fun. Now, what else are you going to say?

KE: I suppose I could have a pop at Labour. That'll go down well.

MW: Why not. Great idea!

KE: OK, how about 'Let's kick Michael Foot's stick away!'

MW: Brilliant, Kenny. Brilliant. You'll bring the house down. Why don't you bring some of those big hands you use on TV? You know the ones.

KE: OK, I'll try. I've already thought of a gag about Maggie!

MW: Marvellous, love. Anyway, don't you worry, we'll have a great afternoon. It's just a bit of fun. Nothing can go wrong. Another drink?

Twenty-nine years later . . .

The Running Horse public house, Davies Street, Mayfair. It's 3.30 p.m. on Friday, 12 October 2012. The authors, James Hogg and Robert Sellers, are interviewing Barry Cryer and Kenny's manager, Jo Gurnett.

BC: What a bloody mistake that was! We were filming on the Friday, and Ev said, 'Michael Winner's invited me to have some champagne and a laugh at some political thing on Sunday.' I said to him, 'Look, Ev, please, mate, don't do it.' He said, 'Oh, Baah, what are you talking about? It'll be fine.' I said, 'I know you, something will happen. I can feel it. Seriously, Ev, DON'T GO!'

JG: But there was nothing he could do. He'd promised. I had to go and collect these huge bloody hands from the BBC and take them all the way up to his flat, which was on the fourth floor! When I got there I said again, 'Ev, you're mad. Don't do it!'

BC: He did though. Bonkers!

JG: The fallout was unbelievable. I had the press on to me all the following day asking how long Kenny had been a Tory, and I kept saying to them, 'Look, he is NOT a political animal. He doesn't know the first thing about politics. Michael Winner got him drunk and persuaded him to do it for a laugh!

BC: The journalists were so cynical though. They knew he couldn't stand Thatcher and they knew he was basically taking the piss out of the audience, but they only reported the 'Let's bomb Russia' and the 'Let's kick Michael Foot's stick away' bits. They conveniently forgot to mention what he said about Thatcher, which was something like, 'I said to her this morning, I did, I said, "Margaret, that's no way to roll a joint!"' But none of them reported that. The next day, on the front page of one of the tabloids, there was a horrible Jekyll and Hyde type drawing of Kenny with the headline: 'The Idiot Face of Conservatism'. They knew full well he was taking the piss, every one of them. I spoke to Ev when he got home and he likened the event to the Nuremburg Rally, for God's sake! He couldn't stick any of them. He was apolitical.

JG: Ev thought it would become tomorrow's fish-and-chip paper, but I told him it wouldn't. I said the best way to counter this was to start turning up everywhere; Labour, SDP, Tory, all of them. 'Ooh yes,' he said. 'That's a great idea. That's what I'll do!' But he didn't. He really should have though.

Young Conservative rallies notwithstanding, Kenny Everett had been dropping incendiary devices all over the shop since 1965. And, almost twenty years after his death, he remains, in the media's eyes at least, one of our most controversial entertainers. Three sackings, several written warnings, two husbands and an incurable disease will testify to this. Yet it's worth remembering that not once did he ever set out to offend anybody. Kenny's biggest crime, if you can call it that, was failing to engage his brain before speaking; in fact he was the master of that particular art. There was no malice-aforethought in play; just a serious case of 'foot in mouth' disease. And although we can't rewrite history, we can endeavour to remind people exactly why Kenny turned up at Wembley that June afternoon. It was the same reason he turned up to every radio or television show he ever produced: to make people laugh – nothing more, nothing less.

Given the hoo-ha following his favour for Michael Winner, you'd have thought he actually had invaded Russia or assaulted Michael Foot. But is a man with a history of being controversial any more offensive when bounding on to a stage wearing big hands and shouting 'Let's kick Michael Foot's stick away' than he would be staring into a large pair of boobs? If Kenny's nemesis, Mary Whitehouse, was out of touch with the mood of the nation, so were those calling for Kenny's head over 'Let's bomb Russia'. The majority of the British public couldn't give a damn what he did on a Sunday afternoon, and those who did see his appearance at the rally knew exactly what he was up to. Billy Connolly summed it up perfectly: 'Kenny was just a man with big hands. He was a dafty man!'

You see, as far as Kenny Everett was concerned, he had a binding agreement with the British public, an agreement that transcended intrusions such as politics and outrage. He trusted us to understand what he was trying to achieve and we never let him down, which is why every attempt made by the media or the establishment to finish Kenny off – and there were many over the years – never came close to succeeding. His responsibilities were to be funny, inventive, impulsive and naughty; and ours were to digest what he did, see or hear it for what it was, and then laugh our heads off.

The purpose of this book is to remind us all that our agreement with Kenny Everett still stands, and is something that should be honoured, ad infinitum. But in order for our book to have the desired effect we must first reacquaint you with the details of said agreement, and make you aware of literally hundreds of new clauses – anecdotes, interviews, facts and surprises, the majority of which have only recently been unearthed – which will reveal how a hyperactive toddler from Liverpool inadvertently fantasized and revolutionized his way into the very fabric of our society.

Being offended by Kenny Everett meant only one thing: you were missing out on something brilliant.

1

A Liverpool Lad

KENNY EVERETT (CHRISTENED Maurice James Christopher Cole) was born on Christmas Day 1944 at the ungodly hour of three o'clock in the morning. It was a home birth, presided over by a midwife who conveniently lived next door. It was an easy delivery, although Kenny would later describe his young self as coming out shaped like a hot-water bottle.

His sister Cate was eighteen months older and can still vividly picture the infant Kenny. 'He was absolutely gorgeous. I remember his very first haircut, he used to have the most beautiful blond curly hair. I just adored him; he was my toy. He was my doll that we probably couldn't afford. I was mad about him. He was lovely until he was about nine or ten, then he became a little brat.'

Home was 14 Hereford Road in the Liverpool district of Seaforth, north Merseyside. In adult life Kenny was scathing about where he grew up, describing the street as 'a bit like a battery farm for humans in the true Coronation Street tradition'. As for the garden, or lack of one, 'if you blinked, you missed it'. Cate doesn't recognize this blunt, almost unfeeling, characterization of her childhood home, but then her brother was always fibbing to the press and defending it by saying, 'Oh, you tell them what they want to hear and then they go away and it's tomorrow's fish-and-chip paper.' Only it wasn't, claims Cate. 'The sad thing is tomorrow's fish-and-chip paper ends up in the British Library and it becomes the Bible of Saint Ev and gets added to and added to, and suddenly it becomes the truth. It's not that he deliberately told lies, he just exaggerated and told great stories, and he was always like that. Even as a child he was very imaginative, and he was always teasing people.'

In reality Hereford Road was your typical suburban street and the house a modest-sized Victorian terrace with small back and front gardens; nothing particularly special, but hardly skid row. There was a bath in the kitchen, Kenny recalled, and every week hot water was boiled on the stove and the family took it in turns to wash, in order of seniority, with Dad going in first. 'It's just as well I didn't have a younger brother,' joked Kenny. 'He'd have been swallowed by the mud!' Another exaggeration, as it turns out, for not only did the Cole residence have a bathroom, it had two! Quite a rarity for that part of Liverpool in those days. Because the houses in the street were over a hundred years old they came originally with no indoor plumbing, just the good old-fashioned outside lav. So Kenny's father, Tom, had one of the bedrooms turned into a bathroom and then later on decided to build another one. 'My father was really quite eccentric,' remembers Cate. 'He used to build things and you'd say, oh gosh, no, not another coffee table, not another cupboard. And this time it was, oh no, not another bathroom.' Built mainly out of wood, the downstairs bathroom formed part of a small extension that ran off the kitchen into the garden.

Kenny also recalled that he and his sister had to share a bed, with his head up one end, and hers down the other. True, says Cate, to a degree. Baby Kenny slept in a cot next to Cate's bed and sometimes would jump out and snuggle next to his sister at night before graduating to his own bed.

Their neighbours and the rest of the families in Hereford Road Cate remembers as, 'very friendly, they were all very civilized, and all helped each other'. These were the nouveau poor; most of them had seen better times and had lost a lot during the war. As one of Britain's busiest ports, Liverpool had been a major target for the Luftwaffe, suffering, like London, its own Blitz in 1941. By the time Maurice came along the German air assault had diminished, although there was still the odd attack, with planes coming in low to strafe the surrounding area and targets like Seaforth barracks, where American troops were stationed. Cate's first toy was a gas mask, 'and Ev's was like a crib gas mask that you could actually put the baby into'. With Hereford Road so close to the docks, not a single house escaped damage. Number 13, opposite the Coles, suffered a hit that blew its roof off. The effects of the war blighted the whole area, with bomb craters in the road and derelict buildings.

Kenny's parents had themselves been bombed out of their previous property during one of the worst attacks in the early years of the war, which demolished every house in the road. Following a bombing raid it was one of the duties of the Home Guard to cordon off the bombed houses and prevent the residents from going anywhere near them. 'Well, my mother wasn't having any of that,' says Cate. 'She went back into this cordoned-off house that had been their home, determined to get her jewellery back. She went up this broken, open staircase to the bedroom, found her dressing table and got her jewellery before she was hunted out by the Home Guard who yelled, "Don't you realize this place is about to fall down on top of you!"'

Elizabeth Cole (born Elizabeth Haugh), known to everyone as Lily, was a real character. 'If you want to sum up my mum in just a few words, think Thora Hird and Margaret Thatcher,' says Cate. 'She was very attractive, with green eyes and red hair, and beautiful skin, and she was very slim and very fashionable. I always wished she would be like a normal mother, roly-poly and up to her eyes in pastry and baked apples, a bit more mumsy and homey, but she wasn't. And she was quite difficult to talk to. You could talk to my father about anything, but you couldn't talk to my mother because she was quite egotistical. You'd start off a conversation and you'd always end up talking about her.'

Behind this façade Lily was a bag of insecurities. Cate calls her 'a little mixed up, really', on account of a difficult and tragic childhood. When Lily was two years old her sister Jane, just a year older, died as the result of a freak accident. She was innocently playing in the park on the swings when she saw her father approaching. Waving, she lost balance and fell off, hitting her head on the concrete ground. As the result of a possible skull fracture, the toddler contracted meningitis and died. The grief was unbearable; her father carried her tiny shoes in his breast pocket for the next six months until he too died; of a broken heart, people said.

Not long after this tragedy Lily and her mother moved into her aunt's house, where Lily was to grow up and enjoy a happy childhood alongside her cousins, who were to become more like brothers and sisters. Sadly, more trauma was visited upon poor Lily not long after her sixteenth birthday when her mother, who had always been quite frail and suffered from a heart condition, died of heart failure. With the sole exception of her husband's, Lily was never to attend another funeral. For much of her life she kept her emotions reined in; if she cried, she cried alone.

Tom Cole, a friend of the family, was a regular visitor to her aunt's house. Tom and Lily often went dancing together and on long walks, and steadily a romance developed. 'My father was very handsome,' claims Cate. 'Everyone said he looked like Jimmy Cagney, and in some pictures I've seen of him in his youth he certainly did. Actually, he was much better-looking than Cagney.'

The couple married by the time they were twenty-one and enjoyed a stable, loving relationship. They were so completely devoted to each other that Cate struggles to remember them ever having an argument or even hearing a cross word between them. This made it difficult for her and Maurice growing up, because they couldn't divide and rule; their parents put up a united front. 'My mother could be something of a tyrant, but Dad was just so patient. I think any other husband might have strangled my mother, but he remained supportive and caring. She was a little bit difficult, a bit sensitive, a bit touchy, a bit fiery. She was a big character and not that easy, but Dad was a saint; he was so loyal to her the whole time, and they were so happy together.'

For a while Lily ran a department at the Prudential Building Society, but gave up work when she had children and became a full-time mother. Much later, when Maurice and Cate were a little older, leaving her bored stiff at home, she had the chance to buy a distant relative's newsagent's business. 'She loved that,' says Cate. 'And she did well with that shop. She liked being there, chatting to the customers. She was a very chatty person, Mum; she never stopped talking.'

Eric Gear, Kenny's bank manager and friend, later got to know Tom and Lily well and recognized that Lily was the dominant one in the partnership. 'She was kind and helpful, but you could see that she was probably the driving force of the family. She was a good organizer, and quite methodical. Now Kenny could be a bit of a scatterbrain when it came to things like finances, but when it came to producing radio shows he had to be extremely disciplined and very methodical. And that was a characteristic that was certainly a product of his mother.'

Lily was also a brilliant gymnast in her youth, and one wonders how much of that dexterity and mobility Kenny inherited. On his television shows he traded in visual comedy to a vast degree, mimicking the movements of rock stars like Mick Jagger and Rod Stewart, or emulating Marcel Marceau in those almost surreal mime artist sketches. Lily's talents in the kitchen, however, were less impressive. Kenny joked, 'She cooked bacon that the government almost commissioned to make warships out of. She knew more ways to murder an egg than any woman alive!'

Tom Cole worked as a tugboat captain on the River Mersey and was of that generation who were thoroughly decent, hard-working, industrious and highly principled. 'He was an absolutely lovely guy,' says Cate. 'And everyone who met him never had a bad word to say about him.'

It was not difficult to see where the future Kenny Everett got his sense of humour from. Eric Gear visited Tom and Lily in Perth, after they emigrated there in the eighties, and his impression was of a very, very funny man. 'In the house, Tom wore a deaf-aid. Well, my brother and I took him out for a drive round Perth, and when we got in the car Tom immediately took his deaf-aid out and began chatting normally. When I asked him about the deaf-aid, he said the wife was less likely to nag him if she thought he couldn't hear her, so he usually kept it in. He was a lovely man, though, and quite mischievous, just like his boy. He was very laid-back and extremely jovial.'

But he was also stoical, as many people were back in the 1940s, and keenly aware and respectful of authority, believing one always had to do the right thing. 'So we were brought up very strictly and with high expectations of our manners and behaviour,' remembers Cate. 'Maurice and I always had to be super polite, well dressed and I suppose you'd say now slightly repressed. We never really stood out of line because you would earn my mother's displeasure, one look from my mother would wither anybody. We were never smacked, one would be brought into line by harsh words and made to feel guilty, so you wouldn't do it again. Nobody would cross my mother. My parents were very strict but very fair.'

Lily particularly doted on Maurice, dressing him up in little dickie bows and smart clothes, including one beautiful white outfit, short white trousers and white shirt, which Maurice ruined one Christmas seeking Father Christmas up the chimney. 'I think Maurice was very happy within the family unit,' believes Cate. 'We were a very close, very loving family. It actually used to annoy us that our parents never argued. Perhaps it was too overprotective. Perhaps we were too cloistered, too sheltered. When we finally left home we were very innocent.'

For a long time Lily's controlling influence extended to not letting her children play out in the street with the other kids. It was the local doctor, who had his surgery in Hereford Road, who finally confronted her about it and said, 'For goodness' sake, you have to let your children out to play!' Far from being horrible, the local kids were great fun and Cate and Kenny got up to all sorts of pranks with them. Cate recalls: 'Almost everyone owned a pair of roller skates and would hang out at this derelict scrap of land. Sometimes there would be fifteen kids hanging off the end of a bicycle as it tore around the tarmac, with the unlucky sod at the back of the line gathering enough momentum to send him airborne. We'd also play simple games like hopscotch, or play with hoops and skipping ropes. You just had to make your own amusement back then, which probably helped Kenny's creative bent.'

Conveniently there was a park at the bottom of Hereford Road and Cate and Maurice spent hours there playing. Sometimes they'd cross the main road and walk down to the beach, where the Mersey lapped against a sandy shoreline. Again Kenny painted a less than romantic image of the place, describing how condoms would wash ashore and that nearby were two sewage outlets pumping waste out to sea, which had a nasty habit of coming back in again with the tide. Yes, Cate agrees, it wasn't quite the Côte d'Azur, 'but it was sandy hills and water – albeit it was River Mersey water, which wasn't that clean – but still one swam and paddled and built sandcastles. We took picnics down there and pitched a tent. Looking back, we had a lot of freedom as children. Actually, we used to go out and play a lot on our own and then come back at mealtimes.'

Often on Sundays they'd join their father for a brisk walk to a park in the Waterloo district of Liverpool where there was a duck pond for little Maurice to sail his toy boat. Other times they'd visit the docks and watch the big liners coming in and out, or enjoy a trip on the ferry across the Mersey. Coming back, they might buy fish and chips at the shop that Cherie Blair's mother worked at. 'Dad was very patient with us,' remembers Cate. 'He spent a lot of time with us, and read us stories. He also had a little Ford car and used to take us out on fun day-trips. And for a special treat he would invite us on to his tugboat, where we would be fussed over by the crew and treated like royalty.'

After the ravages of the war the civic aesthetic of Liverpool had slowly begun to improve, but for Kenny the city would always be a dump, or 'cruddy' as he once referred to it, a place to escape from. Whenever he spoke about Liverpool in interviews it was in derogatory terms, conjuring up a grey and bleak place. These are feelings that find resonance with Cate: 'It wasn't a fun place to grow up in after the war. I never felt comfortable there, and I left when I was nineteen. Kenny left when he was seventeen.'

Kenny always felt strangely out of place in the city, as if he didn't belong, which in a way he didn't. The Coles were not true Scousers with deep roots in the city; the Doomsday Book records that the family originally heralded from Cornwall and Devon, and this particular branch only moved to Liverpool when Kenny's grandfather was in his twenties. 'I remember my grandfather,' says Cate. 'He was very impressive and scary and told tales of grandeur and owning vast tracts of land. We grew up on that, it became family folklore.' He sold up in Devon and was on his way to Australia to start a cattle business when his mother became ill, so they ended up settling in Liverpool. 'I think he was a gambler and a drinker,' says Cate. 'And he married an Irish woman and had five children, most of whom he ignored. He was very strict.'

Towards the end of his life he came to stay at Hereford Road. 'And it was always interesting to go into his room and talk to him,' says Cate, 'and listen to his tales of travel. He'd already visited Australia and brought back a collection of shells and other objects which he used to show us.' Years later some of the Cole family followed in their grand-father's footsteps and set off for Australia. Cate was first to emigrate with her husband and young family in 1983, and she persuaded Lily and Tom to join them in Perth two years later. Cate recalls ringing Lily one night from the balcony of her house overlooking the Indian Ocean and suggesting that her mother and father might wish to leave the cold of Formby for a new life in Australia. Lily replied in a slightly annoyed manner, 'I thought you would never ask!' Ev wanted to live in Australia as well, she claims. 'But he got too sick. He loved Sydney.'

When his childhood came up in interviews, Kenny portrayed himself as a small, weedy boy trying to circumnavigate local gangs who'd shout threateningly, 'What the bluddy 'ell er yooo looking at?' if he so much as glanced in their direction for more than a split second. 'And before you knew it,' recalled Kenny, 'your face was all over the floor.'

This image of a gentle petal of a boy who never really spoke to any-one, was constantly having to avoid bullies and asking his sister to get him out of trouble, is one that Cate simply does not recognize. 'I don't know where all that came from. There were no scrapes, not that I saw or heard about. Yes, he was smallish and slim, and so, so sensitive he picked up on every single vibe, so of course he was going to suffer in a place like Liverpool. But it wasn't a bad childhood. He was always singing and chatting. I always thought he was a very happy child, he never seemed unhappy.'

It's another case of Kenny not stopping to think before speaking to journalists – a dangerous habit that never left him. One doubts it was engineered or carried out in a conscious manner, but he was an entertainer, and when he was talking to the media he wanted to get a reaction. If the truth was boring and wouldn't get a response, he might embellish it a little. However, one porky pie, or shall we say exaggeration, eclipses all others: that of branding his parents as religious zealots, implying they were partly to blame for many of his psychological hang-ups, most notably the guilt trip about his homosexuality which he struggled with for half his adult life. According to Kenny, his family was 'very religious ... extremely Catholic'. They attended Mass every Sunday without fail, and confession once a week. It got to the stage, he claimed, where he had to come up with something sufficiently grand to confess just to keep the priest from falling asleep. Owning up to playing with himself was about as apocalyptic as it got. 'Although if God hadn't meant us to wank, he'd have put our bits and pieces somewhere where we couldn't reach them!'

All the Old Testament doom-mongering of the Church left an indelible mark on young Maurice. It was drummed into him at an impressionable age that God was watching you all the time, like some celestial Big Brother, so woe betide anyone who misbehaved or had less than saintly thoughts. 'I was brought up a true Catholic, that if you do something slightly naughty you go to purgatory for an awfully long time and it's really bad,' he complained during his interview on the BBC's *Desert Island Discs*. 'So if you commit one of these lists of sins and you don't get to confession in time, you'll go to hell FOR EVER. And hell is unimaginable agony – FOR EVER. Fancy telling that to a kid. It's outrageous.' Consequently Maurice was terrified out of his britches and in a near-constant state of neurosis as a child. He worried about everything. 'And if there was a God, why did he make me so thin and spindly?'

Again, the truth is more enlightening than the fantasy. There's no doubt that religion played a significant part in Everett's life, but the culprits weren't his parents. 'Mum and Dad were not religious freaks,' stresses Cate. 'Yes, they had a belief, but they didn't go to church all the time. I know a lot of friends who had evening prayers and used to recite Rosary; it was that sort of time. We never got involved in any of that, and we never had holy pictures hanging up either. In fact, sometimes they didn't go to Mass on Sundays, which actually was a bit problematic for us kids, because at school we had a Mass register and it wasn't just for children, it was for parents. The teacher would ask, "Did your parents go to Mass?" So that was always embarrassing.' If anything, it was years of being harassed by their children that made Tom and Lily go back to church again. Cate can't recall why they stopped going in the first place. 'Perhaps they just fancied some peace and quiet on a Sunday morning. In retrospect, I was happier when they were not in church because my mother was quite outspoken and every time the ninety-year-old priest would stumble on to the altar she'd put out this enormous, "Oh no!" or "Oh my goodness!" She was always in a hurry to get home and do things. She was very outspoken and cringe-making at times.'

No, if there was any religious axe to grind from Kenny it was a result of his experiences at school and of the teachers. 'They were pretty full-on,' admits Cate. 'It was all-pervasive. Honest to God, we could have got a PhD in Catholicism and religious doctrine, when we should really have been concentrating on maths and English and those kinds of subjects. So much of the school curriculum went into religious education.'

From the age of five Maurice had been enrolled at St Edmund's Primary School, a short walk from home. That first day was traumatic; as he watched his mother leave him in a room full of strangers he burst into tears. Reassurance was at hand from one of the teachers, or so he thought. 'There, there, don't cry, little boy,' she said. 'Or we'll nail your knees to the blackboard.'

School was almost as forbidding as church. Here authority manifested itself not as an omnipresent deity but in the nightmare-inducing form of the headmistress, who every morning rose from her desk like a human praying mantis to quiz her unfortunate pupils on the sacraments. 'She was a spinster woman,' remembers Cate, who was also a pupil there, 'with a big long feather-duster, and the feathers at the end of it didn't seem to slow down the swish of the cane. She was such a bully, she was a nightmare. I went back to the school years and years later and she was still pulling kids around by the scruff of their neck and their ears, these poor, timid little five- and six-year-olds.'

St Edmund's was a small school made up of only four classrooms, with old-fashioned wooden benches and desks, and an open fire. Mass was held every week in the school's own chapel, which ran the full length of the top floor and was reached via wooden stairs. So God was literally hovering over the children as they studied, omnipresent.

Cate remembers that Maurice was not academically gifted as a child and did not do well at school. He certainly didn't lack ability, but school failed to hold his interest. 'If he wasn't interested in anything, well, he wasn't interested. I think he lived in his imagination.' In the repressive environment of St Edmund's it must have been tough for any child to embrace the joy of learning. For the most part they were too scared to step out of line or even contribute in class. 'The way the teachers belittled the children,' says Cate, 'you would be too scared to make the wrong answer and wouldn't make the effort in the end. It's a wonder we could string two words together by the time we left.'

Having survived the school week, the big treat at the weekend was Saturday-morning pictures at the local Odeon. Kenny's favourite was always *Flash Gordon,* but he also loved other Republic serials such as *King of the Rocket Men* and *The Crimson Ghost* with its thrills, spills and ridiculously overwrought cliff-hanger endings. It was here one Saturday that Kenny got his first taste of public success. 'Before the film began the cinema manager used to get up on the stage and try and control all these unruly children by having quizzes and competitions,' remembers Cate. 'And Kenny won a skipping competition and I won a singing competition.'

The simple pleasure of Saturday-morning pictures was denied Maurice when his dad decided, for no apparent reason, that he should learn to play the violin. The lessons, given by a grumpy teacher, were not only held at the same time but next door to the cinema. So poor Maurice would see all his mates rush excitedly into the foyer, while he faced an hour of worthless fiddling.

While not exactly a wallflower, Maurice was developing into a shy and reserved boy, not much into physical activities such as sports, preferring to stay indoors with his own company. In that way he took after his father, who was by nature a quiet man. But Kenny carried it to extremes. 'He was very very quiet, very quiet indeed,' recalled Tony Ormesher, who was four years older than Maurice and lived opposite. 'He didn't mix much at all with the kids in the street. When he was eleven, twelve and thirteen he started to go a little bit into himself. I was really surprised in such an introvert person there was such an extrovert trying to get out.'

One friend was a lad who lived around the corner, Peter Terry. A bit of a tearaway, was Terry, and together they'd sometimes sneak into the back of a local grocery store to steal tins of peaches or play postman's knock on the doors of unsuspecting neighbours. Once they climbed on to the roof of the local supermarket. Maurice and Terry also pulled the odd practical joke. The local parish priest, Father McKiernan, was a regular visitor to all local households and would always give Peter Terry's sister Margaret's plaits a little yank as he got up to leave. One afternoon Margaret got her hair cut and, sensing the opportunity for a good wheeze, Maurice asked her to retain the detached plaits. When the priest next visited, Margaret fixed the plaits on to the back of her head so that when he playfully gave them a tug they came off in his hand, accompanied by a scream of anguish from Margaret. After the poor man left in an awful state the children burst out laughing.

If the prankster was born early, so too was the mischief-maker. One day after school Kenny and Cate were walking along the pathway that ran past the side of the school building when Ev saw a brick in a puddle and started playing with it. 'Then he got bored and chucked it over the wall,' remembers Cate. 'And unfortunately on the other side was poor Mike Ahern, who copped it on top of the head. Ev was mortified.' Mike Ahern attended St Edmund's at the same time as Everett, although he was two years older. By a curious coincidence Ahern also became a pirate DJ, had a brief spell on Radio 1 and worked with Kenny on Capital Gold in the nineties. To have two future radio presenters live within 200 yards of each other was a remarkable coincidence.

The natural performer also rose to the surface fairly early on. Cate remembers she and Maurice used to put on little plays and shows and charge all the neighbouring kids a penny to come and watch. When he joined the local scout troop, Maurice appeared in their annual production – playing the part of a woman. This entailed borrowing a red corduroy pinafore dress from his sister, white ankle socks, leather shoes and a long blond wig. 'It was the first intimation I ever got that he was actually brilliant,' says Cate, who saw the play with her mum and dad. 'We went along expecting nothing much, but he was fantastic. He had such stage presence the whole show seemed to revolve around him. I also noticed that it was Ev who prompted all the other kids when they forgot lines.'

One of the happiest periods of Maurice's childhood was Christmas, a time of magic, warmth and celebration. Christmas Day always saw the arrival of Auntie Sadie and Uncle Jack, who used to give the children each a crisp ten-shilling note. Maurice would run upstairs into his bedroom and pin it to the wall, just to stare in wonder at this manna from heaven.

There were holidays to look forward to as well: trips to Ayrshire in Scotland and Llandudno in Wales, where one of their aunts owned a caravan, and Bray on the coast of Ireland near Dublin, as well as an annual jaunt to the Isle of Man. 'I also remember we set off to Devon and Cornwall once,' recalls Cate. 'But because my mother was reading the map we ended up in London!' Wherever they went, poor old Ev would always be travel-sick. 'Car-sick, coach-sick, boat-sick, every kind of sick,' recalls Cate. 'Poor kid. Once we went to Scotland and I actually thought he was going to die. We had to stop all the time – he was in a shocking state. He was a very sensitive boy.'

In the days before television, the radio was for many the only source of home entertainment. Like most families, the Coles would sit around the fire every night and tune into shows such as *Dick Barton Special Agent*, *The Goon Show* and *Take It From Here*, with Jimmy Edwards and June Whitfield. For Kenny, radio wasn't merely a source of amusement, it attained an almost ethereal quality. 'I used to wake up at six o'clock in the morning and listen to the start of radio because I was so entranced by it.' Totally mesmerized by the sounds coming out of the speaker, he'd let himself be taken on a journey somewhere else, somewhere exotic and exciting. 'And then, of course, the transmissions would end and I'd be back in drizzly old Liverpool.' Sometimes he found himself staring fixatedly at the radio even when it wasn't on, this little magic box, trying to fathom where all that sound came from. At night he'd listen to *The Adventures of Dan Dare*, fifteen minutes of wonder which aired five times a week on Radio Luxembourg. Based on the *Eagle* comic strip, each episode started with the command, 'Spaceships Away!' Maurice's imagination would soar as he was taken away to Venus and interstellar battles with the evil Treens.

The dial was almost permanently tuned to the BBC's Home Service, and he'd carry on listening sometimes right up until the end of transmission, when the announcer strayed from the programme's rigid format and set script and began to talk more freely: 'And now I can see the gas lamps flickering in Portland Place, it's time to wrap up for the night.' Kenny loved staying up for that bit, it sounded so cosy and warm, as if the presenter was speaking only to him. It was an early lesson about the power and intimacy of radio.

At school Maurice continued to underperform. About the only lesson that engaged his interest was geography, where he enjoyed learning about other countries, perhaps daydreaming about escaping to a tropical island far away from the grey, cold environs of Liverpool. And so it came as no surprise to anyone when he failed his eleven-plus. The sole object of the exam, it seemed to him, had been to ask all the questions that he couldn't answer, like divide 42 by 6, to which Maurice wrote on the exam paper – *why?* His parents were disappointed but not entirely surprised; 'They knew I had this will-o'-the-wisp mind which flitted from one subject to another.'

So instead of the local grammar school Maurice went to St Bede's Secondary Modern, where physical punishment was rife. Almost certainly Maurice fell prey to the cane since 'they used to cane everybody', according to Cate. 'We also had this despotic headmaster who was very, very tall and frightening-looking, and rather grand about himself, and he used to beat the hell out of the children with a leather strap. It was terrible. Children never went home and told their parents; they'd only have said, "Well, you must have deserved it." That was the culture back then, you put up or shut up. That guy would be hauled before the courts now for his behaviour.'

At St Bede's, Kenny's weedy frame made him an easy target for bullies: 'I spent most of the time at school avoiding the other chaps because they were great hulking brutes; they were practising to be ditch diggers.' Cate says she can't really remember him being bullied, but agrees that 'maybe he felt intimidated. He wasn't a big chap, and he wasn't all that sporty. He was always a bit of a moocher.'

As at his previous school, Kenny didn't form many friendships. One of his few mates was Paul Walker, who lived nearby on Wilson Road. Both quite techy, they gravitated to each other due to a shared hatred of anything to do with physical exertion. Aside from being physically exhausting, Kenny particularly loathed school sports because it meant having to wear shorts, thus revealing to the world his spindly frame.

Looking back now, Walker comments, 'Maurice was quite cultured, even then, and that's probably why he never felt he fitted in. I never recall him being bullied though. He was a delightful lad and quite funny. Very affable. He definitely came over as being middle-class though, but in a very working-class area.' Indeed, while Maurice himself was already exhibiting self-confidence issues, amongst his fellow pupils he was considered clever, combining a quick wit with immaculate handwriting.

Through his love of radio, Maurice had developed a keen interest in music. Near St Bede's was Rosie's, an old junk shop where he spent hours flicking through boxes of old 78 records, buying hoards of them at three pence apiece. In his bedroom was one of those plastic toy record players which he'd been given as a child; wrenching the arm off to allow space for his much larger 78s, Maurice would wet his finger and manually spin the vinyl until it reached the required rpm. George Butterworth's tune 'The Banks of Green Willow' was the first record he recalled ever buying, but the bulk of his 78s were classical recordings. One particular favourite was Laurence Olivier reciting speeches from *Hamlet*. Over and over again he'd play the Yorick speech. 'I just loved the magic of a voice crooning out of a little plastic object.'

Despite his burgeoning interest in music and radio, it's doubtful whether Kenny envisaged a career in broadcasting or indeed knew such a thing was a possibility. At this early stage he had no idea where his future lay.

2

Heaven Calling

ONE AFTERNOON KENNY'S school organized a trip to what can only be described as a religious expo. It wasn't compulsory, no one was forced to go, but Cate remembers most of her class and Maurice's boarding the coaches and off they went. 'And there were all these stalls with nuns and priests encouraging us to join their particular order. Me and my friends came away laughing, saying, no way José. Ev came away with an application form.' It was for a Catholic seminary based at Stillington Hall near York, run by the Verona Fathers, who originated as a brotherhood based in Italy training young men for the priesthood and for missionary work in places such as Uganda and the Sudan.

Cate doesn't believe her brother had any particular vocation to go into the priesthood. As Kenny himself later said, 'It was a choice of either staying at St Bede's and finishing off my training as a mass murderer, along with the rest of them, or going to learn to be a priest and converting people. Can you imagine me converting anybody!'

As a young lad he had been an altar boy and, according to Cate, really enjoyed it. 'He looked so angelic. And he loved swinging the incense. That was theatre, wasn't it.' She can't recall Maurice ever discussing religion or even raising the subject when they were children, though at that age one wasn't encouraged to ask questions. Any expression of doubt would inevitably receive the stock answer: 'It's a question of faith, my child.' Going to Stillington Hall, then, was simply one more fanciful notion that was pushed into his head, helped perhaps by the fact that his friend Peter Terry was already there and reporting back to Maurice how much he was enjoying it. Cate remembers her parents' response to the news along the lines of, Oh golly, are you sure? Well, if it's really what you want . . . 'I think they had to struggle, because it was quite expensive to send him there.'

Maurice arrived at Stillington Hall in September 1956, and it was all rather overwhelming at first. Stillington Hall was an old country house that dated back to the early 1700s. Kenny later recalled that it was like living in a movie set, one of those gothic mansions that turn up in old-fashioned murder mysteries with a grand staircase, balustrades, mahogany panelling and minstrel galleries.

The children all slept in a huge dormitory on the top floor that stretched along the whole front of the house. Maurice hated having to get up early and take a compulsory shower, since there was no privacy whatsoever, no doors on the cubicles, and one was subjected to blasts of cold water. The boys would then hurry along to chapel for morning prayers and communion; though the thin wafer was supposed to remain in the mouth, slowly dissolving as the mind engaged in contemplation of godly thoughts, most pupils were so hungry that they guzzled it down straightaway. After a bible reading it was finally time for breakfast, followed by maths, geography, English, etc.

After lunch there were more lessons or games. Again, Maurice did his best to avoid the latter if at all possible. Football was the favoured sport at Stillington Hall, hardly surprising since many of the priests were Italian; one of them had a relative who was on the books of Internazionale Milano, and he managed to acquire a full strip in the famous black and blue for the school's team. Of course, Maurice tried to stay as close to the edge of the pitch and as far away from the flight of the ball as possible, hoping no one would see him, let alone think of passing the ball to him.

Sport was a mainstay of weekends, too, with pupils playing either football, rugby or cricket. 'Maurice wasn't a great sportsman,' recalls fellow pupil Mike Webster. 'So as an alternative he would spend time in the kitchen garden, eating the gardener's vegetables whilst doing the weeding. Maurice was happier doing this than playing sports. At weekends we would also help the brothers in the stable yard with mucking out.'

Maurice was happiest strolling around the school's picturesque grounds, which included a wooded park that stretched for several acres, soaking in the contemplative nature of the countryside. 'Being a sensitive soul, the quiet, country-house atmosphere was a world away from the rough and tough life in inner Liverpool,' says Webster. 'It was here that he blossomed.' This happened to such an extent that Maurice began developing his interest in performing by putting on little sketches in school productions. These skits, which lasted maybe a couple of minutes, had a similar off-the-wall humour to his favourite radio programme, *The Goon Show*, with the same clever wordplay and cringing puns.

The success of these performances did wonders for Maurice's low self-esteem, according to Webster. 'As he was a quiet, subdued person who didn't like socializing with local children in Liverpool, the fact that he had a willing, attentive audience among the students gave him the confidence to develop his sense of humour without being ridiculed. The voices and the humour developed. During the spring and summer we would amble through the surrounding fields taking in the birdlife and following the river for miles through the fields. It was during this time that Maurice would practise his routine and put on a show while we were ambling along. It was quite evident that even at the tender age of twelve Maurice had a natural comic sense of humour and was a born entertainer. But no one knew where it was going to lead. Including Maurice.'

The standard of teaching, as well as the pastoral care the boys received, was of a high order. Many former pupils who didn't end up as priests nevertheless went on to achieve success in their chosen fields. And Mike Webster, who arrived at Stillington Hall the same day as the twelve-year-old Maurice, is under no illusions as to why. 'The atmosphere at Stillington was calmer than elsewhere because of the small number of students, and because of the style of education of the Verona Fathers. The feel of the whole place was calming, as with only fifty-eight or so pupils it was less hectic than secondary modern schools and a gentler academic pace. Also the nature of the students entering the school added to the overall calmer atmosphere. The discipline was there, but not strict in the normal sense of the word. The staff set an academic example for all to follow and the priests wanted everyone to develop and become "rounded" people. It really was a magical place and was a real adventure for kids from a range of backgrounds.'

Religious instruction at Stillington was fairly intense, as you might expect. Kenny never forgot a lecture given by one of the Fathers about homosexuality, condemning it as a practice that went wholly against nature. 'We cannot accept homosexuality, but we have compassion for the sinner.'

The late afternoon and early evening was spent in private reflection and prayer, and each student was required to go to confession every night, to cleanse the soul for the following morning's communion. Pretty much the only heinous act Maurice confessed to was stealing stationery. He loved to draw, a skill that he carried into adult life, but there was never enough paper in the classrooms so he resorted to stealing it from the teachers' cupboards.

Before the evening meal on Sundays there was benediction, followed by the Rosary, a group of prayers which included fifty Hail Marys. Even on weekday nights they had up to thirty minutes of prayer before supper. But in spite of all this religious doctrine Maurice was happy at Stillington, and when his parents and Cate arrived by car from Liverpool for the occasional weekend visit he took great pride in showing them around. 'We used to really look forward to those trips,' says Cate. 'We'd take him goodies and attend lovely ceremonies in the beautiful old chapel with wonderful music. It was a really enjoyable weekend.'

After just a year, however, Maurice left the seminary under a cloud. Along with Peter Terry and a couple of other boys, he had broken into the chapel late at night and conducted a mock Mass that included drinking several bottles of communion wine; quite a sacrilegious thing to do in such a religious environment. 'We didn't see why the priests should have all the fun,' Kenny said later. 'We didn't understand why we couldn't see what it was like to be a priest.' Obviously the

Fathers realized that somebody had broken in, and as soon as the boys went to confession the truth came out and they realized who the little monsters were. When school broke up for the summer holidays action was taken. 'The Fathers wrote a letter apparently to the Monsignor, our parish priest, asking should we give this boy a second chance,' recalls Cate. 'Unfortunately the Monsignor died and the letter wasn't opened or dealt with, so when the Verona Fathers didn't get a reply I think they thought, just like the BBC years later, oh well, we don't really want a troublemaker back, do we? He was very upset, I do remember that. There was gloom about the house.'

Once that gloom had settled, Maurice pushed religion out of his life completely, referring to it only as a target for ridicule. His naturally inquisitive nature had finally seen behind the façade and recognized it as nothing but a fraud that had preyed upon his child-hood anxieties. Something else clicked with him, something about the collection plate that got passed around the church every weekend. 'I thought, hello, smacks a bit of something or other Ltd. I figured out that the Catholic Church was a business, a very clever one; I wish I'd thought of it.'

Maurice returned to St Bede's, but his apathy for the place and education in general had not diminished and he took not one jot of interest in his studies. His passion for radio and music had now come to dominate his life, combined with an interest in the technical side, with the actual equipment itself and how it worked. Even as early as nine years old he had been cutting out pictures of tape machines from newspapers and magazines and pasting them into a scrapbook. 'Figure that out, Mr Freud,' he joked.

It was part of a natural curiosity that Maurice exhibited from early on in his life. He was inquisitive and forever taking stuff to bits, a clock or kitchen gadget, to look inside and figure out how the mechanism worked. 'But then he wouldn't put them back together again,' claims Cate. 'And that used to make my mother mad. In fact, the only time I ever saw my mother cry was when he dismantled her washing machine – when it was full of washing!'

When the thirteen-year-old Maurice asked his dad to buy him a tape recorder, Tom's answer was unequivocal: 'Not likely, you'll only take it to pieces.' His friend Paul Walker's brother Peter had recently got a Grundig TK5 for his twenty-first birthday, one of the first really good reel-to-reel tape recorders made for the domestic market, 'and Maurice was always coming round and watching my brother play with it,' says Paul. 'He was fascinated.' Eventually Tom capitulated but was rendered speechless when his son asked for another one. The answer was a definitive no. Why did he need two tape recorders? Maurice instead used the money from a paper round to buy another Grundig; already he was thinking about experimenting and mixing sound. All day he played music in his bedroom, taping the latest chart hits from the David Jacobs show on the BBC rather than forking out five shillings at the local record shop for one single with a lousy B-side.

He even came up with the notion of creating his own radio station by requisitioning the front room and piping in his 78s through a speaker, and producing his own version of the *Radio Times*. 'I banned my mum from listening to the BBC, she had to listen to my channel. I only had an audience of two.' Cate remembers it well, the wires hanging all over the ceiling and the remarkable feat of Maurice being able to transmit music and his voice through the real radio, which led to a wicked prank. 'My friend Noelle was visiting me that day and we devised a trick that Maurice's voice would come through the radio saying that we'd all won a prize, some exotic holiday. My poor parents felt so awful having to tell Noelle that it was all a hoax. Her eyes were sticking out like saucers with excitement. It was so realistic; nobody knew it was Maurice in the room next door.'

By this stage one show in particular had begun to exert a huge influence upon the impressionable Maurice: Jack Jackson's *Record Roundabout* on the BBC's Light Programme. Jackson had begun his entertainment career as a band leader in the thirties before becoming a BBC disc jockey in 1948. What was so innovative about Jackson was that between records he would employ silly sound effects and voices, and splice in tapes featuring snatches of dialogue from current comedy shows like *Hancock*. 'Jack was the first person to use those kind of comedy-type inserts from other shows at the BBC,' says DJ

Nicky Horne. 'It was very, very clever. You listen to Jack Jackson now and you think, God, that was years ahead of its time.' It was this bold difference that connected with Maurice, who until then had only heard radio presenters introducing music in that solemn fifties BBC voice. 'He was the first person who sounded like he actually had fun on the radio,' said Kenny, for whom the secret of good radio was always to sound as though you were having a good time. 'All the rest of them were "we'd better behave because we're in Broadcasting House and Lord Reith might drop a brick on us any second", because he was rather severe. But Jack Jackson had a studio in the Canary Islands, so he was free from all this collar-and-tie stuff.' Jackson had emigrated to Tenerife in 1962 and sent his taped programmes by air to the BBC each week.

Inspired, Maurice began to combine records with comedy clips and his own burgeoning humour to create little fifteen-minute shows that emulated the Jack Jackson style, 'but mine were a bit more loony and silly'. His bedroom became his first studio and every spare hour he'd be in there, playing music and refining his editing techniques. Whenever his poor mother attempted to clean she'd find spliced tape stuck on walls and windows with labels warning, 'do not clean this window'. Once she found scrawled over one of the mirrors in lipstick *BBC HERE I COME*. The irony of Maurice hibernating in his room, spinning discs and making tapes, was that the music revolution then taking place in his home city – the birth of the Mersey Beat and the Beatles playing at the Cavern – went completely unnoticed by him. Here was a budding DJ and music lover with the country's most significant music explosion happening on his doorstep – and he missed it!

Maurice left St Bede's with no qualifications and was thrust into the jobs market. His family were certain that his future lay somewhere in the arts because of his creativity; instead Maurice announced he wanted to be a famous pastry chef. 'I think it was another dream,' says Cate. 'He imagined himself as some sort of moustachioed guy in a tall white hat.' Tom knew someone in the catering trade and Maurice was taken on as a trainee at Cooper's bakery. Far from learning the business he got landed with all the rubbish jobs like ten hours a day scraping the fat off sausage-roll trays. 'He hated it,' remembers Cate, 'because he was having to start at the bottom.' After a couple of months Maurice left and applied for a job in an advertising agency called Douglas & Company on Chapel Street in the city centre. Maurice enjoyed working there; the place was full of cheery and friendly people and for the first time in his life he started to open up a little. 'Until then I'd been a clam, but suddenly people were talking to me in a friendly way and taking an interest in me.'

Feeling bolstered, he bought a moped and every morning drove the five miles from home to work, weaving in and out of the rush-hour traffic. Starting off as an errand boy (one assignment had him delivering copy to a pre-Fab Four Brian Epstein), Maurice rose to the heady heights of production assistant. Then one day his manager took a holiday and asked Maurice to look after things while he was gone. While his job carried a certain degree of responsibility, this was too much and he resigned. 'I knew that if the company was left in my hands it would sink without a trace amid a sea of Everett cock-ups.' Maurice found another job relatively easily, a position at the *Journal of Commerce and Shipping Telegraph*.

When he wasn't working, he continued with his tape-making activities. Feeling his tapes deserved an audience beyond family and friends, he'd sent one to Alan Edward Beeby, a columnist for *Tape Recording Magazine*, which Kenny read with relish from cover to cover every month. To his surprise, he received a positive response. The two of them began a regular correspondence. 'They had a very good rapport going,' says Cate. 'I remember letters coming into the house all the time.'

Then came a letter from Beeby which read: 'Maurice, why are you sending me these jolly tapes when you could be sending them somewhere which might do you a bit of good, like the BBC?' Until that point it had never occurred to him that his flights of nonsense and wacky voices might merit the interest of such an august institution. Besides, didn't you have to smoke a pipe and wear Hush Puppies to work for Auntie? Not holding out much hope, he popped his best tape into a brown envelope, penned a suitably grovelling covering letter and posted it to the BBC.

3

BBC Calling

AT TWENTY-SIX, WILFRED De'Ath was the youngest producer at Broadcasting House in 1964. Arriving at his small, nondescript office one morning he saw a package addressed to him on his desk. 'Inside was a tape, so I played it and played it, very loudly, much to the annoyance of my colleagues who were very pompous talks producers all wearing double-breasted suits. They stuck their heads in and said, "Do you mind lowering the volume of that tape?" But as soon as I heard it I knew this guy had got something. I know it sounds like wisdom after the event, but I said, "I think this guy's a comic genius." I remember using that very phrase.'

What struck De'Ath about the tape more than anything else was the sheer professionalism of it. 'I thought it was absolutely brilliant and very cleverly put together.' Entitled 'The Maurice Cole Quarter of an Hour Show', the tape consisted of some silly voices, the Beatles, jokes and topical material such as a snippet of a speech by John F. Kennedy edited in such a way that it was rendered into complete gobbledegook.

At the time De'Ath was producer of *Midweek*, a straightforward thirty-minute magazine programme that went out on Wednesday afternoon on the Home Service. De'Ath thought this Maurice fella would be an ideal guest.

Still working at the *Journal of Commerce and Shipping Telegraph*, Maurice had plain forgotten all about his tape, perhaps having resigned himself to never getting a reply. But then came the rap at the door: a telegram. Telegrams were a rare event in Hereford Road, usually reserved for death notices or momentous announcements.

Eagerly Maurice tore it open and couldn't quite believe what he was reading: 'Tape great. Come to London and be interviewed. Ring Wilfred De'Ath.' Kenny would recall driving his moped to work that morning along the Dock Road in a state of total euphoria, clutching the telegram in his hands, going over the lines again and again, just to make sure they hadn't faded and it wasn't all a dream. When he'd calmed down he called Cate and yelled down the phone, 'I'm going to be on the radio!'

On the appointed day, Kenny arrived in London by train and made his way to Broadcasting House. Walking into the large imposing lobby he called over a commissionaire and asked for Mr De'Ath's office. The producer still recalls the moment the embryonic Kenny Everett walked in. 'He was wearing his first-ever suit. He'd never worn a suit before. He looked very smart, for an eighteen-year-old. I said, "Is that your first suit?" And he said, "Yes, I wore it specially to come down."'

That evening De'Ath invited Maurice to his home in Swiss Cottage. 'I gave him a large gin and tonic and he drank it down like a glass of water. I gave him another one and he drank that down like a glass of water. I said, "You don't have to drink it all at once. You can sip it if you wish." He was a very naive young man, but extremely nice and pleasant. And slightly needy. He brought out a kind of protective instinct in me. I think he was always very needy. He brought out a protective instinct in both men and women. He was very vulnerable.'

De'Ath put a somewhat tipsy Kenny into a cab and sent him back to his rather seedy hotel just off Baker Street, with instructions to return to Broadcasting House the following morning. When he duly arrived next day Maurice experienced, 'my first-ever attack of show-biz butterflies', but these were swiftly banished when he was shown into the studio and his eyes fell upon the banks of tape machines and equipment. This was where he wanted to be, where he felt he belonged.

The compère of *Midweek* was Ronald Fletcher, an old-fashioned type of radio announcer. 'We're going to do something rather unusual today,' De'Ath told him. 'We're going to put this young guy on, we're going to play most of his tape, and then you're going to interview him.' And that's exactly what happened, with the whole thing going out live across the country. The interview went well, with Maurice exhibiting the cheerful irreverence for which he was shortly to become famous. Asked by Fletcher if his parents had any connection with showbusiness, young master Cole replied, 'Oh no, they're quite boring, really.' It was his first on-air goof. 'Mother didn't like that one,' he later confessed. There was also the first of what would be many missiles aimed in the general direction of Liverpool. 'He said how much he hated the place,' remembers De'Ath. 'And he was quite cheeky about the BBC, which given the fact that we were giving him a break was pretty impertinent.' Still, it made for good radio – or did it? De'Ath was rapped over the knuckles for having turned *Midweek* into, horror of horrors, a pop programme. 'I remember the high up telling me off and I got a memo saying you're not to do this kind of thing on *Midweek*. I took a risk and it paid off in a way. I mean, he was very good.'

Back in Hereford Road Lily and Tom listened intently to the broadcast. 'They were delighted, they thought it was great,' remembers Cate, who had already left home by 1962 and was working for a charity organization in London, sharing a flat in Sloane Street. There was an electrical store nearby and Cate hired a radio so that she wouldn't miss her brother's BBC debut either. 'I remember standing in the kitchen in that Sloane Street flat listening to Ev's first-ever broadcast, "The Maurice Cole Quarter of an Hour". He was so excited about that. I thought it went really well, I was very proud of him.'

Brimming with confidence about how well things had gone, Maurice asked De'Ath if he could find him a job somewhere in the BBC. Unfortunately the producer wasn't in any position to help, or as Kenny later joked, 'They had no jobs because David Jacobs and Pete Murray were still alive and expected to live another three hundred years.'

What De'Ath did manage to do was fire off memos to various people he knew, saying could you give this guy a helping hand because I think he's very talented. It seemed to work because two weeks later another telegram arrived at the Cole residence, this time asking

Maurice to return to Broadcasting House for an audition. Excited and nervous, Maurice made the mistake of having a couple of drinks beforehand – well, eight drinks – and staggered into the studio ever so slightly wasted. 'They gave me a bunch of records and said, right, play those gramophone records, one after the other preferably, and speak a little. And I freaked.' There he was, with a group of faceless technical types standing inside a glass booth staring at him; he dried up and could tell by the expression on the producer's face that he'd failed the interview, failed it spectacularly. He returned home crestfallen and depressed. But elsewhere events were unfolding that would ensure the young Maurice Cole got a second chance.

4

Pirate's Progress

I T'S HARD TO imagine today, with music readily accessible in so many different formats, from iTunes to a plethora of radio stations catering to all manner of musical tastes, that back in the early sixties there were few opportunities to hear your favourite records played. Indeed by 1964, the year of Beatlemania, there was one solitary commercial radio station that you could hear in Britain (or rather not hear since the frequency was notoriously unreliable): Radio Luxembourg. This left the BBC dominating the airwaves, and pop music was confined to just a few hours a week on the Light Programme, a station mainly devoted to easy listening, comedy and light entertainment. For an hour at teatime on Sundays there was Alan 'Fluff' Freeman spinning the week's best-selling 45s in *Pick of the Pops*, while on *Saturday Club* presenter Brian Matthew offered a mix of live music, interviews and records for two hours – and that was it.

'There was strict recorded music rationing back in those days,' reveals Rod Argent, founding member of the sixties group the Zombies. 'The Musicians' Union was very powerful and it wanted music to be live, so you had very little recorded music on the radio.' This restriction on pre-recorded content – or 'needle time' as it was known – was a means of guaranteeing work for session musicians, who would perform 'live' cover versions of current hits for radio broadcasts. 'It used to drive us crazy because it was the records that we wanted to hear,' says Argent. 'It was the records that were so beautifully produced and that had the magic sound. I remember the first time I heard the Beatles on Radio Luxembourg and I stayed up all night hoping to hear that record again. That's the sort of thing that you would do. There was no chance of hearing it on the Beeb at the time.' Because Radio Luxembourg was not subject to British law, it wasn't hampered by such petty restrictions and could play whatever it wanted.

Everything changed over the Easter weekend of 1964 with the launch of Radio Caroline, the first of the pirate stations. Broadcasting on unauthorized frequencies from a former passenger ferry that lay anchored three miles off the coast of Essex, it was in international waters and therefore beyond the reach of UK legislation. At last the British public had access to a non-stop output of pop music delivered by a young and thrusting bunch of on-board disc jockeys including Simon Dee and Tony Blackburn.

The pirates were not just a breath of fresh air but a musical revolution, broadcasting loud and proud in open defiance of stuffy old Auntie BBC and the establishment that wanted them taken off the air. Remember, in the mid-sixties there were only two television channels, broadcasting for part of the day, so radio was by far the most popular medium. In many ways the pirates came to symbolize the new, youthful, post-war Britain. As John Peel put it: 'The pirates provided the soundtrack to a lot of young people's lives.' It was a movement that the young Maurice Cole was to be at the forefront of.

That spring an American businessman by the name of Don Pierson was holidaying in England and happened to catch a burst of Caroline. If this was supposed to be the hip alternative to the BBC he wasn't much taken with it. It occurred to him that if he were to set up a radio station that had more in common with the dynamic American Top 40 stations, he could make a fortune. Back home he cobbled together enough backing to buy a Second World War minesweeper 185 feet long and weighing 780 tons, and to equip it with a 50,000-watt transmitter, five times the power of Caroline, and a 212-foot-high radio mast, taller than Nelson's Column, powerful enough to broadcast throughout England and Wales, and even parts of Europe.

The ship – or rust bucket as she was dubbed by those who first looked her over – was the MV *Galaxy*. After several weeks of renovation it departed Miami on 22 October on its long rough voyage across the Atlantic, stopping en route at Puerto Rico and Madeira. Arriving in the Thames Estuary on 19 November, the *Galaxy* anchored itself three and a half miles off Frinton-on-Sea, on the Essex coast, not far from Caroline.

The search for disc jockeys had begun in earnest even before the *Galaxy* had left its American mooring. According to Philip Birch, a Canadian who'd been hired to run the station's sales organization from its London office in Curzon Street, 'We wanted bright sparkling personalities and for the most part British voices, preferably with some DJ experience.' One of the people Birch enlisted to help in this search for talent was Maurice Sellar, who was to play perhaps the most significant role in getting Maurice Cole launched on the radio. Sellar had begun his entertainment career making comedy records for Decca in the fifties, lampooning pop stars such as Tommy Steele and Lonnie Donegan. After that novelty faded he and his manager Roy Tuvey started to make programmes for Radio Luxembourg, quickly establishing themselves as the station's most successful producers and forming their own management company, whose stable of DJs included Brian Matthew and Pete Murray. Such was their impact on the music industry that they were approached by Ronan O'Rahilly, the man behind Radio Caroline, to put money into the venture. 'Which is what we did,' Sellar remembers. 'We bought shares in Radio Caroline and were about to become more involved when we were approached by Philip Birch. He came to our office in Basil Street, in Mayfair, by Harrods, we had a nice set of offices there because we were doing bloody well. He came to see us and said, "I hear you guys have got the tab on everything that's happening on the pop scene. We are fitting out a much much bigger offshore radio ship (he didn't use the word pirate), it's going to be called Radio London, will you find the DJs for us?" Of course we said yes and auditioned several and ended up getting quite a few for them.'

Record promotions man Chris Peers had also been approached by Birch to track down DJs. Peers had been working with disc jockeys for a few years (he now regrets being the person who introduced Jimmy

Savile to the gramophone department of the BBC) and was also in business with Chris Blackwell during the early days of Island Records, so he knew his onions. But where to look? DJs were pretty thin on the ground back then, with the BBC, Radio Luxembourg and Radio Caroline the only employers. Peers' first port of call was therefore Broadcasting House, to ask producers he knew, 'Is there anybody that's sent you tapes that you've rejected?'

Since the Island Records office was at 155–7 Oxford Street, not far from Portland Place, Peers would stroll into the BBC club maybe twice a week after work for a quick drink. 'This one time I was standing up at the bar and there was this tap on the shoulder.' It was Wilfred De'Ath. '"Oh God, Chris," he said. "Do you know, I was going to call you. Have you got a few minutes?"'

'What is it?' asked Peers.

'I'd like to play you a tape.'

So off they went to De'Ath's office, where he played Peers the 'Maurice Cole Quarter of an Hour Show'. Peers has never forgotten his reaction: 'It was fabulous and so original. It was like a junior Jack Jackson. That tape was like a mini-masterpiece. I turned to Wilfred and said, "Would you mind if I take this tape because I'm looking for disc jockeys and I could give this guy a job?"'

Meanwhile, Maurice Sellar was busy sifting through hopeful DJs, and because he'd been a performer he insisted on overseeing the auditions. 'I was looking for something a bit special. I wanted someone to be different than the usual run-of-the-mill type of DJ who just tells you the name of the song and who sings it.' As Sellar remembers it, Wilfred De'Ath had sent him a copy of Maurice's tape, but because they were getting inundated with tapes he hadn't had a chance to listen to it. But when Sellar heard Maurice was coming down to London he agreed to audition him. 'This kid turned up at the City of London recording studios in Aldgate, and he sat down. He was as white as a ghost, thin as a pin. Before we started, he asked, "This is for going out to sea, isn't it? I'm terrible at sea, I get seasick all the time." So I said, "Well, use that in what you're going to do." And when his audition started the first thing he did was pick up a waste-paper basket and went, "I'm on this boat now and I think I'm going to . . . urggh." That was the very first thing he did, and I looked up immediately because by that time I'd seen about seven potential DJs, all of them were rubbish, and I was looking for something special, and he was it. I thought, he's really got something, this boy. After he finished I rang up my partner and said, "I think I've found the new Jack Jackson. This kid is terrific." So Roy said, "Let's sign him up," which we did, we put him under contract.'

There was another reason why Sellar liked this kid. When Maurice walked into the studio he told Sellar that he immediately recognized his name because he'd bought one of his Decca comedy records when he was a kid; it was the Tommy Rot story, which was a send-up of Tommy Steele. 'So I had an instant affinity for him,' Sellar recalls. 'I said, "Great, you're a fan and you've got the same name as me."'

While Sellar passed on his recommendation that Maurice Cole be hired, Chris Peers went to see Radio London's newly installed programme controller, Texan-born Ben Toney, who had a long history in American radio. 'Ben, I have just the boy for you,' he confidently announced, then took out young Maurice's tape and played it. 'I couldn't believe what I was hearing,' says Toney today. 'At the time, I had not heard of *The Goon Show*, but later I found that Kenny was a big fan, and his original tape was a definite take of that show. I had a keen awareness that British humour and American humour were not quite alike, so I played the tape to some of the office force and had them rolling in the aisles. Philip Birch, our manager and sales coordinator, was a rather serious person who when he was excited showed only a glimmer of a smile. I thought if Philip can be amused by Kenny, I will certainly hire him. I can tell you Kenny had Philip fairly roaring.'

From a distance of almost fifty years Philip Birch recalls that initially he voiced reservations about hiring Maurice Cole. 'I thought he was probably a bit too young, but we all were very impressed by his enthusiasm and creativity.' So thanks to the combined efforts of Maurice Sellar and Chris Peers, Maurice was hired for a trial period, initially on half the salary of the other DJs. He couldn't believe his luck.

*

As he prepared for life on the ocean waves, Maurice stayed the night with his sister in her flat in Sloane Street. He had to leave early to get the train to Frinton to catch the tender, which was a little supply boat that serviced the pirate ships. It was still pitch-black outside when he woke at five a.m. to pack his suitcase. Cate got up, too, to make him breakfast, but he couldn't eat it, so nervous and full of anxiety was he about what lay ahead, like a little boy facing his first day at big school. 'I felt so sorry for him,' says Cate. 'He looked dreadful, sleepy, pale and scared. I just wanted to catch hold of him and give him a big hug and say, have a piece of toast.' Finally the time came for him to leave; standing in the doorway, suitcase in hand, Maurice hugged his sister and they said their goodbyes. 'He looked so innocent. He was always so young for his age. When he went to the pirate ship he had the experience of a fourteen-year-old or maybe a twelve-year-old. And I thought, watching him go off into the gloom, that he seemed very young and innocent to be heading out into those unknown waters.'

Within minutes of bobbing up and down on the tender in those choppy waters Maurice felt a stirring in his stomach: nerves had given way to something else. 'The feeling soon identified itself as – here comes the puke.' He was sick three times before the tender even reached the MV *Galaxy*. It wasn't much better when he stepped aboard; the stench of diesel fuel combined with the non-stop swaying reduced him to quivering jelly. 'I was luminous green to the gills.' It was a situation that did not improve for several weeks. 'It seemed to me that the ship was engaged in constant combat with the elements at all hours of the night and day.'

Life aboard was rough in those early weeks as Maurice got used to his new surroundings. He hardly ate anything for the first couple of days and later complained that the cooks were either ex-convicts or Belgians and fried everything in axle grease. The food wasn't quite that bad, but Maurice still didn't eat it. Mitch Philistin, the ship's head steward who also helped out with the cooking, had sailed on the *Galaxy* from Miami and would remain on-board until the ship closed down. He recalls: 'The one thing with Kenny, he didn't eat any of the food. He liked toast with butter and marmalade, and when you gave him food he wanted chips and he put the chips between the bread. We used to do a lot of our own cooking on the ship, he was a very hard man to feed. The original chef was from Haiti, but in the end he had to go back because he said it was too cold. We cooked West Indian food, rice and peas, meat and fish, but Kenny didn't want to eat anything, he preferred to sit there making toast and marmalade.' Maurice did eventually get used to the food – it was either that or dying of starch poisoning.

One of the cooks turned out to be Scottish and rather large and uncouth. On one occasion there was a violent altercation between this cook and one of the DJs and Maurice leapt fearlessly into the breach. 'I flung a bottle of Heineken at the Scot, who promptly turned his marauding attentions on me.' It took several of the crew to restrain him and when everything calmed down the cook was politely asked to leave the ship.

Accommodation was adequate at best. Everyone had to share a cabin, with barely enough space for a wardrobe, a metal basin and a desk. Maurice found himself sharing bunk beds with another young DJ named Dave Dennis, who'd been given the lunchtime show. In April 1965 Dennis was to find fame along with colleague Pete Brady when they helped save a USAF pilot who had been forced to eject from his Voodoo jet during a training mission and landed in the icy North Sea close to the *Galaxy*.

There was little comfort to be had on-board. Interior design was non-existent, there were no carpets or wallpaper, just grey steel corridors and bulkheads. Instead of baths they had to make do with a shower block consisting of tin boxes which, during rough seas, bounced the DJs from one wall to the other. As for the studio, it was located in the bilges, the lowest part of the ship's hull, and was poky and claustrophobic, with an overpowering odour of damp. In time the studio underwent improvements, with better equipment and extra layers of padding to make it more soundproof. But even so, its position at the stern of the vessel meant that when the ship anchored at the bow in fierce weather the studio had a tendency to soar twenty feet in the air when a wave hit. Even in normal weather it was tricky staying upright. Maurice quickly learned that the best way was to hold tightly on to the desk-frame with one hand and operate the equipment with the other.

Shortly before Radio London was due on air Ben Toney paid a brief visit to check that everything was ready to start broadcasting. He brought with him a stack of tape recordings from a Dallas radio station called KLIF; his orders were to ensure that every DJ listened to them in order to acclimatize themselves with the approach and feel of Top 40 radio American-style. The sound Radio London was aiming for was a world away from the affectedness and old-school-tie delivery of BBC jocks, and much more upbeat and vibrant than Caroline.

Looking back, Toney recalls that it was Maurice perhaps more than anyone else who pored over those tapes, listening to them for hours on end, digesting and absorbing them. 'I told him that if he didn't have anything humorous or informative to say on air, shut the hell up and play a record. Of course this is what I told all the DJs. I also told him that there was to be no dead air.' Toney admits that he was tough with the DJs on the ship, telling them in no uncertain fashion what was expected of them. 'I took it a little easier with Kenny because he was young and because he had never been before a mic, other than his home recorder mic. Kenny was a little shy at first because he had not had any experience on radio. He was more or less a young boy off the street. However, it took Kenny very little time to get into the swing of things and to do a better job than most of the other DJs. Within a few months, he became a master at his profession. He was bordering on genius.'

Because of his total inexperience, Maurice was nowhere to be heard when Radio London started broadcasting at six a.m. on 23 December 1964 with Paul Kaye announcing, 'Good morning, ladies and gentlemen, this is Radio London transmitting in the medium wave band on 266 metres, 1133 kilocycles.' It wasn't until the early hours of Christmas Day that his soon-to-be-instantly-recognizable dulcet tones made an appearance, by which time he was no longer Maurice Cole, but Kenny Everett.

Cate recalls her brother telling her how one day he went into the producer's office and was told quite matter-of-factly, 'You have to change your name. Maurice Cole just doesn't cut it as the name of a pirate DJ. Any ideas?' And Ev said, 'Well, there's a guy called Edward Everett Horton that I loved in films, so that's good enough for me, you can call me Everett Horton.' Horton was a character actor with a long career in cinema dating back to the twenties; his wry grin, outrageous double takes and anxious mannerisms had made him a master of drawing-room comedy.

The producer looked at Maurice and thought for a while. 'How about just using Everett? And you look like a Kenny to me, so we'll call you Kenny Everett.'

Interestingly there was a DJ working on local radio in Texas during the fifties called Kenny Everett – a coincidence, no doubt, since it's unlikely our Kenny would ever have heard of him.

Kenny's Radio London debut coincided with the station launching a campaign against drunk driving. Each DJ had been told to draw attention to the perils of being sloshed behind the wheel. Kenny wasted no time in tackling the topic, in a way that was to prove characteristic of his radio style. 'Tonight,' he said, in heavy, whispery tones, 'I want you, before you drive home from the party . . . I want you to get drunk.' Behind the glass, Tony Windsor, the station's senior DJ who'd been posted to oversee Everett's maiden voyage in front of the microphone, could scarcely believe what he was hearing. Kenny carried on unruffled, indeed warming to the subject: 'I want you to get quite drunk – no, not quite drunk, *very* drunk. I want you to get plastered. I want you to get so drunk you can't even find the keys to your car.' Windsor gave a huge sigh of relief; Kenny had cleverly saved himself at the last second. His little escapade was soon the talk of the ship. Fellow DJ Paul Kaye thought it was a great gag, one that made him realize that the station might have a natural on their hands.

Kenny wasn't allowed to bask in the success of his maiden radio broadcast. His fellow DJs swiftly surrounded him and hung him by his ankles over the side of the boat – an initiation ceremony that absolutely terrified him. The boisterous nature of the jocks and their little cliques was something totally alien to Everett. In the early days, before he settled in, Kenny hardly spoke to anyone. Indeed, he would remain something of a loner for his whole stay on Radio London. 'He was very shy and naive,' says Chris Peers. 'Terribly shy. But put him in front of a microphone and bang, he became another person entirely. He was like two different people.'

Radio London made an immediate impact on listeners, thanks in part to that 50,000-watt transmitter. Even on land, a transmitter that size would be considered massively powerful, but being on water boosted the signal, so from day one Radio London had a huge advantage over its competitors. Johnnie Walker, who was living in Birmingham back then and had yet to launch his own DJ career, recalls that it was possible to tune into Radio London, 'but it was very hard to pick up Caroline'. The radical new sound of the station's disc jockeys also contributed to its success. 'Radio London was a class apart,' says DJ Andy Peebles. 'No disrespect to what Ronan O'Rahilly achieved with Radio Caroline, that was a very good operation, and soon there were dozens of other stations of course, like Radio Essex, 271, Radio Scotland and Radio England, etc. But Radio London was an object lesson. It was the perfect business model.'

Most of the shows on Radio London, or Big L as it was affection-ately known, followed a similar pattern: records interspersed by chat, ads and a quick burst of news on the hour, which in truth was a blatant rip-off, as Kenny later revealed: 'Because we had no news-gathering facilities we used to monitor the Beeb's news bulletins, change a word here or there, cross out anything that was difficult to pronounce and read it ourselves five minutes later in a breathless voice that was supposed to sound as though its owner had just rushed in from a massively busy nerve-centre.' The BBC eventually twigged what was going on and deliberately read out a piece of false news, only to hear it repeated minutes later on Radio London.

Yet to be given his own show, Kenny spent most of his spare time checking out the other DJs and learning how everything worked. Determined to make up for his lack of practical experience, he wanted to find out about the theory and operation of all the electronic equipment aboard. Sometimes his questioning was so meticulous in its detail the station's technical boffins had to refer to their textbooks. Not surprisingly, Kenny struck up a friendship with the two radio engineers, both of whom would watch fascinated as he'd dismantle tape machines to get them to run at different speeds or play things backwards. It was constant experimentation. 'Kenny was a wizard, a genius,' recalls Mitch Philistin. 'He was technically brilliant. I called him the wizard, but I think when he first arrived he didn't have much experience in a studio. I think some of the guys like Tony Windsor helped him, taught him a lot. After that he did his own thing.' Mitch also thinks Kenny was way ahead of the game in terms of where the future of broadcasting and music was heading. 'I remember him saying to me that one day instead of vinyl records we'll play all our music on small discs, I remember him saying that.'

Kenny was particularly fascinated by the American-sounding jingles the station played, something new to the ears of British listeners. These hailed from a company called PAMS, a US-based firm that was the world's leading maker of jingles. He loved nothing better than fiddling around with the tapes on his machines until he came up with a result that was totally new and original. 'Kenny would stay up all night and glue tapes together,' recalls fellow Radio London DJ Duncan Johnson. 'He would stay up all night doing things and then sleep during the day.' Kenny didn't see why a jingle couldn't be as melodic and entertaining as a record, and his efforts were of such startling quality and originality that the DJs put him in charge of editing the jingles for their shows. Pretty soon Kenny was dreaming up his own jingles, mixing instrumental backing music with tracks featuring his own vocals. In other words, he was sampling in the days before anyone knew what sampling was; and all on fairly basic equipment.

Most of the electronics in the ship's studio, such as the turntables and the RAC cartridge machines with their big bulky tapes, were run from a single generator. One day it packed up and everything ground to a halt, save for the microphone and transmitter, which were powered independently. Kenny happened to be in the studio all by himself, filling in for someone, so listeners heard: 'Oh dear, we seem to have lost power on the tunes, folks, so I'll just keep chatting away here.' But what to say? 'Well, I started to tell the story of my life,' Kenny recalled in a BBC interview. 'But it shows how young I was – I ran out after thirty seconds! Oh, it was chronic. It was ten minutes before the DJs upstairs, who were casually listening while they were eating, heard the sound of terror in my voice and came running down to tell jokes and things.'

Having found his feet, or rather sea legs, Kenny was given his own show in the early evening. It rapidly became evident how perfectly in tune he was with the sentiment and ethos of the pirate stations, bursting with energy and creativity. As Tony Blackburn observed, 'Kenny came along exactly at the right time for personality radio.' He was the complete antithesis of Auntie BBC, trapped in the stale crustiness of the fifties. Above all, Kenny was funny and the other DJs loved listening to his show. 'He was the funniest man I'd ever heard on radio,' said fellow Big L presenter Ed Stewart. 'He came out with things we all wished we'd said ourselves. He was doing this commercial for a deodorant and he suddenly improvised with, "It's wrong to pong." He was always making up jingles, doing the voice and the harmonies – quite unique.'

When not on the air, there was little for the DJs to do aboard the *Galaxy*. Their options were limited to relaxing in their cabin or congregating on the messdeck, as most of them did, to read, play cards or watch a small black-and-white television. 'They used to get very, very bored on the boat,' says Andy Peebles. 'And to relieve the boredom Kenny used to lock himself away in a production studio. If anything, being isolated on a ship was the making of Kenny. He had nothing else to do but make brilliant radio. No distractions whatsoever.'

The highlight of the week was the arrival of the tender, which brought food, clothes, magazines and cigarettes. Disputes over money did sometimes arise and on those occasions the supply ship would refuse to deliver. Fresh water was usually the first thing to go and the DJs and crew would find themselves with nothing to drink or wash in for days.

The supply ships also brought the latest batch of record releases, although Philip Birch recalls just before Christmas one year severe weather prevented the tender getting to the ship. 'So I hired a helicopter to take colleague Dennis Maitland and myself to hover over the ship. The pilot was very brave but rightly worried that we would be blown into the mast. I climbed out on to the helicopter's pontoon and Dennis passed me an oversize kitbag containing supplies, tapes and records, and most important, Christmas goodies. I lowered these on a long rope into the waiting arms of the smiling DJs.'

5

Kenny and Cash

KENNY WAS SITTING alone in the mess one morning, suffering another bout of seasickness, when a man walked in. Assuming this stranger must be a new recruit, he introduced himself: 'I'm Maurice Cole, but they call me Kenny Everett. I do early evening.'

The stranger smiled and offered his hand. 'I'm David Wish. They call me Dave Cash. Pleased to meet you.'

'Are you a DJ?' asked Kenny.

'Yes.'

'Experienced?'

'Two years in Vancouver,' said Cash.

'That's one year, eleven months and two weeks more than me,' laughed Kenny. 'I'll show you to your cabin.'

After Cash had unpacked, Kenny took him on a quick guided tour. He was delighted that a new consignment of tapes had arrived from the US radio station KLIF, courtesy of Ben Toney. Without delay Kenny put them on and they both sat down and listened. Out of all the material it was *The Charlie & Harrigan Breakfast Show* that piqued their interest. Every morning the pair went through the day's papers for any amusing or interesting stories to liven up the show. Both Kenny and Cash listened for over an hour, drawn in by the American DJs' personalities and sparky repartee, momentarily aghast though at their assertion that the Beatles were two-hit wonders and would never replace 'good old American rock'n'roll'.

After the tapes were finished, both headed back to the mess, where Kenny set about making a fresh pot of tea. Idly chatting away, Cash mentioned that what he really wanted to do, more than being a disc jockey, was to write. Kenny let this sink in for a moment before asking, 'Can you write comedy as good as Charlie and Harrigan?'

'I can try,' said Cash, intrigued. 'What have you got in mind?'

Looking about him, as if he didn't want anyone to overhear, Kenny said, 'If you can write some characters and sketches as good as them, we could do a double show.'

Undaunted by the fact that there had never been a radio duo in the UK, Kenny and Dave Cash set to work. It seemed the obvious thing to do, since Kenny still felt a little timid and nervous in front of the mic: 'Things didn't seem quite so frightening if there were two of us to share the speaky bits in between the tunes.' As instinctively brilliant as Ev was, he lacked proper radio technique; Cash was only too willing to share the expertise he'd acquired during his short time in the business, such as making the listener believe you were speaking directly to them. It's a skill only the best radio presenters acquire, and Kenny became a master in the art.

After a few scriptwriting sessions, undertaken mostly by Cash, along with various rewrites and overnight rehearsals (the only hours the studio was free), *The Kenny & Cash Show* went on air in April 1965. It was an immediate hit, going on to become arguably the most successful show ever on the pirate stations. Cash describes it as 'the most fun I ever had on the radio'.

For Kenny it was an opportunity to introduce an element of slapstick and almost surreal humour to proceedings, in between the records and the usual repartee. Both were huge fans of the Goons, and Ben Toney remembers the boys speaking in Goonish voices and calling each other Neddie, referring to the character played by Harry Secombe.

Unlike most double acts, with Kenny and Cash there wasn't a recognizable straight man as such. 'We had too many comedy characters in the show for just one of us to voice,' recalls Cash. 'It would have been impossible. So I played some of them and so did Kenny. We always tried to have characters with accents very different to our own. That way there was never anyone thinking, Awwh, you can tell it's one of them. One of mine was a Dutch character called Seaman Marks. We were being very deliberately rude, of course, but nobody said a thing and we totally got away with it. It was like Cupid Stunt. It didn't take a genius to work out what we meant.'

By and large, Kenny liked to voice the female characters in sketches, simply because he had a higher vocal range. 'But he was reluctant to do any camp voices,' stresses Cash. 'So it fell to me to voice characters like Camp Danny [a gay cabin boy who ultimately didn't make the airwaves, being deemed too risky by the management]. I loved it. All I did was copy Kenneth Williams, really.'

Then there was Henrietta Dog, a colossally fat woman the captain had brought on board as ballast, who ate everything in sight. Too large to fit through the studio door, Kenny pretended to shout all Henrietta's dialogue from the corridor. She would moan about not having eaten for three minutes – 'I'm bleeding starving!' – and then threaten to sit on Cash if he didn't hand over some cakes. This would be followed by much joshing about: 'Stop it, you fat, hairy beast, you'll sink the bloody ship!' Cue sound effects of timbers breaking and water rushing in. This, along with Camp Danny and much of the other material the pair wrote and produced, never made the final broadcast. Cash recalls: 'A guy called Tony Windsor was the head disc jockey. We were all in our late teens and twenties, he was around forty, so he was the top DJ, and he'd had a lot of experience on Australian radio. He said to us, "Everything before it goes on the air goes past me, all right?"' Some of the stuff we did was pretty near the knuckle and Windsor would say, "Very fucking funny, but no fucking way."'

A lot of the humour derived from sound effects, the sort of thing where a request for listeners to send in an express request would be accompanied by a sudden blast from a locomotive engine. This might seem a bit tired by today's standards, but it was new and fresh back in 1965. It also required glorious ingenuity on the part of the DJs, as Cash explains: 'Radio production facilities on the ship, especially sound effects, were at best limited and at worst non-existent. We had a few tapes of basic boings, thuds and whistles, but anything special we would have to make ourselves.' It was an echo of what the Goons used to do. There are many tales of Spike Milligan hunting around Broadcasting House for suitable objects from which to retrieve the most odd-sounding noises. Kenny and Cash would scour the MV *Galaxy* in much the same way. For one sketch they needed the sound of someone diving into the sea, swimming ashore and back again. Kenny came up with the solution: the station's portable Ampex tape recorder was duly carried into the galley to capture the sound of them filling the sink with water and then dropping an apple into it. When the tape was played back at half the speed, it sounded like something much heavier. For the swimming effect they merely splashed their fingers in the water and added a bit of echo.

Their genius was appreciated by listeners. Nicky Horne, later a DJ with Kenny at Capital, says, 'We'd never heard anything like it before in this country, and actually there's not been anything like it since. It was so clever. You think that they did that in a small ship, bobbing around in the North Sea, sometimes in the most appalling weather, and they were in this rust bucket of a boat that stank of diesel fuel and perspiration, and these two were able to conjure up this world that was both surreal and fascinating, and the wit that came from it was amazing.'

Andy Peebles agrees. 'One of the highlights of listening to Radio London was definitely *The Kenny & Cash Show*. Double-header shows don't always work, but I think Kenny and Dave Cash were very, very special. They had an electric rapport. One of the worst things about double-headed shows is when it becomes patently obvious that one presenter is just trying to outdo the other. You never really got that with Kenny and Cash. Kenny was so quick in terms of response and I think Dave loved every minute of it.'

Within weeks *The Kenny & Cash Show* was required listening for pirate competitors. DJ Paul Burnett, who did the breakfast show on Radio 270, broadcasting from a converted Dutch lugger positioned in international waters off Scarborough, envied the established pirate stations. The Radio 270 ship was smaller than its rivals and therefore even more uncomfortable in rough seas; Burnett once famously threw up live on the air in the middle of reading a script advertising the delights of a bacon breakfast. 'At night you could sometimes pick London and Caroline up,' he recalls. 'And we'd spend hours fiddling with our transistor radios, trying to listen to the likes of Tony Blackburn, Johnnie Walker and Kenny, of course. Kenny was so unlike most of us though. Hand on heart, all we were simply doing was to emulate American radio. We had no concept of anything else, that was the only music radio we'd ever heard. But then you had Kenny doing something completely different. He wasn't copying anyone, really. He was already a legend back in the mid-sixties, believe it or not. Certainly to his peers.'

The reaction to the show, indicated by the fan mail flooding in, was so positive that it bolstered Kenny's confidence and he began taking even more risks live on air, overstepping the mark on several occasions. 'The classic one was Rothmans cigarettes,' recalls Chris Peers. 'Kenny had to do some of the commercials, read them out. I can't remember this particular script but it was for Rothmans cigarettes and he kept coughing the whole time. Well, that created quite a ruckus and I was actually dragged into the Radio London office and told to reprimand Kenny about it.'

On another occasion, after an ad for Birds Eye peas, he came on air and said, 'Oh yeah, I know Birds Eye peas, they taste like bullets.' Again, he was rapped over the knuckles. 'But that's what Kenny did,' says fellow Big L DJ Pete Drummond. 'He didn't give a shit. He absolutely didn't give a shit. He didn't think, Oh, how will this go down? And that's a sign of genius, if you like. He never did it on purpose, he just did it because that was his nature. He was very flamboyant, even then.'

Kenny and Cash would sometimes speak over the records, too – or at least the intros and outros. This style of presenting didn't suit everyone, and there were some listeners who (à la BBC) wanted to listen to the records uninterrupted. Not an unreasonable request, you might think, but when Kenny and Cash received a letter to this effect, they threw their turntables well and truly out of the pram – and with good reason.

In their eyes, the style of presenting to which these people were referring was dead in the water, and came straight out of Broadcasting House via the Light Programme. It was NOT, as the jingle goes, 'the highly successful sound of wonderful Radio London'.

On the face of it, the content of the letter was neither confrontational nor offensive. Then again, asking two of radio's most popular young DJs to stop talking (even for a few seconds) was like asking the Archbishop of Canterbury to stop praying. These chaps had a cause, they were doing their bit to revolutionize music radio. Lest we forget, they were broadcasting from ships for a reason. The very thought of being dragged back to the arid, humourless void that was the Light Programme went against everything pirate radio stood (or floated) for.

Kenny and Cash did not try to hide their displeasure. The author of the offending letter was given both barrels live on air. The diatribe was part-planned, with Cash opening proceedings with a few terse words, followed by a raspberry. Then came Kenny: 'The letter goes, "Could you please tell me why they do not announce the record and then be deathly quiet until the end like other disc jockeys." Well, let me tell you, matey, if you tune in to a certain station called the British Bucket Company you can get all you want because they've been dying for eighteen years.'

And he meant it.

At this point in his life it was rare for Kenny to show his emotions, and to do so on-air was totally out of character. Even when he was annoyed by something, he would usually react with a mixture of exasperation and humour. Not out-and-out vitriol. The dig at the BBC though is quite telling. As much as he loved the Beeb (as he was later to christen it), it offered little in the way of entertainment for anyone under the age of forty. Pirate radio wasn't simply a commercial exercise, it was an expression of freedom and choice – something the BBC could never have been accused of back then.

With eight million listeners, Radio London was now the most power-ful of the pirate stations. Its popularity earned it an integral part in a movie. Filmed with the backing of the Rank Organisation, *Dateline*

Diamonds was a B-picture whose thin plot revolved around the MV *Galaxy* being used to smuggle diamonds between Holland and the UK, with the gemstones concealed inside band demo-tape boxes. Shot in the summer of 1965, the film was released in April 1966 as the support feature to *Doctor in Clover*. Starring William Lucas, Conrad Phillips and Kenneth Cope, *Dateline Diamonds* also included performances from the Small Faces, Kiki Dee and the Chantelles.

To add a veneer of authenticity to the film, both Philip Birch and Ben Toney were credited as technical advisers. They also appear briefly, as does Kenny, playing himself, the only Radio London DJ to do so; confirmation, says Birch, 'of his importance as a Big L presenter'. He even gets a couple of lines and is glimpsed greeting a young Kiki Dee as she steps aboard the ship.

As for interior scenes, a rather fanciful mock-up of the Radio London studio was built, portholes included, at the famous Pinewood Studios. Both Birch and Toney went down for the day and confirm that Kenny came with them. After the short scene was wrapped, Toney recalls they were all invited on to an adjoining stage, where Sean Connery was shooting the latest James Bond movie *Thunderball*. The scene was the climactic fight between Bond and baddie Largo aboard a runaway hydrofoil, a replica of which had been built on the stage. Toney recalls with humour watching as stagehands furiously rocked it from side to side as Connery went through his 007 paces.

Dateline Diamonds may have failed to capitalize on the cultural importance of Radio London, but the station's impact was certainly being felt around the country. It seemed to catch the mood of the Swinging Sixties, even helping to define it. 'The enthusiasm of those early days was something I'll never forget,' Kenney later recalled. 'There really was a sense of pioneering adventure about the whole thing. And the response from the public was sensational. Everyone had their ears glued to the pirates, waiting for the next outrageous joke or the latest hit record, which it would take the Beeb months to play.' Even the station itself became a tourist attraction with swarms of people sailing over on day-trips to catch a glimpse of their favourite DJ taking a stroll on deck and to shout out requests for records.

The pirate DJs were all on a rota system, with three weeks aboard followed by a break where they were let loose on the mainland. The tender would pick them up from the pirate ships and deposit them all at Harwich, where a minibus would be waiting to take them to Ipswich railway station. From there they'd catch a train to Liverpool Street station to be greeted, more often than not, by crowds of screaming girls; the cult of the celebrity disc jockey had begun.

It was while they were on shore leave that the DJs picked up their wages. Most of them received £25 a week – Kenny included, now that he was established – so they'd collect £75 in total, a king's ransom in those days. 'You could have a great week on £75,' recalls Johnnie Walker. 'And you'd bump into each other in clubs or the Red Lion pub in Waverton Street, Mayfair – that was the place where all the pirate DJs used to drink.'

The irony was that most of the DJs never had to spend a penny in London because music publishers and record companies took them out for lunch, dinner, the works. They'd also earn extra dosh making personal appearances or gigging at clubs. Radio London was also quick to cash in on its popularity, sponsoring concerts at the Wimbledon Palais and the already famous Marquee Club, featuring the likes of Lulu, the Kinks, Tom Jones, the Animals, Sandie Shaw and the Walker Brothers.

Kenny and Cash hosted a few of these gigs but not many, as Dave Cash recalls: 'We did the Marquee Club and the Wimbledon Palais together, but that was about it. Kenny would usually go straight to Liverpool as soon as he came ashore. The Marquee Club was great. They'd rename it The Big L Club for the night and all the presenters would turn up for a guest appearance. Kenny didn't enjoy performing in front of a live audience though. He also hated public transport. I used to love double-decker buses and always used to turn up to the gigs on one. Kenny would always get a cab!'

When he wasn't going back to visit his mum and dad, Kenny kept a low profile in London. Occasionally he'd visit his sister, who'd recently got married to Conor, a businessman. One night they were having a dinner party and invited Ev along. 'He was so unsophisticated and new to London,' says Cate. Conor's best man was invited and brought in tow the sister of a second-tier royal. 'She was rather self-important and domineering in the conversation,' remembers Cate. 'Ev made some comment and she tried to put him down by saying, "Do I look like the type who would be interested in pop music?" And he just gave her a long, long look and said, "No, actually, no." It was the timing, the way he looked at her and the way he said it, she visibly withered, and was rather quiet thereafter. I thought, well, you've certainly got something, young man.' This ability to spout acidic put-downs at the drop of a hat is something that Cate believes Kenny inherited from Lily. 'My mother was a very kind person, but she could lacerate someone with her tongue.'

Kenny's profile in London was so low that many of his fellow pirate DJs can't recall ever socializing with him. They'd bed groupies and go out drinking; Kenny wasn't part of that scene at all. 'One suspected on the ship that he wasn't straight,' remembered Ed Stewart. 'I don't think he was quite sure of his sexuality. He never talked about girls. He was shy, a very shy boy.'

Cash certainly knew that Everett was gay. He'd sorted him out a flat in the same block where he lived: Bristol House on Lower Sloane Street in Chelsea. Everett only brought round male friends, never a woman. And Cash was acutely aware that these men were friends rather than lovers. 'Kenny was very naive. He was very affectionate. If he liked you, he loved you. He would often give me hugs. If he disliked you, he hated you. There was no halfway house.'

While they had different social interests ('I was a twenty-two/twenty-three-year-old straight man who was single and had been stuck on a ship for three weeks,' says Cash. 'You figure it out!'), one Friday night he managed to persuade Kenny to come with him to Guys & Dolls, a club on the King's Road. 'I ended up pulling a girl,' recalls Cash. 'And Kenny obviously didn't. So the three of us walk back to Bristol House and as I open my door Kenny begins to follow us in. I said, "What are you doing? You've got your own flat." And he said, "I'll just come in for a coffee." So he came in and had a coffee, but then wouldn't leave! He just sat there telling jokes. He had this girl in hysterics, so she was happy enough. I just sat there trying to catch his eye, giving him a "Look, will you just fuck off?" type look!' The next morning over breakfast it was Kenny rather than Cash who appeared the most offended. 'I wasn't very happy with you going with a girl,' he complained. 'I think it hurt him', is the way Cash remembers it.

While in London, Kenny hung around with a small clique of gay people he'd befriended from the music business. One of them was Jonathan King. They'd first met when King, then still an undergraduate at the University of Cambridge, came aboard the *Galaxy* to plug his single 'Everyone's Gone to the Moon'. It was Tony Windsor who was responsible for turning the memorable tune into a monster hit. 'Tony did the morning show,' says King. 'And I remember him saying, "Here's a record from a good friend of ours and we think it's superb," and he played the song. Then he said, "Isn't that brilliant! I tell you what, it's so brilliant we're going to play it again," and he put the needle on and played it again. Then, he played it a third time! I couldn't believe it. The next time he came ashore I saw him and said, "Thank you! You've made my song a hit. I can't believe you played it three times in a row!" And he looked at me and said, "Do you want to know the truth, Jonathan? I couldn't get the other turntable to work." So my entire recording career was actually started by a malfunction of equipment. It went on to sell four and a half million copies.'

King quickly became an ally of the station and enjoyed giving the DJs female nicknames, as he liked to do with all his male friends. Tony Windsor became Wendy Windsor, for example, and Kenny was Edith Everett. It was a name that stuck and which Kenny continued to use for the rest of his life, often signing letters, 'Yours, Auntie Edith'. Kenny and King often met up and hung out together. 'I used to play him a lot of new music,' recalls King. 'I was the first person to play him the Harry Nilsson records, which nobody in the UK had heard before. They were played to me in Los Angeles by Davy Jones of the Monkees. He very kindly gave me the record, so I brought it back and played it to Kenny and to John Lennon and everybody, and that's how everyone became Harry Nilsson fans.'

King also used to take Kenny down to see his mum in Forest Green.

'Kenny adored my mum and she loved him.' One glorious afternoon they were lying on her lawn, looking up at the sky, when a cloud suddenly obscured the sun. King turned to Kenny and pointed at the offending cloud. 'Vibes,' King said. Just then it began to slowly move away. 'For some reason Kenny thought this was the funniest thing ever and started to use the word constantly. And that's how the word "vibes" came to be so huge in the sixties. It was Kenny.'

Kenny was now regularly ranked in newspaper polls as one of the most popular DJs in Britain. This was largely thanks to the continued success of his own solo show and his partnership with Dave Cash, which had continued to retain its freshness and innovation. The pair of them were doing stuff that nobody else was attempting; they would run competitions like 'the most hated group', and nominate people to be in the 'out crowd' as opposed to the 'in crowd'. They were even given their own regular column in the music press. Ed Stewart recalls arriving in the studio to read the news bulletin when Kenny and Cash opened a bottle of champagne to celebrate their latest ratings. Feeling a bit giddy after one glass, Stewart had to read some awful thing about a politician being assassinated. Looking over the top of the desk he saw Kenny with two pieces of chalk stuffed up his nose and cracked. Unable to control his giggles, they had to put a jingle on.

Most of the fun on the ship seemed to emanate from Kenny. It was probably Ev who wrote the famous sign – 'Please Don't Feed the Disc Jockeys' – and held it up when the day-trippers came by in their boats. But this façade of fun and bubbly energy hid a naive and innocent young man, the timid creature Cate had waved goodbye to in the dark outside her flat.

As he was relaxing on deck with Ed Stewart one afternoon, the Beatles track 'Yesterday' came on the radio.

'Ah, that's a great piece of music, beautiful song,' said Stewart. 'Do you know, Kenny, it's like a musical orgasm.'

Kenny looked puzzled. 'What's that?'

'Well,' said Ed, 'it's like, every time I hear this record I have an orgasm.'

The next day Kenny was presenting his solo show and after playing

'Yesterday' announced into the mic, 'You know listeners, every time Ed Stewart hears this he has an orgasm.' The word orgasm had never been uttered on live radio before and Kenny was instantly dismissed, only to be reinstated twenty-four hours later when the bosses realized he genuinely didn't know the meaning of the word.

This being the era of novelty records, it wasn't long before Kenny and Cash were lured into putting out their own single. TV comedy writer David Cummings, who worked for Dave Allen, Kenneth Horne and Dick Emery, was inspired to write a song entitled 'Knees' after hearing the DJs pontificate on the subject during one of their shows. Kenny and Cash were hauled in for the recording session, and even stayed around for the B-side, for which the backing music was the theme tune to *The Kenny & Cash Show*. As Cummings later recalled, 'Kenny sulked a bit through the recording session with a What-the-hell-have-I-got-myself-into? attitude. Dave Cash was cheerful and seemed to really enjoy it.'

The hope was that the record would at least get airplay on Radio London, but by the time 'Knees' was released in November 1965 both Kenny and Cash had left the station, 'so nobody ever played it any-where,' complained Cummings. 'Unless they were trying to irritate Kenny years later.' Ev hated the record, probably because he saw him-self as something of a musical connoisseur and didn't want to be associated with a novelty record.

That October *The Kenny & Cash Show* had come to a premature end. 'I had a kidney stone which was brought on by the lime deposits in the drinking water aboard the MV *Galaxy*,' reveals Cash. 'Fortunately I became ill whilst I was onshore. They got rid of the stone but the doctor said if you go back on the boat and it happens again it could well be fatal. So I really had to leave the ship.'

Even today, *The Kenny & Cash Show* is fondly remembered. It proved hugely influential, but to a large extent they were victims of their own success. The ad-libs and surreal comedy that formed such an integral part of their appeal often ran counter to the management's preferred American format of Top 40 radio. For instance, they'd sometimes devote hours to playing nothing but the Beatles or the

Beach Boys, earning themselves a rollicking from Ben Toney: 'You guys break format again and I'm kicking your ass!'

'What's a format?' Kenny hit back, quick as a flash. 'Is that something you put down and wipe your feet on? You mean a floor mat, you just pronounce it differently because you're a Texan.'

It could be said that Kenny's self-confidence had begun to border on arrogance. Maybe he thought his popularity was such that he could get away with most anything. Or was it just plain mischief? Either way, he was to be proved very wrong.

The Worldwide Church of God was an American evangelical outfit based in California that paid Radio London a sizeable fee to broadcast a half-hour show called *The World Tomorrow*, featuring the preaching of its leader – or as Kenny dubbed him, 'religious maniac' – seventy-two-year-old Garner Ted Armstrong. 'All the DJs hated *The World Tomorrow*,' recalls Dave Cash. 'We never listened.' Worse, the programme interrupted Kenny's show every night, which pissed him off no end. 'Ev would do four Beatles tracks in a row to welcome the listeners back,' says Cash. 'Not ever knowing how many listeners there would be.'

In addition to finding this a huge inconvenience, Kenny didn't care much for the religious content: 'I'm quite an optimist. He was fire and brimstone. He used to come on and say, "Ladies and gentlemen, the world is falling about your ears, people are being nasty to each other, killing, murder, rape and horror! Send money now and I'll send you a pamphlet telling you how to live better."' After a while, Ev started to hit back, cooing 'Hello, vicar,' as Garner Ted's sonorous tones invaded the airwaves. More brazen was a tape of Ted's sermons edited in such a way as to make it sound as if the preacher was endorsing violent crime. In the end Kenny decided against playing it, but foolishly put on air another tape he'd made where Armstrong repeated the word 'Rape'. When it was heard by a Church of God underling, Kenny was walking on decidedly thin ice. Of course, in today's climate the things Kenny came out with wouldn't raise an eyebrow, but back then it was pretty close to the bone. 'Out on the pirate ships, when Kenny said something outrageous, it was probably two or three days, particularly if there was a storm going on, before anybody could get to him,' says Tony Blackburn. 'And by that time they'd probably forgotten what he'd said anyway.' In this instance, however, Philip Birch was forced to make a personal trip out to the *Galaxy* to reprimand Kenny about his digs at Garner Ted. 'You're a broadcaster,' he ranted. 'You're talking about a guy who is bringing a ton of money in.'

Unrepentant, Kenny continued to make corrosive and disparaging remarks about *The World Tomorrow*, displaying, in the words of Ben Toney, 'a total lack of professionalism'. Then one day in November Garner Ted himself, on a short visit to Britain, tuned in and heard Kenny's acerbic potshots. Without pausing for breath he was on the phone to Birch with an ultimatum: 'Either that little creep goes, or I pull the programme.' Birch had no choice, Kenny was history. It's a decision he still remembers having to make and remains convinced was the right one. 'Kenny was very much a rebel and had to be reprimanded several times regarding adverse comments about sponsors. Eventually it got out of hand and we had to sack him. Not an easy decision.'

Far from being distraught, Kenny was quietly pleased about his dismissal. 'I think he was very nonchalant about the whole thing,' remembers Ben Toney. 'It was my opinion that he had become tired of being on the ship, but he was embarrassed to come to me and resign, since I had given him such a great break in his career. So in the end he forced me to sack him.'

A year bobbing about on the waves in a tin bucket had indeed taken its toll on Everett but his departure was keenly felt both by the station and his fellow DJs, according to Birch. 'I recall the general feeling of sadness among the staff. Everyone could see the need for his dismissal, but no one liked it.' Even Kenny felt a soupçon of, if not quite regret, certainly sadness at leaving a place that had been his home for the last twelve months. As the tender slowly took him back to shore Ev turned on the radio to hear Ed Stewart playing 'The Carnival is Over' by the Seekers and a tear fell down his cheek.

6

Freelance Kenny

THANKS TO MAURICE Sellar's association with Radio Luxembourg, Kenny didn't have to wait long to find a new job. Besides, he'd already made a batch of adverts for the station for big companies like Biro and Beechams. 'And we'd always send them up,' Sellar recalls. 'We didn't send up the product, but we did comedy commercials. We were among the very first to do mini sketches to promote the product, and Kenny would play all the voices.'

It was a weird set-up at Radio Luxembourg. Although the station's output was transmitted from this tiny European country, Kenny's programmes were pre-recorded in London and couriered out, an arrangement he was unhappy with, especially given that he didn't have a studio to play around in. He'd been spoilt at Big L, in the sense that he'd always had a free studio at his disposal, and so was able to prepare and 'create' at leisure. Now, he was studio-less. Worse, so far as Kenny was concerned, it all felt a bit false. 'I wasn't broadcasting from where I said I was, and that just seemed wrong.' This wouldn't be the last time he would have to endure these kinds of restrictions.

The majority of Luxembourg's shows were sponsored by specific record labels, which meant that the only records played during these shows were ones the label in question wanted to plug. Hardly surprisingly, it was a state of affairs that narked Kenny. While he appreciated the value of sponsorship and commercial support, this carried things too far. It was Garner Ted Armstrong all over again, except here they'd swapped high-handed religious dogma for low-quality music.

Hundreds of singles were being released every week in those days, with the vast majority sinking without trace. And for good reason! To all intents and purposes, Radio Luxembourg had turned into a musical graveyard. Somewhere records went to die. Labels would push all the stuff they shouldn't have signed on to the station's unsuspecting listeners (throwing in the odd hit so as to keep them tuned in) in the vain hope that some of it might catch on. Not surprisingly, it didn't. And it made for pretty awful listening. To add insult to injury, Kenny was expected to say how brilliant the records were. He felt a total fraud.

Now that Kenny was living in London, Maurice Sellar had the chance to get to know him properly. 'My wife used to look after him and feed him, Kenny always looked like he needed a meal. My secretary used to nanny him, too, because he was like a lost child in the early days. He would hang on to women who were older than him, more mature women. He was looking for a mother substitute. He appealed to women greatly. Women wanted to mother him and he took advantage of that.' As for his homosexuality, Maurice remembers that the Kenny he knew was desperate to date girls. 'He really was very unsure and confused about his sexuality in those days. He had no idea that he might be gay, or if he did he never let anybody know about it. He did try and form relationships with women. He was completely confused, he had no idea which way to swing, no idea at all.'

Keen to exploit Kenny's success, Maurice got him to host musical themed nights at Tiles, a basement nightclub he'd recently acquired in Oxford Street. 'It was a great place,' says Sellar. 'On one night we had the entire Tamla Motown lot – Stevie Wonder, the Supremes, Smokey Robinson . . . We also had Otis Redding, Ike and Tina Turner, the Who and the Rolling Stones. The club was huge, incredibly successful.'

Kenny played his debut gig there in May 1966, spinning mainly American R&B discs. On immediately before him was fellow DJ Mike Quinn, also playing his first gig at the venue. 'I remember before going on stage walking up and down this long corridor backstage with Kenny going, "Are you nervous?" I said, "Nooo! Are you?" And he went, "Nooo!" We were both putting on this front because it was quite nerve-racking.' Terrifying, in Kenny's case, given that he had developed a genuine phobia of crowds and of performing for a live audience. Torn away from the warm, safe and solitary environment of the studio he felt deeply vulnerable. 'I hate public appearances,' he once confessed. 'I'd far rather be back among my machines.'

Mike Quinn immediately sensed this as he watched Everett from the side of the stage, although he himself revelled in the atmosphere. 'We had an absolutely amazing sound system at Tiles. We had Marshall speakers lined up behind us, racks of them, so when you put the record on, whoosh, this wall of sound hit you. It was a fabulous feeling to be on that stage. But I could see that Kenny wasn't comfortable with the crowd, so he was giving lots of prizes away – that's how he dealt with it, which is clever if you think about it, because you're interacting with the audience and building up a rapport with them. When you're giving people things they're not going to dislike you.'

That first night, Quinn remembers Kenny calling him out on to the stage and in front of the audience asking, 'What's it like to be famous, Mike?' At the time Mike Quinn was one of the co-hosts of a BBC TV pop programme called *A Whole Scene Going* and he had appeared on *Juke Box Jury*, which made him a bit of a celebrity within the burgeoning youth scene. 'So this night Kenny asked me on stage, "What's it like to be a big star?" And I replied, "Well, you'll find out one day, won't you, Kenny?" Because even then I could see his talent, I knew he was good. He was much more than a DJ.'

Maurice Sellar recalls that Kenny was a hit with the customers at Tiles, many of whom came along not just for the live music but for the experience of watching a DJ in action. 'Nowadays you've got Fat Boy Slim and people like that who can pull a big crowd, but in those days a guy who was a DJ was just a guy who stood on the stage and spun discs. He wasn't a star, he was just a guy that got you dancing. Kenny almost preceded the personality DJ. On stage, he had that personality, he would do gags, he worked so hard. And he drew a terrific audience in his own right. So we were doing Kenny Everett nights at Tiles. He was really a big draw. I heard that he didn't like doing live performances, but he certainly didn't show it to me. He'd have a drink or three in our little back office. He was fine.'

Radio Luxembourg was proving less of a success. Kenny wasn't enjoying himself at all and within weeks of joining he was on the lookout for an escape route. Always, one suspects, with an eye on a return to Big L. Freedom came sooner than expected, after Kenny admitted in a magazine interview that he'd once smoked pot. This infuriated Kenny's show-sponsor, Decca, and they, like Garner Ted, rang up the powers that be and demanded his immediate dismissal.

Kenny was thankful, if now unemployed. And he carried on smoking dope, too. Most people in the industry were spliffling quite freely in those days; it was the drug of choice. 'I used to smoke it not so much for the buzz it gave me as for the slightly naughty feeling you got just for doing it,' confessed Kenny. 'It was a bit like farting in church.'

Nor was it his first contact with drugs, or the misuse of them. Back on Radio London he'd overdosed on cough pills after he and one of the technicians experimented with the after-effects of taking too many. Kenny popped fifteen and was zonked out. 'I remember lying in the bunk, trying to figure out how to work my arms and the rest of my anatomy.' And there was this boffin asking, 'What's it like, man. Good buzz?' while Kenny lay there, unable to reply or do anything. He was still in a near-catatonic state when his show went on the air several hours later. Summoning up the energy to clamber to the studio and flop into his chair, Kenny put on a record but quickly realized he was going to be totally incapable of doing anything else, let alone speaking into a microphone and engaging in witty banter. Instead he read a commercial – 'blifghk reg snop tws pfling the grag . . .' It was at that moment his producer came in and carried him back to his cabin.

Within weeks of being sacked by Radio Luxembourg, Kenny was back on the tender, wending his way towards MV *Galaxy*. After several months in exile he was at last back in his favourite place, playing music he adored to an audience who thought he was the best thing since Marconi.

Kenny's return to Radio London in June 1966 was not entirely unexpected. Birch had decided to bring him back 'because we felt he had learned his lesson and the problem wouldn't happen again. Whenever I have had to discharge someone special, it was my practice to try to leave the door open.' So Kenny was back, and as proof of his importance to the station was given the coveted breakfast show.

This time, however, Kenny came face to face with a man he would later come to call his arch nemesis, a man whom he needed no encouragement to ridicule and denigrate in public – Tony Blackburn. Having started his career on Caroline, Blackburn had recently joined Big L and it was here, according to friend and fellow DJ Paul Gambaccini, that Kenny's lifelong antagonism towards him began. 'Kenny told me the story about how on the Radio London boat Tony just walked into the mess one day and announced that he was going to be a big star, and this really rubbed Kenny the wrong way, and I think he just loved sending him up ever after, all from that one moment. Of course, it's also because Tony became the symbol of an entire type of pop presenter. Tony was the incarnation of the spirit of the pop DJ.' Exactly the kind of DJ that Kenny despised; he hated the laziness and cliché-ridden patter of the disc jockey who lamely announced, 'That was Ricky Twinge and the Midwives, the time now is ten fifteen on your groovy platter station, Radio 1, and now a great big biggy from a really outasite band – "You're Too Much" by the Stoatcatchers!' It was Kenny's firm belief that too many DJs believed that this crud was all that was required of them. 'Which it is,' he said. 'Because nobody's used to anything different.'

In one of those great ironies, he literally owed his life to Blackburn. Strolling on deck one night, Kenny thought it would be a jolly wheeze to walk on water. 'Tony says that I was tripping on LSD and I was all set to emulate Jesus Christ's most spectacular stunt.' Blackburn grabbed him and asked what the hell he was playing at. Ev replied that he was Jesus and was about to have a crack at natural water-skiing. Taking him sternly by the arm, Blackburn led Kenny back to his cabin and locked him in.

Kenny's use of drugs had certainly risen a few notches from cough medicine. 'There was a lot of talk about whether the pirate DJs were doing drugs out on the ships,' remembers Johnnie Walker. 'On the

Caroline ship we did actually get into trouble; it was my girlfriend's fault, she gave me three joints to take back. But Kenny was well in advance, I think. The rumour was that Kenny used to drop acid and stand on the boat and look at the stars. Whether or not that was true, it was one of those stories that went around. It was quite a brave thing to do, to kind of surrender your brain for eight hours to go on an LSD trip.'

Walker was at the beginning of what would prove to be a highly illustrious career as a DJ, and before joining Caroline worked on Radio England in 1966. 'I remember I was very nervous on my first broadcast and instead of saying, send your request to Radio England, 32 Curzon Street, London, I said, send your request to Radio London, 32 Curzon Street, England. I was just mortified by making such a stupid mistake and plugging our big rival.' Weeks passed and Walker had managed to forget about his little faux pas when the tender picked him up to go ashore. 'And I saw this little guy with curly hair standing on the deck of the Radio London boat look-ing at us as we pulled alongside,' recalls Walker. 'And he said, "Tell Johnnie Walker, thanks for the plug." And that was my first meeting with Kenny Everett. He made me live through all that embarrassment all over again.'

It wasn't long before Walker's talents were recognized and he joined Caroline. Strangely, he didn't much fancy going to Radio London. 'I think over there it was more professional and the DJs were more into having a career, whereas for the people who worked on Caroline it was more of a way of life, and there was a bit more passion, not so professionally done, the jingles weren't as good.' One thing Walker remembers from his time on Caroline was that most of the DJs on the ship listened to Kenny's show. 'We all thought he was incredible. He was nutty, zany – the word zany could have been invented for Kenny Everett. We just thought he was great. There was nobody else like him. Whereas a lot of DJs, you kind of model yourself on your DJ hero and try and sound like them, but Kenny was just himself. He really was a one-off.'

Kenny continued to have fun on-board the *Galaxy*, where he had befriended David Hawkins, one of the engineers. For a time they rented a flat together in North Audley Street, when they were on shore leave, and Hawkins reveals that Kenny had a girlfriend called Veronica. 'But he was fast coming to the realization that he was gay. He used to call her Knickers. That was her nickname.'

When it was hot the two of them would go swimming in the waters around the boat. 'Kenny was a very good swimmer,' says Hawkins. 'And during July and August we'd often jump overboard and have a dip. Even though it was the dreaded North Sea it was just about bearable. There used to be this bloody long rope which we'd chuck in to the sea, and we'd swim alongside that. The tide was always running at about four knots so if you didn't watch out, you could be in trouble. But we were sensible and we always had somebody watching us, just in case.'

Apart from creeping occasionally out of his shell – though only with a select few, most of them techno boffins rather than his fellow DJs – Kenny continued to spend hours alone in the studio perfecting his show and putting together effects-laden tapes. 'That was the uniqueness of him,' says Blackburn. 'Probably the radio show reflected his brain, which was all mixed up and crazy. He was a crazy person, really.'

As he continued his experiments with sound, electronic phasing became Kenny's new favourite toy. Phasing is a recording technique where you play the same piece of music on two instruments in steady but not identical tempo. The two instruments gradually fall out of unison, creating first a slight echo, then a doubling with each note heard twice, followed by a complex ringing effect, before eventually coming back through doubling and echo into unison. It's been used on many records over the years. 'Kenny could do this live, using two turntables,' claims Bruce Gowers, a television and pop video director who later worked with Everett. 'He'd set two of the same records going, and then drag his finger across one of them to create this phasing sound. It sounds easy, but believe me, it isn't. It's incredibly difficult. Russ Tollerfield, one of the Radio London engineers, told him how it was done, and Kenny went off and perfected it.' While he was at Radio London Kenny created a 'phased' version of the

Herman's Hermits song, 'No Milk Today'. This was played continuously on Big L and listeners eventually preferred it to the original recording. 'He also did the same for the Beatles' "A Day in the Life",' says Gowers. 'So clever. He was ridiculously talented technically.'

Kenny didn't need much of an excuse to play the Beatles. For him they were the consummate pop band. It was the sheer invention in all their tracks, in their beautiful harmonies and adventurous arrangements, that he loved. Rod Argent recalls: 'He had this feature on his radio show where he used to play about a fraction of a second of an opening chord and you had to phone up and say what Beatles track it was.'

Mike Quinn, for one, remembers Kenny never shutting up about the Fab Four, including one bizarre conversation in a car returning from a live gig. 'I think the Beatles should go up in an aeroplane and it should crash and they would all die and they'd be legends for ever.'

'That's a bit strong, Kenny,' went Quinn.

'But they would be, wouldn't they? Be legends.'

Brian Epstein, the Beatles manager, was a big fan of the pirates, especially Radio London, which had become the most sought-after station for record plays. From Big L's inception Ben Toney wanted exclusive plays of new Beatles releases and was forever putting pressure on Tony Barrow, the group's press officer, to get their latest offerings before anyone else. Easier said than done, since the Beatles recorded for EMI, who were foremost in the battle against the pirates. Mysteriously, just before the Beatles released their next 45, someone put an acetate of the record through Dave Cash's letterbox at home. The next time the Beatles released a single, someone handed Kenny an acetate of it in the street. After that, Radio London became the Beatles station – largely because Kenny played them constantly. Ev would be the first DJ in the world to play 'Strawberry Fields Forever', courtesy of a freshly minted copy arriving on-board via Epstein's office.

Kenny's association with the Fab Four, however, was about to get a whole lot more personal.

7

The Fab Five

A COUPLE OF MONTHS after returning to Big L, Kenny was on shore leave when he received a telephone call at his flat. It was Big L programme director, Alan Keen. 'Hi, Kenny. How would you like to go to America and do loads of shows?'

Oh wow, he thought, it was a dream come true, he'd never been to the States before. Oh fabulous, America – New York, Chicago, LA . . . 'What's the purpose of it?' Kenny asked, scarcely concealing the excitement in his voice.

'We'd like you to follow the Beatles around. Thirty-two cities in forty days.'

There was now silence on the other end of the line because Everett had fainted, or so he liked to joke whenever he told the story. 'It was just the best thing. A trip to the States, free, total luxury in fab hotels, and mingling with my idols! So it was just the best phone call ever possible.'

The Beatles 1966 tour of America was to be memorable for a number of reasons. It was dogged by controversy from the outset, on the back of Lennon's ever so slightly inflammatory 'We're bigger than Jesus' remark. Not the best way to kick off a trip around the Bible-belt. It was also to be the Beatles last tour. They'd reached the point where their concerts had little or nothing to do with music – either playing it or listening to it. Instead, it was all about screaming, shouting, fainting, baying, hair-pulling and falling over – and the Fab Four had had enough of it.

Lastly, and most importantly (for us at least), it was where Kenny and the band broke bread and became friends, thus beginning a cycle of relationships and events that would involve parties, arguments, trips (of the acidic variety), interviews, visits to legendary recording sessions, world exclusives, thefts, bespoke jingles, more interviews and a genuine, bona fide love affair.

Firstly though, there was the tour.

Kenny's trip across the good old US of A was sponsored, believe it or not, by Bassett's Jelly Babies. Kenny explained to Beatles historian Richard Porter in 1992 exactly how they came to be involved: 'Well, somebody once threw a Jelly Baby at Ringo during one of their gigs, and he leaned over, picked it up and ate it. At the next gig there were millions of Jelly Babies flying over the footlights, and Mr Bassett heard about this and he thought, Hey, that's a good idea! So he got in touch with Big L and offered to sponsor my trip to America, God bless him! I guess it was lucky they didn't throw something else at them, like condoms! That might have been awkward.'

Only three DJs were invited to follow the tour, all of them pirates. Joining Kenny were Radio Caroline's Jerry Leighton and Radio England's newly hired American jock, Ron O'Quinn. Radio England was the newest addition to the pirate armada and Ron had been brought over from Miami, where he'd been broadcasting on WFUN. He'd only been in the country a few months when he was asked to go back home for the tour. Something he was only too happy to do. 'I was introduced to Brian Epstein not long after I came over to the UK. He subsequently introduced me to the Fab Four, so I kind of knew them. When Radio England first went on air I'd got John and Paul to do some sound-bites for me. The usual kind of stuff – "Hi, this is John Lennon and you're listening to *The Ron O'Quinn Show*." We all got on well though and I pretty much jumped at the chance to follow the tour.'

At around 12 p.m. on 10 August 1966 John, Paul, George, Ringo, Brian, Kenny, Jerry, Ron and the all-girl group the Ronettes, who were supporting the boys on their tour, boarded the Boeing 707, Pan American flight number 53, from London Airport to Chicago. It was a memorable flight from the word go, as Kenny explained in his 1982 autobiography. 'We were taxiing towards take-off in the middle of a thunderstorm at which point one of the engines went kaput and blew up. The Ronettes promptly got off the plane, fearing for their lives. The remaining band of intrepid aviators, myself included, sat pinned to our seats by fear and as we finally took off, I remember John Lennon was gripping the seat for dear life; you could have read a book by the light glowing from his knuckles. I didn't really worry about anything. My only thought was. I'm going to die with the Beatles!'

Once airborne and still alive, Kenny sat back in his seat and tried to relax. It was then that he heard a familiar voice calling, 'Which one's Kenny Everett?' Unable to believe his ears, he answered, 'Here I am,' as Paul McCartney clambered over the seating to introduce himself.

Like most pop bands of the era, the Beatles were huge fans of the pirate stations and appreciated how important they were in keeping pop music alive. After all, where else were they going to get their records played to a mass audience? The BBC's Light Service? All four Beatles had been fans of *The Kenny & Cash Show*, and the fact Kenny was a fellow Scouser didn't hurt either. Strange as it may seem, Kenny was therefore as much a celebrity to the Beatles as they were to him, and the feelings of admiration and respect were reciprocated. Indeed, it wasn't long before McCartney was referring to Kenny as 'one of us'.

Of course, Kenny was excited by the prospect of globetrotting with the Fab Four. But if truth be known he was also absolutely petrified. Yes, he was one of the UK's most popular disc jockeys, and not averse to sharing the odd spliff, but he was also used to spending two weeks on a ship with Tony Blackburn followed by (more often than not) one week at his parents' house in Liverpool. A confident, well-travelled 'Man About Town' he was not.

What made matters worse for Kenny was the realization that, when it came to interviewing somebody, he had absolutely no idea what to do. He also lacked the one thing you really need when it comes to asking people questions: confidence.

Tony Barrow, the Beatles press officer between 1962 and 1968, was the man in charge of the travelling entourage. He remembers Kenny's struggle well. 'I must say that during that tour we kind of nurtured his progress in a way, in that he was quite overwhelmed by the strength of these American DJs, and they were getting all the recording and interview time. Poor old Kenny was waiting his turn politely, but not actually getting a turn.' This ended up working to his advantage, as the Beatles would eventually notice and say, 'We haven't talked to Kenny today.'

Ev was only too aware of his shortcomings and that he was reduced to a bundle of quivering nerves at the prospect of hanging out with the Beatles. 'I had shortcomings stretching in every direction, as far as the eye could see – especially when it came to interviewing. I was the absolute pits! I hadn't worked out that interviewing people involved asking questions which needed answering. Questions were an invasion, especially naff questions like the ones I eventually came up with. I was very lucky because they knew they were trapped with me for the whole tour and so they took pity on me.'

Questions may well have been an invasion, but even the Beatles knew that they needed answering. Just as Kenny put up with his sponsors (to a point) because he understood their importance, the Fab Four tolerated DJs and their ilk, and would do what they had to do – even if it was through gritted teeth occasionally.

It was journalist Maureen Cleave's interview with John Lennon in March of that year that had sparked all the controversy which now surrounded the tour. While chatting about religion for an article in the *Evening Standard*, Lennon had quipped: 'Christianity will go. It will vanish and shrink. I needn't argue about that, I'm right and I'll be proved right. We're more popular than Jesus now; I don't know which will go first – rock'n'roll or Christianity. Jesus was all right, but his disciples were thick and ordinary. It's them twisting it that ruins it for me.'

These days he'd have been pilloried for *not* saying something like that, but surprisingly for the time, nobody in the UK batted an eyelid. It was only when the article was reprinted in the USA several months later that the proverbial began to hit the fan. Ron O'Quinn remembers the fallout: 'As far as I know, his words were taken totally out of context. John talked to me about this and explained what had happened. Billy Graham was due to appear in London around that time and John was having a chat with a reporter which was supposed to be off the record. I'm paraphrasing now, as this was such a long time ago, but the reporter had said something like, "If you were both appearing at the Royal Albert Hall, who would draw the larger crowd, Billy Graham or the Beatles?" And John came out and said what he said. The fallout was immense, of course, and it took a long, long time to die down.'

Lennon then said something quite salient to Ron, which he remembers whenever he hears a Beatles record. 'He said, "Sometimes I'm not a Beatle, Ron. Sometimes I'm just myself."'

When the tour party arrived in the States, Lennon's comments were still big news. People were burning Beatles records and even the Ku Klux Klan joined in, picketing concerts. 'You must be doing something right if you've upset them!' claimed Ron. 'Even the Mayor of Memphis had said that he didn't want an anti-religious group playing in his city. Brian Epstein though, to his credit, said that we'd go to Memphis anyway, and we did.'

Such was the fury of America's religious right that on the eve of the flight out, Brian Epstein almost cancelled the entire tour. It was only after a hastily arranged press conference and an apology that their fears were quelled enough to proceed.

While Epstein and Lennon were busy fending off members of the Ku Klux Klan, Kenny was facing one or two issues of his own. Anxiety about his inability to interview brought on bouts of self-doubt, paranoia and depression. Not to mention homesickness. Help was at hand though, and from a surprising source. 'I would suffer from these Hiroshima-sized attacks of paranoia and just wander into a corner feeling bad for days. Paul McCartney saw all this going on and took pity on me, thank God! He took me into the bathroom of the hotel where we were staying and said, "Why don't you just ask me one question and I'll rabbit on for a bit? Then you'll have enough material for ages."' This was a godsend for Kenny, because McCartney duly gave him an hour's worth of tape, which by careful rationing was spun out to a few minutes' worth every day for the duration of the tour. 'I pretended that I'd done an interview with him every day,' said Kenny, 'but was actually just letting about ten seconds out, thereby saving my Bassett's bacon!'

Kenny's brief on the tour was simple. Relay back to Radio London a daily selection of interviews, listener messages, clips from concerts and as many 'exclusives' as he could 'overhear'. Kenny may well have been, as he put it, 'really crap at interviewing', but his technical wizardry was undeniable, and it was to prove extremely useful.

The whole process of getting his material across the Atlantic for Big L to broadcast was scarcely, as Kenny observed, 'the height of space-age technology'. He would simply attend the concerts, hold a microphone up in the air and tape the boys singing a couple of songs, 'along with the sound effects of a million knicker-wetting teenage girls'. He'd then do a bit of commentary over the cacophony of screams and rush to the hotel to ring Radio London DJ Paul Kaye, who'd be standing in a public telephone box in Harwich. When Kenny's call came through, Kaye would hold up his telephone earpiece to the microphone while Kenny played his tape down the line. 'He'd then take the tapes out to the ship on the noonday tender, edit all the different bits of concert, Paul's interview and advertisements for jelly babies into a half-hour of totally inaudible, incomprehensible crackleness,' as Kenny remembered it. 'The fact that you could hardly hear what I was saying didn't seem to matter all that much because the excitement of hearing the Beatles was what mattered, and the fact that the crackles were at least from America.'

The crackles were indeed from America, as were the screaming hordes that the band and their entourage spent the majority of their time trying to avoid. Attempting to get thirty or so people safely across America while being pursued by rabid teenagers certainly took some organizing. Every destination and every route had been planned months in advance and against the odds the entire operation ran like clockwork – something which impressed Ron O'Quinn: 'The logistics for the tour were astounding, very impressive. But everywhere we went, whether it be a hotel or a venue, it was completely and constantly surrounded by screaming fans. I promise you, there were hundreds of them. Somehow we were all smuggled out quickly and moved on to the next town. How they did it, I'll never know.'

On one occasion Ron was called in to act as a spur-of-the-moment decoy for Paul McCartney. 'We were trying to leave a hotel and there were a huge line of cars parked outside the back, waiting to take us on to the next city. I remember walking towards my car and I suddenly saw Paul running out of the back doors. He saw me, threw his newspaper at me and dived towards his car. About a second later a multitude of fans stormed through the doors. They looked around, saw me – a dark-haired man holding a newspaper – assumed it was Paul and started running towards me. By the time they realized I wasn't Paul (which I have to say didn't take terribly long), he was safely locked away in his limo. I'd seen what it was like being a Beatle, but that was the first time I'd actually been the subject of a charge, albeit mistakenly. It really was truly terrifying.'

Being on a Beatles tour at the height of their popularity was certainly not for the faint-hearted. In addition to the standard bodyguards and police escorts, an intelligence network had been set up, primarily to counter any activity relating to John's religious faux pas. Thankfully there were no extremist attacks to defend against, but it did uncover a plan by a group of fans to ambush the band's limousines on their way to Shea Stadium. The information came through in the nick of time, as the fleet of limos were already en route. A huge armoured Wells Fargo truck was quickly dispatched to head off and divert the convoy before they reached the ambush point. When Kenny, the band and the entourage turned up, they were waved down, piled into the truck and driven safely to the stadium. Pretty exciting stuff.

The tour was packed with incidents of this nature, but the one which had the biggest impact on Kenny took place seven shows into the tour at the enormous JFK Stadium in Philadelphia. Kenny's description of what happened eventually turned into one of his favourite anecdotes: 'I was with the Fab Four in the middle of the stadium, in a caravan, waiting for the concert to begin. The first rows of audience were way back, behind lots of grass about a quarter of a mile away from the stage and the whole area was alive with millions of kids screaming and stamping their feet hysterically. The madness escalated as the concert began and the music was totally inaudible above the screams that came from the crowd. It was all very impressive and awesome, and all highly spectacular until one fan took it into her head to bust through the police cordon which was dotted along the border between the audience and the pitch. The police, of course, hadn't really experienced anything like the heights of hysteria which were gripping the crowd and hadn't, seemingly, formulated a plan for how to cope with a runaway Beatlemaniac. So, hundreds of policemen rushed forward to yank back this Yank, with the obvious result that the thousands of other fans were able to surge forward like the Charge of the Light Brigade multiplied by ten thousand. From where we were it looked like the Atlantic Ocean converging on this little stage – quite the most terrifying sight imaginable. The lads dropped their guitars and hurtled back to the caravan, which was instantly engulfed in the sea of out-of-control teenagers and rocked all over the place, sending everything flying in all directions. We all thought we were going to die, but there was obviously nothing we could do about it so we jostled around inside the caravan, waiting to meet St Peter. Somehow the police managed to control the crowd eventually and we escaped by the skin of our teeth. The four lads were just as scared as me, of course, but they'd seen it all before – only not perhaps at such a high-pitched level.'

Glad as he was to get home, being on tour with his idols had been a life-changing experience for Kenny. It had also introduced him to a whole new culture – a culture that would both fascinate and inspire him for years to come. Ron O'Quinn shared rooms with Kenny for the duration of the tour, and despite them not becoming close (they were competitors, after all), Ron noticed with some glee the effect that being in America was having on Kenny. 'He was in awe of America at the time. Whereas now there might not be a great deal of difference between our cultures, in the mid-sixties there was a huge difference. Europe was still recovering from World War II back then and the USA never really had that, so I think it's fair to say that we were able to move on at a different pace.'

America also had a commercial economy built on advertising and sponsorship, and this fascinated Kenny. 'I think he was one of the few who could see beyond the pirates,' says Ron. 'In the sense that he envisaged a legitimate future for commercial broadcasting in the UK. Not just the radio but television too. He adored American TV. Watching Kenny soak up our culture was like watching a child playing with their first toy. Maybe two days into the tour Kenny was watching television in our room. He obviously loved American radio as well as the TV because he usually had both on at the same time. Commercials were ever-present of course, but back in the sixties a large percentage of the adverts were for over-the-counter products that you could buy at chemists. Anyway, he turned to me during an ad break once and said, "Ron, is there something wrong with American women?" And I said, "No, not to my knowledge." And he said, "Funny, they all seem to have vaginal itch and hygiene problems."'

Though Kenny seldom referred to his transatlantic escapades with the Fab Four, that's not to say the experience didn't affect him. On the contrary. The tour itself was significant in that it introduced him first-hand to a culture which had fascinated him since childhood, and would go on to inspire him for the rest of his professional life. But by far the most salient 'happening' to emerge from the trip, for Kenny at least, was his now burgeoning relationship with the Fab Four. This was something that would have a bearing not only on his professional life but his personal life too.

8

First Love?

O N HIS RETURN to England Kenny continued to keep himself to himself, more often than not preferring the solitude of a studio over nightclubbing. When he did decide to go out on the town, it was very often in the company of Jonathan King. 'We used to go out when he came ashore, out to clubs and for meals. Kenny was painfully shy at the time and very obviously gay – to me, anyway. He knew I was gay, as did all my friends, and I was also quite loud and eccentric. I suppose I kind of took him under my wing really, in a social sense. I made him feel comfortable.'

King did indeed give Kenny the confidence to get out and about more, and the visits to his parents during weeks off gradually became fewer and fewer. And about time, too. Here was one of the country's biggest talents, just turned twenty-two and on first-name terms with the Beatles, the Kinks and God knows who else, and he was missing out on a golden era.

It wasn't as if Kenny wasn't sociable. Yes, he could be shy at times, and he didn't particularly like crowds, but when he was comfortable and in the right company he could mingle with the best of them. Being on the Beatles tour had helped, as had his friendship with King. Socially, Kenny was at last beginning to find himself. But what about sexually? According to Jonathan King: 'Kenny was a virgin when we met. He knew what he wanted but he wasn't convinced. He was always asking me about homo-sexuality though, and he was very curious. He could be honest with me. In those days, being gay was not only illegal, it was something you didn't talk about, especially if you were a celebrity.'

One day in the early part of 1967, Kenny and Jonathan were invited to a party at Brian Epstein's place in Chapel Street. Kenny was nervous about attending the party, but said he'd go if King did. 'I told him we'd have a great time,' says King. 'And when we got there he completely fell for Brian's assistant – a gentleman called Peter Brown, who is now the head of a PR company in New York. Kenny came running up to me and said, "I've met this guy called Peter and he's really nice."' This was a huge moment for Kenny, and fortunately excitement overcame his nerves and a date was quickly arranged. 'He was over the moon,' says King. 'And that's how Kenny got together with his first lover.'

Peter Brown and Brian Epstein had been best friends since the early sixties, when the Beatles were merely a twinkle in Epstein's eye. Becoming personal assistant to the manager of the Beatles wasn't something Peter had necessarily aspired to though, as he relates: 'It all happened in a flash really. Initially, Brian and I were both running a record shop each, both of which belonged to his family. When the Beatles started to become big, Brian and the band moved to London and I stayed behind, running the shops. Eventually things got so frantic down in London that Brian asked me to come down and be his number two. So that was it, I was off.'

It didn't take Peter long to settle into his new surroundings. 'I loved it. We had a beautiful office and it was just Brian, me and a secretary, and that was where the Beatles could come without being mobbed. My job then was working directly with Brian, looking after the Beatles and Cilla Black. Brian made all the decisions, but I was the only intermediary.' This arrangement worked well for Epstein, as he could now concentrate more on the future and less on the day-to-day issues. 'I suppose I was the perfect choice for Brian,' says Brown. 'For a start, he could trust me, and I knew both the band and Cilla well, as they used to come into my record shop. None of them were famous at the time either, so I knew them as just friends and customers really, which also helped.'

Not only was Peter looking after Brian, Cilla and assorted Beatles, but he was about to take under his wing a wiry but extremely well-known DJ. 'I first met Kenny in early 1967. He was an enchant-ing young man and soon afterwards we started having a relationship. Brian was one of the first people to know about Kenny and I, and the whole thing was treated with the utmost secrecy. It was Kenny's first-ever relationship and I wanted to protect him.'

Soon after they became an item, Epstein invited Peter and Kenny to his house in the country for a few days. Also along for the ride were the Beatles and all their respective wives and girlfriends. It was quite a party and, as you'd expect, involved more than a little revelry. 'Kenny was totally blown out of the water because here he was, staying in a house with the four Beatles,' explains Peter. 'But, equally, they were blown out of the water because they were staying in a house with Kenny Everett. They admired and loved him so much and thought he was the best thing ever – Brian included.'

The Beatles were all aware that Kenny and Brown were sharing a room, but nobody cared. 'The Beatles were just impressed that I was having a relationship with Kenny Everett!' remembers Peter. 'At one point during the weekend Kenny had got a little worse for wear, and I'd gone to bed. George Harrison stepped into the breach and made sure he was OK and took care of him.'

Although Peter was four years Kenny's senior and had a great deal more experience than him, he too had struggled with his sexuality from an early age. Unlike Kenny, though, he had decided to accept who he was, and to hell with the consequences. In fifties Liverpool, that was an extraordinarily brave thing to do. 'I also came from a Catholic family and had actually been ordered out of my parents' house in my late teens, when they discovered that I was participating in, as they called it, unacceptable behaviour. Actually, to be fair to my parents, they were very rational about it and said, "If this is true and you are in fact behaving in this way, then you have to promise us that you'll cease to do this and give up any idea of doing it again, otherwise you can't live in our house." I don't know where I got my strength from but I turned round and said, "OK, I'm out of here." I honestly don't know where I got that courage from. Especially as what I was doing was illegal at the time. Kenny loved that story.'

Peter and Kenny had quickly developed a bond, one which was as much to do with who they were as who they had become. 'He had been weaned on a diet of purgatory and hell for all eternity,' remembers Brown. 'And had, like me, been racked with guilt and worry since an early age. How can that not affect you? When he and I got together, though, it was because he was ready. It was the right time for him. And when it came to the physical side of things, which Kenny had no experience of whatsoever, he was comfortable and willing, and that was very important to me. It was a very happy time for both of us.'

At the end of August 1967 Brian Epstein died from an accidental overdose of sleeping pills. The entire country was in shock and the music world left devastated. Apart from the family though, the person hit hardest was undoubtedly Peter. 'It was a devastating situation for me because he was my best friend, and had been for a long time. There was also a huge amount of immediate additional responsibility for me. I was in pieces really.'

Unfortunately, but perhaps predictably, the end of Brian Epstein's life also meant the end of Peter and Kenny's relationship. Suddenly, Kenny's naivety and inexperience lost its appeal. What Peter needed now was a rock – somebody who would see him through this most difficult of times. 'Kenny was quite needy really,' says Peter, 'which is totally understandable, given his history and situation, but he was also quite immature emotionally, and at that time I needed somebody more on my level.'

The day after Brian Epstein died, Brown was alone in his flat when he received a surprising but very welcome visitor. 'I was feeling rotten at the time, really rotten, and then out of the blue Tommy Nutter came to see me. Tommy was an extremely famous tailor on Savile Row and a good friend of mine. He was also emotionally mature, worldly-wise, and made everything seem better somehow. He was also somebody I found attractive. Things just happened naturally.'

Within a few days Peter and Tommy were a couple, and Kenny was single again. It hit him hard. 'When I think back on it, I was a real prick,' says Peter. 'Kenny was enjoying the relationship very much. But

I was in a real state at the time and had to think of myself. Tommy and I suited each other's needs then, and it worked. We were good together, as Kenny and I had been. But Kenny was pretty devastated, I think, and wouldn't speak to me or see me afterwards.'

Heartbroken, Kenny reverted to his old self, with confusion, guilt and denial once again barging their way to the forefront of his consciousness. The new happy and homosexual Kenny was pushed to the back of the closet, where he would remain for the next seventeen years.

Despite the pain, the break-up was clean and uncomplicated, with each going off and throwing themselves into their work. Peter had the Beatles' empire to look after, while Kenny was about to begin a career with the all-new Radio 1. The pair wouldn't meet again until the mid-eighties, ironically only a few months after Kenny had finally come out. 'I'd wanted to see him for years and eventually tracked him down. He invited me round to his flat, which was just off the Cromwell Road, and so I went round to say hello. We were both a bit nervous really, but Kenny was very sweet and funny and clever. I think he was performing a bit though, which was understandable really. And he had a Russian boyfriend, I remember.'

Both Peter and Kenny would no doubt have benefited from having a private conversation, but it wasn't to be. Peter felt he'd never had the opportunity to explain fully to Kenny what had been going on in his mind and the reasons behind their split. Sadly he never got another chance. 'Kenny was one of the most gorgeous people I'd ever met. He was quite famous at the time, yet had so little life experience. That gave him this wonderful vulnerability, of course. But then there was his enthusiasm. He was so enthusiastic about everything. You honestly couldn't have met a sweeter, more adorable person. He was just infectious. All of him.'

After the tour of America, Kenny's relationship with the Beatles had blossomed, and he became a regular fixture at parties, launches and even recording sessions. Throughout the sixties and seventies he managed to be present at either the conception or birth of quite a few hit singles. He was even asked to participate on occasion – playing percussion on Dave Dee, Dozy, Beaky, Mick and Tich's 1966 hit 'Hideaway', and then providing backing vocals on 'Under the Influence', the B-side to Cliff Richard's 1984 hit, 'The Only Way Out'. You can easily find both on the Internet and Kenny's contributions are apparent.

He was far from being just another hanger-on though. Kenny never fawned over these people, which they obviously found refreshing. He was a collaborator, adviser, critic – and even, on occasion, muse – although this was an accolade he would perhaps have to share with LSD and a golf course. 'I once took an acid trip with John Lennon on Weybridge golf course, of all places,' explained Kenny. Lennon and his 'court-jester friend', Terry Doran, had just emerged from the Speakeasy club in London, spotted Kenny and waltzed over to have a natter. 'The two of them were obviously on something, because John was talking completely incomprehensible drivel and Tony was not only understanding what was being said, but replying in the same off-the-planet vein.'

Suddenly a mass of screaming fans descended and the trio beat a hasty retreat into a car and roared away. Kenny was on the back seat, keeping quiet, hoping they would forget about him and he'd get a trip out to Lennon's house in Weybridge, which he'd been dying to take a peek inside. He was in luck. Terry and John were far too busy inventing new languages to notice their diminutive stowaway, and so drove straight to Weybridge. Kenny then timed his reappearance perfectly. 'As we crunched up the drive of John's house, I poked my nose up from the back and said, "Oh I say, you've gone past my flat, what a pity." John said something like, "Life's a bacon butty," which I took to mean, "Come on in, Ken." So I did, into this Aladdin's Cave of a house with acres of grounds and a brace of swimming pools in the bathroom. I'd never seen anything like it and followed the two of them into the kitchen, where Terry produced and cooked up a can of Heinz tomato soup. I thought, Wow, John Lennon eats Heinz tomato soup – how ordinary. I thought he'd have turtles' eggs flown in from Bangkok and caviar freshly rolled on the hips of Filipino virgins.'

Turtles' eggs were off, so Kenny left John and Terry and found a bed for the night. It had been an interesting day, but tomorrow would prove to be more eventful still. 'The next day John asked me if I wanted some LSD. I thought, Yes, John. Anything you say, John. Tell me to turn into a pickled gherkin and I'll do it. So we popped this stuff in our mouths and ten minutes later I was wondering exactly what I was and where I was and why I was and was I why and who where was . . .' Next, Lennon suggested they go for a walk. Kenny remembered it was raining: 'The sort of upper-class fine rain you could only find in posh places like Weybridge.' Somehow the pair of them managed to walk on to a golf course where a helicopter was about to land. 'I've no idea why,' said Kenny. 'And it's just the sort of surreal thing you'd imagine when you are tripping, but it definitely happened. Or was it a bird?'

A few weeks later (on 6 September 1967, to be exact) Kenny attended an eight-hour recording session at Abbey Road Studios, where John and the others were working on three tracks – 'Fool on the Hill', 'Blue Jay Way' and 'I Am the Walrus'. When it got to midnight John was still working on his vocal track for 'I Am the Walrus' and his voice was beginning to show the strain. Producer George Martin suggested he stop for the night but Lennon was having none of it, choosing instead to plough on. Which is why, if you listen to the song, he sounds, as Kenny put it, 'raucous'.

You don't have to be a Beatlemaniac to know at least one of the nonsensical lines from 'I Am the Walrus', but while laying down his vocal track there was one line in particular which Lennon considered especially poignant, as it appeared to have been inspired by that golf course walk at Weybridge. Kenny was sitting in the control room with George Martin when John got to the lyric about getting a tan from standing in the English rain. Lennon stopped and smiled, and then pressed the button to the studio, 'Eh, Ken, remember that day on Weybridge golf course, do you? When we got a tan from standing in the English rain?' Kenny remembered feeling quite embarrassed and told Lennon to carry on singing. 'Come on, you remember, Weybridge golf course,' said Lennon. 'I just looked blank and very red,' recalled Kenny. 'Eventually he got bored and carried on.'

Since their first meeting in 1966 the Fab Four had been extremely good to Kenny. He was therefore thrilled when, towards the end of 1968, he was given the opportunity to repay their generosity.

Every year, from 1963 to 1969, the Beatles produced a special Christmas single which was given out to members of their official fan club. By the end of 1968 the band were spending less time together and it had become nigh on impossible to produce something collectively. Instead, the boys recorded their songs, skits and messages separately, and then handed the lot to somebody else to make them into a record. Luckily for Kenny, he was the first person they thought of. 'I think I was the only DJ that really spent a lot of time in the studio messing around with tapes,' said Kenny. 'I was quite friendly with some of the people who managed them, and one of them said one day, "If we give you some tapes of them messing around, do you think you could edit them so we can release them on a jolly floppy disc?" That was such an honour, I mean, it wasn't given to me as an honour, it was just, Here, can you make something of these? But I considered it to be a great honour as they could have chosen anybody. And it was fun to do.'

Kenny put together the final two Beatles Christmas records, receiving the following credit on the first: 'Kenny Foreverett had a nice time mucking about with the tapes and deserves to be called producer though this is an unpaid position.' And this on the second: 'Soldered into a collective disc by the iron wrist of Maurice Cole'. So, Kenny's first and only credit as music producer was for the Beatles.

The records themselves are strange affairs, almost light versions of Lennon's 'Revolution 9', which appeared on the *White Album*. What was typical of Everett, though, was that as opposed to shouting about it and telling the world he'd produced the Beatles, he almost forgot about it, only mentioning it in a couple of interviews and then almost in passing.

There are two more Kenny-related Beatle incidents worth mentioning here – once again involving John Lennon. The first came about in

1975 when Kenny was at Capital Radio. He'd received a phone call from Lennon, who at the time was convinced he was being trailed by the FBI, and thought the best thing to do was to go public about it. One of the few people he trusted who had links to the press was Kenny, so he picked up the phone and offered him the whole story. Unbelievably, Kenny wasn't interested in the exclusive, and passed it over to his fellow Capital DJ, Nicky Horne. 'The John Lennon interview was quite pivotal really. Years later it was proved that what John had said in that interview was absolutely right: he was being trailed by the FBI. But it was Kenny who arranged that interview. Out of the blue he came to me and said, "Look, I've had John on the phone and he wants to do this interview and he wants to talk about some quite heavy stuff, and I told him, silly sausage, that it wasn't my sort of thing, but I'm sure it's right up your strasse, so I suggested that you go."' And so off Nicky went to meet John Lennon and do the interview. 'At the beginning, when Lennon was warming me up, he was talking a lot about Kenny and how much he respected him, and asked how he was doing. One of the first things he said to me was, "How's Kenny? What's he up to?" Obviously I couldn't thank Kenny enough.'

As Lennon became less interested in making music, Kenny became less interested in Lennon, and by the mid-seventies he was starting to find him a touch embarrassing. It may seem shallow to some, but Kenny had no interest in world peace or the FBI. He just cared about music and his beloved wireless. As much as he adored the Fab Four as people, it was their musical ability and prolific output that really interested him. Whenever he'd interviewed them, his questions were almost always music-led. His technique may well have been poor, and never really improved, but his intention never wavered. He was a fan who wanted to know how the Beatles worked. That was it. He didn't want to talk about conspiracy theories and the like. He was flattered that Lennon still wanted to offer him exclusives, but would have pre-ferred them to be of a musical variety.

The final straw for Kenny came in 1978, when he received a call from Yoko Ono. 'She said, "An angel's been speaking to John, would you like to tell the world?" And I thought, Oh God, here we go, what now?! Basically, they'd had some kind of "visitation" and had been given a message that they simply had to tell the world.'

Once again, Kenny was the first to be called, except this time they wanted him to act as press officer as opposed to journalist, and to contact as many newspapers as possible. 'It was highly embarrassing,' remembered Kenny, 'because I knew that as soon as I rang the newspapers and told them an angel has been hovering over John's shoulder and here's what she said, that they'd just giggle and guffaw.'

Rather than contact the press en masse, Kenny decided to call Tom Davies, a friend of his who worked at the *Observer*. Leaving John's angel out of the negotiations, he asked whether Tom would help. In 2009 Davies wrote an account of what followed: 'Any journalist would be interested in anything John Lennon had to say, particularly as he had long locked himself away in the Dakota in New York. He hadn't spoken to the press in five years. Phone calls were made and I ended up talking to Yoko Ono.' Tom explained that he'd be happy to run their message, and there followed a brisk round of negotiations. 'They said, Would I use their message in full? Would I promise not to comment on it? Would I do this? Would I do that? More phone calls followed and the "Love Letter from John & Yoko", as it was called, arrived, via Kenny, the following morning.'

The Love Letter ran to two foolscap pages. 'Reading it was one of the great disappointments of my journalistic career,' remembered Davies. 'It was pretentious piffle from top to bottom and I wouldn't have used it in a bad week when I'd nothing to write and the deadline was half an hour away. As a species of writing it was best characterized as Jack Kerouac meets Barbara Cartland with quite a few hangovers.'

It emerged John and Yoko had both become involved in what they called 'the wishing process', or 'the spring-cleaning of our minds!' As Yoko Ono put it: 'The people who come to us are angels in disguise, carrying gifts and messages for the Universe. There is love between them, the city, the country, the earth. Their silence is the silence of love and not of indifference. They are all part of the sky, more so than of the ground. They love everything – even the plants, which one of them originally thought were robbing us of air!'

Kenny was mortified. This was without doubt one of the biggest piles of self-indulgent rubbish he'd ever read, and he would be directly associated with it for evermore. Fortunately for him, Tom Davies appreciated Kenny's predicament, kept quiet and simply put it down to experience.

But the PS at the end of John and Yoko's letter very nearly finished them off. It read, simply: 'We noticed that three angels were looking over our shoulders when we wrote this.'

9

Wonderful Radio 1

W HEN KENNY EMBARKED on his 'second coming' with Radio
London, the pirates were already living on borrowed time.
The government was out to suppress them, leaking to the press
unsubstantiated stories about their unlicensed transmissions inter-
fering with legal broadcasters throughout Europe and with the
emergency services. They were the enemy, persona non grata.

Dear old Auntie BBC didn't much care for them either, especially
since they'd stolen so many listeners. During one of their London
visits, Kenny and Dave Cash met up with Jonathan King, who had
been booked to appear on the *Pete Murray Show*, broadcast on the
BBC's Light Programme. When King asked the pair if they wanted to
come along to see how the opposition worked, they replied, 'Oh,
fantastic, we'd love that.' All three of them duly popped along to
Broadcasting House. 'Pete Murray's producer was a chap called Derek
Chinnery, who later became controller of Radio 1,' King remembers.
'Derek was sitting there when we walked in, so I made the intro-
ductions. Pete then saw me from the studio and waved for me to come
in. As soon as I was through the door he said, "My God, is that Kenny
and Cash?" And I said yes. "Awww great. I listen to them all the time.
I absolutely love them. Why don't they come in and do the interview
with you?" Well, Derek's face was a picture, and we knew there was no
way he was going to allow two pirate DJs to be on the BBC. Derek and
Pete had this almighty row that went on for about ten minutes, after
which Derek got his way. So I went on and did the interview on my
own.'

Despite their hatred of the pirates, those in power at the BBC knew only too well that the entire landscape of radio and the listening habits of the nation had changed, thanks to Big L and Caroline, and they would have to change too in order to stay relevant. Privy to the government's plans to scuttle the pirates, the BBC announced its biggest overhaul since the corporation's inception in 1927. Out would go the Home Service and the Light and Third Programmes in favour of what we know today as Radio 2, 3 and 4. And to occupy the space once dominated by the pirates, a brand-new, mainly 'pop' music service was to be created, known as Radio 1.

At midnight on 14 August 1967, the pirates were officially shut down. The then Labour government, led by Harold Wilson, knew the only way to smash the pirates was to draw up a new law. Thus the Marine Broadcasting Offences Act was drafted, which effectively made it illegal for anyone subject to UK law to operate a pirate station. The Big L, Caroline and all the rest were literally dead in the water. Within twenty-four hours Radio London had shut down operations. Ironically, the BBC played the final hour of the station's transmission throughout Broadcasting House. The very last record played was the Beatles' 'A Day in the Life'.

Millions of listeners mourned the loss of the pirate stations. It was as if the soundtrack of their youth had been stifled without their consent. Philip Birch was one of those left wondering what might have been. 'It is unfortunate that this government's attitude towards independent radio has consistently been one of suppression,' he angrily told the press, 'as part of a determined plan to continue the government's monopoly in radio broadcasting.' Gone then, but not forgotten. Their legacy and influence cannot be underestimated. 'Without the pirates, there would never have been Radio 1,' says Nicky Horne. 'Without the pirates there would also never have been commercial radio. Some of those programmes that were on there, they wrote the book, they were the template.' And according to Tony Blackburn, Big L was the best of the bunch. 'I don't think there's been a station better than it, even to this day. It was just unique.'

A few perceptive DJs had already seen the writing on the wall for the pirates and jumped ship long before the shut-down; Kenny was one of them. He left Radio London in March 1967, and his flat in Lower Sloane Street went from a temporary stopover to a full-time base where he would plan the next step in his bid for radio domination. Having heard rumblings of Auntie's new pirate-style pop station, his plans hinged on inveigling himself into the inner sanctum of the BBC. 'You could always get into the Beeb as long as you were carrying something under the arm. I used to carry a ten-inch tape spool. You won't be stopped as long as you have something.'

Such deception wasn't really necessary since Kenny already had an ally within the BBC in the shape of Johnny Beerling, a young producer who was among those tasked with coming up with ideas for the imminent Radio 1. Their paths first crossed in February 1967 when Beerling paid a visit to the Radio London ship. He shouldn't really have been there, but a friend had invited him. When it was discovered a BBC producer had been aboard, the shit hit the fan. By then it was too late; Beerling had gained a valuable insight into how the pirate stations operated – and he was blown away by what he saw. According to Beerling, it was Kenny who gave most of the secrets away. 'He was delighted to show off all the equipment and demonstrate how it worked and what was going on. It was such a different way of working to those of us in the BBC.' On the pirate ships the DJ sat at a custom-built desk with all the technical bits within arm's reach, essentially controlling everything himself, playing the records and the jingles. This was common practice in American radio but totally alien to the BBC, where it was the producer who spun the records while the DJ sat in a separate glass booth reading from a carefully prepared script. 'The whole notion of self-op studios wasn't like anything the BBC knew about,' says Beerling. 'It was a whole different concept. And the idea of cartridge machines with little loops of tape on them and one man controlling everything – incredible.' What Beerling saw that day, thanks in part to Kenny, was to prove invaluable in the creation of Radio 1.

Beerling also came away from the experience with an enormous respect for Kenny; not merely for his abilities as a DJ but for his technical wizardry and passion for broadcasting. Back in London he put in a call to Robin Scott, Radio 1's first controller, suggesting that Kenny was exactly the type of person they should be mining for ideas. A meeting was duly arranged in the early spring of 1967 at a restaurant in Regent Street, near Broadcasting House. It was a lively lunch and Beerling remembers that 'Robin was quick to appreciate the talents of Kenny' as he explained the requirements for 'self-op' studios.

Another of Kenny's suggestions was rather less well received, initially. 'You know,' he said. 'If you want your Radio 1 to sound credible to a young audience or the audience that used to listen to pirate radio, you must have jingles.' Beerling and Scott looked at one another with blank expressions. The BBC had never used anything so common as jingles, but Kenny was at pains to emphasize their importance, and that the people to get them from were PAMS of Dallas, the best jingle makers in the business. In the end that's exactly what happened; the BBC even used a few of the old Radio London jingles, re-recorded to extol the virtues of Radio 1, a clever idea that made the new station sound instantly recognizable.

As Radio 1 began to take shape, Beerling hired Kenny to work on the popular magazine programme *Where It's At*. Broadcast on Saturday afternoons on the soon to be defunct Light Programme and devised by Beerling, *Where It's At* was BBC radio's answer to what the pirates had been doing: a fast-moving show featuring pop music, gossip, comedy and news. No surprise then that Beerling wanted Kenny to be a part of it. The host was DJ Chris Denning, and initially Everett's job was to provide reports and interviews, but he became an increasingly important member of the team. 'He consistently made a very big creative input into the show,' confirms Beerling. Soon Kenny was coming up with catchy jingles, as well as performing in comedy sketches, including some almost Pythonesque mock commercials in which he provided all the voices.

The highlight of Kenny's stint on *Where It's At* took place on Saturday, 20 May 1967 when the programme aired the new Beatles album *Sgt Pepper's Lonely Hearts Club Band* prior to its June release, playing every track apart from 'A Day in the Life' as the corporation had banned it on the grounds that it promoted a permissive attitude towards drug-taking.

George Harrison had earlier invited Kenny round to his bungalow in Esher to listen to an acetate of the album along with some top producers. 'He put it on the gramophone, and we all sat around and this thing started and blew us away, we were completely gone and on another planet. It was a quantum leap, and we thought, music can stop right here, nobody is ever going to produce anything better than this, so all musicians can go back to bed now. It was the best thing we'd ever heard! And George said, "It's quite good, isn't it?"'

Kenny may not have been the first DJ in the world to play *Sgt Pepper* but he did come up with a smashing idea for how to make up for it. Radio London had been the first station to play the album, obtaining an eight-day UK exclusive, airing it on Friday, 12 May 1967. But when Kenny left Big L he took with him the station's only direct link to the musicians themselves, and that was something which he, as well as his new employers the BBC, were more than willing to exploit.

The idea came about when Kenny received an invitation to the album's launch party, held at Brian Epstein's London home on 19 May, eleven days before the record was released. The guest list was, like Kenny, small but perfectly formed, with only a few journalists and industry bigwigs invited. In reality the launch party was nothing more than a glorified press conference, with every journalist or DJ being given a few minutes with each member of the band. Everyone present was armed with either a tape recorder or pad and pencil – except Kenny. He had arrived with a plan.

It had been decided that, on the following day's show, *Where It's At* would broadcast a preview of *Sgt Pepper* and it would be up to Kenny to throw something special together. Not too dissimilar to the 1966 tour, then. But 'throwing something together' was hardly the Everett way. Kenny went in there knowing exactly what he wanted, even taking with him a few lines for the band to read out. He also pre-recorded a skit, telling the story of how 'Lucy in the Sky with Diamonds' came to be written, told in the style of *Listen with Mother* crossed with *The Goons*.

He got almost nothing from George, who had stormed off after being insulted by a journalist, and there was precious little from Ringo, who had never really understood Kenny's unorthodox interview technique, always taking his questions literally and replying in kind. All the hard work would be left to John, Paul and Kenny.

At face value it's merely a preview of an album with a bit of creativity thrown in. But this was *Sgt Pepper* and these were the Beatles. They were also talking to a mate who just happened to be the wireless's greatest ever exponent, in an era when radio was by far the most important medium when it came to promoting and enjoying music. This was definitely a bona fide 'happening' and a real coup for Kenny.

Kenny did one more Beatles special for *Where It's At*, previewing the band's *Magical Mystery Tour* album and again managing to grab an exclusive chat with the Fab Four. The minute the tapes arrived at the studio, they were hurriedly spliced together while Chris Denning was live on the air. Beerling was left chewing his nails that they'd be finished in time.

During the time they worked together Beerling grew very fond of Kenny, although he found it difficult to get close to Ev on a personal level. 'Kenny was quite introverted, really. We'd call him the dormouse because we could put him in the teapot and put the lid on him. I always felt that the later television shows were really Kenny acting a part, whereas on radio he was being himself.' There was also a reckless side to his nature that Beerling identified quite early on. Once when he was about to go off on holiday with his wife, Beerling was taken aback when Kenny presented him with a tab of acid to take along; in the end he chickened out and returned the tab unused.

Such was Beerling's admiration for Kenny's abilities that he trusted him with the job of making a series of promotional jingles that would saturate the airwaves that summer, plugging the forthcoming Radio 1.

It was Beerling who found an empty room on the third floor of Egton House, which stood next door to Broadcasting House, where Kenny could set up his 'wireless workshop'. Equipped with two tape recorders, a four-channel mixer, a couple of microphones and some turntables, Kenny was 'as happy as a pig in the proverbial', says Beerling. The creativity that emerged from this room over the next few years was extraordinary. 'He was a brilliant technical operator as well as having a real talent for invention,' says Beerling. His jingles became something of a trademark at Radio 1, especially his perfect harmonies. Born with perfect pitch, and trading on his experiences as a choirboy, Kenny knew which notes to hit. And his method for layering harmonies remained the same, even after multi-track recording became industry standard. He would record his voice, play it back and sing along with it while recording on to a second tape machine, then repeat the process over and over again until you ended up with a choir of Kennys. The results were often spectacular. 'He had a beautiful choirboy's voice,' said DJ Steve Wright. 'There was always a vulnerability about his voice, and his singing voice I thought was most like him as a person.'

Some BBC engineers, however, took a dim view of a non-engineer making his own recordings. 'At the BBC it was the done thing that if anyone was recording anything it had to be recorded by a proper recording engineer who had been trained in the BBC way of thinking,' says Beerling. 'And here was Kenny, overmoding and distorting and doing all sorts of things that the engineers didn't feel was right. They were very reluctant to see an outsider coming in.'

Overriding their objections, Beerling gave Kenny free rein. He repaid him by producing a collection of memorable jingles to promote the new Radio 1, including this one that ran ten seconds before the station went on air for the first time:

> (*Sound of Kenny singing in harmony, almost without drawing breath*)
> Music at morning time, music at night time,
> and music whenever you feel it's the right time
> to switch on and groove to the sounds that will let you know
> that you are happy that you own a radio,
> and you can tune to the station that gives you
> a plentiful portion of powerful pop
> and is ready to serve you the music non-stop.

So wait for the news that will happily say
Radio 1 is at last on the way. 5-4-3-2-1.

Tony Blackburn may have gone down in history as spinning the first ever record on Radio 1, but the very first voice on the new station was in fact Kenny.

By early September the DJ line-up for Radio 1 had been announced and they assembled on the steps of All Soul's Church, next door to Broadcasting House, to pose for the national press. Most of them had been culled from the pirate ships. Along with Kenny there was Tony Blackburn, Mike Lennox, John Peel (who'd joined Radio London a month before Everett left), Ed Stewart, Emperor Rosko and Pete Drummond, all mixing it up with former BBC Light Programme presenters like Pete Murray, Alan Freeman, Jimmy Young, David Jacobs and Terry Wogan. Looking back, it was quite a line-up of talent. 'And what was funny was the older guys from the Light Programme tried to dress down and the pirate guys tried to dress up!' recalls Beerling.

Finally, on the morning of 30 September 1967, Radio 1 began broadcasting, with Blackburn opening proceedings by playing 'Flowers in the Rain' by the Move. Kenny liked to tell the story of sitting in his flat, listening to the historic broadcast: 'And Tony went, "Hi everybody, this is Tony Blackburn on the *Tony Blackburn Show* playing lots of Tony Blackburn records..." and as soon as he mentioned Tony Blackburn I heard SCREECCHHH, CRASH! Oh my God. I looked outside the window and there was a car sticking out of the showroom downstairs. Somebody had run into this shop under where I lived. I thought, Oh well, if that's the effect it's going to have!'

Despite massive opposition to the closure of the pirates, Radio 1 hit the ground running, doubling the Light Programme audience within a month of its launch. Not much of a feat when you consider its main competitors had been nobbled. And there was still residual resentment that this replacement service wasn't anywhere near as good. 'The BBC playing records and trying to get in on the act seemed very unhip to us,' says Rod Argent of the Zombies. 'Stations like Caroline and

London were the hip people, really.' Philip Birch was heard to mutter, 'This government imitation is the greatest tribute of all,' momentarily forgetting perhaps that the pirates, especially Radio London, were themselves carbon copies of American stations.

In spite of all his help and influence in the development and launch of Radio 1, Kenny would not be rewarded with his own daily show. Worse, he was spitting hairballs that his arch nemesis Tony Blackburn had secured the coveted breakfast spot. The fact that 'safe' DJs like Blackburn, who fitted easily into the BBC way of doing things, had got the top jobs infuriated him and this gnawing sense of injustice would ultimately escalate into a burning hatred of the corporation.

So where did the BBC top brass decide to place Kenny, arguably the most popular and certainly the most creative of the pirate DJs? Tucked away in a Tuesday lunchtime slot, hosting an hour-long record review programme called *Midday Spin*. And he wouldn't have got that if it hadn't been for the determination of a young producer called Angela Bond who'd previously worked in the old Light Programme's Gramophone Department. At a production meeting she raised the question of Kenny landing the *Midday Spin* gig to executive Mark White. 'Well, actually no,' White admitted. 'Everett's rather difficult to handle and we can't think of anybody who will be able to look after him . . .' White paused momentarily before looking directly at Angela. 'Why, are you volunteering?'

'If it means the difference between having him and not having him, then yes, I'm volunteering,' she replied.

It's incredible to think that without Angela's intervention Kenny might never have been employed at Radio 1. As her daughter, Sue, explains in an email to the authors: 'Mum always said that Kenny was ahead of his time with his innovative radio style and great talent. She has told me that the BBC were reluctant to employ Kenny as they thought he was too erratic and only agreed to take him on if she was willing to act as his producer and keep him under control, which she gladly agreed to do.'

Angela's role in the development and success of Kenny as a DJ at Radio 1 cannot be underestimated. She brought out the best in him and as a partnership they worked brilliantly together. Like Ev, Angela loved radio people and adored her craft. She was warm, friendly and blessed with a terrific sense of humour. She also wore colourful head-gear, until a colleague told her that only lesbians at the BBC wore hats. Remembering Kenny years later Angela said, 'He had this wonderful, mischievous sense of humour. He would look at me from the corner of his eye like a little imp.' Significantly, Angela was almost twenty years older than Kenny and so perfectly fitted his practice of seeking out mature women to act as mother substitutes. When asked to sum up their relationship, Johnny Beerling says, 'Angela was a lovely lady who mothered and encouraged Kenny for many years.' Sadly Angela Bond passed away in January 2013.

Stuck in *Midday Spin*, a show whose rigid format gave him little room, if any, for his brand of anarchic spontaneity, Kenny felt lost and unloved, 'seething every morning as I'd hear Tony Blackburn doing his three-hour daily breakfast show. Aaargh!' It was around this time that Wilfred De'Ath got back in touch and invited Kenny to his house for dinner. They hadn't seen each other for about three years, and De'Ath struggled to recognize the callow youth making his first trip to the capital. 'My wife and I liked him very much when we first met him because he was a vulnerable young man,' he recalls. 'But we didn't like him as much this time. I thought he'd become rather big headed; inevitable, I suppose. So it wasn't such an enjoyable occasion. He was still a pleasant guy, but he spent the whole evening bemoaning the fact that he hadn't got all the publicity that Tony Blackburn was getting. We had a nice evening but he'd been a bit spoilt by success, I thought.'

Kenny wouldn't remain on the sidelines for long. After much badgering by Angela Bond he won himself a two-hour Sunday morn-ing show that December, and also played a prominent part in Radio 1's Christmas Day broadcast, when he was reunited with his old sparring partner Dave Cash. It was a great idea to bring the mavericks back together, but soured by over-efficiency on the part of the BBC. Auntie insisted that the DJs must script the entire show before it would be allowed on air, thus diluting the freewheeling spirit of mad invention and spontaneity that had made them such a success on

Radio London. And yet they still managed to offend someone, as Dave Cash confirms: 'The management thought our show too near the knuckle!' Radio producer Kevin Howlett was only eleven years old when he heard the show and hasn't forgotten it. 'They kept threatening to play "A Day in the Life" by the Beatles, which was still banned at that point. They'd keep playing little snippets from the song, without including any of the lyrics. I think it was too radical for Radio 1 and Johnny Beerling said, "Don't put Kenny and Cash together again!" Kenny was bad enough on his own, but he and Dave used to egg each other on and I think they terrified the BBC.'

For Kenny this meddling typified his new employers. Already he was talking about the 'doomy atmosphere' at Broadcasting House, with its cloistered halls, labyrinthine corridors and faceless suits behind multitudes of anonymous doors. 'Really, to be a good Beeb person you need to be a superb clerk, marvellous at filing,' he jeered, pointing out that there were far more administrators on radio programmes than actual creative talent, people whose job it was to file voluminous typewritten data about how long records lasted and whether the programmes got out on schedule. 'It's all run by Hitler.' Comparing the BBC to the Third Reich was a trifle extreme, but it's an indication of the depth of Kenny's feelings early on in his career. Already he feared that his creativity was in danger of being suffocated beneath layers of bureaucracy: 'Nothing can be done without going through a ridiculous amount of red tape.'

Nevertheless, with Angela Bond behind him, Kenny flourished in his new slot. As ever he was determined to push the boundaries of the medium and challenge the preconceptions of listeners, becoming, for instance, the first DJ to play classical music between pop records, not to mention blasts of George Formby or Busby Berkeley melodies. Every week Angela Bond would go down to the BBC record library and scan the dusty shelves for unusual pieces of music that she knew would appeal to Ev; anything from big band sounds to comedy and classical. 'And he'd come in and the first thing he did, before he even said hello, his eyes would immediately go to this pile of records on the corner of my desk.'

Armed with all these vinyl goodies, Kenny would disappear into his wireless workshop. 'He loved the technical side,' said Angela. 'He lived, breathed and ate it.' Hours later he'd emerge with the most beautifully crafted and downright nutty soundscapes to punctuate his show, creating an almost unique atmosphere for his audience. 'I always thought that the stuff Kenny put into his shows was as interesting as the records he was playing,' says Beerling. Or, as Angela put it, 'He lived in this world of fantasy when he was making his bits and pieces. He was a verbal cartoonist.'

For instance, he'd take some bland music or obscure song and sing his own vocals over it. Steve Wright, one of Kenny's most ardent fans, remembers him playing around once with a B-side to a Clodagh Rodgers hit. 'He took the intro, which was basically a little fifteen-second piano piece, tripled it up so it now ran for forty-five seconds, and sang a jingle over it.'

He'd try out any idea that caught his imagination. In 1970 Kenny was given a new song by the great Matt Monro, somebody he thought highly of. The song in question, 'We're Gonna Change the World', was quite a departure for Monro, swapping his usual swooping ballads for something in the 'pure pop' line. Kenny loved the song and played it at every given opportunity. Although it didn't chart, it became what was known as a 'turntable hit'.

Weeks later, Kenny unearthed an out-take of Matt's vocal from the recording of the song which ends with him collapsing into a huge coughing fit. To the majority of us, hearing one of the greatest singers of a generation spluttering his way through a song would be at least mildly amusing, an audio version of *It'll Be Alright on the Night*. But to Everett the tape was like golden thread, material he could spin into something amusing; or, in this instance, something which would wind up both the BBC and the Musicians' Union.

The skit begins in the style of a fifties news bulletin with Ev telling the listeners, 'It's just been announced there's going to be a musicians' strike. Until we hear more here's some music.' Next we hear the intro to 'We're Gonna Change the World'. A few seconds in, Kenny speaks again, this time as a Musicians' Union shop steward shouting,

'Everybody out, come on!' This is followed by the sound of footsteps, until it appears everyone except Matt has left the room, leaving Matt singing a cappella – cue the out-take. When Monro reaches his inevitable coughing fit, Ev interjects again with, 'I knew he couldn't keep it up . . .'

Incidentally, when a Musicians' Union strike did occur ten years later, Kenny got right behind the cause, even joining the strikers on the picket line!

Comedy was always a vital component of Kenny's appeal, and he was never shy in acknowledging his debt to *The Goons*, especially their use of surreal humour and imaginative sound effects, although he insisted that they merely provided stimulation for him to develop his own brand of comedy. Certainly his radio shows were populated with a gallery of Goon-like characters, and some of his early silly voices, especially those of spivs and hysterical women, have more than a whiff of Peter Sellers about them. In his new Radio 1 show the cast of characters included a garrulous old man who lived in the deepest, darkest recesses of the BBC's gramophone library, a postman who 'delivered' all the latest releases, and a somewhat lecherous crone called Gran, 'a very wise, sophisticated old bat,' who played ancient records and gamely argued with Kenny about how the tunes were better in her day. All these characters would be performed by Everett himself. Often he'd stay at Broadcasting House until late on Saturday night, when the place was almost deserted, recording voices for the following day's show. Later on he introduced a 2001-style authoritarian computer, which he voiced with the aid of a vocoder.

By far the most celebrated of these characters wasn't a work of fiction voiced by Kenny but the spouse of a BBC employee. Angela Bond had been chatting with the woman in the BBC canteen when she introduced her husband, a resting actor called Bryan Colvin, who spoke with a highly cultured voice. Angela turned to Kenny and said, 'What a marvellous voice. You must have him on the show. He could be your butler.' Kenny's eyes lit up. 'Yes, and I'll call him Crisp.' The Jeevesian butler became a mainstay of the show, invariably trying to calm Kenny down as he was chased around the studio by Gran.

As he had done on Radio London, Kenny created his own world, one so utterly captivating that listeners regularly sent in letters addressed to Crisp and Gran. It certainly made an impression on the young Kevin Howlett, who went on to carve out a career in radio himself, working for the BBC before forming his own production company and making several radio documentaries on his hero Everett. 'It was so imaginative. You know that old cliché about radio being the theatre of the mind, well, I completely fell into that Kenny Everett world. You had Crisp and Gran, who were the comedy characters. There was one particular show which I vividly remember. Crisp and Gran locked Kenny out of the studio. That was the idea behind the whole programme. Crisp would say, "Well, madam, shall we play another gramophone record?" And she'd reply, "Ooh, Crisp, yes pleeeeease." And all the time Kenny's banging on the door, trying to get back into the studio. I thought that was wonderful. He painted all these pictures of this grand butler, Crisp, and this mad Gran. The guy who played Crisp had a very natural wit, which I think helped a lot.'

There were also pre-recorded sketches, with Kenny again taking on all the voices. Increasingly fed up with the Beeb's bureaucratic incumbents, its 'old-fashioned ideas and out-of-date equipment', he'd take sideswipes at his paymasters, painting a picture in the listener's mind of Beeb mandarins as old duffers entombed in cobweb-strewn, wood-panelled offices, lost in a time warp circa 1936. It was a cliché he was still playing around with in his TV sketch shows of the eighties. It's a portrait that wasn't too far removed from the truth, according to Johnnie Walker, who followed Kenny to the corporation. 'We used to laugh at the BBC, they were just complete idiots. They were so old-fashioned. All this great music had come along and they'd sort of done nothing about it, they hoped it was a fad, a fashion that would go away after a couple of years. I remember Douglas Muggeridge, who took over from Robin Scott as controller of Radio 1, saying to me once, "You know what, Johnnie? I think really, with hindsight, looking back, I think the BBC totally underestimated the impact of the Beatles."'

Within a few months Kenny's Sunday show had become required

listening and he was being lauded by the nation's critics. As Gillian Reynolds said in a *Guardian* article on Ev: 'His programmes are consistently funny and inventive, owing something to the Goons, something to Wodehouse, but most to Everett's infectious sense of humour.' In a *Financial Times* article, Tony Palmer wrote: 'Most pop people consider Everett the first real genius of radio.' This was a key statement, for Kenny's appeal ran across the board, from the general public to the movers and shakers in the music industry.

Rod Argent agrees that he was enormously respected: 'Artists like the Beatles and later Queen and all the people that he championed, they can tell someone who knows what he's talking about with music and who's got a genuine enthusiasm for it. And you don't always get that these days with presenters, who are quite often just celebrities and the music is almost an afterthought. Kenny was one of a few DJs who were enormously knowledgeable about music and enormous fans of music, and that for me is where a DJ should always come from.'

Within the ranks of Radio 1 itself, Ev was equally admired. Alan Freeman even went so far as to call him 'one of the network's most valuable assets'. David 'Kid' Jensen, later a highly successful DJ, was at Radio Luxembourg when Kenny was on Radio 1 and was a huge fan. 'I was amazed by his creativity and imagination, but what really stuck out for me as a fellow DJ was the effort he put into each show. His shows just flew by and I was always left wanting to hear more. He made compulsive, compelling radio. What marketing people these days call "Appointments to listen".'

10

Lady Lee

I'T'S A MEASURE of the calibre of parties and the kind of circles Kenny was moving in during the mid-sixties that he found himself one evening sitting on the floor in the front room of Brian Epstein's house with Ringo Starr, John Lennon, George Harrison and Klaus Voormann, the well-regarded German musician and graphic artist. Or rather, he was poleaxed on the carpet, 'my brain floating on another planet in an LSD-induced trance'.

George Harrison had only recently returned from a trip to India, where he'd been studying sitar under Ravi Shankar. Bearded and barefoot, he arrived at the party resplendent in all manner of beads and bells. According to Kenny, whenever Harrison moved he sounded like Tinkerbell.

By this point Ev had consumed a few gins and joints and had become somewhat introspective. Instead of joining the other partygoers in trying to cajole Kenny with 'Come on, you'll be OK, give us a hug' type reassurances, George decided to recite a few uplifting verses from the Bhagavad Gita before advising Kenny to begin practising yoga.

Given Kenny's previous experiences with religion, this wasn't such a good idea. As it became obvious that Harrison's wise and wonderful words were falling on decidedly deaf ears, a woman joined the gathering and began passing around a joint. When it reached Guru George, instead of smoking the thing he simply carried on reciting.

Irked at seeing her pot go to waste, the woman remonstrated, 'George, you're hogging the joint!' When Harrison told her to piss off, she replied undaunted, 'That's very un-Christly of you, George.'

Apparently marijuana can induce merriment, and the sight of George (who was beginning to become a bit of a religious bore) hitching up his lungi and making for the door reduced Messrs Lennon and Starr to helpless giggles, with John literally falling off his chair. Even Kenny managed a laugh.

That evening in 1966 would imprint itself on Kenny's memory as the first time he laid eyes on Lady Lee, the woman who in a few short years would become his wife.

Born Audrey Valentine Middleton on 14 February 1937, one of three daughters to a Sheffield fireman, she was still in her teens when she married a junior professional footballer. When her new husband was called up for his National Service, she went back to live with her parents for a while before running away to London, where she had several affairs and drifted into showbusiness as one half of singing duo Lee and Michelle. Though she never quite made the hit parade, Lee lived a glamorous life on the periphery of the cultural explosion of the early sixties, becoming friends with Michael Caine and Brian Epstein, and sharing alcoholic breakfasts with Keith Moon.

She'd also begun a passionate affair with singing sensation Billy Fury, Britain's answer to Elvis. Fury was mobbed wherever he went and often Lee was in the midst of it. Once she took him to see her family in Sheffield; within minutes word had spread and about fifty people gathered outside the house. In an effort to smuggle him out, they requisitioned a neighbour's motorbike and dressed Billy up as a woman, wearing Lee's mum's coat and a headscarf. 'We walked out,' remembers Lee. 'I was just behind Billy, and a bunch of them followed us. It was scary, and one of them went, "It's him, get him!" That's when the motorbike we had on standby pulled up, Billy jumped on and off he went and then they looked at me and said, "Get her, he can't get away without her!" And they all chased me. I ended up punching this one girl. I bloody had her. It was me or them. And we were only out visiting my mother.'

The next time Kenny remembered meeting Lee was in a flat in Fulham owned by a record producer friend called Don Paul. Again, everyone was sitting around smoking pot (this was the sixties, remember), when Lee and Billy Fury invited them all back to the mansion they shared in Sussex. It was a pad Kenny got to know well over the coming months as he was frequently invited there for weekend parties. He'd sit in the garden with the others to drop acid and check out while basking in the summer sunshine. One eventful afternoon a BBC producer turned up with that weekend's supply of LSD and purple hearts secreted in a small tin. Suddenly, the tranquillity of the day was interrupted by the piercing sound of a police siren which seemed to be heading their way. Panicking, the BBC producer threw the contents of the tin as far as he could into a wooded area beyond the environs of Fury's neatly manicured lawns. As the shrill noise of the siren gradually melted into the distance, the guests looked with accusing eyes at the BBC man and for the next few hours everyone searched in the long grass and bracken on their hands and knees. Only one pill was ever found, which was carefully cut up into small pieces and shared out. 'Silly days,' Kenny later confessed. 'I wouldn't like to go back, but I wouldn't have missed it either.'

As their paths kept crossing Kenny and Lee grew quite chummy. They'd talk for hours, he made her laugh and they had fun together. 'We laughed a lot,' she says now. 'In fact we never stopped laughing, that was our big attraction, we just fell about in hysterics.'

Almost from the beginning Lee knew that Kenny was gay. 'When he used to come to me and Billy's house, all the other guys would be downstairs and I'd be upstairs and he'd come and sit in my bedroom and watch me get made up, watch me get dressed, he'd just sit there. He used to follow me around like a little creature. I took no notice of him in the end because he was always there.'

All the more confusing, then, when Lee began to notice Kenny exhibiting an attraction towards her. 'He would be all over me sometimes, unnaturally all over me. And Billy got really annoyed and very jealous.' One night Fury returned home from a gig and Ev was sitting on the couch with Lee's legs draped over him and he was running his fingers up and down her thigh as if he were playing the piano. 'Billy went ape-shit,' Lee recalls. 'He was convinced we were having an affair. I said, "You've got to be joking, he's a queen!"'

A bit of a nuisance, too. 'He used to break everything he touched. He just had no sensitivity back then, and no etiquette.' Fury had bought Lee a very expensive antique Japanese fan and it was displayed magnificently spread out on the wall. 'And it was on a wall for a reason,' says Lee. 'Well, Kenny yanked it off and started imitating Madame Butterfly, waving it around and fanning himself with it, and it snapped. He never apologized or anything – he didn't think it mattered. I threw him out and barred him.'

She couldn't get rid of him, though. He was on the phone, endlessly pleading, 'I promise I won't do it again,' to which Lee would reply, 'No, you're banned.' And she meant it. 'I didn't want to see him ever again. In the end I felt sorry for him because his friends could all come to the parties and I'd say to them, "But don't bring him."' Lee finally caved in after he sent her a letter on which he'd drawn a myriad of broken hearts and tears. He was forgiven and allowed back into the fold.

Between the laughter and a friendship that was gradually growing stronger, Kenny opened up to Lee in a way he'd never done to anyone else. He spoke about many of his physical hang-ups: he was convinced that no one could find him attractive, that he was too skinny and weedy. In the mire where his sexuality was concerned, and finding fewer and fewer answers to an ever-growing list of questions, he started to turn more and more to drugs. Throw in a few gin and tonics and a dash of self-doubt and you've got the makings of a grade one depressive. Ev was forever discussing the merits of topping one-self, and once, during a party at the house, while in the throes of an LSD trip, he announced his intention to commit suicide. Fixing him with a look, Lee told him, 'If you are going to commit suicide, could you please vacate my premises, indeed vacate the area, because it would be extremely inconvenient for us all.'

It was a flippant response to, let's face it, a flippant suggestion, but Lee was only too aware that Kenny had severe emotional issues and lacked self-confidence, regardless of the massive success he'd achieved as a DJ. In quiet moments she tried her best to reassure him and boost his self-worth. 'You're not unattractive,' she'd say. 'But you have to give good value in life. If you keep boring on about how you're pathetic and how you want to commit suicide, no one will want to be with you.' Her home truths seemed to work and for a while at least Kenny appeared content in his own skin. Indeed, when Lee and Billy Fury separated at the end of 1967, after eight years together, it was Kenny's shoulder she cried on, and he was a source of strength as she fought to cope with the emotional repercussions: 'He surrounded me.'

Having helped her get back on her feet, Kenny was vitriolic when Lee began dating again. Jealous of the other men in her life, he'd turn up unannounced at her flat, usually when she had someone over for a quiet romantic dinner, and hurl a volley of waspish put-downs that caused a few suitors to flee into the night. 'One by one, Ev destroyed them,' says Lee. 'It was a planned strategy. He would arrive at odd times of the night, knocking on my door. He'd bait them, make them look small and spend all his time running them down. Whatever they did, he would belittle them. He was very good with words, brilliant with words.'

Kenny was smitten, and it's probably safe to assume he'd never felt emotions like this towards a person before, and maybe surprised even himself that the person in question was a woman. An entry in his diary during this period read: 'To Lee, the only woman in my life. A jewel, a flower, an essence of all that is good and lovely. An island in a sea of horror and agony, of despair and crippling fatigue and boredom. She and she alone can bring happiness and solace into my worthless and empty life. I would kill for her – kill d'you hear, KILL.'

Kenny liked to think of himself as something of a romantic and his courtship of Lee – for he believed it to be a courtship – was filled with walks in the country and afternoons spent knitting on village greens. His body alive with new emotions, Kenny confessed to Lee his confusion over his sexuality and told her he found homosexuality distasteful. 'Men aren't built for men,' he said. He also blamed God for how he was born, just as he'd earlier blamed the Almighty for making him spindly and weak. 'Homosexuality is a mortal sin,' he pronounced. 'And I know God will punish me for it.' Having spent years in showbusiness Lee had come across many homosexuals and had lots of gay friends, so she tried her best to reassure Everett that it wasn't a mortal sin, and that gay people could lead happy lives and enjoy stable relationships together. Kenny, however, was unconvinced and often spoke of his desire to be 'cured'. One of the ways towards rehabilitation, as he saw it, was to take the plunge and experience a physical encounter with a woman; maybe then he'd see the light. 'But I didn't in those days have the first clue about how to approach a woman and entice her into my bed. I was yer actual innocent virgin.' When it came to women, of course.

Not long after Lee broke up with Billy Fury, she and Ev had gone on a motoring holiday around the Continent, and Kenny spent practically the entire two weeks dreading the possibility of nocturnal fumblings, quite oblivious to the fact that Lee was not looking for any romantic entanglements in the wake of the break-up. 'We'd often go to three or four hotels until I could find one which had two vacant rooms,' he later admitted. Yet he'd exhibit fierce jealousy whenever Lee got chatting to a waiter or another man. His hormones were so out of control it was as if he couldn't think straight – certainly not when he was behind the wheel: they crashed three times during the holiday, colliding with a car, a lorry and even a deer!

One night, according to Lee, they were given a double room and Ev's personality shifted alarmingly. He grew moody and verbally attacked her. The two of them ended up having a blazing row, with Lee baffled as to what had caused it. Only later did she realize it was the threat of sharing a bed; Kenny couldn't handle the possible physical repercussions or the emasculation of being rejected. 'If Ev felt threatened or foolish, he would attack. If he felt he was going to be rebuffed, or someone was going to turn him down, he would attack. That grew to be the habit. He would attack before you could. He was rather like a frightened little animal.' In the end they popped some acid and stayed up tripping all night.

Both of them struggled to deal with the situation. Each had formed a genuine affection and love for the other, but with no satisfactory outlet for those feelings they were left floundering in a state of confusion. Lee in particular was confounded as to how and why she'd fallen for a man she knew to be gay, but she could think of nobody else she wanted to be with.

The all-important first physical connection came courtesy of a chemical reaction. Kenny and Lee were tripping at Ev's flat when it happened. 'He suddenly looked at me and lit up,' Lee remembers. 'He declared I was the most beautiful thing he'd ever seen.' Lee later came to believe that both of them reaching an LSD-induced high was Kenny's way of getting close, of unlocking that barrier. Lord Birt, former Director-General of the BBC, recalls that back in the days when he was plain John Birt, television producer, Kenny once told him that acid helped him find women attractive, and in effect cured him. 'That's what he wanted. Kenny wanted to be "normal", he wanted to be heterosexual and he wanted a marriage, and that's how he found Lee.'

The next day Ev poked his head round the door of Angela Bond's office to proudly announce, 'I've done it.' Quick as a flash he was on the phone to friends with the news, too. Even more seriously, he'd arrived at the conclusion that he wanted to marry Lee, he'd found his soulmate, the person that he wanted to spend the rest of his life with.

In spite of his relationship with Lee, it was fairly well known at the BBC that Kenny was gay. Wilfred De'Ath had arrived at that conclusion within a day of meeting him back in 1964. 'I'd met various homosexuals at Oxford and in the army, and I knew immediately that he was gay. He just wasn't interested in girls. He pretended to be interested in girls, but you could tell that he wasn't really. This went through to 1967 when I met him again and he told my wife and I about all the girls he'd had, but it didn't seem to ring true. Obviously when he became famous we discussed him at the BBC and all of my colleagues said the same thing: he's obviously homosexual but hasn't faced up to it.'

There was also an incident in the late sixties that convinced De'Ath of Kenny's homosexuality. 'He asked me to meet him at the London Hilton, some posh bar, and he was with an extremely beautiful girl. He was drugged up, I could tell; he was obviously on drugs by this point. You could see this very sexy girl was proud to be with Kenny Everett, but she whispered to me at one point after we'd had a few drinks, "He's not interested in me," and I thought, well what a waste.'

As Kenny continued to flourish at Radio 1, one of his earliest benefactors decided it was time they parted company. Maurice Sellar and his partner Roy Tuvey had branched out into writing television comedy, where they would achieve great success with the likes of Spike Milligan, Jimmy Tarbuck, Frankie Howerd and the Two Ronnies. But what to do with Kenny? Maurice recalls: 'I said to Roy one day, "We can't let Kenny float on his own here." So I took him to a very success-ful agent and a great friend of ours called Harold Davidson. Now, Harold Davidson used to look after Frank Sinatra when he came to this country and had some very big stars on his books. And I said, "I want you to take care of Kenny, because he's going to be a very big star. And I think your agency's right for him." So they took him on.' It would prove to be an important decision, and it would lead to one of Kenny's most coveted and significant friendships.

Amidst all the surreal humour, the jingles and the wisecracks, Kenny was keenly aware of the importance of playing the right music on his show. He had strong views about music and got incredibly excited when he found something new that he liked, regardless of style or potential popularity, and he couldn't wait to play it to his listeners. 'He would break all the rules in the early days of Radio 1, playing several songs by the same artist in the same show,' says Kevin Howlett. 'Or playing the same song again and again. Nobody else really did that.'

Ev's musical taste was fairly eclectic. He was a big fan of the American singer-songwriter Harry Nilsson. Today Nilsson is best remembered for the single 'Everybody's Talkin'', which was the theme tune to the film *Midnight Cowboy*, but back then he was the darling of the British music scene and both John Lennon and Paul McCartney were among his fans. Kenny had been introduced to Harry by John Lennon and the two had struck up a friendship. Kenny even covered two of Nilsson's songs, 'Without Her' and 'It's Been so Long', which were released (without troubling the charts) as a single in 1968.

Nilsson was an extraordinarily talented and creative man, but he also drank a lot and could at times be quite a difficult character. One day he was scheduled to be a guest on Kenny's show, but instead of playing it safe by churning out platitudes and a few easy questions, Kenny decided to put Nilsson's talent to the test and prepared a backing track before challenging the singer to improvise to it live on air. The backing track in question was a loop consisting of the opening two bars of the Bee Gees song 'Craise Finton Kirk Academy of Royal Arts', which had appeared on their third studio album.

'I surprised him with it live on the air,' remembered Kenny. 'I said, "Harry, we've got a piece of music here and you're going to sing along to it, NOW! Ladies and gentlemen, Harry Nilsson."'

What came next is one of the most sublime pieces of musical improvisation you're ever likely to hear. Recognizing the tempo, Nilsson suddenly begins singing the lyrics to one of his own songs, 'Morning Glory Story', over the top of Kenny's loop. Despite the track being in a much higher key than his song, Nilsson remains undeterred and sings the lyrics beautifully. Note perfect, in fact. In today's music terms it would be described as a Bee Gees/Nilsson/Everett mash-up.

Kenny's never-ending quest to create brilliant radio superseded not only Nilsson's reputation as being difficult, but also the ambition of every other DJ in the country. Nobody else would have dared put such a big star on the spot like that – especially one who might easily have got up and walked, or worse still clouted him one.

In a delicious example of semi-dramatic irony, the next time Harry appeared on Kenny's show he barely said a single word and ignored every question Kenny posed. Only when he signed off did Nilsson spring into life. 'Thanks for having me, Kenny. I've enjoyed it.'

Another musical favourite was psychedelic outfit the Idle Race, featuring a young Jeff Lynne. Kenny regularly played them on his show when no other Radio 1 DJ, save John Peel, would go near them. He was even appointed the band's honorary fan club president. Jeff Lynne went on to form supergroup ELO in the seventies and again Kenny was a big fan.

Ev also played a hand in turning Dionne Warwick's 'Do You Know the Way to San José?' into a big UK hit, playing it, at Angela Bond's suggestion, when the record company had given up hope it would ever chart.

Kenny was now clocking in regular audiences of five million, his show perhaps the most influential on radio in the late sixties. On a roll, he was given a new daily evening slot to start in July of 1968. His Sunday show ended on a high on 9 June with another interview with the Beatles conducted at the Abbey Road studio. This interview reeks of historical significance. The Beatles were still the biggest band in the world and were a week into recording their seminal double LP, *The White Album*. The Fab Four are in fine comedic form, with Lennon firing off a succession of surreal wisecracks, although one pun about the recent assassination of Robert Kennedy was wisely omitted from the broadcast.

After several minutes of random playfulness, Kenny asks if John and Paul would sing him a jingle, and they do just that, improvising something on the spot. Later on George and Ringo enter the studio, and Kenny gets a second jingle, this time sung by Ringo to the tune of 'Goodnight Sweetheart'. This one's topical though, and refers to Kenny's first sacking from Big L, with the lines: 'Goodbye Kenny, it's good to see you back, Goodbye Kenny, we hear you got the sack!'

The whole interview is a hoot and drives home just how fond the Beatles were of Everett. How many DJs or journalists could pop in to Abbey Road and leave with two improvised jingles, not to mention a jazz/lounge rendition of 'Strawberry Fields'?

Foreverett, as Kenny's new show was called, went ahead without the stewardship of Angela Bond. She believed moving to a daily slot was a mistake, that the high standards Kenny had managed to achieve would be difficult to maintain over such a gruelling schedule. While much of Kenny's show was unscripted and off the cuff it generally took two or three days of preparation and at the end of each broadcast he would be emotionally and physically drained. Angela was worried he was taking on too much and that her replacements didn't know how best to handle his talent. Kenny waved her concerns away and forged ahead regardless.

Within a few weeks cracks began to appear. Kenny started turning up unannounced in Angela's office complaining that his new producers were trying 'to get inside my whole body and work it themselves'. He was exhausted, unable to churn out conveyor-belt genius in the quantity that was required to fill a daily show. Angela Bond agreed to come to the rescue – but on one condition. She told her bosses she would only do it if Kenny was given one of the most prestigious slots on the schedule – the Saturday morning show. They agreed.

One eighteen-year-old wannabe DJ who got to know Kenny around this time was Nicky Horne. Along with many of his contemporaries, he'd been inspired towards a career on radio because of the pirate stations. 'My heroes were always on the pirates, like Kenny and Cash. The DJs on Radio London opened my eyes; if I'd been a bit older I'd have loved to have gone out and worked on that boat.' By chance Horne had met up with Chris Grant, who did trailers for Radio 1, and together they decided to try a two-hander show, à la Kenny and Cash. One Friday night after everyone had gone home Grant stole his way into the Radio 1 studios, completely against all the rules, to edit the tapes. By chance Emperor Rosko was in that night and as he was walking past the edit suite he heard Nicky Horne's voice and went inside. 'Who's that?' he asked. 'It sounds remarkably like Kenny Everett.'

'This is a young guy called Nicky Horne,' replied Grant. 'He's an aspiring DJ, we're working together on this programme.'

'I want to meet him,' said Rosko. 'And I want to meet him tomorrow.'

Everett followed Rosko on Saturday mornings and always took the rise out of the American-born presenter, never failing to win the handover. 'What Rosko wanted was someone who sounded like Everett to kind of put Kenny on the back foot,' recalls Horne. 'So I met Rosko the next day and within three days had moved out of my parents' house and he'd offered me a job as his assistant. And that's how it all began for me. I'd go with Rosko to Radio 1 on a Saturday and of course I'd see Kenny.'

For a young DJ to observe at close quarters master practitioners like Everett and Rosko was a rare opportunity. Towards the end of Rosko's show Kenny would arrive in the studio opposite and start his preparation. 'I could see him from our cubicle,' recalls Horne. 'And he would be rehearsing with all of the carts, because all of his voices and all the inserts and stuff were on tape cartridges. He would have so many of them and they would all have to be in perfect order because there were only three cart machines at Radio 1 and sometimes he would need five, so as soon as one finished he would have to plug in the next one. He had to be incredibly well organized.'

Kenny's natural environment was sitting in a room on his own with a microphone, surrounded by all of this paraphernalia; that was his domain, his kingdom. 'He would come alive when that microphone was on in the studio,' says Horne. 'The energy level would increase phenomenally. I never really saw him get nervous. There were other DJs who would literally shake before they went on, their hands would shake, but then as soon as the red light went on and they were in network, as it was referred to at Radio 1, the shakes would go. Not Kenny. He was in his element.'

David Briggs was one of Kenny's producers at Capital in the early seventies, and agrees that watching him perform could be an incredible experience. 'I can't think of any other broadcaster who could bring into a studio the same amount of excitement yet calmness that Everett could. It was mesmeric to watch. He was totally in control yet you got the feeling that absolutely anything could happen. He was unbelievable.'

11

Kennyvision

I T WAS INEVITABLE that one day somebody would try and coax Kenny away from his radio studio and on to television. The idea of Kenny appearing on the box had been mooted as early as 1966, when he and Dave Cash had been approached about making a Kenny and Cash quiz show for ATV. And according to Mike Quinn, Kenny made a brief guest appearance in 1967 on *Come Here Often*, a lively magazine programme for children produced by Rediffusion. It was a comedy skit and Kenny was dressed up as . . . Jimi Hendrix! 'I was getting changed in the dressing room,' recalls Mike, 'when Kenny called out, "Mike, Mike, look!" I turned round and said, "My God, you look just like him." There he was with the guitar, the hair, the clothes, everything. And that would have been the first time Kenny dressed up on television, too. He did like the television scene. He said to me after the show, "Do you think the producer liked me? Do you think she'll use me again?" He took the television very seriously. There's no doubt that Kenny wanted to be a star.'

The person who gave Kenny his first proper break on television was Oxbridge graduate, former building-site labourer and newly promoted producer at Manchester's Granada Studios, John Birt.

Liverpool-born Birt had started at Granada as a production trainee in 1966, before finally getting his break on the current affairs programme *World in Action*. There he was responsible for suggesting and bringing to fruition a ground-breaking episode in which Mick Jagger, William Rees-Mogg, the Bishop of Woolwich and several others gathered together to discuss Jagger's recent arrest and subsequent trial for drug offences.

But despite his successes, Birt soon became tired of current affairs, and together with fellow Granada graduate Andy Mayer began to conceive a new entertainment show based around what they'd both like to see on television. Granada's then head of programmes, David Plowright, loved their initial outline and duly commissioned a pilot. Two years and three series later, *Nice Time* had proved a big success, and was to be the precursor for all manner of magazine-type shows. After seeing one of the three surviving episodes, *Nice Time* can be summed up as a cross between *That's Life* and *Play Away*.

According to John Birt, *Nice Time* was 'a celebration of working-class humour and popular culture which used real people to entertain'. Broadcast from August 1968 in the Sunday teatime slot, it always began with a musical item: 'A choir of George Brown lookalikes singing "My Way",' recalls Birt. 'Or some George Formby impersonators with ukuleles singing "I'm Leaning on a Lamp Post".' These were usually followed by location items where presenters would ask old women in Blackpool to tell them about their first kiss, or ask a group of male pensioners to improvise a western-type shootout.

Any of this ring bells? Esther Rantzen must have been taking notes.

On the face of it, it's not really surprising that *Nice Time* proved popular. The format was fresh, production values high and it was being produced by the future Director-General of the BBC! It also boasted a team of budding young writers that would cost a king's ransom were you to try to hire them today, among them Clive James, Tim Brooke-Taylor, Michael Palin, Terry Jones and Graeme Garden.

As for the show's presenters, they were every bit as eclectic as the format. In addition to experienced TV man Jonathan Routh (who introduced Britain to *Candid Camera*, a hugely popular television programme based on an American format, which ran for seven years from 1960) and *Coronation Street* actress Sandra Gough, the show's two main presenters were Kenny and Germaine Greer.

Germaine remembers her audition for the show well: 'I was teaching at Warwick University when Andy Mayer, who was a friend of mine, asked me to come up to Granada and audition for a new comedy series. I bought a day return and set off. The audition consisted of interviewing people who just happened to be around – a make-up person or a singing monk. I made up ridiculous interviews, was told that I had got the job, had been booked into the Midland Hotel and would be needed in the studio the next day. I said I wasn't right for the format, didn't want the job, and had my return ticket and a proper day job to go to. The rest is history, because obviously I was persuaded to do it.'

In Kenny's case, his role on *Nice Time* had been planned from the show's inception. John Birt had long been a fan of Kenny's, but got quite a shock when they eventually met: 'We'd actually lived parallel lives!' claims Birt. 'Kenny and I were born fifteen days apart in the same area of Liverpool. I went to the Catholic grammar school and he went to the Catholic secondary modern. His parents moved to Formby and so did mine. We spent our childhoods living within a mile of each other but never met, and I didn't find all this out of course until I offered him the job on *Nice Time*. But we had an awful lot in common, and undoubtedly must have passed each other in the street scores of times.'

Pleasantries and coincidences aside, Birt was extremely excited at the prospect of introducing the Wireless Wizard to a new medium. But what of the transition? Fronting a TV show was a very different proposition to making radio – especially if you were a young, shy perfectionist who was used to working alone. John Birt had no doubt that Ev could handle it: 'You shouldn't underestimate Kenny's creative confidence. This was a young man who had lived alone in his own mind, in his room with his tape recorders, expressing himself. But his genius was quickly recognized and he was comfortable with his artistic expression.' Birt was aware of Kenny's shyness, but had quickly worked out that it was by no means all-pervasive. 'He was not some-body who wanted to stroll into a large room and dominate it. He was shy in that sense. But he wasn't shy with the people he worked with. When you were together with him he was very easy and relaxed. He was self-confident about his own ability. Not vain or immodest about it but just a natural self-confidence.'

Like many we have spoken to, John Birt believes Kenny's talents stretched far beyond any studio. 'He was a true artist. Long before the digital era Kenny could create and craft hours of exceptional broadcasting, full of wit, insight and humour, completely single-handedly. He was also a true critic. He understood popular music and he understood what "good" was, and had already become a highly influential person, much respected by the people whose records he played. So he was both highly expressive himself in a comedic sense, but also beyond that, a real player in the music industry.'

What might have seemed a gamble turned out to be a bit of a masterstroke on Birt's part, as new boy Kenny delivered everything he'd hoped he would and more. Not only were they getting a huge creative talent, they were also getting a grafter. 'He was wonderful to work with,' remembers Birt. 'He was hard-working, flexible and reliable – all the things people might not think he would be – and not a prima donna in any way. We worked him very hard and he was a great companion. Very honest and very self-aware. He was also extremely game and would try anything. *Nice Time* was very youthful in its enthusiasms and we always did something at the end of the show each week which was very much of its time. As an example, somebody would say, "If you live in Smith Street in Stockport, look out of your window and you'll see a big furniture van. Go and bang on the back doors and a brass band will march forth and play for an hour." And that would actually happen!'

While all this was happening one of the *Nice Time* presenters would be making their way to Smith Street to host the event. 'You'd have dozens of people running up Smith Street,' says Birt, 'banging on the doors of a furniture van as a brass band began to play. But Kenny or Germaine would have absolutely no problem at all in going to Stockport on a cold winter's afternoon and presiding over such an event. These bits would not be televised, by the way, it would just happen.'

The partnership between Kenny and Germaine Greer was, at first glance, an odd one. On one side you had this tall, super-intellectual, self-confident Australian academic who even then was a world authority on Shakespeare. And on the other you had this short and slight DJ who had none of Greer's educational upbringing or erudition.

'But they actually got on really well,' claims Birt. 'And I think the main reason they got on well is that Germaine really admired Kenny.'

Birt's right. Germaine Greer was indeed a fan. 'Kenny was the only member of the team I did want to work with,' explains Greer. 'I lived in Leamington Spa at the time and Kenny used to pick me up on the way north to Manchester and we'd sit in his tiny red car with the quadraphonic stereo turned up full blast listening to that week's rock releases. After that it was all hard work. I knew Kenny was a genius, but I'm not sure how I knew.'

Greer also admired Kenny's attempts at rethinking the conventions of broadcast media. 'He wanted viewers and listeners to understand how stereotyped and stultifying these were, so he made his own jingles and invented his own voices and masks. We were always trying different ways of doing things. We introduced one episode with our backs to the camera, for example. Also, when the number of writers increased we started to be told what to do and what not to do, so we both rebelled and kept improvising.'

The appeal of *Nice Time* cut across all ages and professions, it was watched by children, old people – and musicians. 'It went out at five p.m. on a Sunday when rock musicians were just waking up,' says Greer. 'I could get a backstage pass to anything, even the Rolling Stones, just on the strength of the show.'

Nice Time came to an end in June 1969. It had been an experiment in almost every single way, but it had worked. Naturally with something so original opinions had been divided, but with *Nice Time* these had eventually become comical. In the 'For' camp we have esteemed critic Philip Purser, who described the show as, 'One of the three best television programmes of all time.' Not bad! And for the 'Againsts' we have author Len Deighton, who wrote to the then head of Granada suggesting that those responsible for the programme must be 'the worst people in the world'.

Regardless of Deighton's assertion, *Nice Time* featured some memorable moments, such as Tim Brooke-Taylor's revival of the Backwards Walking Race which ran from Macclesfield to Buxton (hundreds took part, each with a guide walking forward). During another episode, Germaine Greer was asked to hand out *Nice Time* T-shirts from a van in Wigan, but only to people accompanied by a dog. Again, hundreds turned up, with every breed imaginable in attendance, from Alsatians to Pomeranians. Within minutes Germaine was stuck in the middle of a full-scale doggy riot.

John Birt was relaxing at home when he received a telephone call from a distressed Germaine Greer. 'I have only ever smoked pot half a dozen times,' says Birt, 'and this particular afternoon had been one of them. As Germaine explained the situation to me, her words were almost drowned by a cacophony of barking in the background. My brain was fuzzy, my thinking slow. I could barely focus on a course of action. I took Germaine's number and encouraged her to stay put. The police eventually escorted her to safety and we compensated the residents. Germaine never complained. To her it was a great adventure.'

Kenny and Germaine had formed an unexpected, unconventional and surprisingly successful alliance, but the relationship came to its natural end soon after they stopped working together. 'When the series finished, because we were all bored with it, I went my way and Kenny got married,' explains Greer. 'It was pretty clear that Kenny was gay but I don't think he had quite figured this out for himself. When he began to turn up with Lee, I was puzzled. As I recall he stopped driving me to and from Manchester and retreated into a private space. Maybe it was Lee who removed him from my searching gaze. He was a Catholic boy and coming out must have been horribly hard for him. I think acting out his homosexuality was traumatic for him. He certainly didn't want me deciding the issue. By the way, I didn't start working on *The Female Eunuch* till 1969.'

Not long after *The Female Eunuch* was published in 1970, Kenny was asked to write a tribute to Greer – which he did, and exactly as you'd expect. The book went on to become an international bestseller and an important text in the feminist movement.

It was thanks to John Birt and *Nice Time* that Kenny was given the opportunity to try his hand at becoming a pop star. His previous effort with Dave Cash, which was nothing more than a novelty song,

Left: Maurice James Christopher Cole – long before he became Kenny Everett.

Below: He talks to the animals – Kenny on holiday in Dorset with sister Cate in 1949.

Below left: On holiday in Wales, 1952, with father Tom and mother Lily.

Below right: One of Cate's favourite photos of her little brother, taken at St Edmund's primary school in 1949. 'He was such a good-looking child. Adorable.'

Above: A new intake of pupils arrive at Stillington Hall (**below**) in September 1956. Kenny's reasons for attending were simple. 'It was a choice of either staying at St Bede's and finishing my training as a mass murderer, or learning to be a priest!'

Above: Kenny and pals share a joke with one of the Verona Brothers – although he still doesn't seem to get it!

'Can you imagine me converting anybody?!' Kenny, second left, with some fellow budding missionaries at Stillington in 1957.

Above: Kenny at a gig in West Wickham around 1965. 'Gigs are like banging your head against a brick wall – it's great when it stops.'

The Wireless Wizard in 1965.

Left: Stardom was actually closer than anyone could have imagined. One of Kenny's first publicity shots from Radio London.

Below: Kenny admitted that he was terrible at sea – a fine choice, then, to be a pirate radio DJ.

Yearning for Stardom!

Above: 'Don't forget, we loved each other.' Kenny and Lee on their wedding day.

Below: John Birt with his first wife, Jane, at Kenny and Lee's wedding. 'I managed to avoid the punch, thank God.'

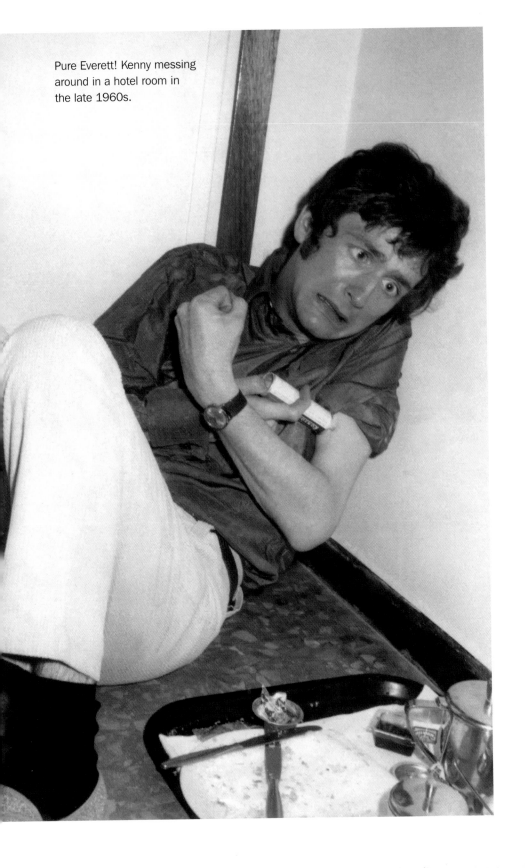

Pure Everett! Kenny messing around in a hotel room in the late 1960s.

Above: The original Radio One DJs. Kenny's in the back row, third from the left.

Below: Kenny, Cate and his nephew Peter at Cowfold in the early 1970s. Despite not having a regular radio show at the time, it was to become one of the most productive periods of Kenny's career.

At Capital Radio in the late 1970s. Although he had more freedom at Capital, Kenny still got himself in trouble on a regular basis.

had been something Kenny had reluctantly gone along with and then done his best to forget. So how did Birt persuade him to take a second stab at pop stardom? It all came about thanks to a bunch of striking technicians at Granada. 'I think this particular strike lasted six to ten weeks,' recalls Birt. 'During this period nobody had anything to do, so Andy and I decided we would write a *Nice Time* song which we could use for the show. We got together at my flat in Altrincham – where, incidentally, Kenny would almost always stay when he was doing the show – and wrote the words to the song. A friend of Kenny's wrote the music.' We're unsure whether it still exists, but they also made what would today be called a 'promo'. 'This involved Kenny being suspended from a crane, and hiked up about a hundred and twenty feet into the air,' remembers Birt. 'He was extremely brave and you'd never be allowed to do it now. The song was very much of its time though, and although we maybe didn't realize it at the time it was heavily influenced by *Sgt Pepper*.'

Unlike the Kenny and Cash debacle, *Nice Time* is actually well worth a listen and shares the same high production values that the programme itself enjoyed. The man charged with producing the single was Wayne Bickerton, who went on to co-write 'Sugar Baby Love' for the Rubettes. Bickerton has fond memories of the recording: 'Kenny was wonderful. I remember he kept following me into the control room and making lots of suggestions. He'd go back up to the studio, have a word with the musical arranger and come back down with a load more suggestions. In the end I had to ask him to go back to the studio and concentrate on doing his vocals. He was a very sweet and enthusiastic pain in the arse!'

Within a day Kenny had cut his debut single as a solo performer, and everyone involved was pleased with the final product. Stylistically, the song fits into the 'soft psychedelia' bracket, sounding like a cross between the Beatles and Jeff Lynne's band, the Idle Race. Even more impressive, *Nice Time* was at one point passed off as a rare Beatles song, apparently entitled 'Bye, Bye, Bye', which is what Kenny sings as the song fades out. Praise indeed.

12

Wedded Bliss

M ANY OF KENNY'S friends and colleagues were dumbfounded when they heard he intended to marry Lee. As the wedding date loomed, the concerns of his family grew to such an extent that they could no longer be ignored. His brother-in-law Conor urged Cate, 'You have to call him in and try and talk sense to him, this is going to be a disaster.'

Cate asked Ev to her house where she gently made her feelings known. While expressing support and her desire for his happiness, she asked whether he was certain that his feelings for Lee would last. Pointing out that his bride-to-be was seven years his senior, a worldly woman, she questioned whether Lee was 'the right fit' for him.

To Cate's horror, Kenny went back and told Lee every single thing she had said: 'He could be very naive. But nevertheless we were invited to the wedding.'

Lee herself had raised concerns about whether the marriage should go ahead. In a private taped interview that Everett conducted with Lee and her husband John Alkin in 1983, which has never been broadcast or made public, Kenny was unusually candid about the situation. 'Lee said to me, "We can't get married because you're gay." And I said, "Oh no, after a couple of years it'll suddenly fall into place and I'll go, of course, women, they're fab." But it never happened.'

Also, not to be too flippant, it was the kind of thing you did in the whacked-out sixties. 'Don't forget also, we loved each other,' stresses Lee. 'It was as simple as that. He declared his love for me by marrying me, and I declared I loved him by marrying him, and that is what we did.' Kenny recognized the day as one of the most special in his life by deciding not to shave again, growing the familiar beard that he kept for most of his life.

As for the ceremony itself, which took place on 2 June 1969, it perfectly encapsulated what the Swinging Sixties was all about. For a start, they hired a double-decker bus to transport all the guests to Kensington Registry Office. Lee wanted to go on the bus with everyone else but her best man, Tony King, wouldn't hear of it. 'Never! Not if I'm best man, not if I'm giving you away, never. We're having a coach and white horses.' It was duly arranged, along with a driver in top hat and tails.

In another bizarre touch, the reception was held first, since the bride and groom wanted to make a quick getaway after the ceremony. But then somebody spiked the punch. 'I had this dressmaker,' recalls Lee, 'and his best friend was a drag queen who was halfway through a sex change operation so couldn't go to the wedding, and she spiked the punch. We were all absolutely gone.'

Rather the worse for wear, everyone turned up at the registry office, with Kenny and Lee arriving in style in their horse-drawn carriage. Lee wore a lovely lace dress and carried her chihuahua instead of the usual wedding bouquet. Kenny was resplendent in an Edwardian suit with a pink cravat. 'It was very embarrassing,' he later admitted. 'You attract a lot of attention, crawling slowly along Kensington High Street in a horse-drawn carriage.' The press lapped it up, of course, and the ceremony made all the papers.

Jonathan King recalls: 'At the wedding, I spent all the time saying, "This is a terrible mistake," and a friend of mine kept saying, "Jonathan, this is not a tactful thing to do, be quiet." He was right, of course, but so was I. Years later, in the late seventies, I interviewed Kenny for Capital Radio and I remember saying during the interview, "Do you recall me saying at your wedding that it was all a big mistake?" And he said, "Yes, I do. I only wish I'd listened to you!"'

Kenny and Lee went on honeymoon to Jersey, along with a gay couple, Don and Alan, who got married at the same ceremony – standing directly behind Ev and Lee and taking silent vows, since this was before same-sex civil partnerships. Like Lee, Don and Alan had partaken of the punch. 'Ev hadn't had any,' remembers Lee, 'and went to bed early. I was up all night with Don and Alan going – wahey! When Ev got up in the morning we were still going – wahey! It was only then it started to dawn on us that something was wrong. It was a strange wedding. It should have been a warning.' Cate remembers Kenny complaining that he was slightly hurt about being left alone the first night of his wedded life, while Lee partied with Don and Alan.

The couple set up home together in a flat in Holland Park, which they shared with a veritable Noah's Ark of pets. There was Lee's chihuahua, two cats, a Great Dane and an African grey parrot, which took an instant dislike to Kenny. Whenever it heard him arrive it would fly over to the plate rack beside the kitchen doorway and hang upside down until Ev reached the kitchen, when it would swing out and bite him.

Jo Gurnett, Kenny's future agent, remembers that parrot all too well. 'When Capital Radio provided a mews house for them in St John's Wood, this bloody parrot used to sharpen its beak everywhere. All the wood on the side of the stairs had gone – he'd chewed that – and most of the carpet. Ev would lie on the settee and it would fly over, land on his chest and start chewing his ear. It was an absolute menace – almost feral! It used to fly at them when they walked through the door. Whenever I visited I used to say to Ev, "Don't let that bloody thing come anywhere near me!" I love animals, but that parrot was manic!'

It's easy to suggest that this menagerie served as a substitute for children, except that Kenny didn't want any and Lee couldn't have them. When Kenny used to visit Cate, his young niece would wrap herself round his neck and he'd carefully but determinedly pull her off by the scruff of the neck and place her at arm's length on the floor saying in his best camp Noël Coward voice, 'You'll make somebody a wonderful wife some day.'

A few years into their marriage, adoption was considered. 'Ev and I didn't know whether we might be missing out on something,' says Lee. 'We talked about it and then we went through all the vetting. But when they rang up to tell us we could come and choose one, the pair of us realized it wasn't what we wanted at all. It was a good thing, it was clearing for both of us. He wanted to know whether he really wanted it. Of course, the minute they said, "Right, you can choose one," we bolted.' The subject of children was never raised again.

13

Another Sacking

WHILE RADIO 1 listeners continued to love Kenny's irreverent style and sense of danger on air, Angela Bond was conscious that he could sometimes go too far. Yes, this unpredictability was an integral part of his appeal, but it could lead to the occasional lapse into bad taste or mockery gone too far. When that happened, Kenny would be summoned to face Robin Scott, like a child ordered to the headmaster's office. Angela therefore had to walk a delicate tightrope, giving Kenny enough freedom to operate while at the same time trying to curb his worst excesses. 'Look, Kenny,' she'd say. 'You know what the BBC's like. Don't say shit, bugger, arsehole, piss, cock, fart. It's got to be in good taste.' Ev would invariably wave away her concerns, making the same mistake he did at Radio London, believing he was invincible, bullet-proof.

Kenny's enmity towards the BBC had given way to total disillusionment over what he saw as the failings of Radio 1, which had neither the soul nor the passion of the pirate stations it had tried so hard to emulate. 'They didn't allow you to have it,' says Johnnie Walker, who felt much the same way as Kenny. 'They kind of squashed it out of you.' It also lacked the pioneering spirit of stations like Radio London. For Kenny there was no sense of fun or enjoyment, and he resented the way DJs were denied the freedom to express themselves. The cosy blandness that was de rigueur at Broadcasting House simply wasn't conducive to the station Radio 1 needed to be: cutting edge, radical and in tune with the times. The atmosphere was totally wrong, largely due to the fact that the place was run by people who didn't know anything about pop radio. 'Pinstripe prunes in offices miles away,' said Kenny. Did the BBC really think that two hours of Jimmy Young in the morning and Terry Wogan in the afternoon was what the nation's youth wanted to hear?

Refusing to remain quiet on the matter, Kenny went public. And as usual, tact wasn't on the agenda. In an interview with *Melody Maker* he condemned Radio 1 as 'awful – really revolting'. The suits went mad. Johnny Beerling attributes Kenny's apparent hot-headedness to the fact that he often spoke his mind without a thought for the consequences. While that may be true of many of Kenny's utterances and deeds, on this occasion he knew exactly what he was doing.

The issues identified by Kenny were in fact perfectly reasonable and the BBC hierarchy saw sense and asked, 'OK, tell us what's wrong and we'll try to do something about it.' For starters Radio 1 was based within Broadcasting House and spread all over the building like supermarket margarine. 'You have to walk down about eighty-five corridors before you get to the bit you want,' complained Kenny. And when you got there you were surrounded by staff from other branches of the organization, which resulted in 'feeling as though you're in a cross between a hospital and a prison'. This meant Radio 1 had no chance to cultivate its own identity. 'It should be run as a separate service,' observed Kenny. And to this end he suggested it be housed in a completely separate building. The bigwigs blanched at that. 'Oh, well, er, yes, it's a good idea, but there's nothing we can do about it, is there? It would mean ripping out phones and changing people's offices around.' Kenny must have rolled his eyes heavenward. 'But it would be a better service in the end,' he insisted. 'Because Radio 1 would be separate.' Radio 1 did eventually move to a new building, Egton House, across the road from Broadcasting House, but not until 1985.

Another mistake, according to Kenny, was that Radio 1 shared news broadcasts with its sister stations. Kenny would be in full flight on his show and then have to cross over to the news and the listener would suddenly hear the voice of some extremely plummy octogenarian newsreader and everything would come to a grinding halt. 'The whole thing lacks zip, enthusiasm, atmosphere and speed,' was Ev's view. What was required was a two-minute blast of news more in keeping with the 'pop' sensibility of Radio 1, and perhaps a sixty-second news flash on the half-hour, along with traffic and weather bulletins throughout. In other words, exactly what happens in today's radio, where the newsreaders usually fit in with the presentation of the show or the DJ.

Plainly the BBC didn't want to take any of Kenny's ideas seriously and so he kept voicing them in public. Finally he was hauled in front of the executive elite and made to sign a document in which he pledged to stop making adverse comments in the press. Of course, the minute a reporter came up to him in the street and asked for a statement, off he went on another rant. To another journalist he said, 'I'm terribly sorry, but I've signed a piece of paper which says that I won't speak to the press about how awful Radio 1 is.' The next day's headline ran: BEEB GAGS CUDDLY KEN. Another reprimand followed.

Such behaviour exasperated his bosses. Chris Peers, who had helped Kenny on the road to stardom, was good friends with Radio 1's controller Robin Scott and often popped into Broadcasting House during this period. 'Robin always used to say to me, "You're the fella that we've all got to blame for having this guy."' Said in jest, no doubt, but with more than a grain of truth to it. 'But of course they all thought he was great,' says Peers. 'The guy was a real talent.'

Gagged he may have been, but Kenny's anarchic sense of humour wasn't so easily quelled, and ultimately it was this that proved his undoing. In the spring of 1970 Kenny discussed live on air rumours surrounding a celebrity's wife being made pregnant by another man. It was a clearly libellous statement, although luckily nothing came of it. At the end of the broadcast Angela Bond calmly took Ev to one side and whispered, 'Lovey, you've got to be careful.' That's all she said. Kenny however was incensed the matter had even been brought up; to him it proved she was no better than the rest of them. He stormed out, demanding that Angela be removed from her post as his producer. It was an act of incredible petulance, especially after everything she had done for him. Because he was a star, Kenny got his way and Angela was moved elsewhere. He may have won, but it was to be a hollow victory since there was now no one who knew how to control him. Angela herself held no bitterness towards Kenny; she understood that the real enemy, the dragon he intended slaying, was the BBC, an institution that he had come to despise above all others. It was a self-destructive path that he was hell-bent on following.

Losing Angela Bond did more harm than Kenny could ever have imagined. In truth, when Kenny threw his toys out of the pram with Angela, the suits should have given him a big hug, told him he was wonderful, and let him whine for a bit before kicking his arse and sending him back to work. Providing it was done in the right way and by the right person, his anger would have subsided and he'd more than likely have ended up apologizing and getting on with it. Instead he was indulged, for all the wrong reasons – and by somebody who knew nothing about the reality of the situation. Whoever he'd gone to had simply wanted him out of their office.

Kenny didn't know how lucky he was to have Angela until it was too late. Johnnie Walker, who'd recently arrived at the BBC, was in a far worse situation with his producer. 'We'd never had producers on the pirates. None of us could understand what a producer did, and mine used to sit in the studio with a stopwatch! He'd be timing links, making sure I was getting to the news on time, and worrying about what time you should be putting your records on, so all your spontaneity would just be crushed. But Angela totally got Kenny and understood him and really allowed him to be who he was. He was very lucky in that respect.'

To err on the side of caution, two producers were chosen to replace Angela: Teddy Warwick and Derek Chinnery, the man who years before had rejected Kenny at his first BBC audition. Chinnery's overriding memory of Kenny was how he would arrive at the studio with barely minutes to spare before his show started, clutching a hoard of tapes he'd worked on, hurriedly rewinding some of them before the red light flashed and he was live on the air. It was a quite deliberate ploy, this mad scramble, intended to give his performance an edge, to feed on his adrenalin.

This practice of arriving late was ultimately to backfire on Kenny big time. Since the start of Radio 1 Ev had complained to Robin Scott about the poor standard of equipment. 'Robin, you must get the equipment we had on the pirates, they've been using it for years in America. It's tried and tested, it's lovely, you just have to flick a button and there's the record instantly. It's all fabulous, darling.' Scott would usually mumble something along the lines of, I don't know, the expenditure, all that money stuff. But Kenny kept on hassling and hassling him. As was his habit, Kenny arrived for his show with two minutes to spare and walked into this totally new studio Scott had ordered to be built overnight. 'And I didn't know which switch did what, or anything. And Robin was there watching, the bum, and I was pushing all the wrong buttons and nothing was coming out.' After ten minutes Kenny admitted defeat and gave up. 'I crawled out of the studio on my knees, about three inches tall.'

Chinnery recalls one occasion when Kenny ran out of steam with ten minutes still to go before he was due to hand over to Emperor Rosko. His tapes had all been used up and, as always at the end of a broadcast, Ev was exhausted, physically and emotionally spent. He'd nothing left, no ad-libs, no gags, no sketches, no silly noises. Nothing. 'Let's just stop,' he said to Chinnery. 'Rosko's here. I'll hand over now.' Chinnery was dumbfounded. 'Why, Kenny? Play a couple of records, for God's sake.' Reluctantly almost, Kenny filled the dead time by spinning discs. 'He felt his role was more than just playing records,' said Chinnery. 'He had to have something productive or amusing to put in.'

However fine a pair of producers Chinnery and Warwick were, they lacked Angela Bond's restraining influence. Kenny continued to sail pretty close to the wind until finally, almost inevitably, he went too far. It had become a tradition on Big L for Kenny to try to corpse the newsreaders, and he'd carried the practice over to the BBC. He once introduced newsreader Peter Jefferson by saying, 'Here comes Peter Jefferson with his airplane,' alluding to the rock group. He then listened in stunned disbelief as Jefferson delivered the horrific news of a plane crash. Keith Skues often used to end up with the weekend shifts and dreaded having to sit opposite Kenny to read his news bulletin, 'because I knew he'd be up to some trick or other. He'd either start removing his clothing or on one occasion setting fire to my script!' Skues managed to get through the headlines, but during the sports announcements had to pound on the paper to stem the flames.

Kenny wasn't averse to mocking the actual news, either, especially the lame practice of ending a bulletin with an amusing or banal topical story. On 18 July 1970, the final news item concerned Mary Peyton, wife of Conservative Minister of Transport John Peyton, having passed her driving test. Kenny couldn't resist chipping in: 'Probably crammed a fiver into the examiner's hand.' Oh dear. It was a relatively innocuous throwaway line, one that would hardly raise an eyebrow today, but in 1970 the high-ups took a dim view. In less than forty-eight hours Kenny was gone, given the boot on the express orders of the BBC's managing director of radio, Ian Trethowan. Chinnery did his best to calm things down, suggesting Kenny vanish for a bit of gardening leave until the controversy subsided, but Trethowan was adamant: 'He goes.' Kenny was at home when he was telephoned personally by Douglas Muggeridge, who'd replaced Robin Scott as the controller of Radio 1, a man even more rigidly con-ventional and old-fashioned than his predecessor. 'Well, Kenny,' said Muggeridge. 'The time has come for the parting of the ways.'

One of the first things Kenny did was contact Jonathan King, who in turn got in touch with his publicist. Within the hour a horde of journalists descended on Everett towers. King also suggested buying a crate of champagne for the press to guzzle down to ensure favourable coverage. It worked; the reports that appeared in the next day's papers were wholeheartedly on Kenny's side, with the Beeb emerging as the villains – how could they sack that lovely Cuddly Ken?

The reaction to Everett's dismissal within the BBC was predictably fraught. 'We were outraged about it,' remembers Johnnie Walker. 'How ridiculous and stupid to get rid of somebody so talented. But it was very typical of the BBC, they like to hire somebody who's a bit zany and is going to get lots of people listening, but when it gets a little bit close to the edge they don't back them.' Tony Blackburn remembers bumping into Kenny not long after hearing the news. 'He told me, "I've been sacked." And I said, "Actually, Kenny, I'm not surprised, really. You pushed it a bit too far." He'd been given four or five warnings and he didn't believe them. I remember him even saying to me, "When they sacked me they were very apologetic." They really didn't want to sack him.'

Angela Bond and other producers voiced their strong disapproval over the decision and asked for his immediate reinstatement. To many of them it smacked of the BBC reverting to that fifties maiden aunt image it had tried so desperately to shed. It also demonstrated a degree of naivety on the management's part: surely the BBC didn't expect to provide a pop station geared towards youth culture without a degree of irreverence and establishment-knocking, something that pop music has always been about.

As the man responsible for bringing Kenny into the BBC and championing his talents, Johnny Beerling, while accepting that the driving-test jibe was the final straw, was furious about the sacking. In his view it severely damaged everything they had been working to build up in Radio 1 and diminished the BBC in the eyes of the young audience that they were trying to gain credibility with. On 23 July he made his feelings known in a letter to Trethowan. 'I can hardly deny that, during his BBC career, he has been a source of controversy and occasional embarrassment by some of his comments both on the air, and to the press. But against this one must weigh his talent. I quite genuinely believe that he is the most talented and creative disc jockey/entertainer of our time.' It didn't do any good. Incredibly, the most creative and popular DJ on air was out of work.

Kenny was inundated with messages of support from listeners and colleagues. Dave Cash and Alan Freeman phoned him personally to say how sorry they were, while others went public. John Peel, not averse himself to criticizing the BBC, said, 'I shall miss Kenny on Saturday mornings; now there's nothing to listen to.' David Jacobs, in a stern letter to the press, described Kenny as, 'One of the few talented presenters of record programmes in Britain today.' And fellow Radio 1 jock David Symonds said, 'I regard Kenny as the Spike Milligan of our generation. He has a similar outrageous, zany sense of humour. You just can't gag people like that.'

Very few people were aware of the fact, but Kenny's cheeky remark about the Transport Minister's wife was not the only reason for his dismissal – though it served as a useful smokescreen. It wasn't until years later that the full story emerged.

From the outset, Radio 1 was hamstrung by the BBC's appeasement of the Musicians' Union, limiting the amount of airtime that could be devoted to vinyl. Unlike the pirates, who could play as many records as they wished, the BBC were required to fill 25 per cent of airtime with live music. This guaranteed regular employment for British musicians such as the members of the Northern Dance Orchestra, who would be hired to cover the latest Beatles or Stones hit, but was unpopular with people who would have preferred to hear the original. 'They sound terrible,' Kenny would complain. 'Worse than that, they sound like the Northern Dance Orchestra.' Not only did this practice dampen the enthusiasm of DJs and listeners who had to put up with these duff cover versions, it put a dampener on the whole atmosphere of a show.

When the BBC entered into delicate and fraught negotiations to increase the number of records it could play, the Musicians' Union complained about Kenny's constant barbed remarks. 'It was getting to the situation where he was seriously upsetting negotiations,' confirmed Teddy Warwick.

So was Kenny a sacrificial lamb, sacked to appease the Musicians' Union? A couple of weeks before his sacking and before his remarks about the Transport Minister's wife, Everett complained on air that Radio 1 had commissioned the jingle company to sing all their DJ's names – except his. To demonstrate this, he played the 'offending' jingles live on air, after which he declared, 'Anyway, I've done my own,' and proceeded to play it. This does beg the question: had the BBC already decided to get rid of him?

Whatever the reason behind the decision, Warwick, like most of his colleagues, felt Auntie had made a monumental mistake. 'My view was that Kenny should be seen as a sort of court jester as far as the BBC was concerned. And the BBC is a big enough organization to allow itself a court jester. Even if Kenny occasionally said things that the BBC didn't like, this role suited him and it suited us, and I think the BBC would have gained a lot of respect by having somebody who was as talented as he was, who occasionally seemed to step out of line.'

In spite of all the support he received, Kenny felt aggrieved that he had ended up a lone voice in his opposition to how Radio 1 was being run, since he knew other DJs felt the same way. 'I did suppose some-one would join me,' he told the press. 'I suppose they thought, let him moan on our behalf – we'll keep quiet and keep our shows.'

One can't help thinking that there was something inevitable about Kenny getting fired by the Beeb. 'He was a genius,' says Johnny Beerling. 'But saying that he was also a loose cannon and he could be difficult. He certainly pushed his luck with the BBC.'

The real beneficiary of all this was an up-and-coming DJ by the name of Noel Edmonds who ended up with Kenny's slot, becoming at twenty-one the youngest jock at the station. Beerling happened to be with Edmonds in Weymouth for an outside broadcast when the call came through from Mark White, Radio 1's head of programmes: 'Noel, we want you to take over Kenny Everett's Saturday show from next week.' It was the chance of a lifetime, but at the same time a terrifying prospect to replace such a hugely popular figure. It was to Beerling that Edmonds turned for advice. 'Johnny, what shall I do? How can I hope to fill Everett's shoes?' All Beerling could say to the young DJ was to be himself and the listeners would be won over, which of course they eventually were.

The press didn't help. On his first day in the job the *Evening Standard* wrote: 'Heaven help poor Noel Edmonds, who, from today onwards, has been given the unenviable job of governing in the ten-till-twelve spot in the wake of the deposed enfant terrible of Broadcasting House.'

14

Kenny Everett's Explosion

After the success of *Nice Time*, Maurice Sellar wrote to Kenny congratulating him and telling him how much he'd enjoyed the show. Everett replied within the week; Maurice still has the letter today. It reads: 'Dear Mo [Maurice and Ev always used to call each other Mo. 'I never called him Kenny,' says Sellar], thanks for the congrats. It's ridiculous how well things are going. I've had lots of offers of telly and have had the job of turning them all down, because I've discovered that TV is just not my scene, wireless is much more flexible and that's where my only broadcasting interest lies. Signed Kenny Everett, Edith, the Wireless Wizard.'

It took one of Kenny's heroes to change his mind. Shortly before his sacking from Radio 1, Barry Took, who was head of everything at LWT, got in touch with Kenny. 'Barry had written *Round the Horne* and all kinds of other stuff and I thought he was fab – a comedy genius, really. When he told me what he had planned I just said yes.'

Working with the man who had co-written one of his favourite radio shows sounded fantastic, but the money LWT were offering was also quite attractive, and just happened to match the amount Kenny needed to buy a new home studio. The purchase was an ironic one though, as Kenny observed soon afterwards. 'I earned enough money from a TV show to pay for the equipment so I could improve the sounds I was doing for wireless – and then I go and lose the wireless show!'

What Took had in store for Kenny were three different series which would be made back-to-back. With luck, one or more would catch on and a TV star would be born. It didn't quite work out that way, but *The Kenny Everett Explosion* (1970), *Making Whoopee* (1970) and *Ev* (1970–71) are all interesting pieces of television, with the latter bearing more than a passing resemblance to Kenny's breakthrough series, *The Kenny Everett Video Show*.

Kenny began working with LWT in June 1970. *The Kenny Everett Explosion*, which was broadcast a month later, lasted ten episodes and was, according to Kenny, 'a bit rubbish'. For a start the format seemed to have been devised along the lines of: 'Let Kenny do whatever he wants, providing it doesn't cost much.' LWT obviously thought that if you left Kenny in front of a camera long enough, genius would abound and magic would be made. Not a bad idea really, if everything good he'd ever done had been both spontaneous and down to him and him alone. This obviously wasn't the case though, and as well as taking hours and hours to prepare, Kenny's work had often involved input from people like Dave Cash, Angela Bond and Johnny Beerling. The only familiar face Kenny had with him on *Explosion* was Bryan Colvin, who had played Crisp the Butler on his Radio 1 show.

The cracks began to appear within a few episodes. Kenny, already deeply unhappy, was all too aware that he was facing the prospect of his first ever flop. And with his name not only in the title but all over the credits as well, there was absolutely nowhere to hide. When they got to episode six, the director declared he'd had enough and jumped ship. In an effort to salvage the situation, LWT decided to give rookie director Bruce Gowers his big chance. Luckily for LWT, and in particular Kenny, he snapped their hands off. 'The original director of the show had a nervous breakdown,' explains Bruce, who went on to become a hugely successful director of TV shows and music videos – and who directed the promo for 'Bohemian Rhapsody', one of the earliest pop videos. 'I don't know if Ev sent the director crazy, or [it was] just the pressure of doing the show, but I was brought in to make the remaining four episodes and help turn everything round. I hadn't been directing more than a year. I was a huge fan of Radio London and was a massive fan of Ev's, so it was a dream come true for me. I'm not saying it was all down to me, but things certainly improved and the final few shows were well received. Ev was also a lot happier. We just wanted to get the series out of the way though and move on to the next.'

The second of Ev's three ventures at LWT was a bizarre little programme called *Making Whoopee*. The stars of the show were Bob Kerr's Whoopee Band (an offshoot of the Bonzo Dog Doo-Dah Band) who each week would play a selection of songs at the Half-Moon pub in Putney. It was Kenny's job to introduce each song, and that was about it, really. Six episodes were made in all, and it's safe to say that any Whoopee made didn't make it past the saloon doors.

After a couple of weeks off, Kenny and Bruce sat down and began to plan the third and final series, and because he was involved from conception, Kenny felt much more comfortable and enthusiastic than he had on the first two. He also now had more experience and a creative and extremely keen colleague. The resulting show was, it's fair to say, way before its time. If anything though, *Ev* readied Kenny for what was to come eight years down the line.

Bruce Gowers still has a great deal of affection and enthusiasm for his work with Kenny, and remembers the final series quite vividly: 'Each show lasted thirty minutes and would feature a sketch or two and some star guests. We had a real mix of people on the show. One week we had Barbara Cartland, then the Bee Gees. It was very eclectic! Then we'd always have two or three specially made music videos. These were wonderful. What we'd do is basically choose a song, listen to the lyrics and make a video based around the story. Kenny would always play all of the parts though, and was the only person who'd ever appear in them. I remember we made one for "Feeling Groovy" and "Why Don't You Write Me", by Simon & Garfunkel. We also did "Patches" by Clarence Carter. That one was about a boy whose father dies and he has to look after his mother and work hard. Kenny played the son, the mother and the father. The next one we did was "Mama Told Me Not To Come," which was a Randy Newman song recorded by the Animals. Tom Jones covered it, I think.

Next time you hear that song though, listen to the lyrics and try and imagine Kenny acting it out. There was no studio audience on *Ev*, by the way. It was just Kenny, the crew and me.'

So *Ev* was a precursor to *The Kenny Everett Video Show*, only with a smaller budget? 'That's about right,' says Bruce. 'Very much so. But it was certainly not as sophisticated.'

Once Kenny had found his feet in television, he could at last begin to embrace the technology more, just as he'd done in radio when he'd joined Big L. Bruce Gowers was only too happy to help him experiment. 'He realized you could do visually the same kind of thing on television that you could do on radio. You know the kind of thing, multi voices and multi characters all in the same shot, etc. We'd use chroma key a lot, which is where you superimpose an image or video on to a coloured background. We once did something like this with the album cover of *Bridge over Troubled Water*. We basically made it look enormous, as though it was a hundred feet high. Kenny then walked on and said, "Hail to thee, oh S&G," and then a bloody great hammer came down and smashed it into smithereens. It would probably look dreadful today and very dated. But back then it was cutting edge, and it really got your imagination going as to what you could do next. It was Kenny who came up with the Simon & Garfunkel idea, not surprisingly.'

Creativity aside, Bruce also remembers Kenny being rather good at forgetfulness. 'I used to have to pick him up from his flat on the way to the studio – otherwise he'd be late. That's if he'd remember he was working, of course! He actually got lost on his way to work once.' Neither has Bruce forgotten the menagerie of animals Kenny and Lee kept, especially that parrot, and the extraordinary fact that it used to call the dog. 'It had learned its name, which just happened to be Knickers. It would say, "Knickers!" It also used to do an exact impression of their phone. They had one of those slim phones and the parrot would have them fooled constantly.'

Like *Nice Time*, *Ev* lasted two series and provided a handful of memorable TV moments. Not least Kenny's video for 'Mama Told Me Not To Come'. Barry Took had every intention of signing Kenny up on a long-term contract, such was the improvement on *Ev*, but unfortunately he left LWT before he could action the move.

By early 1971 Kenny had four TV series to his name and had also got to work with some of the best young talent television had to offer. Had he got the TV bug? No he hadn't, but he now appreciated its worth a bit more and in a few years would be ready to give it another crack.

When Kenny was sacked from Radio 1 he was just twenty-five years old, yet he'd been the undisputed king of music radio for over five years. Until then he'd had everything: fame, adulation, famous friends, a wife – money. He and Lee had enjoyed a good life.

They were living in a beautiful fourteenth-century farmhouse close to the village of Cowfold in Sussex. As idyllic as Petal Cottage was, it was badly in need of renovation and was as much a project as it was a home. Renovations cost money, of course, but in addition to their 'project', Kenny and Lee also had their menagerie to support. When asked about their dependants, Kenny listed 'four chicks, a Great Dane, three cats, two hens and a cock, Duckie!'

Lee was convinced the place was haunted. Originally it had been three cottages before being converted into one big house. Ev and Lee slept in a room at the far end, but when that was being renovated they moved into a bedroom at the other end. 'I couldn't sleep at all,' admits Lee. 'In the chimney we found all these children's shoes with hobnails in them to ward spirits away. The place was haunted as hell.' After doing a bit of research Lee discovered that an old woman who used to live in the far cottage had gone mad and been locked up in that very room.

Despite the ghosts, Petal Cottage was a great place to host parties and entertain friends. Bruce Gowers was one of the first people to come down and visit. 'Paul McCartney's album *Ram* had just come out and Ev was absolutely blown away by it. I turned up at his place in Sussex one afternoon and he wanted to play it to me. So he rigged up his stereo next to the window, we laid down underneath a tree in his garden, lit a huge joint and off we went. I don't remember much about the album but I do remember thinking, shit, this is strong stuff!'

One memorable Christmas, Ev's parents came down to stay along with Conor and Cate, who drove up from London. Jonathan King even turned up! 'My mother was as high as a kite,' recalls Cate. 'They were all smoking pot and eating Christmas cake with marijuana seeds inside. It was the best Christmas my mother ever had, because she was a very uptight lady, and she was stoned out of her mind for three days eating this cake and inhaling everyone else's smoke. And Lee was saying, "Cate, take some of my Christmas cake home with you." And I said, "No thanks, Lee, it doesn't really do that much for me." And there's my mother going, "Cate, don't be so rude, we have to take some of Lee's homemade Christmas cake." For years she talked about that Christmas as the best she ever had. She was about ninety when I finally said, "Mother, that's because you were high as a kite." She said, "I was not!"'

Kenny was initially kept quite busy after being sacked by Radio 1, at least until the end of the year. He'd been pre-recording shows for Radio Luxembourg since 1969, and was contracted to do so until the end of 1970. Sponsored by Esso, these shows were rather short affairs lasting just under thirty minutes, but they're enormous fun and feature some of Kenny's most inventive jingles. They also highlight perfectly his genius for making every second count. We're unsure as to why Luxembourg decided not to renew his contract, but it certainly wasn't a case of him being fired.

There was also a contract with LWT to fulfil, so until February 1971 Kenny was out most days making TV shows. Unfortunately, he wasn't bringing home any money. That had dried up weeks ago. Kenny had accepted the LWT job several months prior to being relieved of his duties at Radio 1 and had spent the £4,000 they'd agreed to pay him on a state-of-the-art home studio. Had he not been given the boot, everything would probably have worked out wonderfully, but by early 1971 the Everetts were on their uppers.

Had Kenny been asked to provide a job description during this period, the one position he'd have been able to legitimately claim, as well as TV presenter, would have been 'magazine columnist'.

During the early seventies some of his most lucrative work came from contributing to women's magazines. Between 1970 and 1972, *My Story*, *Love Affair* and *Jackie* (all now defunct) had Kenny on their books as a regular contributor. There may even have been more. *Love Affair* and *My Story* were purveyors of fine romantic fiction; both had invited Kenny to become a guest columnist for a few months. *Jackie*, on the other hand, had asked him to co-write a two-and-a-half-page weekly comic strip, entitled 'The Life & Times of Kenny Everett'. These were meant to be comic interpretations of real-life events, and featured 'happenings' such as his wedding to Lee and his sacking from Radio 1. One slightly later edition featured a strip called 'He's a Secret Rug Addict', which told of Kenny's short-lived but expensive habit of purchasing luxurious rugs!

Kenny's association with this genre continued throughout the seventies and early eighties. Even his hilarious but not entirely factual autobiography of 1982, *The Custard Stops at Hatfield* was serialized in the ever-popular *Woman* magazine.

For those who've never read *The Custard Stops at Hatfield*, it is precisely what you'd expect the autobiography of Kenny Everett to be. Not overly long, occasionally rude and teeming with great anecdotes, some true and some not. Although it bears Kenny's name and captures his voice, it was written by one of Kenny's best friends and one-time producer at Capital, Simon Booker. 'We went off to a hotel somewhere, supposedly for a week, to write it,' remembers Simon. 'Kenny had the attention span of a gnat though, so we actually lasted about a day and a half. I'd follow him around the grounds with a tape recorder and I'd prompt him with questions. After that I did lots of other research and wrote it over several months.'

The book's working title was 'Buy this Book', which was very 'Kenny' and would probably have worked well. The eventual, slightly more cryptic title came from one of the original taped conversations with Simon: 'We were talking about the difference between the North and the South and how posh it is down South. Kenny said that you get cream in the South and custard in the North, so we decided on *The Custard Stops at Hatfield.* On publication day, my then wife, Kara, gave me two cats and they were named Custard and Hatfield.'

According to Simon, Kenny never even read the book. 'He certainly never read it all the way through. He used to say, "I know what happens, darling, why would I want to read it?" He did all the talk shows to promote it though, which was brave!' Kenny was close enough to Simon to know that there weren't going to be any nasty surprises. 'I think he trusted me completely and knew that I wasn't going to write anything which might make things difficult. He also hadn't come out at that stage, so I made sure we glossed over all that. We were quite candid about drugs though.'

Kenny and Lee scraped through the first half of the winter, but by early February the financial situation was getting desperate. Fortunately, in mid-February Kenny received a welcome offer to make a one-off TV show, but from a somewhat unexpected source. BBC2 wanted Kenny to appear in an episode of their new 'fly on the wall' series, *One Man's Week*, in which a well-known person submits to being followed by a camera crew. Other subjects from the first series included Richard Ingrams, Humphrey Lyttleton, John Peel, J.B. Priestley, Barry Took, Godfrey Winn, John Aspinall and Michael Foot, who as yet had no stick to kick away. This would be good publicity of course, but more importantly, it would bring in much-needed cash.

From the BBC's point of view the invitation was bizarre and completely inconsistent with what had occurred previously. For starters, Kenny's sacking a few months earlier had been the corporation's most notorious dismissal. And not long before that, Robin Scott, who had been the controller of BBC2 since 1969, had called for Kenny to be reprimanded over his use of a BBC2 out-take on one of his Radio 1 shows (this will be covered later in the book). The BBC was either having second thoughts about Kenny or it had serious communication issues.

Kenny's episode of *One Man's Week*, like many of his radio shows, has recently surfaced after being presumed wiped. The programme begins by showing us how Kenny is taking to rural life by having him lead us round his vegetable patch while explaining the merits of growing cucumbers, cabbages, potatoes and sausages.

After this we get a tour of the farmhouse, which is absolutely stunning, though probably in pretty much the same state as it was when they moved in. This life obviously suited Kenny, but only to an extent. Whatever new venture he launched himself into would initially be the best thing ever – there were no half measures with Ev. He'd pictured himself escaping to the peace and quiet of the countryside and thought it would be an antidote to the hectic pace of life in London, but it wasn't long before he was bored with all that peace and quiet. Despite being labelled as shy, Kenny was in fact extraordinarily inquisitive and very much a people person. He was just wary when it came to choosing the people he wanted to surround himself with. His love affair with the country would continue for the rest of his life, but it wouldn't be too long before he would be pining for the city again.

By far the most fascinating part of the *One Man's Week* is when Kenny sits down to interview Kenneth Williams. One can only assume that this happened at Kenny's behest, but his behaviour is interesting, in that it is very different to how he ever behaved with a musician. It didn't matter who it was or how much he loved their music, when Kenny interviewed musicians, with perhaps the exception of Lennon and McCartney, he sounded bored – and, on occasion, waspish. Though he had a good ear and a superb voice, he was not a musician, and therefore he could not relate to them in the same way he could to a fellow entertainer, especially one who had been such a major influence on him. Many cite Spike Milligan as being Kenny's primary comic influence, but Williams isn't far behind. *Round the Horne* had an enormous effect on the young Kenny, and when it came to creating their comedy characters on Big L, Kenny and Cash took more inspiration from *Round the Horne* than from any other show. Kenny knew the scripts inside out, had an extensive knowledge of Polari, the language used by the overtly camp characters, Julian and Sandy, and could do passable impressions of all Williams' characters. Thus his manner as he interviews

Williams is almost gushing, and he hangs on his hero's every word.

Apart from the animals and an occasional film crew, Kenny and Lee had two additional house guests at the start of 1971 – the session guitarist Joe Moretti and his wife, Pina. Joe was a musician of some repute and had been around since the late fifties. Born in Glasgow in 1938, Moretti moved down to London in his teens and began hanging out at the now legendary 2i's Coffee Bar in Soho. There he met the likes of Jet Harris and Tony Meehan, who he would later record two Top Ten singles with, 'Apple Jack' and 'Scarlet O'Hara'. But by far his best known work had been on three number one singles: Tom Jones' 'It's Not Unusual', Chris Farlowe's 'Out of Time' and Johnny Kidd & the Pirates' 'Shakin' All Over'.

Having a musician of Joe's quality around while he was 'resting' wasn't to be lost on Kenny, and when the two weren't decorating or go-karting on the village green, they'd be locked inside Kenny's studio. This was the first time Kenny worked with a musician. He and Joe even began writing and recording an album together, a smidgen of which (a song that appears to be called 'Texas Dan') can be heard on *One Man's Week*. How much they completed is unknown, as Moretti unfortunately passed away in 2012, but we're hoping to find more as we begin to go through the two hundred or so reel-to-reel tapes Kenny left in his private archive.

It seems the majority of their work together was jingle-based. As we said, Kenny had never worked with a musician on a one-to-one basis before, so this was a very different experience. Moretti subsequently laid down dozens of backing tracks for Kenny, all of which he put to good use.

As a thank you for his stay at Petal Cottage, Moretti recorded a double A-side single as a tribute to Kenny and Lee, which was released in 1971. Lee's track is called, appropriately enough, 'Lady Lee' and Kenny's, 'Little Evvy'.

The producer of that single, Mark Wirtz, was also a friend of Kenny's and had become his first studio-based collaborator back in 1969. Wirtz had been responsible for writing the 1967 hit single 'Grocer Jack', which had been championed by the pirates, and had got to know Kenny through Moretti. Wirtz was a producer for hire by this time and in 1971 had recorded tracks for hundreds of different artists.

Wirtz was the first record producer Kenny really got to know, and he remembers being bombarded with hundreds of questions. 'Kenny was more interested in production than I ever was. I enjoyed producing records but after a while it just became work. He was so enthusiastic though, and I tell you what, he was a good little producer. He was very basic, of course, and would have struggled producing a band, but he could have learned very easily. In fact it would probably have taken minutes!'

Not long after meeting Mark, Kenny asked if he could accompany him on the odd recording session. Wirtz didn't see this as being a problem, as long as he didn't get in the way. 'Kenny's enthusiasm could be infectious but also quite annoying,' remembers Wirtz. 'He was only used to working in a very basic home studio, so was in an environment which was new and exciting. He wanted to learn everything there and then. Too many questions!'

Visiting studios was nothing new to Kenny, but up until now he'd always arrived in his capacity as a DJ and had therefore always been required to conduct an interview or something. This was master-and-pupil stuff, and he was there to learn.

As useful as the experience undoubtedly was to Kenny, Mark Wirtz isn't surprised that he never went on to become a producer. 'I think Kenny did learn a lot from our time together, but he was always happiest on his own. As far as I know, he only ever collaborated with me and Joe, and we were his friends. If he'd turned up at a big studio to produce a band he'd never even met or heard of before, I don't think he'd have coped. He definitely wouldn't have enjoyed it!'

Wirtz has hit the nail on the head. Kenny wouldn't have lasted five minutes as a jobbing record producer. He'd have been fine working with one or two bands perhaps, à la George Martin, but to get to that position he'd have had to 'work the studios'. No chance.

Mark Wirtz emigrated to the United States in 1971, but not before he and Kenny had the chance of co-producing a series of jingles together. These were made for the Tea Council of Great Britain and as far as we know were never played on a radio station. In fact we're at a loss as to why he was asked to make them in the first place. Mark can't recall that particular detail, although he does remember producing them with Kenny. 'Wow, that was over forty years ago. I remember Kenny asking me to help him, and we made a whole batch of them. We got Joe Moretti to write and record one for us, which had a Scottish theme to it. Kenny wrote and voiced the rest, I think. We used all kinds of backing tracks. His studio was very basic, so there was only really so much we could do. It was all great fun though. I still listen to them quite often!'

It really must have been fun. The jingles are wonderfully diverse and the production has a definite polish to it. One of the most entertaining tracks has a historical flavour. In it, Kenny plays Queen Elizabeth I, who is greeting Sir Walter Raleigh on his return from North America:

Forsooth Sir Wal, thou hast done well, what wouldst thou wish for
  thee?
No trinkets, Ma'am, he said with charm, but let us all have tea.
The courtiers all then had a ball and scoffed it down with glee.
For if you're wise you'll realize, there's nowt as nice as tea!

Another makes reference to Engelbert Humperdinck, or, as Kenny had christened him, Ingle Dingle Humple Dumple. Hump's inclusion in the jingle had materialized because of a feud between the two, which had started after Kenny made disparaging remarks about one of Humperdinck's records live on air. He'd done the same thing with Tom Jones weeks before, accusing him of wearing trousers that were too tight for him and singing songs from a bygone age. Jones had the good sense to ignore him. Humperdinck, on the other hand, felt he had to respond, and did so via the press, thus kicking off a war of words that would be conducted either on air or via the tabloids. Kenny wasn't the only one guilty of spreading an anti-easy-listening doctrine; he just happened to be the most vocal. It backfired on him, though, when people like John Lennon began describing that kind of sentiment as musical fascism! The joke had gone too far and it was time for Kenny to back down.

By way of apology, Kenny played one of Humperdinck's songs on his next show, commenting afterwards that he thought it was a good song and was sung well. Fortunately Humperdinck had been listening and immediately responded by sending a telegram to Kenny, which read:

Thanks Kenny
   That was nice
   Hump

15

Local Radio Star

KENNY SPENT THE first half of 1971 in 'radio silence'. Luckily for him, his absence from the airwaves was lamented by David Wayne, station manager at one of the BBC's new local stations, Radio Bristol. Like many, he saw Kenny's enforced hiatus as a travesty, but for him it presented an opportunity, and he decided to make a move. David spoke about the experience on the radio documentary, *Kenny Everett – The Local Radio Years*: 'I just rang him up. I put the idea to him and he thought it was quite a wheeze. So I had a meeting with him and we decided that the best way to do it was for the shows to be pre-recorded. I'd then pick them up from Bristol Temple Meads station on a Friday, play them through to make sure they were OK, and then broadcast them on the Saturday morning.'

David asked Kenny to make four one-hour shows. And, while not overly enthusiastic about the remuneration on offer, Kenny was thrilled to be creating again: 'They're putting me on Radio Bristol. Four hours at £12.10 an hour. I look on it as a cuddly little station on which I'll be able to groove on.'

But before Kenny could groove, David would have to get past Kenny's old adversary, the anti-everything MD of BBC Radio, Ian Trethowan. 'There was a huge internal row. I still remember the chilly moment when Ian Trethowan rang me and cross-questioned me about what I'd done. He asked me whether I'd ever looked at Kenny's file. I didn't know there was a file, but apparently it said that Kenny was not to be re-engaged without a conversation with the managing director.' Wayne, who had always operated on the understanding that local radio managers were autonomous, stood by his decision. 'I was going to put him on the air because I thought it was in the best interests of the station, whereupon Trethowan said, "On your head be it" – which I'm sure it would have been, if anything had gone wrong. In fact nothing did go wrong and the rest is history.'

It had been an extremely brave move on David's part, and overcoming Trethowan had been a genuine David & Goliath moment. BBC local stations were extremely parochial back then. They had few members of staff, minuscule budgets and even smaller audiences. The whole concept was still quite experimental – as was Kenny's appointment, of course. This was akin to Accrington Stanley signing David Beckham.

Kenny was all for experiments, it was part of his nature. Yes, the audiences would be tiny, but this didn't even register with him. Would any of his former colleagues at Radio 1 have agreed to such a move? It's doubtful. John Peel, perhaps; he and Kenny were the two DJs who genuinely allowed 'cause' to come before career.

There's no denying that this was a huge step down. This hit home when Kenny read an outline for one of Radio Bristol's shows: 'The idea is that anyone in the West with a claim to fame may appear. We'll be meeting the world bowls champion, the captain of Britain's sea-angling team, a Gloucestershire man who claims he's spoken to men from outer space who are frequenting Cirencester Common and numerous others who reckon they're champs in some way or other.'

When he turned up for the Radio Bristol press conference, Kenny happened to have with him the film crew for *One Man's Week*. They were shooting as he took a question about his sacking from Radio 1, and he turns to the camera and says, 'Isn't it strange that I'm being filmed by one end of the BBC about being sacked by the other?' In reality, there was layer upon layer of strangeness: Kenny was being filmed by BBC2 while answering a question about being sacked by BBC Radio 1 while at a press conference promoting his new show on BBC Radio Bristol. Farcical stuff.

Farce or no farce, Kenny was making radio again. The programmes he produced for the local BBC stations vary massively in content, as he was often without a brief, playlist or any idea of whom he might be broadcasting to. This meant that he was ostensibly making the shows for himself, and so these are, on occasion, intensely personal affairs. Whatever he was thinking, watching, listening to or laughing at went in, and they're quite unlike anything he'd produced previously. One of the more interesting examples is from Christmas 1972, when he was asked to make a sixty-minute show for BBC Radio Medway, now part of BBC Radio Kent. Apart from the prerequisite station jingles, Kenny includes no fewer than five songs by the Beach Boys, Rossini's 'William Tell Overture', the theme tunes to TV shows *The Persuaders* and *Match of the Day*, at least four digs at the BBC and a particularly disgusting joke about Jonathan King. A fascinating insight into the mind of Kenny Everett, week beginning 18 December 1972!

Lee remembers how thrilled Kenny was to be back on the air. But he'd only been hired to make four shows, and that wasn't going to pay all the bills. She had to try and help him build on the momentum. 'It didn't matter how small a Beeb. It was the Beeb, and that was all that mattered. He was over the moon! I actually think he'd have done it for nothing. After he made the four shows for Radio Bristol, I suggested he try and syndicate them, and he did in the end. I also encouraged him to contact some of the other stations.'

Fortunately for Kenny, who couldn't sell a black cat to a witch, he didn't have to knock on many doors. Word had got around about local radio having its own superstar and in the autumn of 1971 he was contacted by his hometown station – BBC Radio Merseyside. This time around he'd be asked to produce a series of two-hour shows for which he'd be paid the princely sum of £20 a time.

Victor Marmion was Radio Merseyside's head of programming at the time, and even though he belonged to a different generation to Kenny, he was still puzzled by the BBC's decision to sack him. 'I wasn't a particular fan of Radio 1,' he explained on the *Local Radio Years* documentary, 'but I was of Kenny Everett and used to listen to him when he was on. When I heard he'd been dropped by Radio 1, I must admit to being pretty put out. I thought it was a very pusillanimous decision by the BBC. Then I heard that Radio Bristol had used him once or twice so there was obviously no absolute ban on him.'

Kenny's Merseyside roots also played a part in Victor's decision to contact him. 'I felt very strongly that the output of the station should be reflective of the area. We might not have been so interested in another DJ, but Kenny was quintessentially a Merseysider, so I thought it would be a terrific idea to get him.'

Even though he hadn't been fond of the place as a child, Kenny did feel an affinity for the people of Liverpool and went out of his way to make the Radio Merseyside shows special, producing an array of bespoke jingles and skits that the station could hitherto have only dreamed of acquiring. One jingle in particular had the whole area in hysterics, when Kenny made an advert for the station featuring a bogus public service announcement warning the people of Liverpool about a new disease that was sweeping the area – Merseysitis! 'From dithering grannies to unprotected youngsters, I've seen people rolling around in the gutters screaming for another fix of Radio Merseyside!'

Kenny also used his programmes on Merseyside to reply to his mother's letters. 'In reply to your last letter, Mother, my answers are Yes, No, No, Yes, Don't know, How dare you? Not blooming likely and, Would you like a three-legged Great Dane for Christmas?'

And if somebody wrote in asking for a birthday greeting to be read out, more often than not Kenny would record a personalized rendition of Happy Birthday, complete with four-part harmony. It was pure quality.

The next station to call on Kenny's new-found community-based broadcasting expertise was Hampshire's BBC Radio Solent. Today Radio Solent has a weekly audience of around 285,000 listeners. Back in 1972, however, the number would have been closer to 285. Despite this, within a week of signing Kenny up, Radio Solent had in its possession a jingle that, had it been required to name those involved, would have listed:

The Beatles & Kenny Everett
Music: Lennon & McCartney
Lyrics: Everett
Produced by Kenny Everett

As Solent was – and still is – by the sea, Kenny decided to take the vocal track off 'Yellow Submarine' and replace it with the following:

> Radio Solent by the sea, with a jolly show for you and me
> Cuddly Ken is in the chair, playing lovely sounds on the air
> Gather round (gather round) without delay (without delay),
> listen closely now, to all he says
> Playing discs for you and me, on Radio Solent by the sea
> *Chorus*:
> Kenny Everett on Solent by the sea – Solent by the sea – Solent by
> the sea.

Unfortunately, this particular parochial partnership wasn't to last, and ended with one of the most bizarre examples of censorship ever seen on British soil. Kenny had submitted a show in which he'd used clips from American radio, something which had inspired him since listening to those Charlie & Harrigan tapes on Big L. American radio was commercial though, and this, according to somebody at Solent, was anti-BBC. Anti-BBC? Commercial radio had already been given the go-ahead in the UK, so it wasn't as if banning a few moments of audio from a visiting superstar was going to change things. It's also worth mentioning that the four other BBC local stations Kenny worked for at the time all broadcast the same show without complaint or comment.

Shortly after this, a different 'somebody' decided it would be a good idea to inform the national press that they'd sacked Kenny Everett. Pleasant as its 285 listeners undoubtedly were, BBC Radio Solent was not Radio 1, London or Luxembourg, and apart from a few column inches here and there, the story, such as it was, died.

*

By 1972 there were twenty BBC local radio stations, all operating autonomously and with varying degrees of professionalism and success. One of the more experienced was Kenny's own local station, BBC Radio Brighton, which today is part of BBC Southern Counties Radio. Radio Brighton had begun broadcasting in 1968, and boasted Desmond Lynam among its early presenters.

In common with the other BBC local stations, Radio Brighton only broadcast at certain hours of the day, not developing a full daytime schedule until the mid- to late seventies. The programmes they did produce were quite focused, and there was little in the way of music or humour.

Phil Fothergill was an assistant on the station and remembers Kenny's show being somewhat luminous. 'The whole of Radio Brighton was like a very mini Radio 4, and so to suddenly have these Everett shows appear in the schedule was rather bizarre to say the least, especially as the manager of the station wanted something a little bit more reverent. But he knew that the publicity involved would actually be worth the embarrassment as far as he was concerned.'

But to Phil the PR opportunities counted for nothing. As far as he was concerned Kenny was the best DJ in the business, and he was elated to have him on the station. That elation was taken to another level, however, when the station manager asked Phil to be Kenny's producer. 'I was a bit star-struck because Kenny was a hero. And then they said to me, "We think we're going to take this show and we want you to be executive producer." Well, that was ludicrous, of course. What they basically meant was go up and collect the tape.'

Collect the tape? This was even better, as it meant Phil might get an opportunity to watch his hero work. And, thanks to Kenny's unique brand of timekeeping, he did. 'Whenever I went up to collect the tape it was pretty likely it wasn't ready. But that wasn't a problem. He'd just say, "Sit down over there, will you?" and he'd produce the programme in front of my very eyes, and it was like magic, to see somebody as professional as that when I was just a youth. I was also amazed at how much kit he'd had built especially for him. He had compressors which would change the sound of your voice, and varying speed tape recorders. Great big green things, they were. He called those, "my tanks".'

Phil's counterpart at Radio Merseyside, Barbara Taylor, didn't have the luxury of being able to drop in and watch their show being made. For her it was a trip to Liverpool Lime Street station where she'd meet the Saturday morning train from London. 'I used to hate Saturday mornings. I used to wait for the London train to come in so I could collect the tapes. Sometimes they couldn't find them and I'd say, "My God, you've got to find them, otherwise I'm going to have two hours of dead air!" There were at least two occasions when I got on-board with a guard and we tried to find the tapes. Fortunately for me, we always found them.'

But that was only the start of it for Barbara. When Radio Merseyside began airing Kenny's show it went out unchecked. That soon changed, however, after it was realized that some of the material was perhaps a little risqué. It would be up to Barbara to ensure that any stray naughty bits were edited out beforehand. 'The boss said, "This has got to be listened to before it goes out." But sometimes I might not get back from the train station until eight thirty a.m. and it was due on air at nine a.m. I had half an hour to edit a two-hour tape! So I used to listen to as much of the first half as I could, and then let it go out while I edited the second half. It was a near thing, more often than not.'

Fortunately for all concerned, Kenny couldn't tune in to BBC Radio Merseyside. Had he been able to, he'd have realized that his show was often being cut to shreds, and would probably have gone spare.

As if able to sense what was happening, Kenny sang the following lyric on a version of Cat Steven's 'Moonshadow' which he made for one of his Radio Merseyside shows:

> And if I ever lose my mic
> If I can't say what I like
> Then I'll leave the BBC.

In between him getting the sack from Radio 1 in 1970 and then returning there in 1973, Kenny's primary source of income had been – the BBC. Slightly baffling perhaps, but perfectly true. Fortunately he had a lot more friends than he did enemies at the corporation and there were, it seemed, even more people willing to go toe to toe against Ian Trethowan.

In addition to the stint on local radio and his turn on *One Man's Week*, Kenny also became part of the writing/presenting team for BBC2's satirical show *Up Sunday*, along with Clive James, John Wells, Willie Rushton and James Cameron. *Up Sunday* came right at the end of the sixties satire boom and was a spin-off from the arts programme *Late Night Line-Up* – as indeed was *One Man's Week*. As well as a rather stellar cast of writers and presenters, *Up Sunday* boasted a jaw-dropping list of regulars, including Eric Idle, Peter Sellers, Spike Milligan, Vivian Stanshall, Max Wall and Richard Murdoch.

Sadly, few episodes of *Up Sunday* survive, but it was described by the wonderful TV-Cream website as being, 'A legendarily last-minute affair, with scripts knocked up hours before totally live transmission, sometimes not at all.' *Up Sunday* also had a 'laid-back' running order so that Everett and Co. could drop or cut short anything they got bored with, which was pretty much everything! One imagines Kenny must have felt very much at home.

Despite finding favour at BBC2, it appears Kenny's biggest fan at the Beeb during this period was a senior producer at Radio 4 by the name of Richard Gilbert. Gilbert, who produced the magazine show *Start the Week*, saw a role for Kenny on his show and had no qualms whatsoever about hiring him. And so he did, with Kenny becoming a long-standing fixture on the programme. He even created the first (and possibly the only) jingles ever made for Radio 4!

Start the Week was in those days presented by Richard Baker, and it would be Kenny's job to provide a series of excerpts and links for the show. He was given a free hand and there was no censorship, as such. The only request was that Kenny remained mindful of the audience to whom he would be broadcasting. Kenny was happy to comply, of course. The last thing he needed was to be sacked by one of the people trying to save him. That would indeed be 'biting the hand'.

Ever the canny old dog, Kenny decided he'd use the platform to launch a new campaign that would (hopefully) get him back on national radio. He'd tried this before, not long after he was sacked, but it had quickly died a death as he was without a show of any kind. Now that he'd got it back, he was determined to try again. The whole exercise was disguised with a thick veil of comedy, of course, but the sentiment was serious. He wanted his old job back!

Neither Gilbert nor any of his colleagues at Radio 4 batted an eyelid when they heard what Kenny produced. This was because they too wanted to hear him back on Radio 1, and even though some of it might have been seen as a little anti-BBC, his 'campaigns' and 'appeals' were all aired on *Start the Week*, and were also included on his shows for the local stations.

One of the funniest (that we've heard) was broadcast at Christmas in 1971. With 'Deck the Halls' playing in the background, Kenny reads out the following message:

> Can you see this happen?
> Can you stand by and see this crime perpetrated?
> This Christmas, as you're cramming food down your face, spare a thought for Everett.
> Send money now to the Keep Ken Alive Fund, Squalor Mansions, Rat Alley, Cowfold.
> Richard Baker will give you the address at the end of the programme. Won't you, Richard?

Later there was:

> And now, friends, an appeal on behalf of the 'Bring Back Cuddly Ken to Radio' campaign. Yes, friends, ever since my sacking in 1970 . . . By the way, what do you think of my sacking? Oh it suits you, darling!

Lastly there's his 'BBC Bum', one of the most hilariously insightful thirty seconds of radio you'll ever hear. It parodies the BBC hierarchy's incompetence at decision-making, as well as its policy of employing 'too many chiefs and not enough Indians'.

The skit begins with Kenny asking the question: Can you say Bum on the BBC?

Older voice: Hang on, I'll check . . . (*cue footsteps, followed by knocking on a door*) Can you say Bum on the BBC?

Much older voice: Hang on, I'll check . . . (*cue slower footsteps followed by knock on door*) Can you say Bum on the BBC?

VERY old voice: Hang on, I'll check . . . (*cue even slower footsteps followed by knock on door, door opens*) Can you say Bum on the BBC?

God-like voice: YES.

Kenny: Thank you. Bum bum bum bum, etc.

The links on *Start the Week* were less duplicitous affairs, and came as a series of musical vignettes. One, 'An Ode to Richard Baker', is a sixty-second song congratulating Baker on his previous announcement: 'It had Pace, Class, Razzamatarse!' The audience absolutely adored it, and although they could never allow him a regular show of his own, Gilbert and Radio 4 rewarded Kenny's hard work and creativity by asking him to make a special one-off Boxing Day extravaganza.

Everett on Everett went out on Boxing Day 1972 and is rightly regarded by many as one of the finest radio shows he ever produced.

Kenny's final invitation from Gilbert was to appear as a co-presenter on the Radio 4 children's show *If It's Wednesday, It Must Be*, a sort of junior version of *Start the Week*. Hosting the show was the acerbic and extremely unpredictable Kenneth Robinson, probably the only man in radio who had been sacked more times than Kenny. The Bonzo Dog Doo-Dah Band's Vivian Stanshall was the show's other ever-present guest alongside Kenny. Other contributors included renowned alcoholic and full-time hellraiser Jeffrey Bernard; satirist and musician Miles Kingston; nocturnal DJ Annie

Nightingale; eccentric poet Ivor Cutler; experimental composer Ron Geesin; hippy poetess Lady June; and, for one episode, a very young Harry Shearer, better known as Derek Smalls from *This Is Spinal Tap*. As all were on their very, very best behaviour, it somehow worked and quickly became a cult favourite with listeners of all ages, eventually running for three series.

Though they have been dubbed Kenny's 'wilderness years', in terms of the quality and variety of work he produced they were arguably the most fruitful of his career. He had appeared on BBC2, LWT, Radio 4 and a total of six BBC local stations. It was a chaotic period though, and despite managing to keep his head above water, the lack of financial security was beginning to trouble him. If he was to continue progressing as he had been, things would have to change quickly.

16

Produce Me Out of Here

EVEN WITHOUT A regular slot on national radio, Kenny should have been earning a fortune from voice-overs and commercial production. He had his own studio and a lot of time, enthusiasm, experience, and a not inconsiderable amount of talent. The jobs should have been pouring in. The fact that they weren't was the fault of his agent.

Like most of the country's big-name DJs, Ev was represented by the Harold Davidson Organisation, but the person who was supposed to be looking after him had become a liability after developing a serious drink problem. This wouldn't have had as much impact if Kenny had a regular show in place, but maintaining a steady flow of bookings for voice-over work required constant dialogue between potential clients, the agent and Kenny, and that wasn't happening. Kenny knew that enquiries were coming into the agency, but they weren't filtering through to him. As it turned out, things were even worse than Kenny realized, and companies were avoiding asking for him because of his agent's behaviour.

In mid-1972 Kenny wrote to Harold Davidson, informing him that he intended to leave the agency. Davidson, who had been unaware of the severity of the problem, immediately took action. The agent in question was relieved of their duties and encouraged to seek help, while Harold set about finding a replacement. Luckily, there was a candidate close at hand.

Jo Gurnett was a friend of Harold's who had until recently been working for Philip Solomon, a music impresario who owned Major

Minor Records, whose hits included 'Je t'aime . . . moi non plus' by Serge Gainsbourg and Jane Birkin. He was also on the board at Radio Caroline and managed several bands. A keen horseman, Solomon also owned a stud farm in Northern Ireland. When he sold Major Minor Records to EMI, he'd asked Jo if she'd like to go over and work there for a while. 'I thought I'd give it a go, but I didn't last long,' she remembers. 'You can only see so many mares being serviced by stallions! So I went back to London and not long after I arrived I bumped into Harold Davidson. I'd always got on very well with Harold and he'd always said that if I ever needed a job he'd employ me. Fortunately, when I bumped into him, he had this vacancy looking after the DJs, so I said I'd give it a go.'

Although she had no experience as an agent, Jo had honed her skills as a negotiator and was used to handling artists and groups. Dealing with a bunch of DJs would be a pushover in comparison. And so it proved to be. Jo took to her new position like a duck to water, and continued looking after the likes of Sir Terry Wogan, Steve Wright and Ken Bruce right up until her retirement.

But on joining Harold's organization, the main focus of her attention would be Kenny. So far as he was concerned the situation hadn't been resolved and he was still intent on finding alternative representation. 'I think he'd become so fed up that he was considering leaving the business altogether,' remembers Jo. 'It was a desperate time really and I had to handle things very delicately. I think he'd lost all confidence, both in the agency and in himself, and that needed to be rebuilt. Then one day, not long after I started, I got an enquiry for him to do a voice-over. So I rang him up and that was the start. He was so thrilled though. Things had also become pretty desperate financially, I think. But from then on, his situation started to improve.'

Indeed it did. Kenny's confidence rapidly returned as work began to trickle in again and, for the first time in two years, he was able to shift his focus from financial concerns to rebuilding his career – again!

It is impossible to overstate the importance of Kenny having the right person looking after his affairs outside the studio. And, had it not been for Jo stepping into the breach at the Harold Davidson

Organisation, we may well have been writing a much shorter book. The words vulnerable and vulnerability came up again and again throughout our research – never in the context of Kenny's work, but in terms of his struggle to cope with day-to-day life.

The broadcaster and journalist Matthew Parris met Kenny in the mid-eighties, a period when he was experiencing a great deal of personal upheaval (the details of which are covered later), and observed: 'I suppose the mistake I would have made about him, and this is so often the case with geniuses, is that with his work he showed such judgement, such timing, such a sharp intellect, such an ability to distinguish between what would work and what wouldn't work, such poise, such precision, that I would have assumed he would have been the same with his private life, and he would have the same wisdom and the same judgement as he showed in performance. But evidently he didn't, and of course it's very common that people don't, but I always find it very hard to believe.'

The phrase 'Behind every great man is a great woman' could well have been written for Kenny. Over the course of his life he enjoyed the love and protection of four women: Lee, his sister Cate, Jo and his friend Cleo Rocos. Each brought something very different into his life, their support mattered to Kenny, and prevented him from going under – which is what would have happened had they not been around.

Jo was a rock for Kenny; they spoke on the telephone almost every day until the end of his life. 'It didn't matter where he was or whether he was working or not, there would always be a call going in from either him or me.' Jo didn't just manage Ev's career, she managed his life. There's no doubt about it, Jo was exactly what Kenny needed, both professionally and personally. 'We were inseparable really. I became his agent, manager, mother, everything. I did his shopping for him. Especially food shopping. I used to spend half my life popping in and out of Marks & Spencer. I also used to go to Harrods and buy his towels and his bed linen. The truth was he didn't like to go out on his own, because if he did he'd be accosted by someone demanding, "Oh, go on, you funny bugger, make us laugh," and he couldn't handle it. I even had to go to the loo with him, if we were in a public place. The amount of times I had to stand outside a gents loo waiting for him! I went absolutely everywhere with him, to every single job – regardless of where it was, what it was or how long it took.'

It wasn't until Kenny formed a great working relationship with Barry Cryer and Ray Cameron on the Thames TV shows of the late seventies that Jo saw Kenny begin to handle himself a bit better with the public. 'But you could see the panic in his eyes, when he was in a large group. He would always sign autographs though. He never, ever refused to sign an autograph.'

In the early eighties Kenny was invited to a Hi-fi & Audio show at Wembley Conference Centre with his Radio 2 producer Geoff Mullin. They arrived and were welcomed on to the Sony stand, and then the Panasonic stand, and then another, before eventually settling down somewhere to rest. 'So we're sitting there, intently listening to some pretty serious hi-fi equipment,' recalls Mullin. 'And I'm suddenly aware that people had started to recognize him and are beginning to gather round. Then one person stuffs a piece of paper in front of him and says, "Can I have your autograph, Kenny?" So he signed the bit of paper, looked at the ever-growing crowd of people, turned to me and whispered in my ear, "Geoffrey, produce me out of here!" Anybody else would have said, "Let's go," or whatever, but not Kenny. It made me howl. So I made our excuses and off we went. He really didn't like crowds at all.'

It was one of the reasons why Jo knew that Ev would never have countenanced being the subject of *This is Your Life*. 'Jo,' he'd warned, 'I would rather have red-hot nails pushed into my eyeballs.' It wasn't just the public exposure, his life laid bare for all to gawp at; it was the fact it would have pushed him out of his comfort zone. 'He would have loathed it,' says Jo. 'You know, a teacher he couldn't remember – it was too long ago. He really just lived for the moment. That television show's done, let's move on. He wasn't at all nostalgic. He did talk about the past, but not much.'

For Kenny the past was a closed door. There's no better illustration of this than a story from Paul Walker, his old school friend. Paul's younger brother, Peter, was once directing a show at the BBC and spied Kenny holding court in the canteen. 'Peter had known Maurice too, of course, way back when we all grew up in Liverpool. So as he walked past him he said, 'Hello, Maurice, how are you?' And Maurice, or Kenny as he was then, just cut him dead. He looked at him and then turned away – completely ignored him. There's no way he wouldn't have remembered Peter, so he must have put Maurice to one side and that was that.'

Two years of comedic campaigning and relative good behaviour eventually paid dividends for Kenny, and in March 1973 he was invited back to Radio 1. There were to be conditions, however. For a start he wasn't allowed to appear live on the station under any circumstances. The suits may have mellowed somewhat, but they were still wary of him and 'real-time Everett' was some way off. It seemed Kenny's rehabilitation was far from over!

A compromise was reached whereby he would pre-record his shows at home and send them in by post or by courier. They lasted an hour, and went out every Saturday at 10 a.m. Paul Gambaccini shared the same producer as Kenny and remembers his fellow DJ having the odd timing issue. 'Teddy Warwick was Kenny's producer then, and he was also my executive producer. And I remember him saying how naughty Kenny was because he would send in the tapes and they would not be precisely the right length. This was an hour show and they'd be fifty-seven minutes or fifty-nine minutes or sixty-one minutes.' Kenny blamed this on the fact that the machine which times how long a piece of tape lasts didn't work in his studio at home. 'And so Teddy would have to do some surgery by either adding a bit of music in a way which was unobtrusive or somehow editing a piece of music. But he adored Kenny and made it clear that this was well worth it.'

When Teddy set about editing Kenny's shows it was all about keeping to time, which is a large part of any producer's job. But there were still people within the BBC who insisted on censoring him. Certainly there were times when edits were in order, but the majority of these examples are as harsh as they are mind-boggling. One cut in particular baffled absolutely everybody, especially Kenny. 'The nervous old Beeb still chopped out the strangest bits from my tapes. There was one instance when I played a record by the Four Tops called "Ain't No Woman Like the One I Got", and I said, "That's the Four Tops with 'Ain't No Woman Like My One-eyed Love'," and they chopped it out! I suppose they thought they'd get a lot of letters from complaining one-eyed women!'

Kenny wasn't completely anti-censorship. He agreed that there was a time and a place for everything, give or take. But surely even his nemesis-to-be, Mary Whitehouse, wouldn't have taken a Stanley knife to that?

Examples such as this showed that, despite the truce, nothing had really changed. Kenny was still capable of making terrific radio shows that attracted vast and loyal audiences, and the Radio 1 hierarchy were still capable of making appalling decisions as to what was acceptable for broadcast. The vast majority of people at Broadcasting House were there to make the best radio possible, and in the vast majority of cases they did. These people were talented, experienced and knew their audiences inside out. Did they really need the old guard at the top? It's debatable. And one can only speculate as to what Radio 1 might have sounded like had they simply been allowed to get on with it.

Kenny's second and final stretch on Radio 1 came to an end in September 1973. He'd had six months back in the fold and had enjoyed almost every moment. But there was a new challenge waiting for him.

17

What a Capital Idea!

It's really most amazing that the station which we're
crazy over has a sound that's absolutely new.
There's radio this, and radio that, oh what a bore,
but there's never been a stereophonic station before.
Bringing you all the hittypoos and bringing you all the fun,
Capital brings you all the stars and jollity by the tonne.
If anyone asks you why you're smiling, just remember, pal,
Stereophonic Radio Ca-pi-tal.

Lyrics to one of Kenny's first Capital jingles

RADIO 1 (AND the rest of the BBC, for that matter) simply weren't
ready for Kenny Everett. He was one of the most unique talents
the Broadcasting House side of the corporation had ever had on its
books, and with people like this you need to offer more than just
indulgence.

Johnny Beerling and in particular Angela Bond had done an
amazing job in nurturing Kenny's talent, and, for a time, had managed
to restrain him. If it hadn't been for them he'd probably have been out
within a week. Unfortunately though, in order for this arrangement to
work long-term Kenny also needed a Tony Windsor or a Philip Birch
at the helm, somebody whom he admired and who didn't always
communicate via memo or telephone. Somebody who could put a
gentle arm around him and explain with conviction why he should or
shouldn't do something. 'Programme directors, I think, treated Kenny
with kid gloves,' says DJ Nicky Horne. 'Not because he was a huge star

and they were frightened of him. He was treated with kid gloves because I think everybody knew that he was as delicate as a butterfly and that if you were to say something to him in the wrong way he'd get really, really upset. And that was part of his utter charm.'

Contrary to popular belief, Kenny could be fine with authority – just not the Beeb's kind. He operated according to simple criteria: those at the top must know the industry, be able to communicate and, most of all, be accessible. He wouldn't always do as he was told, of course, but as long as he respected the bosses, there'd be more good behaviour than bad. If he couldn't respect them, however, he couldn't work with them. The saying 'no respect for authority' generally refers to somebody being unruly, but you do sometimes have to take a step back and examine why those in authority fail to command respect.

The suits at the Beeb knew little about music or personality radio, only communicated via boy-scout runner and were about as accessible as the queen's toilet. The only people who genuinely respected them were those who aspired to be one of them.

Directly after his sacking from Radio 1 the BBC began to lose control and the situation grew embarrassing. Ev had gone from mocking the organization quite openly on Radio 4 to having the head of BBC Radio trying to prevent him from broadcasting to an audience of twelve on a local station.

If somebody with Kenny's temperament gets even a sniff that those above him have lost control, they're going to exploit the situation. Not necessarily for any specific gain or reason, but because they can. And, that's precisely what Kenny did. Hence the enfant terrible of the air-waves became more interested in putting the boot into the Beeb than creating great wireless. The continuing mismanagement had riled him to the point where he'd become bitter and more than a little obsessed.

If he was ever to get back to doing what he did best, he would need a new and totally different environment. Somewhere that was all about the wireless. A few familiar faces would be nice, as well as bags of talent, artistic licence, great facilities, a degree of direction and an all-prevailing sense of fun and the ridiculous.

As importantly though, he needed to be able to respect the

hierarchy. And, if he could get along with them, well, so much the better.

Since the demise of Big L, Kenny had been itching for commercial radio to be given the green light in the UK. Commercial TV had started way back in 1955 and, as far as he was concerned, it was high time radio was given the chance to catch up. Given the ridiculous lengths it had gone to in scuppering the pirates and solidifying the Beeb's monopoly, this was unlikely to happen under a Labour government. Support would have to come from the other side of the house.

In their 1970 election manifesto, Ted Heath's Conservative Party promised to introduce 'local commercial radio' to the UK. When they came to power in June that year they were true to their word and began to push through the Sound Broadcasting Act (1972). This would in turn create the Independent Radio Authority, whose remit would be to award nineteen radio licences throughout the UK. London and the Home Counties were granted two of those licences – with one primarily news and the other general entertainment. Capital Radio (or Radio Capital, as it was initially known) won the entertainment licence and the London Broadcasting Company (LBC) won the news licence.

Kenny had prophesied the arrival of legitimate commercial radio as long before as 1966, when virtually nobody else in the UK thought it would ever happen. When it finally came to pass he was ready to jump on-board. 'I always knew that commercial radio would hit land,' Kenny said in 1981. 'Even when I was on the pirates I thought it was a natural progression. I didn't know it would happen so soon though. When I was at the Beeb I heard rumblings, so I thought, Hello, you better get girded up, Ken. So I bought a stereophonic attachment for my studio and I was all ready. My loins were girded when it happened, and there it was in stereo [Radio 1 had always broadcast in mono]. But I've always been fascinated by commercials. They're little cameos of brilliance. They're like little shows.'

Those running the Capital application had assembled a team worthy of winning Oscars and Grammys, let alone radio licences.

Lending their considerable weight to the Capital cause were the film director and producer Bryan Forbes; Beatles producer George Martin; actor Dirk Bogarde; and the actor and director Richard Attenborough. This 'luvvies love-in' must have impressed, as the application was successful, and at 5 a.m. on 16 October 1973 Britain's first commercial 'entertainment' station began broadcasting.

Capital's debut was more Radio 4 than Radio Fun. After an almost Churchillian introduction from Richard Attenborough, there followed a three-minute rendition of the National Anthem, complete with verses which most people never even knew existed. Those who hadn't yet fallen back to sleep were then treated to Capital's station-jingle, which had been written by George Martin and performed by the group Blue Mink. Simon & Garfunkel's 'Bridge over Troubled Water' was the first record played, followed by a rather sleepy welcome from DJ David Symonds.

Symonds had been a colleague of Kenny's at Radio 1 and says they were lucky to start broadcasting when they did. 'We were not ready at all. Only a short time before we were due to go on air there was a guy with his legs sticking out from under the desk. They were actually still wiring the desk shortly before I was due on air. We hadn't even had a dummy run on it and only made it by the skin of our teeth. I'd been up all night and I was so tired I actually fell asleep in the toilet. Somebody found me upright facing the urinal with my head against the tiles. By the time I was due on air I was exhausted. There really was a pioneering spirit though!'

Although Attenborough assumed the role of chairman at Capital, the man responsible for the station's output was programme controller Michael Bukht, better known as TV chef Michael Barry from the programme *Food & Drink*.

DJ Nicky Horne joined Capital a month before they went on air. 'We were an incredibly close-knit team. In fact before we went on air, camp beds were set up in the music studio so that we didn't have to go home. We were working so hard to try and get everything ready. The atmosphere was wonderful.'

It didn't matter who you were, everybody mucked in, even the chairman. 'Richard Attenborough would come in with Indian take-aways for thirty people,' remembers Horne. 'That was quite something, being fed by Richard Attenborough! Michael Bukht was also an amazing man, and it was he who brought us all together.' When it came to recruitment, Bukht's approach was rather un-conventional. 'He hired people as much for their personality as their broadcasting ability,' says Horne. 'If Bukht thought they'd be good for the team, he'd have them, and regardless of experience. I remember him once saying to me, "I didn't pick you because you're a good DJ, Nicky, I didn't pick you because of that, because you're not! I picked you because you're a nice bloke, now fuck off and be a nice bloke on air."'

Bukht's vision with regards to programming was even more radical. He intended Capital to be a full-service radio station, so there was a 'talks' department, presenting interviews and documentaries, a daily soap opera, a classical music programme, a rock show, a children's show, a show for older listeners featuring music from the forties and fifties, a daily phone-in with the agony aunt Anna Raeburn, a jazz programme, the Greg Edwards soul show, a sports department and Roger Scott's 'people's choice', giving listeners the chance to select a track to be featured for the week. And virtually every show went out live.

As well as a unique vision, Bukht also had the temperament and build of a Silverback, and was not to be crossed. In his office he had a talkback box and if he heard something he didn't like he'd scream down the DJ's headphones, almost blowing their ears off. This also applied to Kenny of course, and he and Bukht had regular run-ins, the vast majority of which were centred on Kenny's refusal to work to a playlist. 'I tried to reason with him,' explained Bukht, 'but I always got the same answer: "People tune in to listen to ME, Michael. They like what I like, so I choose the music."' Bukht was loath to admit it, but Kenny was right. 'He was a complete one-off. I couldn't let anyone else act like that, for the simple reason they probably wouldn't have been able to pull it off. Kenny was just Kenny.'

Bukht was an extraordinarily dedicated programme controller. It didn't matter whether he was at home or in the office, in a meeting or on the phone, he'd always have Capital on. This worked in terms of maintaining quality, but it could also be bad for his health – especially when Kenny was on air.

One day in 1977, at home listening to one of Kenny's weekend shows, Michael heard: 'After the news we're going to do the competition, folks, and this week's prize is . . . a FERRARI, yeeaaah! All you gotta do is phone in, answer a simple question, and you could be a winner!' Bukht went white. This wasn't America, where radio stations were allowed to give away cars and yachts; the Independent Broadcasting Authority had imposed a strict limit as to how much could be spent on prizes and in 1977 that wouldn't have stretched to a Robin Reliant, let alone a Ferrari. 'The maximum prize value you were allowed to offer was about thirty-five pence,' joked Kenny. 'And there I was, giving away a Ferrari! I set the competition, asked the listeners to phone in and sat back while telephone exchanges all over London blew a fuse as thousands and thousands of people dialled the Capital number, all desperate for the Ferrari.'

While London went Ferrari-mad, the Independent Broadcasting Authority went mad at Bukht. A minute after Kenny announced the competition they were on the phone asking what the hell was going on. Capital was London's biggest station and this was an extremely serious breach of policy.

The moment Kenny came back on after the news he let on that the Ferrari in question was in fact a Dinky Toy. Hostilities between Bukht and the IBA ceased and everyone stood down. It had spoiled his bloody weekend though! Kenny was nonplussed. 'Nobody really thought I was actually going to give away a real Ferrari. That's just stupid!'

Kenny always talked fondly of Bukht. He was Capital's spine, and had created an environment where Kenny could practise his art with a sensible amount of autonomy. Throughout the years much has been made about Kenny not enjoying this freedom at Capital, with many claiming that he yearned for the adrenalin rush that comes from broadcasting under the constant threat of rebuttal. In truth, Kenny received a host of verbal and written warnings at the station, and it's rumoured there was an actual suspension, although we haven't been able to substantiate this.

The fact remains, Kenny delivered some of his finest work during his time at the station. Being at Capital enabled him to mature both as a broadcaster and, for varying reasons, as a human being. He'd matured professionally at the BBC, thanks primarily to Angela Bond and the BBC archive, but at Capital it was more about the people, and from the moment he joined he was surrounded by an ensemble of 'wireless-heads', all of whom liked and admired him.

The youngest of the original Capital DJs was Nicky Horne. Having started as an assistant at Radio 1, Nicky worked at Capital for thirteen years, before moving on to stations such as Radio 1, Classic FM, Virgin Radio and Planet Rock. Nicky joined Capital on his twenty-third birthday and, in addition to Kenny, was working with the likes of Dave Cash, Tommy Vance and Dave Symonds. 'It was just like a dream come true. Here I was on the same radio station, with a daily show no less, as Kenny Everett. This is a guy that I'd idolized on Radio London, who I'd done everything in my power to emulate and to copy, which is why Emperor Rosko wanted me in the first place on Radio 1, because I sounded like Kenny.'

Horne was so obsessed by Kenny that he would practise for hours, trying to perfect the impersonation. But that wasn't what Michael Bukht wanted. He wanted Nicky Horne! 'When I joined Capital Michael Bukht made all of us, but me particularly, go through a process which lasted for about three weeks where he would make us record links and then would analyse the links and say, "I want you to be real, I want you to be you, I want you to tell the truth." So I would do a link sort of sounding like Kenny and he'd say, "That doesn't sound like you, it sounds like somebody else, be you." And he gradually peeled the layers of this personality that I'd developed, which was ninety per cent Kenny and ten per cent Rosko, and then allowed me to be me. But I'd idolized Kenny so much. I really wanted to be Kenny!'

The early presenter line-up at Capital was almost as eclectic as the programming itself, and featured the likes of Gerald Harper, Robin Ray, Michael Aspel, Tim Rice, Tommy Vance and Sue Cook.

The very first person Bukht hired at Capital was Kenny's mate and ex-Big L partner, Dave Cash. Cash was brought in as a DJ, of course, but also as a production manager, and he was immediately given the task of helping Bukht recruit the best talent broadcasting had to offer. 'Michael Bukht wanted me to line up everyone I thought he should get in for an audition. So I said, yes, fine. Everyone assumes that the first guy I phoned was Kenny. In fact it wasn't, it was Tommy Vance, because he had commercial production experience. Kenny was the second though. Then when he came in and met Dickey they fell in love with each other immediately. The "Oh daaarrlings" were everywhere! And Kenny started calling him Dickeypoo, which everybody then copied!'

Before all the pink gins and the air-kisses, Kenny had to meet the man in charge. His manager, Jo Gurnett, remembers that trip to the Euston Tower: 'A lot of people like to think that Kenny's first meeting at Capital was with Richard Attenborough. It wasn't though. It involved Ev, Michael Bukht and me. Capital was just a shell at the time and Ev and I turned up there, climbing over wires and walls and things. They were such nice people though. I think Kenny warmed to all of them.'

Kenny did warm to all of them. Capital was everything he had hoped a legitimate commercial radio station would be. He agreed with the programming direction and was surrounded by a team of enthusiastic, like-minded people. Presenter Mike Smith, who joined the station in the late seventies, remembered Kenny as being the office joker. 'Our open-plan production office – called the Playpen – was where Ev ran wild on Fridays. If you hadn't been soaked by Kenny doing a run-by with the plant sprayer, you simply were not part of the fun!'

Kenny's broadcasting career at Capital began as it had finished at Radio 1 – with a weekend show, pre-recorded at a farm in Wales where he and Lee had recently moved. Despite it not being live, this had worked well at the Beeb and during his last stint he produced some brilliant shows. Not so at Capital, however. His debut show for the station is altogether quite staid. It's not a bad show by any stretch of the imagination, but there was definitely something missing. Fortunately for everyone concerned, the initial 'adult contemporary' music policy for Capital's breakfast show was backfiring and the station's initial audience figures were poor. 'People are very much creatures of habit,' says Dave Symonds, Capital's original breakfast DJ, 'and however much you publicize something, it's word of mouth that counts, and that takes time. People also have to come round to an idea. I think that the music policy was good though. I don't think Radio 1 was playing album tracks at the time and quite a significant part of our playlist was album-orientated, so Capital did offer a genuinely alternative diet.' This particular diet was starving London of what it really wanted, and Capital's listeners were leaving in their droves. Kenny lamented the change in music policy, but could understand the move. 'I really did prefer the early music,' he said in the late seventies. 'The rest of the world's caught up now, and they're all playing groovy stereophonic stuff. We used to sit in the studio though, thinking, Great, this is for me, while all the audience were sitting listening to Radio 1!'

The poor listening figures forced Bukht and Attenborough to take action. The music would have to change, but so would the geographic location of their star DJ. Kenny was ordered to London. 'Forget about all this sending shows by train,' they said. 'Get down here and do them live. You and Dave Cash, you're going on the air together.'

As far as the station was concerned, moving Kenny to London was a masterstroke, and not merely from a programming point of view. If you have somebody as talented and well respected as Kenny Everett on your payroll, you want to have them around the place. It breeds confidence and provides inspiration, and for a start-out station like Capital, that was crucial.

Until Capital began broadcasting, Big L had been the country's most successful and well-respected commercial station (albeit an offshore one), and the most popular show during its three-year existence was *The Kenny & Cash Show*. People of a certain age talk about it to this day, but in 1973 it was fresh enough in people's minds to be seriously considered for a second outing (though technically it was to be a third outing, taking into account their single-show stint at Radio 1). Bukht and Attenborough thought it was worth a try. If nothing else it was bound to stir some interest, and it would also be a nice 'doff of the cap' to Big L.

After a huge advertising campaign the all-new *Kenny & Cash Show* went on air and was an immediate hit. While happy about being reunited with Cash, Kenny wasn't exactly thrilled with the change in music policy. 'We played all sorts of dreadfully common music!' he once admitted. 'And of course the ratings went whoosh!'

Although they were now used to broadcasting almost exclusively on their own, it didn't take Kenny and Cash long to re-establish the rapport which had once made them the most talked-about people in radio. One of the many people listening to the new Kenny and Cash was their soon-to-be colleague, Peter Young. Peter joined Capital in 1975 but before that had been a huge fan of the pirates. He couldn't wait to hear the all-new Kenny and Cash, but admits it wasn't quite up to the standard of the original. 'The new Kenny and Cash worked, up to a point, but it didn't have the same anarchic quality as the pirate version. That was what made them great, really. It was still a lot of fun though.'

Peter has a point. Back in the day, Kenny and Cash had a virtual monopoly when it came to anarchic behaviour on the airwaves. When the partnership re-formed, fans of the previous incarnation were expecting more of the same. It wasn't to be, however. Both were a little older and in Dave's case, a little wiser. This time around the people of London would have to make do with 'Kenny & Cash Lite'.

Despite being a bit of a disappointment on the anarchy front, Capital's *Kenny & Cash Show* still had a genuine edge to it and became a welcome alternative to the rather sanitized Noel Edmonds offering over on Radio 1. The show also produced several instances of broadcasting gold. On April Fool's Day 1974, Kenny and Dave decided to do an entire programme as if they were back on Big L. This was no tokenistic tribute; they were determined to do it properly, and went to enormous lengths to ensure the show sounded exactly the same as it had on the *Galaxy*.

Their attention to detail was almost forensic. There were references to Big L programmes, supposedly to be broadcast later that day, adverts for Big L T-shirts, on sale from 17 Curzon Street for only twelve shillings and sixpence – 'Buy two!' – original Big L jingles, as well as sound effects of transmitter interference and tenders, which kept barging into the side of the boat while delivering supplies. Even the playlist was authentic (although Bukht took some persuading), and included a selection of hits from Big L's early Fab 40 shows. Adverts were read out for old gigs and personal appearances; according to Kenny, Ed Stewart and Dave Dennis would be introducing Marianne Faithfull, Herman's Hermits, plus Brian Poole and the Tremeloes at the Starlight Ballroom this coming Saturday. They even had digs at Radio Caroline! Only the adverts were current. The whole exercise sounds completely effortless and was truly an astounding piece of broadcasting.

Despite the fervour surrounding the reunion, cracks began to appear within a few months, and it wasn't long before Kenny and Cash was reduced to just Kenny. One of their engineers, a young chap called Clive Warner, recalls: 'At the time I had a night job at Capital running the master control room. That was where we fixed microphones and things. At the end of my shift I used to go straight on to *Kenny & Cash* as an engineer. I was pretty exhausted but I was young, so could just about manage it. It was also something to look forward to at the end of the night. As the weeks went by I began to notice changes in Dave. He began to get bags under his eyes and he seemed to lack concentration.'

What was happening to Dave was nothing more than good old-fashioned parenthood. The sleepless nights that went with having a baby daughter were the last thing a breakfast DJ needed. After a few weeks he could take no more and reluctantly asked for a transfer to a daytime slot. It was a sad end to British radio's first on-air partnership, but at least they had the satisfaction of finishing on a high.

Kenny remained friends with Dave Cash for the rest of his life.

Though they stopped working together on the breakfast show, they continued to meet once a month at Mario's restaurant near the Euston Tower. Their relationship had been built on a shared love of music and comedy, and their personal lives rarely clashed. On the rare occasion this happened, however, it was an uncomfortable experience and new parameters would have to be quickly drawn. Dave Cash explains. 'I had a young daughter of about eighteen months old at this time and Kenny used to come to Sunday lunch with us every week. My wife and I had a deal with regards to changing nappies. Whoever was closest did the deed. One Sunday baby Emma did the full works and I had to subsequently change her nappy in front of Kenny, and this really freaked him out. The next day he said, "Listen, this Sunday lunch idea's nice, but I can't take you as a dad." I said, "Yes, but she's my daughter, what am I supposed to do?!" So he said, "OK, why don't we have lunch at Mario's every month? You don't bring your daughter and I won't bring my boyfriends." And so that's how it was until quite near his death, really. I was never totally comfortable with him being homosexual, and he was never totally comfortable with me being heterosexual.'

Dave recalls the pair of them coming out of Mario's one afternoon and spotting a young and very beautiful couple. As they watched them go by, Cash said, 'What a beautiful arse.' And Kenny went, 'Yes, hasn't he!' Both men cracked up laughing.

When Dave shifted shows, Kenny agreed to carry on solo for the foreseeable future. Up to then, his on-air behaviour at Capital had been almost exemplary. The pre-recorded shows weren't a problem, of course, and when he'd been broadcasting with Dave Cash he was too busy being one half of a partnership to be controversial. Kenny live and on his own, however, was a different proposition. While he wasn't daft enough to swear on a breakfast show, he could be partial to the occasional lack of judgement. Clive Warner was the man who inadvertently set him up. 'I had been watching *Monty Python's Flying Circus*, which was very popular at that time. I connected a tape machine to the TV and recorded the funeral sketch. It was in extremely bad taste but very funny. It's based around a man who brings his dead mother into a funeral parlour. So begin lots of references as to how they can dispose of the "stiff", including, I think, eating her!'

Clive put the sketch on to a cartridge tape and gave it to Kenny the next morning. 'He thought it was extremely funny,' remembers Clive. 'So funny, in fact, that he decided to play it live on air going into a commercial break. Directly after the break the switchboard began to go mad. We received hundreds and hundreds of calls, all complaining about the sketch. I remember at one point they actually shut the switchboard down as it just couldn't cope.'

A few days later the Independent Broadcasting Authority wanted Kenny and Clive's heads. The volume of complaints they had received had been huge. Not only that, the opening chimes from the Python sketch were allegedly quite similar to those used by LBC, and so 'mocking the competition' was added to the list of charges. 'Both Kenny and I received an official warning,' says Clive. 'But it could easily have been a lot worse. It was my fault really. I could have been responsible for yet another sacking!'

Kenny was a huge fan of *Monty Python's Flying Circus*. 'That makes me laugh more than any other television programme,' he told the author Jeremy Pascall in a 1973 interview, 'because it explores new areas of humour. Even if it's done badly, it's new and never boring.'

Kenny raved about things like the Spanish Inquisition sketch and their 1975 film, *Monty Python and the Holy Grail*, and his love for Python was reciprocated. Lee remembers some of the members of Monty Python getting quite excited on meeting Kenny. 'We'd been invited to a recording of a theatre show. I think it might have been at the Drury Lane. We were sitting in a box and a couple of Pythons came in to say hello. I honestly can't remember which ones. But they were over the moon that Kenny was laughing. I remember them leaving saying, "Yes, we've got him."'

Until the late sixties Kenny's favourite comedy fare had been *The Goons* and *Round the Horne*, but by the early seventies his tastes had begun to widen, especially after working with the likes of John Wells and Clive James on *Up Sunday*. This programme had exposed Kenny to satire, which became one of his favourite forms of humour. He revelled in its use of irony, sarcasm and ridicule, which had been the cornerstones of his own brand of waspish fun.

Kenny was also gravitating towards some of the more traditional mainstream performers of the day. 'When Morecambe and Wise are on form they have no equals,' he said in 1973. 'They don't seem to think about what they do, they just rush in and do it, which is marvellous, because if you're going to stop and think about what's funny you get very hesitant and unfunny.' In fact, Morecambe and Wise had to work extraordinarily hard to perfect that air of spontaneity. Unlike Kenny's own TV shows at Thames, which genuinely could be quite spontaneous, every sketch that Morecambe and Wise ever performed would be rehearsed for days, sometimes weeks. Even when they had guests on their show, it was a prerequisite that they rehearse for as long as was needed. With Kenny, the star would be handed a scrap of paper in their dressing room about ten minutes before filming.

Much later, Kenny enjoyed watching the odd sitcom, and he was absolutely bonkers about *The Larry Sanders Show*. 'I introduced him to it one day and the next morning he came in raving about it,' recalls fellow DJ Paul Burnett. 'From then on, whenever an episode was aired we'd watch it, and then meet up the next day and spend hours reliving what we'd watched, repeating all the dialogue, etc. We knew every word. We were proper anoraks!'

People who worked in showbusiness really took to *The Larry Sanders Show*. 'It was very "knowing" about the industry,' explains Paul, 'about fame and everything else. It was documentary-like. I suppose it was the chat-show version of *Spinal Tap*.'

Kenny was so taken with it that he wrote a fan letter to the show's star and creator, Garry Shandling. 'I remember him confessing this to me one day,' says Paul. 'It was the only fan letter he'd ever written. He never got a reply though, which I think pissed him off a bit! It's doubtful Shandling received the letter, but even if he had he wouldn't have known who he was.'

But as Kenny's admiration of satire, surrealism, slapstick and sitcom took off in the early seventies, he was falling temporarily out of love with one of his earliest comedy heroes, Spike Milligan. 'I'm not so keen on Spike these days,' he admitted to Jeremy Pascall. 'He seems to be going on more of an "I must save the world" kick. Like all geniuses he has a fit every now and then. But he was most people's primary inspiration.'

What Kenny was referring to was Milligan's now famous attack on an art exhibition at the Hayward Gallery in 1971. One of the exhibits consisted of an aquarium full of catfish, oysters and shrimps, which were due to be electrocuted, and all in the name of art. Milligan, who was a keen animal rights campaigner, took umbrage at the exhibit and had attacked the aquarium with a hammer.

Kenny was always uneasy about allowing causes, however good, to infiltrate entertainment. When Capital Radio started their Help a London Child campaign in the mid-seventies, he initially saw it as an unwelcome diversion, something that would get in the way of doing what he was paid to do. It wasn't that Kenny was uncharitable, he simply didn't appreciate how much of an impact radio could have in raising funds and awareness. He assumed it was just tokenism. Once converted, he went on to become one of Help a London Child's most fervent campaigners, and would spend days preparing special episodes of Captain Kremmen and the like, which would be used to raise money for the charity.

18

Charley Says

BY THE MID-SEVENTIES Kenny's career was flying. In addition to the radio gig, he had his pick of the best voice-over jobs – and not all of them twenty-minute sessions for Birds Eye Fish Finger adverts. Then in June 1975 he was offered a job that would last the best part of four years.

Celebrity Squares was a popular TV game show which had originated in the USA. The set featured a giant noughts and crosses grid with nine boxes, each one occupied by a celebrity who would have to answer a question when nominated by a contestant. Bob Monkhouse hosted the show and regular guests included the likes of Arthur Mullard, Willie Rushton and Frank Carson. As the show's announcer, Kenny was required to introduce the celebrities and announce the prizes, etc. Though not the most exciting job in the world, it was easy money and Kenny appeared on all 138 episodes between 1975 and 1979.

While making *Celebrity Squares*, Kenny struck up an unlikely friendship with Bob Monkhouse. 'Bob was always ringing Ev, asking for funny quotes and daftness,' remembers Lee. 'He liked clever people, people with a quick mind, and he and Ev were always swapping jokes and chatting about comedy. They bounced off each other really well.'

In the years since *Nice Time*, Kenny had evolved a love–hate relationship with television. Prior to *Celebrity Squares* he'd presented *Top of the Pops* – an experience he absolutely loathed, according to Jo Gurnett: 'He couldn't stick doing *Top of the Pops*. He only made a few episodes in 1973, not long before he left the BBC for Capital, but would quite happily have made none. It was all, "Stand here, stand there. Now say this into this camera." It was chaotic, but not in a "Kenny" way. There was just no fun. I think the atmosphere as a whole was also quite unfriendly.'

One of the problems was that working in television took Kenny way out of his comfort zone. For Ev to enjoy and indeed tolerate the experience, it was imperative that he be surrounded by people he trusted. The move 'behind the cameras' for *Celebrity Squares* suited him; the relative calm of a sound booth was a welcome change to the pushing and shoving he'd experienced in front of the cameras on *Top of the Pops.*

It helped too that Jo Gurnett would always accompany Kenny to the *Celebrity Squares* set at Elstree Studios. 'We'd sit in the sound booth overlooking the studio and we'd play Scrabble and sip brandy. He'd have gone out of his head with boredom if I hadn't gone with him.'

Having somebody there to chat to must have been welcome, as Kenny had to wait up to an hour before being required to speak. Not all of their conversations remained private, however, which caused more than a little embarrassment. 'I remember filming one episode,' says Jo. 'We were having a chat about the Green Cross Code Man. One of us must have seen it on telly the night before and we were making all kinds of comments about him, saying that he was either very well hung or that he wore an enlarged nappy that was full of bananas. Anyway, after a while we began to notice these howls of laughter coming from the studio, so we looked down and realized it was all aimed at us. Ev had left the microphone on and they'd heard every word. Some of it was positively pornographic!'

Journeys to and from the studio weren't without incident either. Jo recalls one occasion when 'Ev decided that he needed to stop and get his car washed. It was winter and the car was mucky, which he didn't like at all. Anyway, we pulled into a garage with an automatic car wash, he paid his money and in we went. There was water and soap spurting everywhere and these enormous brushes whirring round.

Then it suddenly hit us – Kenny had his roof down. He had a convertible BMW and the bloody roof was down. We'd been talking so much we hadn't noticed. That was it though, it was too late. We, along with both the inside and the outside of the car were well and truly washed. We were absolutely saturated. I remember we smelt rather nice though.'

Not long after that they were involved in a car accident on their way to Elstree. Jo didn't come out of it too well, but Ev was relatively unhurt. 'When we got to the studio they wouldn't believe us,' Jo remembers. 'They said, "Rubbish! You're always late. It's just a bad excuse." We were never that late though. I eventually had to drag them into the car park and show them the damage to the car. Not to mention the damage to me! The accident wasn't Ev's fault, I should point out.'

When they weren't crashing or getting soaked, Kenny and Jo were partial to the odd spying mission. Everett absolutely loved people-watching and he and Jo often went for a drive and parked just off the King's Road to study passers-by, muttering to each other, 'Ooh, I wonder what he does?' Or, 'Why's she wearing that?' Or, 'I bet they're having an affair!' They'd sit there for a good couple of hours. 'Life fascinated him and so did people,' reveals Jo. 'For all his shyness he actually adored people.'

In addition to the ubiquitous quiz shows and commercials, voice-over artists get some strange job offers. One of the strangest Kenny received came when the animator Richard Taylor (of *Crystal Tipps and Alistair* fame) was asked to make a series of public information films. These government-commissioned short films ran from 1945 to 2005, covering all manner of subjects from the art of crossing the road to how to dispose of an old fridge. Along the way they became a part of our cultural fabric, and today enjoy a huge cult following.

When a 2006 survey asked 25,000 people to name their favourite public information film, twenty-two of these British nuggets of nostalgia featured on the resulting list. They ranged from Rolf Harris exhorting us to 'Teach Them to Swim' before waving goodbye with his big toe, Edward Judd ordering us to 'Think Once, Think Twice, THINK BIKE', and Kevin Keegan ushering kids across the road wearing a hideous chequered sports jacket. But the celebrity cameos could not compete with the animated films. And of these the most popular, voted for by 10,000 of the 25,000 who were polled, was a series called *Charley Says*.

Made in 1973, the *Charley Says* series (complete with the warning growls and meows voiced by Kenny) delivered often-stark messages in a darkly comic way. They were produced by animator Richard Taylor, who had been approached by the Central Office of Information. 'They asked for some films warning pre-school kids about domestic dangers. They listed the dangers they wanted to focus on, and asked me to come up with ideas, the key feature being that they would not be presented in such a way that they would cause imitation among children.'

The inspiration for *Charley Says* came from a thirties comedian Taylor remembered from his childhood who always had a little girl with him on stage whose lines usually began with, 'So-and-so says' and for some reason that had always stuck in his memory. 'So, after I'd decided on using a little boy and a cat called Charley, the strapline "Charley says" just followed, and I rather think it worked.'

Once Richard's idea had been approved it took him six weeks to make the films. It was also his idea to use Kenny. 'I was a big admirer and he had a good reputation as a voice-over artist, so I decided to get in touch with him and see if he'd do the job. He was a big animal lover, liked the idea and so was happy to oblige. It was also something different, which was really what Kenny was all about.'

As with many of Everett's voice-overs, he preferred to do the recording at his own home studio. 'When we met up I gave Kenny the script and the timings for Charley, and off he went. He then rang me up with some ideas, which he duly performed over the phone, and we eventually decided upon the one used. The conversation must have sounded very strange to anyone who was listening at his end. Anyway, he then simply recorded them at his home studio and sent them over.'

Six films were made in all, educating British nippers about the dangers of playing near water, playing with matches, talking to strangers brandishing puppies, playing in the kitchen, pulling table cloths at tea parties and not telling your mum where you're going.

Thanks to the Internet (something Kenny would no doubt have made good use of) all six are easily available on YouTube.

Kenny went on to make one more public information film in 1981. 'Children Overtake', another animated effort, features Augustus Windsock, 'the oldest living cyclist in the world', demonstrating how to overtake a parked vehicle. While not as memorable or interesting as the Charley films, it will no doubt ring a bell in the heads of a few thousand forty-somethings.

For the connoisseur of this form of nostalgia, the *Charley Says* films are without doubt the gold-top of seventies 'responsibility broadcasting'. They also gave Ev (albeit posthumously) his highest ever position in the UK charts, when in 2003 British band the Prodigy sampled the voices from one of the films to use on their single 'Charly', which reached number three. As a pioneer of the art of sampling, one can't help thinking that Kenny would have been chuffed to bits.

19

Cock-ups and Dramas

WITH BACKERS SUCH as Bryan Forbes, Richard Attenborough and Dirk Bogarde, it was inevitable that Capital Radio would have its own drama department. This was an extremely bold experiment though, as was the decision to set up a news department instead of relying on bulletins supplied by the IRN (Independent Radio News). The only other station which could boast drama and news departments was Radio 4, and they did nothing *but* news and drama. Sadly this statement of Capital's overall ambition was let down by an unfortunate lack of direction, and by 1975 both departments had been closed down.

Money had also played a part in the closure of news and drama. Capital's ambitions were simply too big to be sustainable, especially in the depressed economic climate of the seventies – although one suspects they would have struggled to maintain such diversity of programming in any economic climate. 'They were trying to do too much,' explains Dave Symonds, 'although what they did was very good. The evening talk shows with Alan Hargreaves were good. The sport coverage was good. I'm not sure about the drama though. It was all of the *Mrs Dale's Diary* variety. I don't think they were ever going to threaten Radio 4. It was all a bit lightweight.'

By the mid-seventies Bukht, Attenborough and Co. had ditched their original remit of being all things to absolutely everybody and instead decided to focus more of their efforts on becoming a classier and perhaps edgier version of Radio 1. But before that rethink came about, Kenny was given a chance to brush up on his acting skills.

Actress Jenny Hanley, best remembered for co-presenting the seventies kids' TV show *Magpie*, made a number of appearances for Capital's short-lived drama department, and remembers working with the talented but often elusive Mr Everett. 'We did a series at Capital about a lonely hearts agency, and my radio husband and I were running this agency with a computer, which was voiced by Kenny. Kenny was a canny bird, in that he would always get freebies wherever he could. He was inventive too and seemed to know a great deal about modern science and gadgets.'

Not long into the series Kenny discovered that there was a new machine available that could make his voice sound even more metallic. 'Until then he'd been inhaling helium and then speaking into an old voice modulator,' remembers Jenny. 'He absolutely adored helium and seemed to use it all the time. It can't have been good for him.'

It might not have been good for him, but Kenny certainly loved the stuff. For years he'd been using machines to make his voice sound high-pitched and squeaky. Now all he had to do was inhale toxic gas! Fortunately, Kenny's love affair with helium was sporadic enough for it not to harm his lungs, which can happen if you inhale too much. He'd occasionally take some to a party, swapping 'bring a bottle' for 'bring a canister'. That always went down well. But by far his most inspired helium-related incident was the one which featured in an episode of *The Russell Harty Show* in 1981.

Kenny and Russell had met in 1972, when Harty was a producer and occasional presenter on *Aquarius*, LWT's predecessor to *The South Bank Show*. Kenny had been asked to film a segment entitled 'Kenny Everett's London', which was billed as 'A personal impression of some lesser-known London monuments to good and sometimes bad taste'. He obviously impressed, as a few months later he was invited back – this time to discuss classical music.

He and Harty got on well, and from 1976 onwards they started making tit-for-tat appearances on each other's shows.

Kenny's fellow guest on this particular show was a surprisingly timid Penelope Keith, who, upon realizing Kenny has a canister of helium and isn't afraid to use it, slowly moves her chair away from him. This probably wasn't a bad idea, as after Kenny takes his first inhalation, he immediately sets about trying to persuade Harty to imbibe. 'Have a go, you'll love it, love.' To his credit, Harty inhales a lungful, and as the two begin a verbal exchange in what must be at the very least a Top C, Penelope Keith turns from slightly nervous giggling guest to slightly annoyed matriarch. Harty is the first to be chastised: 'Russell, you'll shrivel your vocal cords for ever – no more. NO MORE, RUSSELL!' Then she turns on Kenny, whom she seems to believe is a bad influence on poor Russell. 'No, don't do any more. DON'T DO ANY MORE!'

After warning the audience not to try this at home, Harty then brings the show to a close. 'Can I just tell one more joke?' pleads Kenny, and before Russell can refuse, he embarks on the gag, leaving his host in a nervous limbo.

'The boy stood in the chip shop, eating red hot scallops, one fell down his trouser leg . . . and scalded him on the ankle!'

As Harty and Penelope laugh – no doubt breathing huge sighs of helium-free relief – Kenny hushes the audience and shouts, 'Missed his bollocks completely!'

Back to Jenny Hanley and Capital: amazingly Kenny managed to persuade the powers that be to invest in this new machine that could modulate his voice, regaling them with all kinds of possibilities as to what it might do. As soon as the machine arrived, however, he decided that it was too big to be kept in Capital's studios and would be far better off in his nice, 'much roomier' studio at home. After somehow getting the machine home, Kenny then decided that as the new machine was no longer based at the station, there was no need for him to attend the scheduled recording sessions. He simply asked for his lines in advance, recorded them at home and dropped them in at his leisure. 'He could do his bit at whatever time he wanted to, got paid for the session and had a new voice modulator thrown into the bargain,' remembers Jenny. 'He was very, very canny. Periodically we'd get a little note, which would be left in the studio before one of the sessions – something obscure like, "I hope you're having as much fun as I am", which was only meant to rile us!'

*

Although never forming a regular on-air partnership again, Kenny did develop a good rapport with several of his colleagues at Capital, but not necessarily the ones you might expect.

Broadcaster and musician Robin Ray had been at the station since the beginning, first presenting a show called *A Time for Lovers* where, in his own words, he would, 'introduce poetry and music for late-night sweethearts'. According to Kenny it was 'dead naff', but it was, for a time, extremely popular. Ray also presented Capital's classical output, and over the years used an array of different shows to ply his trade. He and Kenny had a lot in common, not least a love of classical music. Robin also had a wicked sense of humour and was a hopeless giggler. This amused Kenny no end and he always took great delight in seeking out examples of Ray giggling on air, and then playing them to his audience. 'Isn't he sweet, listeners? Take him out for lunch and regale him with cheques and money and things. He'll giggle for you!'

Kenny always took great delight in people corpsing or cocking up, and over the years assembled quite an impressive archive of out-takes and bloopers. This was also for the benefit of his listeners, of course, and he would periodically play his favourite blunders, much to their delight. One of the first out-takes he ever used featured Paul McCartney, recorded while playing (or trying to play) the piano intro to 'Martha My Dear'. The out-take itself isn't especially funny, as it simply features McCartney messing up and starting again. So, rather than mocking McCartney, Kenny tells the audience he's been up all night practising the song and just couldn't get it right. It was a simple gag but beautifully executed.

The blooper Kenny used most on his Capital shows was perpetrated by his replacement at Radio 1, Noel Edmonds, whom Kenny had always considered to be a little bit too 'whiter than white'. Edmonds had been recording a commercial and had fluffed one of his lines. As is often the way, before beginning a new take he begins to list words beginning with the letter F. God only knows how Kenny got hold of this – or any of his out-takes, for that matter – but he played it, delightedly exclaiming, 'See, folks, he's human after all!'

Only one of these 'lapses' ever got Kenny into trouble. Well, almost. Back in 1969 when he was still at Radio 1 he had procured a set of out-takes featuring BBC television presenters. One of these had the legendary sports commentator, David Coleman, losing his rag with a cameraman. After fluffing an announcement at the start of *Grandstand*, Coleman decides it's the cameraman's fault and begins tearing into him. A genuine tirade ensues in which Coleman becomes more and more irate: 'Keep your bloody camera straight! You're running all over the bloody studio. Pull your bloody finger out.' The outburst carries on for well over a minute and climaxes with an exasperated Coleman declaring, 'I've never seen such a bloody carnival in my life!'

David Coleman had been fluffing announcements and throwing tantrums since the late fifties – indeed, he is regarded as the doyen of gaffs, earning him the distinction of a fortnightly salute in the form of *Private Eye*'s long-running feature Colemanballs.

Kenny was thrilled and couldn't wait to include it on his next show. Robin Scott, who was now controller of BBC2, heard the show in question and was incandescent with rage. He immediately called his successor, Douglas Muggeridge, claiming Kenny had gone too far and had been unprofessional in using the out-take. Muggeridge duly asked to see Kenny about the incident, but he was unapologetic. Nobody had complained, apart from Scott, and it had made a lot of people laugh. It was just a bit of fun! As for being unprofessional, maybe it was, a tiny bit, but nowhere near as unprofessional as yelling at a cameraman.

Though Kenny's knowledge of classical music was nowhere near as encyclopaedic as Robin Ray's, it was nonetheless quite extensive. He'd been playing classical music on his shows since his days at Radio 1, and was one of the first pop DJs to do so.

Paul Gambaccini remembers classical music being introduced to pop radio, and laments its passing from the genre. 'Kenny and Alan Freeman were the first to introduce it. Alan Freeman would use bits as mood amplifiers and he was sublime in that respect. And as I say this

I'm getting very sad because I'm thinking about how almost all young DJs today don't have a clue as to the potential of the art; how you can create effect with so little, as long as you're using your head. But Kenny was more likely to play a longer classical selection, and in that sense he was probably unique because those of us who were classical enthusiasts, in addition to being popular music enthusiasts, would have classical programmes, but never tried to mix them.'

For Kenny, part of his decision to play classical music came from a desire to stave off boredom. 'I'd get bored if I just played pop records – and the audience notice if you're bored. So I like to amuse myself and my audience by playing unusual things. I think I was the first DJ to play classical music amongst all the pop. Because it's pretty!'

After becoming hooked by the genre from the age of six or seven, Kenny then took against classical music when he started to attend St Bede's. There he was told that you had to listen to classical music because it was good for you – and that was never going to go down well with Kenny. But by the late sixties he had rediscovered the genre. 'I thought, hey, this deserves an airing, this Mozart stuff. You need to have something out of the ordinary, a nice contrast to the general run of pop.'

The only way a pop DJ could get away with a diversion of this nature was if the audience trusted them, and Kenny was one of the few DJs who enjoyed such a relationship with his listeners, the other notable exceptions being Roger Scott, John Peel and Paul Gambaccini. They too had audiences who had bought into their taste and judgement, but there is a fundamental difference between them and Kenny. Whereas Scott, Peel and Gambaccini championed the music, Kenny championed the music and the medium. When a record finished on John Peel's show you couldn't wait to hear what he was going to play next, whereas with Kenny you looked forward to hearing the next record, but you couldn't wait to hear the bits that went in between, be it a jingle or a Captain Kremmen.

When Kenny began playing classical music, nobody questioned his choice or judgement. The BBC may not have always trusted what he was going to say, but they did trust what he was going to play. He always figured that people listened to his shows because they liked what he liked, regardless of genre.

One of Kenny's favourite classical pieces was the Overture to *Ruslan and Lyudmila* by the Russian composer Mikhail Glinka. Those familiar with radio but not necessarily classical music might recognize this as the theme to Radio 4's comedy *Cabin Pressure*. But before playing the overture on his show, Kenny couldn't resist giving it the Everett treatment. This comprised of a specially recorded introduction which went, simply: 'Yum diddle um diddle um diddle um diddle um . . .' As ridiculous as this may sound, the intro works and the two join seamlessly. This then became a running gag, and every subsequent piece of classical music Kenny played would receive its own 'Yum diddle' or 'Bum tiddle' intro, and quite often, even an outro!

At Capital, Robin Ray and Kenny quickly formed a teacher/pupil type relationship. Ray began by introducing Kenny to lesser-known composers such as Jacques Ibert and even took Kenny to his first opera at the Royal Opera House. As the conversations flowed, so did the concepts. Both felt passionately about introducing classical music to a wider audience, and thus, over lunch one day, they began devising a vehicle whereby they could showcase the genre to a hitherto un-classical audience. The result, *The Best of Both Worlds*, was broadcast on 20 December 1979 and fulfils their brief to the letter. It's educational without being patronizing and includes a heady mix of rare and popular classics; one or two pop songs, some flirting, ribbing and lots of near-the-knuckle humour. They even undertake an on-air 'mash-up', blending Dvorak's 'Humoresque' with Stephen Foster's 'Swanee River', with Robin singing one tune and Kenny the other, simultaneously. And it works, much to Kenny's delight. Then Ray finds a professional recording of each and plays them simultaneously. Their pièce de résistance, however, is an impromptu a cappella version of Radio Luxembourg's close-down song, 'At the End of the Day', sung in the style of the Goons.

Before they could make any more of these shows Kenny would be on his way out of Euston Tower. It's a great shame, because this coming together of 'mischievous but earnest polymath' and 'puckish, acerbic genius' could and should have provided hours of essential listening.

Another of Kenny's unlikely 'rapports' at Capital began in 1974 when the station unveiled their new mid-morning DJ: Michael Aspel. Kenny was thrilled at the appointment and offered to write and produce his show jingle:

There's a chap called Michael Aspel
He's going to grace your wireless waves
He's coming soon to Capital, to make you housewives rave
He's got a voice that's smooth as honey, and he's nearly six foot eight
So forget your troubles and be gay,
he'll be with you every day
from nine until middayeeeeeeeee!

Michael Aspel (or Michael Asprin, as Ev christened him) had been an acquaintance of Kenny's since 1968, when he hosted the request show *Two-Way Family Favourites*, a successor to the wartime show *Forces Favourites*, which linked families with relatives serving abroad. In programming terms it was the antithesis of Kenny's show, exchanging anarchy and chaos for sentiment, calm and Acker Bilk.

The show was broadcast at noon every Sunday directly after Kenny's. Because Aspel was broadcasting across Britain and Germany, he was unable to take part in any pre-show chat as only half his audience would know what the heck was going on. Kenny, on the other hand, had no such constraints and could say whatever he jolly well liked. He was quick to take advantage: 'Ooh, 'ere she comes,' he'd say, as Aspel went on air. 'She's carrying a beautiful new handbag made of lettuce leaf, with diamanté and radish-encrusted tiara, tilting fetchingly over his left eyebrow.' Aspel, not surprisingly, almost always got the giggles, much to the consternation of his audience overseas.

He eventually got his own back on Kenny though, deciding to come clean and explain to all his listeners why he'd been breaking into fits of giggles every Sunday. 'It's because I'm being picked on by this awful Kenny Everett, and until now I haven't been able to retaliate.' At first Kenny was mortified, thinking Aspel was branding him a bully! Fortunately he quickly realized what was going on and breathed a sigh of relief. 'He's actually a very funny man, that Michael Asprin.'

Six years later, when Michael jumped ship to Capital in 1974, hostilities between him and his pint-sized adversary resumed. His new mid-morning show once again followed Kenny's, but this time things were on more of an even keel, as Aspel was able to retaliate freely to Kenny's goading. It soon became obvious that Kenny wasn't the only one blessed with a quick and acerbic wit, and so began a succession of mid-morning handovers which were to leave the listeners in stitches and, more often than not, Kenny reeling. He hated to admit it, but Michael Aspel was, as he later put it, 'Queen of the put-downs!'

Fellow DJ Peter Young recalls one particularly memorable Everett/Aspel handover: 'I remember them once having a sound effects war live on air. Aspel was broadcasting from a studio at the Ideal Home Exhibition at Earls Court and Kenny was in his studio at the Euston Tower. During the handover Aspel must have said something slightly rude, and Kenny said, "How dare you, Asprin. Take that!" and you suddenly heard this ZEEEEEUUUUUUUMB sound. Aspel retaliated immediately with a WHAAAAAAAAAAAAARP. It went on for about ten minutes in all. It was all totally off the cuff. Superb entertainment!'

Despite all the ribbing, a great mutual respect existed between Kenny and Michael. Kenny made Aspel laugh like a drain and he appreciated what Kenny had done, and was doing in the name of radio. For Kenny, it was Aspel's voice that made him want to rhapsodize about his friend. In his opinion Michael's was the epitome of broadcasting voices and he could quite happily sit and listen to him for days.

When Kenny eventually moved from weekday breakfast to a weekend show, he took the opportunity to use Aspel on a regular feature. 'Michael Aspel's Joke Spot' comprised pre-recorded gags, many quite risqué – not what you'd expect to hear from Capital's mid-morning housewives' pin-up. That was the joke, of course, and as a feature it worked wonderfully, becoming a genuine appointment to listen. Michael Aspel's delivery, incidentally, was exemplary; Kenny later commented that he could easily have made it big in comedy.

We're unsure as to how it came about, but around this time Kenny and Michael made a record together entitled 'On Love', released as a flexi-disc in 1974. It's one of the most bizarre but fascinating things you'll ever hear, and consists of Kenny and Michael chatting about love and their respective experiences thereof. The record begins with Kenny and an uncredited woman supposedly making love on a very noisy bed. As they approach 'the end', all manner of bangs and explosions can be heard, before a breathless Kenny climbs off the bed, walks over to Aspel and says, 'Aaaaaah, that's better, Michael. Now, what did you want to talk about?'

Kenny was so enamoured of Aspel's voice that he decided it would be a great idea to sit him down in his home studio, hand him some books and ask him to begin reading. Kenny would record the exercise, and voilà! He'd have his favourite books read to him by his favourite voice, and could listen at home or in the car. Since Kenny wasn't a great reader (he didn't have the attention span) this would be perfect.

Albeit unknowingly, Kenny was about to invent the audio book. Such recordings did exist at the time, but not commercially; those available were intended specifically for the visually impaired and could only be played at libraries or schools. How things have changed! Thirty-eight years on, it's a multi-billion-dollar industry.

When friends got to hear about his brainwave, they immediately encouraged Kenny to commercialize it. Given his fame, contacts and expertise, he could have had an extremely profitable business on his hands in a matter of months, with the potential to sell it on for a vast profit.

This, not surprisingly, was precisely where Kenny lost interest. How dare they encroach on his personal life – and why was everybody so obsessed with money?

When Kenny joined Capital his brother-in-law Conor suggested that he ask for shares in the station. It was a request the board would undoubtedly have agreed to, but Kenny's terse response was, 'No, absolutely not. Money is a dirty word!' Had he taken Conor's advice (and lived beyond 1995), he would have become a very rich man. In 2008, after a merger with GWR, the Capital Group was sold to Global Radio for £375 million!

This highlights Kenny's complete indifference to wealth. He wanted merely to have enough money to enjoy a decent lifestyle, and, if he wanted, treat his friends and family. He hated the effect massive amounts of money had on people, and was never driven by it. Apart from when he signed for Thames in 1978, it was something he rarely took into consideration when deciding whether to accept a job. He left that side of things almost exclusively to Jo Gurnett, his manager. Whatever she managed to negotiate on his behalf would invariably suit him just fine. 'He was awful with money,' remembers Jo, smiling broadly. 'He didn't know what anything cost and I think it amazed him sometimes that people were willing to pay him so much money. When he did the BBC TV shows in the eighties, there were a lot of strikes at the time, and quite often he'd go in to record and be sent straight home again. He'd then ring me and tell me what had happened, and when I explained to him that he was still getting paid he'd say, "Really?" I remember once ringing him up about a voice-over. When I told him how much the job was worth he said, "All that, just for saying a few words? It's mad!"'

Despite constant requests from his fans, and despite the fact it seemed a natural progression from his work in the studio, Kenny always rejected the idea of recording an album. Although not a musician, he was a consummate vocalist and a dab hand in the studio, and he'd proved that he could turn his hand to writing a melody or two. So why not give it a go? Kenny's response was, 'Why spoil things? . . . I like working alone. I don't want a crowd.'

There was, however, one especially pushy friend of Kenny's who wouldn't take no for an answer: Elton John. In 1973 Elton founded his own label, Rocket Records, and began signing a plethora of artists including Neil Sedaka, Cliff Richard, and Kenny's old friend from the Zombies, Colin Blunstone. Desperate to see what would happen if you put Kenny Everett into a recording studio (as opposed to a radio studio), Elton offered him a recording contract. Kenny accepted and they began to discuss ideas. What they eventually settled on was an album in the form of a radio show. Kenny would be the DJ, of course, but he would also sing all the songs, which would be written or co-written by Elton. The deal was even reported in *Billboard* magazine. Unfortunately, as is often the way with these things, the idea fell by the wayside.

Kenny's only regular extravagance was eating out. He adored going to restaurants and must have patronized hundreds during his lifetime. Jo recalls one particular favourite: 'We used to go to a very, very posh restaurant on Queen Street, which is just off Curzon Street in Mayfair. We'd always turn up just as they opened their doors, and they'd let us in wearing T-shirts and jeans and things. We were always quite scruffy, but for some reason they didn't seem to mind. They always used to have a chap playing the piano, and when Kenny had finished his meal he'd get up and have a little dance. He'd do his thing for a few minutes and then say to me, "Come on, darling, let's have a little dance, shall we?" and I'd get up and join him. He wasn't performing to an audience, as we were usually the only ones there. I think it was just the scene – the pianist, etc. It just got him in the mood.'

One of Kenny's other preferred eateries was a slightly more 'starry' restaurant in Beauchamp Place, Knightsbridge, called Ménage à Trois, a name which would come back to haunt Kenny in the mid-eighties, and not for culinary reasons. The restaurant was owned by Antony Worrall Thompson and was, for a time, Kenny's favourite restaurant. His producer at Radio 2, Geoff Mullin, remembers eating there with Kenny on several occasions. 'It was an extraordinary place. It was very modern and always had a great atmosphere. But they only served starters and desserts. No main courses. That was its gimmick, I suppose. So you'd usually have a few starters and then go on to dessert. It was very popular for a while and somewhere celebs would go to be seen.'

Although Kenny loved his food, according to Geoff he was equally happy eating a Pot Noodle as he was a poulet au pot. 'Kenny loved high-end food but he loved Snack Pots and things like that just as much. It was all new back then, and I think it fascinated him how it would cook in just a couple of minutes. Again, it was instant! Kenny was the king of instant.'

On the domestic front, Lee and Kenny had abandoned their farm in Wales. It was another of those great ideas that didn't survive the test of time. Or as Lee put it: 'It was a disaster.' Kenny had a predilection for developing crushes on men who were all too obviously straight. It had started on *Nice Time*, when he lusted after one of the cameramen, and there had been a number of instances since, all of them ending the same way.

One of these 'crushes' was Charlie, their odd-job man at Petal Cottage in Sussex. It was Lee who had come up with the idea of moving to Wales, where land was cheap and Lee and Kenny could set themselves up on a little hill farm surrounded by their animals.

'Never mind the style of life,' Lee says of the experience now. 'Because life stopped when we got there. Nobody coped with it at all.' The hill farm was literally in the middle of nowhere. There was a neighbouring farm but the inhabitants were anti-social and insisted on always speaking Welsh in their presence.

They'd all moved in together, including Charlie and his young kid and pregnant wife, but according to Lee he wasn't much help on the farm. 'Charlie did nothing. He did bloody nothing.'

Matters came to a head when Charlie's wife took their child and went home to Sussex. Lee and Kenny stuck it out for a while longer, but eventually it got too much and they packed their bags and returned to London: 'I said, "Sorry, I'm not milking another cow." I was out there milking like some mad woman. Although, to give him credit, Ev loved milking. He was great at milking.'

As they waited to sell the farm Kenny and Lee took out a bridging loan and purchased a converted inn, the Old Red Lion, in the village of Cherington, which is situated in the heart of the Cotswolds. They bought the house from Oscar-winning actor Hugh Griffith, a fact that tickled Kenny, especially when he heard about Griffith's illustrious house guests: 'Hugh had been matey with Richard Burton who had often come to stay at the house, bringing with him Elizabeth Taylor, so when we moved in I was thrilled to bits to be sleeping in the same bed in which Liz Taylor had kipped, and to be placing my watch on the same bedside table which had once groaned under the weight of her jewellery and false teeth. I'm easily impressed.'

Griffith had left the old pub sign in place even after turning it into a home, and Lee and Ev decided to carry on the tradition. One afternoon they were shocked to find two hikers in the middle of their kitchen, looking for the bar. 'They'd gone through the gate and straight in because we didn't use to lock the back door because it was as private as hell,' recalls Lee. 'We had a good laugh about it.'

Lee was convinced that the Old Red Lion, like Petal Cottage, was haunted. This time it was the room at the top of the house. Tommy Vance came to stay one night and his hair was standing on end in the morning; he complained about footsteps and God knows what other noises that had kept him awake for hours. 'I wouldn't sleep up there,' admits Lee. 'We used to put people up there for fun.'

These ghostly happenings didn't deter Kenny from building another home studio, replete with cartridge machines, equalizers, signal compressors, quadrant faders, multi-track tape machines, amps and other gadgets. Often he'd drag Lee into the studio when he needed a female voice, or if she had friends round for tea he might barge into the lounge asking, 'How can I make the sounds of eyeballs being ripped out?' Most irritating of all was his habit of using sundry household appliances. 'It was a case of, where's my iron? Where's my whisk? Everything would disappear out of the kitchen and it would be in the studio,' says Lee. 'I'd be cooking and I'd reach in a drawer for something and it would be gone, and I'd think, oh no.'

In that regard he'd been a liability since their first home together in Holland Park. When he was shooting his LWT shows, Lee came home one evening to find a camera crew and six fat women running round the bed with scarcely anything on, like something out of the *Benny Hill Show*. This after they'd set fire to her grand piano during a sketch where Kenny plays on the keys so frantically they catch light. 'I used to complain all the time,' laments Lee. 'But it didn't make any difference, it went in one ear and out the other.'

20

A Cry for Help

As WELL AS a substantial pay rise for Kenny, Capital had provided the Everetts with a beautiful mews house in St John's Wood, a stone's throw from Abbey Road Studios. All Kenny had to do was get to bed early, try to stay sober, do his show, and he'd be free to do whatever he liked at weekends. But as was so often the case with Kenny, what came to pass was the complete reverse of how things were supposed to be. This time, however, his actions would have consequences far more serious than any suspension or sacking. It wasn't his career he was taking chances with but his health, both physical and mental – and it would very nearly be the death of him.

Sleeping had started to become a problem for Kenny in the mid-sixties, not long after he stepped aboard the *Galaxy*. The causes were most likely anxiety-related, but his habit of knocking back gin and tonics and acid tabs only exacerbated the condition. Even so, it wasn't a major problem. Almost everybody he knew had trouble getting to sleep every now and then. You just took a pill and off you went. Since Kenny seldom had to get up before midday, it was manageable.

With the breakfast show, midday turned into a 5 a.m. start. Instead of retiring at 9 p.m. with a mug of cocoa and a good book, Kenny was hitting the town with a vengeance, as if trying to make up for the three years he'd spent in rural seclusion. Invitations to parties and events were pouring in, and he accepted almost every one.

Even when Kenny wasn't out on the town, he was finding it hard to sleep. This was partly down to the sleeping pills he was taking, a sedative-hypnotic drug called Mandrax.

In his autobiography, Kenny explained that Mandrax was not like other sleeping pills. 'I'd take one at about seven o'clock in the evening. The pill would make me buzz before it started to send me off to sleep, so I'd think: Hey, let's party, and I'd have a drink or six, which mixed with the pill made me stagger around in a state of unconscious awakeness until about four in the morning.'

To counter his tiredness Kenny tried cycling to work, which was about three miles door-to-door. This, unfortunately, had the opposite of the desired effect, and by the time he reached the studio he could hardly breathe, let alone broadcast. So, rather stupidly, Kenny began taking amphetamines. And this wasn't just occasionally, it was every weekday.

Clive Warner was one of the first to notice a change in Kenny's behaviour. As his engineer, he was present at every show. He was also invariably knackered, having usually been up all night working in the master control room. But as Clive would sit there bleary-eyed, nursing a strong black coffee, Kenny would be buzzing around as if he'd just woken up from a hundred-year sleep. 'Kenny came out of the starting gate like someone had lit gunpowder under his arse. It was bad enough when Dave Cash was around, but after Dave's departure Kenny sped up even more, as if the handbrake had been removed, and it became – for me at any rate – practically impossible to keep up with him. But with no Dave there to break things up, it was just constant Kenny. Don't get me wrong, it pretty much all worked as far as the listener was concerned. I just had trouble keeping up with him.'

Usain Bolt would have struggled to keep up with Kenny on speed, so poor Clive didn't stand a chance: 'There were times when the programme was moving so fast it was practically impossible to tell what he was going to do next. There was just a constant flurry of hand gestures and shouts. I had to get used to the idea that adverts would be requested with a split second to go and without any prior warning. One day one of the other jocks took me to one side and told me that Kenny used to take speed before coming in to do his show, and then after it, he'd drive back home and drop a load of downers to counter-act the speed and allow him to sleep.'

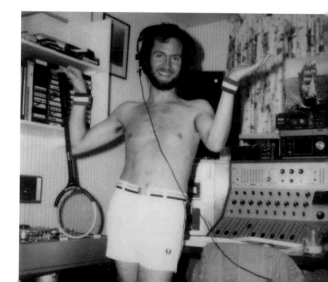

Top: Kenny, Lee and their Great Dane, Basil, in the kitchen at Cowfold.

Centre: Farmer Ken mucking out his dairy herd. According to Lee, Kenny loved milking the cows and was actually quite good at it!

Right: 'Ev was a terrible squash player. He used to enjoy going berserk around the court,' said Geoff Mullin. Inside his home studio after a match in 1978.

Below: Kenny and Tommy Vance formed *MightyMouth*, a commercial production company in the mid-1970s. The logo was designed by Kenny.

Above: Kenny by Kenny. A mid-1970s design drawn by Kenny himself.

Below: 'My mission? To boldly go where no hand has set foot.' Kenny's first depiction of Captain Kremmen, drawn in the mid-1970s.

Kenny Everett Tommy Vance

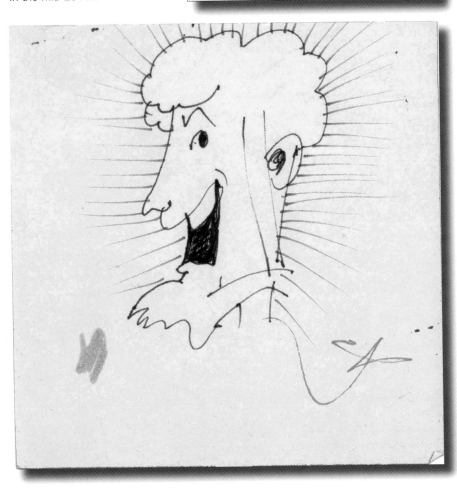

A publicity shot from the early 1970s. 'Kenny was definitely broadcasting royalty ...'

Right and below: Two of Kenny's characters from *The Kenny Everett Explosion*, 1970.

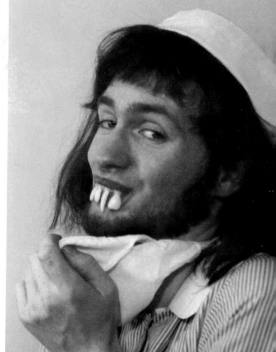

Above: Barry Cryer, Kenny and Ray Cameron in 1980. Theirs was one of the most consistent comedy partnerships ever, enjoying ten consecutive years at the top.

Left: Barry Cryer said, 'Cliff was marvellous. Week after week, he'd turn up and be lambasted.' Kenny and Cliff in one of their quieter moments, in 1982.

Right: Kenny and Benny Andersson at the launch of Abba's greatest hits album, *The Singles*.

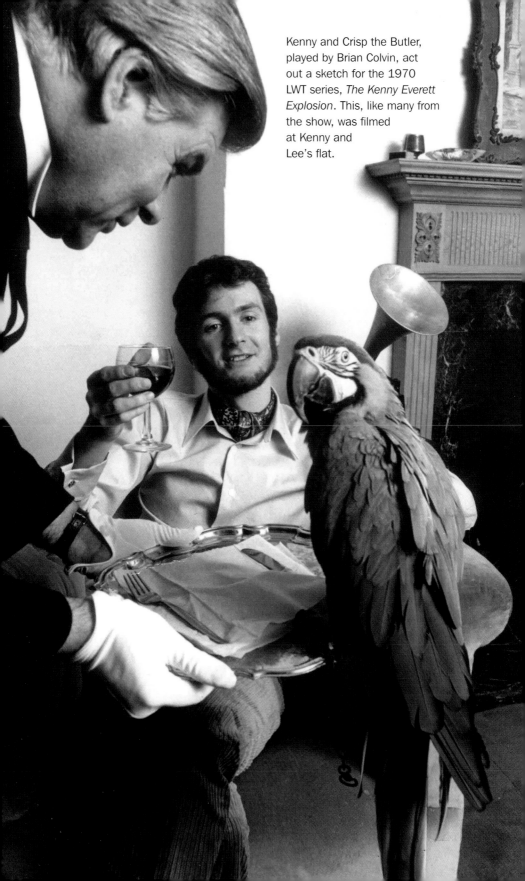

Kenny and Crisp the Butler, played by Brian Colvin, act out a sketch for the 1970 LWT series, *The Kenny Everett Explosion*. This, like many from the show, was filmed at Kenny and Lee's flat.

One of Kenny's home-made Christmas cards from the mid-1970s.

Above: John Alkin: guitar and vocals. Kenny Everett: vocals, percussion and darts. Kenny and John, whom Lee married after she and Kenny separated, enjoy a sing-song in the late 1970s.

Below: Kenny, Lee, John and, of course, Elton John at Lee and John's wedding reception, which was held in a fish and chip restaurant close to the registry office.

Pepe (**left**), Kenny and Nikolai (**right**) having fun in the pool in 1986. The three men had a complex relationship which was not as one-dimensional as the press would have liked us to believe.

Left: Bon appetit! Casa Ken's set menu for the evening.

Below: With his and Lee's dog, Knickers.

RESTAURANTE DE CASA
DE KEN

Chef: Pepito
Aids de chef: Nikita

FIRST COURSE

Stringy things in strange sauce

SECOND COURSE

Strange lumpy objects with a rather dangerous
smell

THIRD COURSE

Hairy warm objects that
move around the plate

FOURTH COURSE

Coffee and drugs

It may have been obvious in the studio, but while researching the book we listened to shows from this period, expecting to pick up on a more frenzied Kenny or perhaps the occasional lapse where he was slightly incoherent, but his performances are as steadfast and exemplary as ever. It's impossible to say how hard he had to work to achieve this, but his ability to beguile an audience while experiencing such extreme inner turmoil is quite astounding, and may have been his one salvation – a chance to escape the anxiety and insomnia for a couple of hours. Kenny wasn't simply suffering for his art; he was fighting for it. These 'little victories' were cosmetic though, as the more drugs he consumed the less efficacious they became, so he'd take more and more. Each show was eating away at him.

Kenny managed to maintain the façade for over a year, but inevitably the drugs took their toll. His memory and concentration were the first to go. 'A year or so of constant Mandrax did me no good at all. My brain started to wander all over the place, leading to mistakes that I wasn't even aware I was making. I'd introduce records that weren't there, forget appointments, forget names (even more than usual) and think I'd finished doing jobs which I hadn't even started.'

On air his trademark exuberance was maintained right up until a week or so before matters came to a head in May 1975, when he slowly began to morph into a style better suited to an overnight shift.

Lee had left Kenny alone in London while she was in the Cotswolds with his parents, who were down on a rare visit; he was due to drive over and see them at the weekend. After attending a showbiz event, he'd returned to St John's Wood inebriated, disconsolate and forlorn. Sleep deprivation on its own can play havoc with the mind, but when mixed with alcohol, drugs, stress and depression, it can be fatal. Every thought and emotion is magnified by ten and sleep becomes more elusive than ever.

Their house was situated close to a Chinese restaurant, and after taking his usual three pills Kenny lay on his bed listening to the sounds which invariably followed closing time. These could be loud on occasion, but were the sort of sounds you got acclimatized to after hearing them on a regular basis. But tonight everything seemed amplified, as if played through a loud speaker. In his disturbed state of mind, what happened next seemed a natural step: 'My reasons for staying alive became blurred. The thought of popping my clogs didn't seem to matter any more. I was in a woolly world where death seemed to be the next step, so I popped a load of pills into my mouth, laid back and waited for the Pearly Gates to come into view.'

In between taking the pills and shaking hands with St Peter, Kenny picked up the phone and called Aiden Day, Capital's then head of music. Kenny would later claim that he was simply saying his final farewells, but a more likely explanation is that he wanted Day to get him to hospital. This is what happened, of course: Day immediately phoned for an ambulance, then made his way round to the house. Within twenty minutes Kenny was on his way to the Royal Free Hospital in Hampstead. Aiden then called Lee and Jo, neither of whom could get to the hospital until the following morning, so Day drove over there himself and stayed with Kenny until they arrived. Jo was first through the door, and on seeing Kenny felt a mixture of emotions. 'When I arrived he looked absolutely desperate, the poor love. I don't think anybody realized just how bad things had become. He was exhausted and so sad. But I think he felt embarrassed more than anything else.'

As soon as Lee arrived, a plan of action was put together. Some kind soul at the hospital had informed the press that Kenny had been admitted, so the place was teeming with journalists and photographers. 'In the end Lee and I smuggled him out of hospital in the service elevator,' remembers Jo, 'along with all the dirty laundry. When we eventually got out we found my car, pushed him into the back and sped off.'

Once they got to St John's Wood everything was calm and quiet – but not for long. 'Somebody at the hospital had tipped off the press again and within a few minutes of getting him inside the house they were crawling all over the street outside and ringing the bell, "Is he alive, is he dead?" This went on for ages, so in the end I got hold of a screwdriver and disconnected the bell. I didn't know what the heck I was doing, but it stopped it.' It was going to take a lot more than this to deter the reporters though, and on realizing that the bell no longer worked, they began hammering on the door. 'In the end he asked me to go down and speak to them, so I went down and told them he was very much alive and well. They didn't believe me, of course. I grabbed a camera from one of them (who I knew) and took it upstairs. I then took a photo of Ev smiling next to a cardboard cut-out of himself, took the camera downstairs, gave it to the reporter and said, "There you go. There's your proof. He's absolutely fine."'

After the madness had died down, Jo remembers telling Kenny that this couldn't happen again. '"You've got to stop doing this, Ev," I told him. "I'm not a PR person and I'm not used to handling the press!"'

On the same day Kenny escaped from hospital, Michael Bukht spoke to the press. He told them that Kenny had been overworking and he'd accidentally taken one too many sleeping pills. The ruse worked, and the press bought the story.

Prior to coming out in 1985, Kenny had always blamed his alleged suicide attempt squarely on his sleeping pill dependence. Even in his last-ever interview in 1995 he said, 'I was stupid, perhaps even out of my mind at the time and took a lot of sleeping pills.' But when quizzed by Sue Lawley on *Desert Island Discs* in 1993 he gave a very different reason. 'I fell in love,' he said.

There is perhaps an element of truth in what he told Lawley, but instead of love being the root cause, it's far more likely it was one more contributing factor, exaggerated by his overwrought condition until it seemed unbearable. Because the fact is, Kenny was always falling in love. Or at least he thought he was. Before he came out, his objects of desire were almost exclusively heterosexual men, which caused a whole heap of problems. 'Most were infatuations really,' claims Jo, 'and would sometimes only last a few days. But some of these infatuations obviously led to rebuttals, and his initial reaction was always one of hysterics.' Kenny was generally swift to bounce back, sometimes miraculously so, but his recovery depended on being able to pour his heart out to either Lee or Jo.

Jo recalls one of these late-night distress calls from Kenny: 'He'd been in the Cotswolds I think and had been rejected by somebody, and I got a very tearful call from him saying he was heartbroken and could he come over. I said to Ralph, my husband, "We'd better get up, Ev's on the way." So he said OK and we both got out of bed. Ev then arrived, still very tearful, and I gave him a brandy, put him into our bed and lay on there with him for an hour or so. All the time my husband's sitting in the living room, nodding off. Anyway, after an hour Ev suddenly sits up and says, "I feel so much better now. Thank you, my petite choux," which was one of his names for me, and off he went into the night, happy as Larry.'

Paul Gambaccini was also aware of Kenny's propensity to become infatuated, which he saw as one more manifestation of his overall vulnerability. But Paul is also of the opinion that what ultimately saved Kenny from imploding was his relationship with his studio: 'There would be moments of infatuation when he met new people that he thought, oh, maybe I'm going to have a relationship with this person, and that constitutes some kind of positive feeling, but it was almost always unrealistic. The difference was that he and the studio was realistic, he could be in there surrounded by his favourite records, his favourite gadgets, and he'd have total freedom. What's not to like? And he actually did produce masterpieces.'

Jo Gurnett is adamant that the 'suicide attempt' wasn't intended as such. 'I'm not convinced that he intended to kill himself. He was very low and very depressed, but I don't think he actually wanted to die. It was a classic cry for help.'

Ev had been talking about suicide to anyone who'd listen since about 1966 (not long after he began smoking pot and taking LSD), but it was mostly an attempt to garner sympathy. Sure, he did wonder about suicide – when he was under the influence. The irony is that back then he used drugs to escape; now he was taking them to survive. Whether the overdose was intentional or not, had Kenny not received help at this point in his life the chances are he really would have wound up dead, and not necessarily by his own hand. A diet of sleeping pills, LSD, pot, alcohol and speed was not conducive to survival.

Lee confirms that when she first met Kenny he was already on prescription sleeping pills and suffering the inevitable side effect:

depression. After worrying for years about the amount he was taking, she confronted his doctor and threatened to take action: 'If you give him any more sleeping pills, I'll have you.' Within weeks Ev was in hospital having his stomach pumped.

Cate knew that her brother suffered from bouts of depression and self-doubt but doesn't believe he was a depressive. 'Although I think at stages in his life he had a lot to be fed up about. When Lee was down at their farm in the Cotswolds and Kenny was all the time in that flat in St John's Wood, I used to worry because I knew he wasn't eating properly, and I knew he wasn't sleeping properly, and I know he was taking pills because he couldn't sleep. I often thought, poor guy, but there wasn't much I could do about it because I was in Wimbledon with three small children of my own to look after. But I knew he must have been unhappy and very lonely.'

The news of his hospitalization came as a horrible shock to Cate, but she's convinced the overdose was accidental. 'I'm pretty sure myself that he didn't sit there and think, I'm going to end all this, I'm going to take an overdose. I think he was just fed up, thought, God I'm going to obliterate myself for the next two days, and the minute he felt himself slipping too far he called someone. Well, you don't do that if you're absolutely intent on killing yourself.'

His colleagues at Capital knew Kenny took drugs on occasion, and some may have been aware that he was on sleeping pills, in much the same way they knew he was probably gay. But such was Kenny's brilliance at appearing perfectly normal on air (most of the time) not one person at the station had an inkling that anything was wrong. 'I was not aware that there were any issues, that there were any problems,' says Nicky Horne. 'And so it did come as a huge shock. The initial story was that he'd just taken a couple more sleeping pills than he needed to, but then it suddenly became quite clear that it was more than that and the management at Capital were very concerned. They were concerned for his mental health and welfare, and I know that they pulled out all the stops and did everything that they could to help him get better.'

Kenny took about six weeks off in all, and during that time he at long last began to wean himself off the pills which had blighted his life. It was to be a slow and extremely painful process. 'Lee was collecting a prescription for me at the local chemist one day,' explained Kenny. 'And she noticed a pamphlet called "Sleeping and Not Sleeping", which explained why sleeping pills are the pits and how you can get a good night's sleep naturally.'

This happened to be exactly what the doctor (or the chemist) ordered, and the pamphlet provided Kenny with the advice he needed to finally get him back on something resembling an even keel. The hardest part was coping with the withdrawal symptoms from coming off Mandrax. 'When I came off the pills, I had three months of nightmares,' remembered Kenny. 'For the first week I couldn't sleep at all; I just stared at the ceiling. When I did eventually manage to nod off, I dreamt I was awake, staring at the end of the bed where there was a woman with straggly hair and razor-sharp teeth, eating her way up my feet, legs and body.' Kenny would wake up sweating and shivering, trying to separate the horror of what he'd dreamt from what was happening. Six months would go by before he finally got a good night's sleep.

As he began to return to his old self (whatever that was), Kenny started taking on more work. When the opportunity to make some shows for Dave Symonds' new Portsmouth-based station, Radio Victory, came along, Kenny leapt at it. 'I went down there when I left Capital,' remembers Dave. 'I'd always wanted to programme a radio station. I'd fallen out of love with presenting and wanted to see what it was like on the other side of the desk, so to speak.' Dave was able to do exactly that at Radio Victory, and ended up raiding his former employers for staff. 'First off I poached Russ Tollerfield, who had been one of the engineers on Radio London. Then I took Paul and Tricia Ingrams out of the news room. I had an incredible staff.'

Symonds then contacted Kenny and asked him if he'd do a Sunday-morning show for him. 'They were carefully crafted shows and they were totally station-specific. Kenny wasn't lazy, either. He didn't just stitch together a few off-cuts from some of his other shows. It was all totally new.'

Following Kenny on Radio Victory was another old colleague from Radio 1, Don Moss. Moss was from the David Jacobs school of broadcasting, and perfect fodder for a good tease. 'During the last five or ten minutes of his show, Kenny used to take the piss out of Don,' remembers Symonds. 'He was absolutely merciless, and as Kenny was on tape Don couldn't respond – and this really annoyed him. Once Kenny knew about this, it made him worse!'

At Capital it was Peter Young who became the butt of Kenny's putdowns. 'I was very flattered that Kenny bothered to mention me at all!' claims Peter. Among his favourites were:

'Thank you, Peter, for a truly unbelievable show. I was listening on the way in and I thought: I don't believe this!'

'Thank you, Peter Young. Number one in the ratings – the navy ratings!'

'Thank you, Peter Young – a monument to ineptitude!'

On one occasion, Peter managed to return the favour: 'I left him speechless once. He was in another studio and we had a handover after the news. I cracked some mild joke and he said, "God, you're funny today." I replied, "I thought I'd better get the gag in quickly, before you cut me off in my pri—" and just left him sitting there. There was a five-second pause before he said, "Thank you for that old joke."'

21

A & R Kenny

Kenny's relationship with the music business continued to flourish throughout the seventies. It wasn't just that he was an important and well-liked figure in the industry; artists respected his musicality and proficiency in the studio, and they loved his irreverent interview style – a refreshing change from the usual fawning technique. The only musician Kenny ever came close to fawning over was John Lennon – and even then it was all quite mutual. (According to Lulu, the attraction was also physical: 'One of the first things Kenny ever said to me was that he fancied John Lennon.')

The significance of these friendships became even more apparent when he moved into television. Having David Bowie appear on your show performing 'Boys Keep Swinging' was one thing, but then having him chase you around the studio, prodding you with a violin bow was quite another. No other DJ on the face of the earth could wangle that. Kenny always put his influence to good use.

But it wasn't just about being chased by David Bowie, or flying around America with the Beatles. One of the most overlooked aspects of Kenny's life in music was his ability to discover and even on occasion nurture new talent.

Early in 1974, while at Capital, Kenny took a liking to a Scottish glam-rock band called Iron Virgin. Their single, 'Rebels Rule', was played constantly by Kenny – and it's a genuine foot-stomper of a song. Although it was popular with his listeners the song failed to become a hit. The group then re-recorded the song, as a thank you to Kenny, changing the title to 'Stand Up for Kenny Everett'. Unfortunately, that too failed to chart.

A few months later, while held up at traffic lights, Kenny noticed a man leaning out of his car and waving at him. Kenny rolled down the window and the man said, 'Kenny, please, you've got to listen to this—' He then proceeded to play a tape on his car stereo at full volume.

Kenny listened for a while, liking what he heard. 'Who is it?' he asked.

'He's called Chris Rainbow. He's new. I'm his manager.' By this time the motorists behind them were getting impatient, so Chris leapt out of his car and handed Kenny the tape. 'Please give me a call. My number's on the tape!'

When Kenny got home he played the tape again. There was just the one track: 'Solid State Brain'. It was very melodic, with intricate harmonies and was extremely catchy – perfect Everett material. But despite the undoubted quality of the song, it had yet to receive any airplay. This, in Kenny's view, was a travesty, so he took the tape into Capital the very next day and played it on his show. He was adamant that his listeners would go mad for the song, just as he had. As he'd said to Michael Bukht a few months previously, 'They like what I like.' And they did.

Rainbow's label, Polydor, was quick to respond. 'Solid State Brain' soon became a hit. The majority of sales were in the London area, of course, but that didn't matter, there were enough people buying the record for it to chart.

Keen to meet this new melodic maestro, Kenny rang the number on the tape and asked his manager if Chris would like to come in to do an interview. 'Chris would be delighted to come in,' he said. 'But an interview might be difficult as he suffers from a pretty bad stammer.'

'No matter,' said Kenny. 'If he can't talk to me on air, he can sing to me instead.' Over the following months Chris became a regular guest on Kenny's show, singing live as opposed to talking. The people at Capital became so fond of Chris that for a while he became the station's 'musician in residence', and in addition to playing his music they had him record jingles for them, as did Kenny.

Kenny's most notorious musical discovery was a song which, on its original release, had been banned by the BBC – not unlike Kenny himself! Released in 1976, 'The Lone Ranger' by Quantum Jump was quickly chosen as Tony Blackburn's record of the week. The gentleman responsible for writing the song was the band's lead singer, Rupert Hine, who today is a celebrated record producer. Hine clearly remembers the joy of imminent success quickly being eclipsed by severe disappointment. 'One moment we were told it was Blackburn's record of the week and the next we were told it had been banned.'

Apparently the Beeb took exception to the line, 'Maybe masked man he a poofter, try it on with surly Tonto'. What was this – the BBC sticking up for homosexuals? Sadly not. Their objection was not that it might cause offence to the gay community, but that it referred to homosexuality – a topic that was strictly taboo. 'I think that was the first and last time the word poofter has been used in a pop song,' says Hine.

A second reference, this time to drugs, also caused alarm in the corporation: 'He smoke pipe of peace with Tonto, put his mask on back to fronto.' It's a great lyric, and it beggars belief that the BBC felt they had to step in and censor it, or else the nation's children would be lost to the evil weed for all eternity. I ask you . . .

Sadly, there was nothing anybody could do about it. 'The Lone Ranger' quietly slipped from number 26 in the charts, where it had been before the ban, to absolutely nowhere, leaving Rupert and his band mates with nothing but dreams of what might have been.

Well, not quite. Naughty bits aside, there was something unique about 'Lone Ranger', and that was its introduction. 'The song was originally recorded with just a short one-bar intro,' recalls Rupert. 'Then a chap at the record company said, "If you could just jazz up the front a bit, that'd make it stand out."' Hine had heard this line so many times over the years. It was stock-in-trade stuff. But now they were suggesting it for one of his own songs! 'This really annoyed me. Partly as a two-fingered salute to the record company, I was on the loo one day, reading a classic loo book, *The Guinness Book of Records*, and I came across this word for the longest place name in the world, which was:

Taumata-whaka-tangi-hanga-kuayuwo-tamate-aturi-pukaku-piki-
maunga-horonuku-pokaiawhen-uaka-tana-tahu-mataku-atanganu-
akawa-miki-tora.

'It's the name of a town on St John's Island which is just off New Zealand.' Rupert had a go at pronouncing the word and thought it sounded very rhythmical, but he wanted to know how it sounded when pronounced correctly. 'At the time I was working with Manfred Man's Earth Band, whose singer Chris Thompson hailed from New Zealand, and I asked him if he knew the word. Fortunately he did and he read it out. I was right, it was very rhythmical. I asked him to write it out phonetically and I recorded it the next day, before completely and arbitrarily shoving it on the beginning of the record. I then handed it to the record executive and said, "Here's your exciting fifteen seconds." The irony being that he was absolutely right: it made the record! The song was catchy enough, but people only ever talk about "that word". Even though it's ninety-six letters, once you've learned it, it's hard to forget!'

It most certainly was hard to forget, and while Rupert was perhaps getting fed up with having to recite it, there was one man who was already making plans to use it on his radio show. 'It was around the time of the song getting banned that Everett first heard it,' explains Hine. 'After that he contacted me and asked if I'd record different versions of the word. He wanted them all done in different character voices. The most memorable was when he requested that I do it as a typical British Rail platform announcement. That was fun. It went something like:

> The train at platform 12 calls at Ashford, Epsom and
> Taumata-whaka-tangi-hanga-kuayuwo
> tamate-aturi-pukaku-piki-maunga
> horonuku-pokaiawhen-uaka-tana-tahu
> mataku-atanganu-akawa-miki-tora.'

This became a running gag on Kenny's show and he used the

recordings in a variety of situations. Then, in 1978, he decided to take 'the word' with him to television. 'He'd been playing and using it almost constantly for two years, and had kept the song alive,' says Hine. 'But when he went to television, he began using it as the intro to his show, which was amazing.' The people at Thames came up with an animation of a mouth saying, 'Taumata-whaka-tangi-hanga-kuayuwo-tamate-aturi-pukaku-piki-maunga-horonuku-pokaiawhen -uaka-tana-tahu mataku-atanganu-akawa-miki-tora,' which was used to open each episode.

Having the song played intermittently on Capital Radio was one thing, but having it (or at least the intro) played every week on television, and in front of millions of people, was quite another. Interest in the song rocketed and in 1979 Quantum Jump (who'd split up some time earlier) were invited to re-form and help make the song a hit. 'The first thing we did, on Kenny's insistence, was to re-record the song,' remembers Hine. 'The original version was recorded live and so wasn't particularly steady. Kenny suggested that if we re-recorded the song, and made it much tighter, it might also appeal to the dance audience, which would result in it being played in nightclubs. He was completely right. The second recording is a much better arrangement and is the only one that would have worked in 1979.'

'The Lone Ranger' eventually peaked at number 3. 'It took a very long time to get there though,' says Rupert, 'and took months creeping up the charts. This meant that it did very well sales-wise and sold about five hundred thousand copies. Bear in mind that you only need to sell about fifteen thousand to get to number one these days. Half a million was very impressive. It was really that record and that success which changed my career. After that everything became big and I had several multi-million selling records back to back, but I had nothing like that before my association with Kenny. So I would thank Kenny for a lot of the success in my career.'

Despite this association, Kenny and Rupert only ever met in person on two occasions. 'Both times it was in a recording studio. The first time was when he came in to watch us re-record "The Lone Ranger", and the second was when I was working on Captain Kremmen. Kenny had asked me and my then partner, Simon Jeffs, if we'd record the incidental music for Captain Kremmen, and so we ended up creating some electronic versions of classical pieces, which is what Kenny had asked for. We used lots of different synthesizers and it was enormous fun. Kenny had a thing about synthesizers, and I remember him coming in to watch us work. He was adorable though, great fun. Certainly in the context of music. He was a cross between passionate and funny, which I always think is a wonderful mix.'

Without doubt, the biggest song Kenny ever played a hand in turning into a hit was 'Bohemian Rhapsody'. Love it or loathe it, Queen's anthem is probably the most famous rock song ever recorded. It catapulted the group to superstardom and has gone on to sell close to nine million copies worldwide.

Things could have been very different though – had it not been for one Maurice James Christopher Cole.

Though they had three sell-out tours behind them, three successful albums and two hit singles, by 1975 Queen were flat broke. When journalists visited them at their flats to conduct interviews they brought bottles of wine with them. Not because it was expected (it wasn't), but because the band genuinely couldn't afford to buy it themselves. Understandably, they had started to become bitter and disillusioned with the industry. If they were going to progress, something had to give. The band decided an immediate change of management was called for and, after much deliberation, they approached Elton John's manager, John Reid. Reid had an excellent reputation within the industry and had broken Elton John into the all-important American market. He immediately agreed to represent them, saying, 'Right, boys. I'll look after the business. You go off and make the best album ever.'

The band duly went into the studio and began work. As well as a producer and a couple of engineers, the sessions were attended by Queen's new roadie, Peter Hince. Peter had known the band since they supported Mott the Hoople in 1973 and would stay in their employment until 1991, working on every album and every concert until

Mercury's death. Peter remembers the period well, and recalls a certain bearded DJ popping in to say hello. 'Kenny was around a lot in those days, always bouncing into the studio to see what was going on. He was like a kind of whirling dervish and couldn't sit still for two minutes. He loved being in the studio though and seemed to thrive on watching people create music. He was a good friend of the band and I think he got to know them through Elton John.'

Kenny was also a keen supporter of their music, says fellow DJ Peter Young. 'He was playing Queen long before "Bohemian Rhapsody". I think the first record of theirs he played was "Seven Seas of Rye", so he was there right from the start. He probably felt in a sense that they were a follow-on from the Beatles, which were his number one love. Queen had those harmonies and they had the catchy tunes and the catchy riffs.'

This was also the beginning of his friendship with Freddie Mercury. 'He got on very well with Freddie, of course,' says Hince. 'As well as them both being gay [although not publicly], they were into the same kind of music and were both interested in studio techniques and production. It was a good match.'

As *A Night at the Opera* neared completion, the band were growing nervous. It had taken months to make and was at that time the most expensive album in history. Peter remembers it all getting out of hand: 'I think we used seven studios in London alone. We had different members of the band in different studios at the same time, scattered all over the city. In a single day I could be required to go from Sarm Studios in the East End over to the Roundhouse in Chalk Farm, down to Olympic Studios in Barnes and then to Scorpio, which was underneath Capital Radio. It was absolute madness.'

EMI had originally earmarked bass player John Deacon's song 'You're My Best Friend' as the first and probably only single from the album. It was a well-written, radio-friendly pop ballad coming in at just under three minutes, and definitely Top Ten material. The band, however, didn't agree. They put forward Freddie's 'Bohemian Rhapsody' as the first single, which would then be followed by 'You're My Best Friend'. EMI opposed the choice, as did John Reid. It was far too long, for one thing, coming in at just under six minutes. Radio stations simply wouldn't play it. An edit was suggested but the band vetoed that idea. If it was going to be released as a single, it would go out in its entirety.

The only people who considered 'Bohemian Rhapsody' a potential single were, it seemed, the band. Brian May had taken a copy round to his good friend Noddy Holder, in the hope of garnering support. Unfortunately Noddy said the same as everyone else: 'You haven't got a hope in hell.'

John Reid also played it to Elton John, who simply asked, 'Are you fucking mad?'

The playback for *A Night at the Opera* took place at the Roundhouse studio (a playback is an exclusive preview of an album attended by DJs and industry bigwigs). EMI executives and staff were in attendance, along with specially invited members of the music press and DJs. Kenny was there with Paul Gambaccini, who remembers the significance of that occasion. '"Bohemian Rhapsody" was the last track, so by that time people had pretty much got in their minds what they thought the single should be, which was "You're my Best Friend". So they were satisfied there was a hit. And then there was this huge thing at the end, and I think a lot of people on first listen – because after all it's a lot to digest – just thought, oh, this is a very pleasant self-indulgence. But of course to Kenny it was more than a self-indulgence, it was – the way! He could hear something that other people did not yet hear. It was multi-layered, the kind of thing he was doing in his own studio.'

To Kenny, the length of the song was completely immaterial. 'Forget it, it could be half an hour long. It's going to be number one for centuries!'

Within hours Everett called Freddie Mercury to congratulate him on his masterpiece. Given all the negativity surrounding the record, Mercury had begun to have doubts. Kenny couldn't believe his ears and set about trying to reassure him. 'It was like Mozart wondering if his next concerto was any good,' remembered Kenny, 'when of course it was utter genius.'

The following day he went to visit the band in the studio. Firstly to offer them support, but secondly to see if he could snaffle a copy of his new favourite song. The song's producer, Roy Thomas Baker, recalls: 'Kenny said they should have a new position for it in the charts. It shouldn't be number one. It should be above that, at half. That's where it should be, it should be at number half!'

Breaking every rule in the book, Baker and the band gave Everett a copy of the record, but under the strict instruction that he wasn't to play it on air. But telling the enfant terrible of the airwaves not to play his favourite record was like telling a pig not to eat. Kenny made his promise, gave them all a wink and left.

Once he had 'Bohemian Rhapsody' in his grasp there was only one thing he was going to do with it. Actually, that's not strictly true – there were fourteen. Fourteen being the number of times Kenny played the record on his show over the next two days (although not always in its entirety), with, as Peter Hince recalls, Mercury in attendance in the studio.

Kenny began by playing a few seconds here and a few seconds there. 'Dig this, listeners. This is SO fab and groovy. I promise you've never heard anything like it.' He then played the entire song. And then he played it again, and again and again. *The Kenny Everett Show* had become the 'Bohemian Rhapsody' Show. Capital Radio's switchboard was inundated with callers, all wanting to know where they could buy this astounding new sound. They came in person too, hundreds of them, waving pound notes and terrorizing the receptionists. Nobody had ever seen anything like it before – certainly not for a record.

It didn't take EMI long to see the error of their ways and the initial doubt was soon to be replaced by dough. 'Bohemian Rhapsody' was released to a grateful nation (and an even more grateful band) on 31 October 1975. It spent nine consecutive weeks at number one, spawned an epoch-making pop video and changed the face of rock music for ever.

The music press showed slightly less enthusiasm for the song. In fact it's fair to say they were downright vitriolic, which was par for the course whenever Queen released a record. The now defunct *Melody*

Maker came up with the most amusing quote, accusing the band of, 'contriving to approximate the demented fury of the Balham Amateur Operatic Society performing the *Pirates of Penzance*.' Queen's stock-in-trade reply remained the same, and was echoed by both Kenny and the record-buying public – 'Fuck 'em!'

Prior to its release, Everett had been the only person who 'got' 'Bohemian Rhapsody'. Everyone else involved, including Mercury, was either too close to the song or had something riding on it. Not Kenny. He didn't have any of these shackles. To him it was simply a piece of genius, something to be savoured.

Queen would always be grateful to Kenny. Rarely had a group incurred the ire of the music press more, and over the previous twelve months allies had been thin on the ground. Kenny's faith in the band and their song had been resolute, surpassing anything they had previously experienced, and from then on Queen never looked back, selling over 300 million records and becoming one of the most successful chart acts in history. Like Kenny, they continually dared to be different. It didn't always work, but when it did, records were usually broken.

While Kenny had been force-feeding the nation 'Bohemian Rhapsody', the band had been rehearsing for a world tour, which would start the following month in Liverpool and take them to all four corners of the globe. Even in those days Queen shows were extravagant affairs, featuring enormous lighting rigs and all manner of pyrotechnics. Arguably the most crucial part of any rock concert is the intro. Before the band come on, something has to set the mood and ensure the audience are on-side.

Well aware of his friend's dexterity in the studio, Mercury decided to give Kenny a call and see if he'd oblige. Kenny was absolutely thrilled. His work would now feature at the beginning of every concert during the entire *Night at the Opera* World Tour. A meeting took place at which he was given a brief, and off he went to his studio.

What Kenny eventually delivered was something uncharacteristically understated yet totally appropriate. As the house lights dim you suddenly hear an orchestra tuning up. After fifteen seconds or so the maestro taps the baton, the orchestra quieten and a voice announces, 'Good evening, ladies and gentlemen, and welcome to a *Night at the Opera.*'

22

The Bottom Thirty

SINCE THE EARLY fifties, countdown shows have been a staple on music radio. Mini song contests designed to let us know who's sold the most records or gained the most votes. Kenny himself used to co-present Capital's Top 100 with his colleague Roger Scott. This was a huge broadcasting event in London and attracted massive audiences.

Up until 1977, every countdown there'd ever been on radio had 'counted down' to what was the most popular, or what the listeners considered 'the best'. But what about the worst?

Kenny had developed a penchant for, as he called it, crud. Bad records. Musical B-movies. Tunes that were so bad, they were good. If the Light Programme was 'Ovaltine for the ears', as he once described it, this was absinthe. Not content with playing the odd turkey and taking the rise out of it, Kenny launched one of the funniest and most original radio shows ever produced: *The World's Worst Wireless Show*.

The idea for a radio show teeming with crud came from Kenny's engineer, Jon Myer. Jon spent fourteen years at Capital and would go on to become the first head of music at BBC 6 Music. He recalls: 'Kenny used to have a feature on his weekend show called "The Capital Memory Module". This was basically just a tape of a load of oldies cleverly edited together. One day the tape contained an old "death disc", which is what they used to call a particularly bad record. I think it might have been Jan and Dean's "Dead Man's Curve". Kenny came over the talk-back and said, "God – they made some awful records back then!" and without thinking I replied, "You should do a whole programme of them."'

Kenny was a spontaneous and reactive individual who knew a good idea when he heard one, so the moment the tape had finished he went straight back on air and invited his listeners to scour through their record collections and send him all their tat. Bearing in mind he was only broadcasting to the Greater London area, Kenny still received over one thousand contributions in the first couple of days, the kind of response usually reserved for *Blue Peter*'s milk-bottle-top appeal.

The recordings came in all shapes and sizes – from old tapes and flexi-discs found on the front of magazines through to 78s from the thirties. But the list of perpetrators is extraordinary, and can more or less be divided into three sections. First off there's the 'Celebrities and Thespians' section: people trying to cash in on a particular success, or just trying to cash in. Among them Jack Warner, William Shatner (obviously), Leonard Nimoy, Shirley Anne Field, David McCallum, Hughie Green, Tommy Vance, Bob Monkhouse, David 'Diddy' Hamilton, Tony Blackburn, Hayley Mills and Reginald Bosanquet.

Next we have the established acts, or the 'people who should know better' section. And make no mistake, they're all here on merit. Here we have the likes of Elvis Presley, Simon & Garfunkel, David Essex, P. J. Proby, Jim Reeves, Del Shannon and Shakin' Stevens.

But the last and most enjoyable section is the 'Unknowns and Hopefuls'. People who had made a record in the earnest belief it would lead to bigger things, never suspecting they were completely tone deaf. Records like these were what the shows were all about, as the acts themselves were novelties, as well as the records.

So the concept was there, as was the source material. But that alone wouldn't make a radio show. Jon Myer explains: 'Anyone else who had simply played a load of dreadful records would have created something unlistenable. It would take a genius like Kenny to make it entertaining.'

Jon's right. Simply playing twenty-odd awful records back to back would indeed have been unlistenable. It was up to Kenny to create an environment worthy of these crimes against musicality. The result, not surprisingly, is sheer perfection, a radiophonic hybrid of Hammer Horror and the Goons. This, incidentally, is a pretty fair collective description of the music.

The first *World's Worst Wireless Show* was broadcast on Saturday, 30 January 1977. It lasted one hour and featured seventeen stinkers. But the crud kept coming in, so another show had to be planned, and then another. By the time the third show went to air it had been expanded to two hours and featured twenty-seven records.

Its success exceeded everyone's expectations. What had originally been intended as a bit of fun quickly morphed into the most talked about radio show in the UK. 'When the press got hold of the show, we started receiving crud from all over the place,' Kenny later said. 'We had some from Birmingham and Glasgow, even a couple from overseas. It really caught on. At last, people had somewhere they could dump all their bad records!' It had been a long time since a music-based radio show had taken such a hold on the public's imagination. And for bad music? That was pure Everett.

Rather than settling for simply churning out more World's Worst episodes, Kenny came up with the idea of making things competitive. Once again he put out an appeal to his audience, only this time he wasn't looking for flops but votes. Over ten thousand listeners wrote in to cast a vote for the worst record they'd ever heard, and from that came the now fabled Bottom 30. Or, as Kenny duly christened it, Cuddly Ken's Countdown of Crud. The show would go out live, and at 2 p.m. on Saturday, 24 May 1977, some poor bugger would be crowned winner.

The poor bugger in question was supposedly an American singer named Jimmy Cross, with a song from 1965 entitled 'I Want My Baby Back'. The title probably has you imagining some godawful piece of bubble-gum pop. If only! This is something far worse. Or far better, if you're Kenny Everett.

It tells the story of a man and his girlfriend who, while driving back from a Beatles concert, are involved in a car accident. He survives but sadly his 'baby' perishes. Not being able to live without her, he decides to dig her up so they can be together. The song ends with him joining his 'baby' in her coffin, and as he closes the lid he sings a final muffled chorus of 'I've Got My Baby Back!'

The World's Worst Wireless Shows and inaugural Bottom 30 had been such huge successes that in 1978 the compilations label, K-Tel, decided to release an album celebrating Kenny's creation. Pressed rather inventively on to green vinyl, and released under the nom-de-plume Yuk Records, *The World's Worst Record* invited you to, 'Cringe along with us and listen to some of the most tasteless sounds around. Pain can be fun!'

K-Tel had initially intended to release the Top 20 of the Bottom 30, so to speak. But copyright issues forced them to settle for a slightly bastardized version. It appeared that even people with awful voices had egos, and some of the artists K-Tel approached weren't too thrilled at being included. Featuring on a radio show was one thing, but being immortalized on green vinyl was quite another.

One artist who had no such egotistical hang-ups was 'the legendary' (his words) fifties and sixties crooner Jess Conrad. According to Jess, he was named 'Britain's Best Singer' by *NME* in 1961. How times have changed. The undisputed 'King of the Crud', Jess's songs featured in all six of the shows and he had an unassailable three entries in the inaugural Bottom 30. Not bad for a megastar (his words again) from Brixton. His trove of absolute stinkers included such classics as 'This Pullover', 'The Big White House' and 'Why Am I Living?' (Which is exactly what Kenny said when he'd finished playing the record.) Despite his limited vocal range, Jess's looks and mile-wide smile somehow saw him through the sixties. Always derided as being 'a bit naff', he was sensible enough to cash in on this reputation as a crappish crooner and make it part of his act. The new Jess Conrad was all about exaggerated ego, extreme vanity, self-deprecation and a good sense of humour. And because of this persona, he was probably the only professional act in the UK who had what was required to profit from this new-found infamy.

When people started sending in Jess's records, Kenny launched a 'Where's Jess?' campaign, asking listeners to let him know if they'd seen the great man. 'Kenny always mentioned me on his show. I think he had a crush on me,' says Jess, modest as ever. 'He was always asking, "Where's Jess?" But to tell the truth, he actually introduced a whole new generation of fans to me. I suddenly started getting teenagers coming to my gigs and buying my records. They also started coming to my charity football matches.'

When K-Tel were compiling *The World's Worst Record* they asked Conrad's record label, Decca, for permission to use the recordings. 'For some reason they refused,' says Jess. 'Out of the twenty or so records featured on the album, three were by me, so Kenny's people asked me to re-record all three tracks – which I duly did. They paid the bill for the recording and I was very well rewarded.' Jess even got a call from his bank manager about it. 'I remember him calling me up and commenting on how much money Kenny Everett had made me. Since he started talking about me on air and playing my stuff, my popularity had gone through the roof. So, who was I to complain?'

With a low boredom threshold, not to mention an intrinsic loathing for nostalgia, it would be three whole years before Kenny could be persuaded to make a follow-up to the original Bottom 30. But in March 1980 he began appealing for 'fresh crud'. Though still broadcast only in the London area, the new Bottom 30 nevertheless made the national press and resulted in thousands of people throughout the UK pleading with London-based friends and family members to record the show and send it on.

23

Captain Kremmen

A
S FUNNY, INVENTIVE and, on occasion, 'iconic' as Kenny's TV characters were to become, they never really made it past a sketch, save for the odd appearance on *Parkinson* (Cupid Stunt) or on the 1983 comedy single 'Snot Rap'.

If one creation could be said to truly define Kenny, it's Captain Kremmen, a parody of Flash Gordon, Dan Dare and all those other square-jawed space heroes. Created initially for the radio, the character encapsulates everything he held dear: the medium, science fiction, comedy and a sense of the ridiculous – or as Kenny once described it, 'sound effects and smut'.

The general consensus is that Kremmen first came into being circa 1976 on Capital. However, according to Dave Cash, that date's about nine years out. 'Captain Kremmen was a regular on our show for about the last three months of our run on Big L. Back then it was more of a sketch than an episode, and sometimes would only last a few seconds. We got it off the ground in about the summer of 1965. We'd always done silly characters and wanted to do something 'spacey'. We were both huge fans of *Dr Who* back then. That was our favourite. We tried to come up with some good strong character names (Dr What, being one) for our space hero but nothing really worked.'

Then out of the blue the boys received a tape from Gary Owens, a popular DJ and voice artist in the States who would later make it big on TV's *Rowan & Martin's Laugh-In*. Somebody had sent Owens a tape of *The Kenny & Cash Show* and he'd loved it. In return he sent them a letter of encouragement: 'Great show! You guys are pushing the boundaries. Keep pushing!' along with some drop-ins from a comedy library called Superfun. Drop-ins are short pieces of audio that you can 'drop in' to help break up a show. 'When we listened to this tape it was littered with five-second vignettes – mock adverts, all for a company called Kremmens,' recalls Cash. 'The one we remembered most went: "Kremmens Snuff Company invites you to put their business up your nose." We just looked at each other and said, "That's the one!"'

The Superfun drop-ins had been produced by the celebrated voice artist Mel Blanc and his son Noel. In a career spanning almost sixty years, Mel, who was known as 'the man of a thousand voices', created some of the world's most recognizable voice characterizations, including Bugs Bunny, Tweety Pie, Sylvester the Cat and Barney Rubble in *The Flintstones*.

His son Noel can pinpoint the genesis of the Kremmen name in even more detail. 'My father and I had begun producing Superfun in the mid-sixties, and it went on to contain around eight thousand vignettes. Bob Arbogast, who was a very well-known voice artist, came up with the name Kremmen and we used it on quite a few of the vignettes. It was a ubiquitous name that we used everywhere, like the Acme Company in *Road Runner*.'

Kenny was mad about the Superfun library and would dip into it on a regular basis for the rest of his broadcasting career, using hundreds of the vignettes on his shows.

After *The Kenny & Cash Show* came to an end, Captain Kremmen was stored away in the recesses of Kenny's mind while he got on with building his career. Years later, firmly entrenched at Capital, he at last had the financial security to dedicate less of his home-studio time to lucrative voice-overs and focus instead on being inventive. The jingles were still flowing like wine, but that wasn't enough. Kenny needed to be challenged again. He wanted to work on something character-based, but also on something that could stand up on its own. Creations like Gran on Radio 1 had been fun, but they were recurring, peripheral characters, designed to complement whatever he was doing at that moment. When he resurrected Kremmen, it was for a stand-alone serial; something he'd tried his hand at as early as 1968.

Kenny's first attempt at an ongoing comedy serial was 'Dick Dale, Private Doctor', a parody of *Dick Barton, Special Agent* which ran on the Light Programme and Radio 1's *Where It's At*. In 1972 he created 'Rock Salmon, Special Investigator' for Radio 4's *If It's Wednesday, It Must Be . . .* Another Dick Barton spoof, Rock Salmon, soon descended into a weekly excuse to have a dig at Mary Whitehouse – no bad thing, but in the absence of storylines it was more 'saucy anarchic five minutes' than detective parody.

Kremmen was destined to be Kenny's alter-ego, save for a few minor physical and vocational discrepancies. Born in Liverpool on 25 December 1950, Captain Elvis Brandenburg Kremmen was six feet ten inches tall, had an IQ of 498, and in addition to being a space captain was a concert pianist, supreme athlete, diplomat and genius. Each week, he and his busty, sex-mad assistant Carla would travel the universe fighting the likes of Queen Iris and her blancmange-like Krells, ably assisted by their evil scientific aide, Gitfinger, and their trusty spaceship technician, Gonad.

Captain Kremmen wasn't just any old creation, it was a piece of Kenny. You could probably say the same about his jingles, each one lovingly constructed over a hot tape recorder or two, but those were made for specific audiences or organizations. Kremmen, on the other hand, was made by Kenny, for Kenny. He was living out his childhood fantasies directly through his art, without having to compromise on humour.

Best of all, it was created in his favourite place, his home studio, using a heap of records and cartridges which he referred to as his 'Kremmen-aids': silly sound effects that come up at the press of a button. 'There's one monster sound that I didn't do,' Kenny once admitted. 'I think it was probably recorded at the zoo. Then there's a modern monster sound that reminds people of a belch, which isn't surprising because that's exactly what it is! It happened when Tommy Vance and I were looning about in the studio. He felt a burp coming on, so I recorded it. I twiddled with the dials and put the tape machine into playback, so the sound reverberated. Then there's that blood-curdling scream that is featured so often. That was easy. I just stuffed my wife in the oven!'

Kenny introduced Captain Kremmen to his public in 1976, and although he stopped making the serial in 1980, he would continue using it right up until 1988, when he switched from Capital to its new sister station, Capital Gold.

Kremmen was a hit with the listeners from the outset, and gave Londoners yet another reason to make sure they tuned into Kenny's show. Fellow professionals were also hooked. 'It was absolutely sensational, Kremmen,' says Peter Young. 'Nobody else could even attempt to do anything like that. I loved it. He did get into trouble with Kremmen once. There was a joke on one of the episodes which wasn't very well received. Kremmen's boss said, "I'll take you to my club one day, Kremmen. I'm a country member," with the response, "Yes, sir, I'll remember."'

In 1976 sci-fi and comedy may have seemed strange bedfellows, but that was only because nobody had ever tried it before. The serial was such a huge and instant success that spin-offs were suggested almost immediately, turning Kenny's first space serial into his first franchise. Not his idea, of course. Kenny honestly couldn't have given two hoots, choosing creative over commercial possibility any day.

As well as LPs featuring episodes of Kremmen, by the late seventies you could also buy iron-on transfers, watches, T-shirts, patches, badges, key rings, dolls, comic books and slides for the iconic seventies toy, View-Master. It even ran as a comic strip in the London *Evening Standard*.

In an interesting twist of fate, the man who became Kremmen's biggest fan and most fervent champion was also the man who had indirectly given Kenny and Dave the name. A man who was also one of Kenny's earliest heroes.

Kenny had first heard Mel Blanc back in 1948, when his then favourite DJ, Sam Costa, used to play the Tweety Pie character's signature tune 'I Tawt I Taw a Puddy Tat' on his BBC radio show. Thanks to Sam, the song became a huge hit, going on to sell around two million copies worldwide. It was Kenny's introduction to silly voices, pre-dating the Goons by a good five years. A quarter of a century later, Ev and Mel had not only become friends but also business associates. Noel Blanc explains: 'My father, Vincent Price and I came to England many times in the seventies, mainly to do work for Armed Forces radio and television. Kenny met Mel and me and we struck up a friendship. Vincent was often in London because his wife was based there and he and Kenny became close friends, too, so whenever Mel and I came back to London we'd meet up with Kenny and Vincent. We'd either go to his house or to Capital, and we'd all watch him perform.'

Much as Mel and Noel Blanc admired Kenny the DJ, they admired Kenny the voice artist even more. 'As far as Mel and I were concerned, he was the best voice artist in the business. He was a brilliant voice artist. Mel especially was a very, very big fan of his. Believe it or not, as a voice artist Kenny performed a lot like Mel.'

On one of their early visits to Capital, Mel humbly offered to voice some show-trails for Kenny, using several of his Looney Tunes creations. As you'd expect, Kenny rushed Mel into a studio before he had a chance to change his mind. An hour or so later Mel had recorded a selection of bespoke promotional trails as Bugs Bunny, Daffy Duck, Tweety Pie, Porky Pig and Sylvester the Cat.

By now, Kenny had a library of bespoke trails and jingles featuring some of the biggest names in the entertainment business, including the Beatles, Harry Nilsson, the Zombies, Roy Wood, Cat Stevens and now Mel Blanc. It was a collection he would continue adding to. When Kate Bush agreed to do a jingle for him she was too busy to come into the studio so instead recorded her tribute down the phone. It went, 'I wonder if people appreciate what Kenny Everett has done for England. Not only is he one of the greatest intellectual wits and humorists of the century, but he's the greatest sex symbol since James Dean. Aren't you, little Kenny Pooh?'

The moment Kenny played Kremmen to Mel Blanc he was immediately hooked and requested tapes of every completed episode. Kenny was happy to oblige, and also extremely flattered. Indeed, such was Mel's admiration for the show that he managed to get it syndicated in the United States. 'We had so much faith in Kenny,' says Noel. 'We both considered him a genius. He was doing things that we in the States hadn't even thought of. He was changing voice structures and stuff, totally ahead of his time. Mel and I were astounded. He may have been influenced in the beginning by the USA, but by the mid-seventies he was far more advanced than anyone over here. There was nobody else in the world that could do what he was doing. Mel and I thought we were state-of-the-art and we were running a full-time production company, but we were nowhere near Kenny.'

Kenny's friendship with Vincent Price was also founded on mutual respect and admiration. Price found Kenny charming and impish. And, like Mel and Noel Blanc, he was a fan of his work both as a DJ and as a voice artist. 'Vincent loved Kenny and they got on famously,' remembers Noel. 'Kenny made him laugh hysterically. He was like Vincent's jester!' For Kenny, it was far more straightforward. 'He's Vincent Price. What's not to like?' Kenny loved Price's films, of course. What self-respecting horror fan didn't? But as with Michael Aspel, it was Price's voice which really drew Kenny in. A mere sentence from the great man would have Kenny in raptures. 'Vincent's voice is mesmerizing,' he once proclaimed. 'And it's instantly recognizable. The whole world knows it's him.' But Kenny never dreamt that Price might be willing to work with him. To Kenny, Price was a film star; though he'd done radio in the past, he was in a whole different league to a 'jobbing' voice artist.

'Vincent Price did a lot of radio with us,' remembers Noel Blanc. 'He did an enormous amount of voice work. One project he did for us was called *Odyssey*, which consisted of two hundred and sixty mini horror stories that were all a minute and a half long. Then we did another two hundred and sixty that were two and a half minutes long. I believe Kenny often used some of them on his radio shows on Capital.' In fact, over the next twenty years, Kenny used almost all of the *Odyssey* vignettes on his shows.

Kenny ended up working with Vincent on several occasions. Usually he'd ask him to record a horror vignette he'd written himself, or the odd comedic line. 'Kenny was always using Vincent Price,' remembers Peter Young. 'He used to have this running gag. At the end of a random sentence he'd say, "Even Vincent Price says . . ." then he'd press a button and you'd hear Price say, "Hello, I'm Vincent Price." That was it. This went on for years!'

There was one other 'voice' from this era that Kenny found irresistible. Barry Clayton had one of the most recognizable voices of the seventies and eighties and is perhaps best known (to music fans at least) for voicing the intro to Iron Maiden's classic 1982 hit 'The Number of the Beast' – a job, incidentally, that had originally been offered to Vincent Price. Price's fee for the work was reputed to be £25,000, so Clayton was hired instead (dubbing himself with the nickname, Vincent 'Cut' Price).

Clayton was employed full-time at Capital. As well as presenting their *London Tonight* news programme, he acted as an in-house voice-over artist, something Kenny took advantage of more than most. 'Oh yes,' recalled Barry. 'Kenny would regularly stick his head around the office door, grab me and drag me behind a microphone to read something outrageous.'

Kenny would often sit Clayton down in his studio mid-show, hand him a script and ask him to read something out in a particular voice, live on air. 'Right, now do "sexy",' Kenny would say. 'Sexier! Go on, really sex it up!' This was all done purely for Kenny's own enjoyment, of course!

Though he'd achieved massive success with the radio serial, merchandizing and USA syndication, there were still two frontiers Captain Kremmen had yet to explore – the singles charts and television.

As with the merchandise, the idea to release a Captain Kremmen single didn't come from Kenny himself. In this particular instance the person with the pound signs fluttering before their eyes worked for the music publishers Essex Music.

One of their clients, the ex-Manfred Mann multi-instrumentalist and composer Mike Vickers, had written the music Kenny used as the theme tune for Kremmen. Somebody suggested that he and Kenny get together and release the track as a single. 'I'd recently made an album of library music called *Electronic Music*,' remembers Vickers. 'I was very much a pioneer of the Moog synthesizer in this country and I'd made the majority of the album using one. I think Kenny was also a big fan of the Moog and he probably used a lot of library albums on his radio shows. He began using a track off that album as the theme tune to Captain Kremmen. The track was called "Retribution".'

Vaguely reminiscent of Joe Meek's old sixties hit 'Telstar', 'Retribution' fits so well that it could easily have been made for Captain Kremmen. But while it made a great theme tune, it would need work if it was to become a single. 'The people at Essex had suggested that I stick some of Ken's stuff over the track,' explains Vickers. 'I had to leave that up to him really, so began to rework the original track by putting on some new drums and bass guitar. I still hadn't met Kenny at that point but went into the studio and began work. Eventually a date was arranged for him to come in and do his stuff, and that was the first time I met him. It didn't go well though. He just froze up. He was very uncomfortable performing in front of other people. He tried but it just didn't work. In the end he went home and recorded his parts in his own studio. He didn't even come in for the remixing.'

The result of their labours – the original track, plus a selection of superb Kremmen sound-bites slapped on top – transforms the piece from a latter day 'Telstar' to a camp sci-fi version of *Shaft*. Although it didn't win them any platinum discs, 'Retribution' still reached a respectable number 32 in the charts. What really brings the whole thing to life, however, is the video, which Kenny and Mike made especially for *Top of the Pops*.

It can't have cost more than £4.50 to produce, but is great to watch and fits like a glove. It begins with Kenny, as Kremmen, sitting at what looks like a set from *Blake's 7*, twiddling knobs and looking busy. Kremmen's vocals then come in, 'My mission – to camply go where no hand has set foot. To explore new vistas, quash new monsters and make space a safe place for the human race – for I am CAPTAIN

KREMMEN!' Then the main theme is welcomed with the words, 'He's so hunky' – cue Kenny looking straight to camera, snarling and flexing his muscles.

We then see him suspended in front of a space backdrop by a glaringly obvious harness, while he flails his arms and legs pretending to run in space. Poor old Mike Vickers need not have turned up; he appears for no more than a few seconds, playing an electric piano while dressed like Biggles. The BBC obviously couldn't afford two space suits.

By 1978 the *Captain Kremmen* serial was synonymous with Kenny's radio shows. Thus when he made the transition to television it seemed only natural that his superhero should come along for the ride. At Kenny's suggestion it was decided that Kremmen would get the animation treatment and Thames duly approached Cosgrove Hall.

One of Britain's most treasured and well-respected animation studios, Manchester-based Cosgrove Hall were responsible for the internationally successful series *Danger Mouse, Count Duckula* and *The Wind in the Willows,* all featuring the voice of actor David Jason. Other gems, which to this day evoke fond memories, include *Chorlton and the Wheelies, Jamie and His Magic Torch, Alias the Jester* and a superb feature film version of Roald Dahl's *The BFG.*

In common with Nick Park's Aardman Animations, Cosgrove Hall productions always have a quintessentially British feel. This made them an inspired choice when it came to the task of animating a character created by the quintessentially British Kenny Everett.

The resulting films – an astoundingly imaginative hybrid of drawn and 'live object' animations – do justice to both character and creator. This is all the more impressive given the speed at which Cosgrove Hall worked, sometimes completing an entire cartoon in as little as two weeks. In animation terms, that's extremely swift.

For once the time constraints were dictated not by budget or workload but the erratic timekeeping of Kremmen's occasionally delinquent creator. One of the founders of Cosgrove Hall, Brian Cosgrove, remembers the lengths they had to go to just to begin work: 'Kenny wasn't the most disciplined of people. In the business of animation you need your soundtrack quickly so you can animate to it – especially when you're working to deadlines. Kenny was a devil for not doing his until the last minute. We had many cases where the director had to travel down from Manchester at the very last minute, while we still had just about enough time to do the animation. He'd knock on Kenny's door and have to insist that he did the track while he waited. Being such a skilful person, he did do it. He never once sent them to us a fortnight early. Good Lord, no! Maybe he needed the pressure to get the creative juices going.'

By now Kenny's flying-by-the-seat-of-your-pants work ethic had become the norm. Not ideal when you're working within a deadline-led industry. Fortunately for Kenny, Brian Cosgrove was all too willing to adapt: 'It's very difficult to put a rein on people like Kenny. You can't discipline them and say, You have to do it this way. With some-one like that you have to take what you can get and work around them. I can understand how he must have rubbed a lot of producers up the wrong way, because they were used to handling people who did as they were told, and I don't think Kenny was ever that.'

Indeed not, but even when Brian's director did have to knock and wait, he came away with not only a good soundtrack, but a lesson in sound production. 'Apparently Kenny would just sit down in his studio with his discs and tapes and things all on shelves, and he'd be reaching to all points of the compass, grabbing whatever he needed. Then he would ad-lib that episode of *Captain Kremmen* and it would be perfect. After an hour and a half he would just hand the thing over and that would be that.'

Despite the timing issues, Cosgrove Hall's interpretations of Kremmen are exactly what you'd expect to see if Kenny himself were the animator. And, given their initial brief, you can't ask for more than that. 'The timing used to put us on the back foot a lot and so we had to be very creative in how we represented whatever his mind was conjuring up. I remember there was a one-eyed alien in one of the tracks and we finished up breaking an egg into a frying pan, frying it, and shooting that as the one-eyed alien. It sounds rather stupid but it seemed to work.' It was this kind of mad, frenzied creativity that

Brian Cosgrove ended up really enjoying. 'We would have liked more time to produce them, but then again, if we had, would it have been as good?'

Captain Kremmen's final adventure began in 1980, when *Kremmen: The Movie* went into production. 'Movie' is a slight misnomer, as it's only twenty-five minutes long. And, despite the best efforts of all concerned, it's a far cry from the film they originally set out to make.

The short films made by Cosgrove Hall had been such a success that Kenny's TV scriptwriter Ray Cameron suggested an animated movie. They knew it was going to be expensive to make, but it would still be cheaper than a live action movie. With Kenny at the peak of his success, Ray was confident finance wouldn't be an issue. After a couple of weeks of searching, however, it soon became apparent that the opposite was true. Securing finance for any film in 1980 was nigh on impossible, especially in the UK.

The feature-length *Kremmen: The Movie* was therefore cut to twenty-five minutes, rendering the film's cinema potential as nothing more than support fodder. That said, it was still the big screen, which was somewhere Kenny hadn't been seen or heard since his 1965 cameo in *Dateline Diamonds*. Ultimately the project became an extension of his TV show, with Ray producing the film, co-writing the script with Barry Cryer, and Kenny working his magic with the voices and sound effects. That just left the animation.

The original idea of hiring Cosgrove Hall had gone out of the window when the budget was revealed, so a low-budget alternative was sought. They turned to a young animator called John Sunderland who had animated the titles for TV programmes including *OTT*, which was basically *Tiswas* for adults, and *3-2-1*, a popular game show starring Ted Rogers. John was both excited and intrigued at being asked to meet Ray and Kenny, and assumed it had something to do with the TV show. 'I sat there wondering what the connection was. Did they want me to create the titles for a new project, or maybe even the next television series? After the opening chit-chat, Ray asked to see the contents of my portfolio. He seemed to love what he saw. After that test had been passed it was down to business and he outlined the project.'

Once made, explained Ray, *Kremmen: The Movie* would be released as the B-film to *Can't Stop the Music*, Allan Carr's vehicle for the Village People, who were then at the height of their popularity. 'The trouble was,' remembered John, 'according to Ray, it was a load of absolute crapola and its producers knew it and were expecting it to bomb big time.' Regardless of how popular the Village People were, to survive past opening night, *Can't Stop the Music* (or Please Stop the Projector, as Ray had retitled it), would need all the help it could get.

The film's distributors had already planned for the national release to fall on the same night as the London release. That way the producers could bank on at least one profitable night before word got out how dire the film was. But the danger was that people would walk out and demand a refund, so they needed a strong second feature, something with a big UK name attached to it. Captain Kremmen to the rescue! '*Kremmen: The Movie*,' proclaimed Ray. 'The B-film that doesn't need a feature!'

He had no sooner finished explaining all this to John when Kenny walked in. 'I think my eyeballs fell out of my head,' remembered John. 'The Jesus of the jingles just walked in the room and came and sat next to me on the sofa. "Hi, John," he said, shaking my hand. "So you're the chap who's going to make our epic, are you?" I suddenly relaxed and turned to look at him. He was genuinely friendly with no edge to him. After looking through my portfolio he said, "Ah, piccies and biccies," and he picked up the plate of biscuits and offered me one. It sounded just like something he'd say off the TV!'

To say John found it surreal having a chat and a biscuit with one of his heroes is an understatement. 'He didn't seem quite real in 3D, in his cowboy boots, jeans and pearl-buttoned plaid shirt. It was as though he didn't belong in the physical world, as though he'd just stepped out of the television for a bit for a stretch. And he didn't strike me as "zany" or "madcap" or a BBC anarchist – all the things the media said about him. He was just very pleasant and obviously very smart.'

When Kenny had asked John a few questions about his experience and background, Ray suggested he have a look at more of John's work. 'I dug deeper in the folder and showed both of them the development work for Dusty Bin and for the TV titles for *3-2-1*,' says John. 'As Kenny had now warmed to me, it was sort of assumed that I'd be making the film and soon we were talking about how and where it would be produced.'

John wasn't sure if he was ready for making a movie, regardless how short it was, and wondered how Ray and Kenny would react if they could see where he worked – in a back bedroom on Kirkstall Road in Leeds, surrounded by smelly laundry and baby clothes! 'I sort of made it up as I went along and told them my intention would be to bring a team together and establish the animation crew, but this was a different game to producing a short TV title. We'd make it up in Leeds, I explained, where it wouldn't be as expensive. And as my "premises" weren't big enough (they would have been without the cot and the laundry basket), I'd probably rent a building for the duration and enrol some production management people to handle the business side of things, leaving me free to do the design and direction for the film. I sounded just like what I imagined the "real thing" sounded like!'

That all seemed to make rudimentary sense to Kenny and Ray. 'I'd impressed myself – a very dangerous thing,' said John. 'The trouble was, although I wanted to come over as competent and understanding of the whole process, I didn't know if I really could pull it off, especially in Leeds; hardly the animation capital of the world. I knew I was most likely digging myself a deep hole.'

Before John could dig himself any deeper, common sense took over. 'I put the brakes on and said I couldn't give them a complete yes there and then. Not until I'd checked out the feasibility of the project. This, I said responsibly, was too big a deal to screw up. It was like telling Jesus that you didn't want to join his gang!'

At that point Kenny left, saying he hoped to see John again soon. Ray followed him out into the hall and came back saying that Kenny really liked his stuff and that, if he could do it, the job was his. Before he left that afternoon John and Ray had a read-through of the script. 'It was OK, not great, but very Kenny,' John recalled. 'There were lots of characters and double entendres. Some of the characters were from the TV show, like Dr Gitfinger and Carla, and there were some new ones too. I could see most of it in pictures in my head, which was a good sign, and I added some suggestions, just to see how they would be taken. Funnily enough, after that first meeting I hadn't clicked that Kenny was gay. I was still naive in that direction. If I had, there were gags and innuendos in the script that would have made a lot more sense to me. I wondered why Ray kept laughing!'

Kenny 'borrowed' the plot for *Kremmen: The Movie* from one of his favourite *Star Trek* episodes, 'The Doomsday Machine', which centres around a huge machine that consumes planets. Kremmen's mission in the film is the same as Captain Kirk's – to find said machine, turn it off and save the universe. It's all perfectly watchable stuff, and probably served its purpose in helping lure people into the horror that was (and is) *Can't Stop the Music*. You can't help wishing they'd waited though. In order to animate well you need a realistic budget and lots of time. Kenny and Ray had neither, so what chance did it have?

Given the relentless commercialization of Kremmen, Kenny should have become a very rich man. Instead he came away with pennies, having been ripped off by several dubious characters and even some supposedly reputable organizations. Although frustrating, it didn't really matter to him and he rarely referred to it. As far as Kenny was concerned the people who'd ripped him off would have spent the money by now and would be looking for a new scam. He, on the other hand, had spent six years zooming about the universe, being rude, having great fun and playing every sci-fi character imaginable. There was only one winner really.

24

Off to Thames

A s HEAD OF Light Entertainment at Thames since 1968 Philip Jones had overseen some of British television's most popular programmes. He lured Benny Hill from the BBC, revived the old telly favourite *This is Your Life* and was responsible for a slew of popular sitcoms including *Bless This House, Love Thy Neighbour* and *Man About the House*. He had also nurtured the early career of Tommy Cooper. Always on the lookout for new talent, Jones asked his teenage son if there was anyone he and his mates wanted to see on TV. Without hesitation the answer was – Kenny Everett.

While he'd already done a moderate amount of television work, Kenny had never really enjoyed it, even going so far as to once admit some of it had been torture. He was a radio man, pure and simple, and when Jones offered him the chance to star in his own TV series he was sceptical. It took a guarantee that he would have a top team of creative talent to guide and steer him in the right direction to clinch the deal.

Jones wanted Bruce Gowers at the helm for the series. Since directing Kenny for LWT back in the early seventies, Gowers had gone on to shoot the video for 'Bohemian Rhapsody' and worked on numerous television shows. 'I get a call from Philip Jones at Thames. He said that he'd just signed Kenny Everett, knew that I'd worked with him, and would I consider doing the show? Now, right at the same time I'd also been offered a job with NBC in New York called *Headliners with David Frost*. I have to say that I was in a genuine quandary as to what to do. I actually called Kenny up and said, "Look, Ev, they've offered me your show but I've been offered this thing with David Frost in

New York. What do I do?" And he said, "Take the New York job. It'll be better for your career." So I went over and never came back.'

Thwarted, Philip Jones then contacted Royston Mayoh, who'd worked on the *Tommy Cooper Hour* and *David Nixon Show*, and had a reputation for keeping within a tight budget. In other words, he'd a knack for making something look bigger and better than it was. 'Philip Jones called me in and said, "Look, I've booked Kenny Everett from radio and, to tell the truth, I don't know what to do with him." Well, I couldn't do anything with him either, as I was working with Bernie Winters at the time. But I remember thinking to myself, Thank fuck for that! Last thing I needed was a DJ.' Mayoh passed.

Jones's third choice turned out to be inspired. David Mallet had been a staff director at the BBC, working on *Juke Box Jury*, when he defected to Yorkshire Television in 1969 to help create the sketch show *Sez Les* for stand-up comic Les Dawson. On the cusp of a career as a supremely innovative pop video director, Mallet was the perfect choice. He drove up to see Kenny at his farm in the Cotswolds, and after lunch the two men went for a long walk. They connected almost immediately, finding they both shared the same vision for the show: to translate to television the irreverent zaniness of Everett's radio programme. Mallet was to label Kenny, 'A sort of rock'n'roll Monty Python.'   .

After the meeting, Mallet drove back to London, mulling over possible writers for the show. One name kept popping up: Barry Cryer. Mallet and Cryer had worked together on the long-running comedy panel show *Jokers Wild*, and by the late seventies Cryer had established himself as something of a comedy institution, having written for the likes of Morecambe and Wise, the Two Ronnies, Billy Connolly, Dave Allen and Tommy Cooper. Cryer already knew Everett, having been approached by Angela Bond about the possibility of doing a radio programme together. Though nothing came of it, Ev and Baz had kept in touch.

With Cryer on board, they set about generating ideas. One of these was a sketch featuring a pastiche game show, and Canadian stand-up comic Ray Cameron, who had worked on *Jokers Wild*, was brought in to help. 'Then after we'd chatted for a bit it became obvious that Ray should work with us full-time,' says Cryer. 'In fact, David Mallet and I were having a pee at the time, when the idea just came to us. And that's how the team got together.' It ended up being a highly significant trip to the men's room, since Barry and Ray would write for Kenny for the next ten years.

As a trio, Kenny, Barry and Ray worked in near perfect harmony. Cryer can remember only one occasion when he argued with Everett, and that was over the name of one of the characters, a spotty ne'er-do-well Kenny wanted to call Sid Snot. 'I said, "Surely we can do better than that! Honestly! Sid Snot!" Boy, was I proved wrong. Kids absolutely loved it.'

It was the cavalcade of comedy characters that helped set *The Kenny Everett Video Show* apart from many of the other comedy offerings on television when it launched in June 1978, taking over the slot vacated by *Opportunity Knocks*. Sid Snot was joined by Angry of Mayfair, a seemingly respectable city gent who would rant about society's ills and then turn from the camera to reveal knickers, stockings and suspenders; Brother Lee Love, a maniacal preacher with enormous hands (Kenny still taking the piss out of Garner Ted Armstrong?); and fastidious French Lothario Marcel Wave. 'When it came to creating Marcel Wave, it was Ev who said he should have a plastic chin to cover his beard, and he was spot on,' confirms Cryer. 'That was so important.'

Another feature that placed the show firmly into the unmissable category were the guest appearances by music stars who turned up to perform their latest hit or, better still, appear with Kenny in a skit. 'We were the musical version of *Morecambe and Wise*,' says Cryer. According to Mallet, the stars wanted to appear on the show for one simple reason: 'They loved Kenny Everett. Also those artists had a similar sense of humour, a rock'n'roll sense of humour, and the rock'n'roll sense of humour hadn't been on telly.' Elton John, Wings, the Police, Bryan Ferry, Kate Bush, Rod Stewart, Thin Lizzy, 10cc, Elvis Costello, Gary Numan were among those who featured, along with Dusty Springfield, who was hung up in chains above a steaming cauldron and whipped by Kenny.

The undoubted highlights were Freddie Mercury, dressed in leather à la Sid Snot, entering the Eurovision Violence Contest, where he proceeds to jump on Kenny, bringing him heavily to the floor whereupon the pair of them roll around like ten-year-olds. And David Bowie performing the classic 'Boys Keep Swinging', after which he's confronted by Ev's Angry of Mayfair who complains, 'I fought in the war for people like you. And I didn't get one!' It was inspired lunacy and star power on a grand scale. Perhaps its only equal in world television at that time was *Saturday Night Live*.

Leo Sayer remembers his guest spot on the programme with great fondness. He'd guested a few times on Kenny's radio show, but had found his host difficult to strike up a rapport with and consequently never got close to him. 'I don't think many of us did. He and I only ever exchanged small talk, or threw Goons impersonations at each other across the studio floor. I liked him a lot, and I did try to engage with him, but he was shy and always off up in the clouds somewhere. Looking back, he always seemed quite a private person, and I don't think conversation was one of his strong suits, but it didn't need to be. I admired him greatly as he was an amazing character – a chameleon with all his voices, and a trailblazer with his radio jingles.'

A real favourite of the show, and someone who guest-starred more than any other musical performer, was Sir Cliff Richard. 'Cliff was marvellous,' recalls Cryer. 'Week after week he'd turn up and be lambasted. I remember on one show, Ev was talking to camera and you suddenly see Cliff passing behind him in a wheelchair, looking all old and dowdy, and Ev says, "Ah, there's dear old Cliff, on his way to make-up." He was such a good sport.' The reason Sir Cliff Richard subjected himself to what on the surface appeared to be humiliation was because he totally trusted Kenny, he knew whatever the sketch or comic business was, it wouldn't be a send-up – the audience would be laughing with him, not at him. 'I got soaking wet doing that show,' remembers Sir Cliff. 'And hung up by my thumbs. You knew that Kenny was going to be outrageous. But there was no malice involved whatsoever. And as a fellow artist I felt totally comfortable with him.'

When asked to appear on the show, he'd had no hesitation: 'Kenny was one of the most genuinely funny people I've ever met. He was very much like Eric Morecambe in that regard, just a naturally funny person.' Unless it was a musical performance, which required camera set-ups and several takes, Sir Cliff would arrive at the studio, walk on set and do the sketch with no prior rehearsal. 'Kenny would already have an idea. He'd say, "This is what we're going to do, this is what I'll say, if you want to say something you can, you're going to start singing 'Living Doll' and I'll come on and wheel you out of the studio." I knew basically what was going to happen, so it didn't actually need a great deal of rehearsal. He just needed my permission to do it, and of course there was no way I was ever going to say no, because he always chose the right thing. I'd get there and he'd say, "This is the idea, I'm going to hang you up by your thumbs and swing you across the studio." He always knew exactly what he wanted. If you're going to do something that comes across as an ad-lib, one of you has to know exactly what you're doing, and he was always the one in charge.'

Only in an atmosphere where two artists have complete faith in each other can you get away with the things Kenny inflicted on his guests. Like hanging Sir Cliff from the ceiling. 'Actually they tied the knot round my wrists, and I held on to the rope as they swung me across the stage and Kenny said, "Ladies and gentlemen, it's the end of the show and I'm going to leave you with a cliff hanger." I had these welts on my hand right through to the next day. I don't remember him telling me that he was going to whip me, either. He was a funny man, no doubt about it.'

Another uncomfortable moment for Sir Cliff was when he recorded a video for his hit 'Carrie': 'Kenny made me wear my collar up and they wouldn't let me put it down even though they had a rain machine going full blast and the collar was acting like a funnel down my back. I got absolutely drenched.'

Perhaps fearing payback, Kenny had his suspicions when in 1984 Cliff invited him to sing backing vocals on a new record. 'I'd heard Kenny singing on his radio show, on those fabulous jingles he used to make, but he really thought I was setting him up, getting my own back on him. I did a song called "Under the Influence" written by a friend of mine and I asked Kenny to do the harmonies. It was fantastic, he was a good vocalist. I don't know how he would have sounded as a solo vocalist, but certainly he knew harmonies, and just came in and did them and it was great fun, we had a good laugh. But he did tell me afterwards that he thought I was going to pull a trick on him because of what he'd done to me.'

Apart from that day in the recording studio, Sir Cliff can recall only one other occasion when he and Kenny met outside of filming the TV show. They never had lunch, never met socially, never formed a friendship beyond the studio walls. 'The only time I remember sitting down with Kenny was with some people at my Christian arts centre group,' recalls Sir Cliff. 'He came along one day and had a chat and we all discussed life and philosophized a lot. And he was very funny with everyone.'

Nevertheless it's with huge affection that Sir Cliff looks back on his involvement in the video show. Like the charity record he later made with the cast of *The Young Ones*, it offered a chance for Cliff to reinvent himself for a new audience and also to dispel a few misconceptions: 'It's good to do these kinds of things sometimes because the public sees you as being ordinary for once, they see you as a real person, that you're not some jumped-up, arrogant guy that doesn't want to be made a fool of. I mean, *The Young Ones* hit me on the head with a mallet, for crying out loud!'

Just as memorable as the star guests was the raunchy dance troupe David Mallet discovered. Kenny wasn't convinced by the idea initially, and reserved judgement until he saw Hot Gossip in action. After a few minutes he got them big time. According to their choreographer, Arlene Phillips, he often turned up at rehearsals. 'Kenny would watch our dance numbers and enjoy them and loved being surrounded by the dancers. I had complete licence to create whatever I wanted, but the naughtier the better as far as he was concerned. Kenny had little interest in dance, only the dancers, but it was Kenny who named us "the Naughty Bits" and that name stuck with us.'

Mallet, putting to good use his savvy pop video sensibilities, directed all the dance sequences. Arlene Phillips recalls his contribution as vital to their success: 'He set out to break all the rules of dance on television and in doing so helped create the storm that blew Hot Gossip into the public eye.'

Predictably Mary Whitehouse blew a fuse at all the leotard crotch-thrusting. Whenever she wrote a letter of complaint to Philip Jones it would magically find its way to the press, thus giving the show a massive publicity boost. 'When I first heard about Mary Whitehouse complaining about the group, I was shocked,' admits Arlene. 'I certainly didn't think someone should be complaining about dance being sexy when there was so much violence on television at the time, apparently going unnoticed.' Years later, Barry Cryer met Mrs Whitehouse at a reception and said, 'Thank you, thank you. I worked on the Kenny Everett show and you made us.' She walked off in a huff.

Some of the comedy sketches could be equally as offensive, although Kenny and his writers admitted to built-in self-censorship which prevented them, most of the time, from 'miscalculating' the limits of taste. That didn't stop the complaints pouring in, as they did after Kenny's send-up of Barbra Streisand performing while her prominent nose gets ever bigger until it engulfs her whole body and she starts banging into columns. To achieve the effect several different-sized polystyrene prop noses were used, the last being especially heavy, with a metal bar inside for leverage. 'It took all my meagre efforts to get it off the ground,' revealed Kenny. 'We crashed into a camera with it in the end, I remember. It was a good sketch, though we got a lot of complaints from Golders Green.'

Kenny's impersonations of pop stars were a recurring theme. There was Elton John, whose trademark garish glasses grow to a ridiculous size during a song; and Rod Stewart, whose leopardprint-clad arse grows to Hindenburg proportions until he ends up floating in the air. But perhaps the most famous, and funniest, sketch was the one featuring the do-it-yourself Bee Gees kit, where he swallows a series of pills until he sprouts the hairy chest wig, buck teeth and falsetto voice of the famous Gibb clan. When Barry and Ray came up with the idea, Kenny immediately rushed off to make a Bee Gees demo for the sound people. 'He came back after an hour or so with this little cassette in his hand,' recalls Barry. 'And he and I took it to the sound people. I remember Ev modestly handing it over and saying something like, "This is the kind of thing we have in mind. It's just a guide, but I hope it helps." The man put it in the machine, pressed play and sat back. Well, you could tell he was dumbfounded. He just pressed the stop button and said, "We can't do better than that. That's perfect. We'll use it." Ev was absolutely thrilled. So the Bee Gees impression you hear on the sketch was knocked up in an hour by Ev. Amazing.'

Visual humour was an important element of the show and some of the stunts proved hazardous. For one sketch Kenny was dressed as a punk-rock singer, with the Pretenders as his backing band. At the end of the song Kenny had to plunge his microphone through the camera lens, in reality a sheet of Perspex in front of the camera. 'When I pulled my hand back, there was a bit missing, blood all over the studio floor and bits of thumb flying around the room.' He was rushed to Casualty, patched up and sent back to the studio to carry on filming, where he was happy to learn the next sketch involved an exploding violin. The effects team had rigged a button for Kenny to activate the explosion, but it had inadvertently been placed directly over the powder box. Again Kenny was whisked off to hospital with burnt and blistered fingers. 'When they sent me packing they must have wondered what on earth I got up to in my spare time.'

The Kenny Everett Video Show was recorded without a studio audience, a decision taken by David Mallet – and a radical one too, especially for a comedy show. 'I didn't want a studio audience because they can impose a different sort of timing on an artist, and Kenny was much more intimate than that.' The day they began shooting it sounded dead without any audience, and then somebody in the crew laughed and Mallet thought, Got it! 'After that, we just used the crew. I said, "No, to hell with it, we're all going to laugh out loud during the jokes." ' The crucial thing was that nobody was required to laugh, it was all genuine and spontaneous. 'It was the only show I ever worked on where the people watching were never asked to laugh or applaud,' says Cryer. And it was unique, one of the things that made the programme stand out, personalized it, in a way, as if you were somehow in on the joke. 'Sometimes we did two or three takes and it just got funnier,' recalls Mallet. 'And you can recognize my laugh, you can recognize Barry Cryer's laugh, you can recognize Ray Cameron's, and I can even recognize some of the cameramen. Remember, the crew had been used and abused for years doing *Opportunity Knocks* with Hughie Green and things that they really loathed. Then suddenly here was something of their generation (everyone was in their late twenties, early thirties), and somebody they liked and genuinely thought was funny.'

One person more than happy to perform in front of banks of empty seats was Kenny, who still found performing live in front of an audience extremely difficult. Yes, he could sometimes face up to his phobia if the occasion merited it, like the time he was asked by Barry to hand out medals at a local charity run. 'Ooooooh, Baah [Ev always called Cryer Baah], of course I will!' And true to his word, he showed up. 'Because Ev absolutely hated crowds, when he turned up I hid him away in the pub so he wouldn't be bothered too much,' recalls Cryer. 'And then all the runners eventually turned up for the presentation ceremony, and he walked out of the pub, got himself together, and came back in the pub as Kenny Everett the TV star. "Helloooooooo, darlings, are we all out of puff?!" I never forgot that though, because it wasn't his scene at all and he didn't enjoy it. But he came and did it for us and he was marvellous.'

Kenny had long since given up live DJ appearances following a particularly unpleasant experience, which he related to Chris Tarrant one evening when they were chatting about the business. 'Kenny was very shy and actually quite nervous of anybody bigger than him, which was virtually everybody, and he remembered vividly the last time he did a gig. It was somewhere in the Midlands, he went to this disco, you know – Tonight Kenny Everett live on stage at eight o'clock – and this enormous man who called himself Mr George came up to him and said in a deep voice, "Hello, Mr Everett, I'm a great fan of yours and if there's any trouble in my club, don't worry, Mr George himself will handle it." And Kenny was going, "Oh that's fine, thank you very much." So he goes into his dressing room and is sitting there thinking,

Oh my God, what am I going to do? I don't want to go out there. It was a big crowd. And he heard this enormous crash and a few screams, and he peeked out of the door and there was Mr George, being carried past on a stretcher with blood streaming down his head. So Kenny said, "Sod this," and jumped in his car and drove home. And he said he never, ever did a disco appearance again.'

Throughout its run *The Kenny Everett Video Show* regularly achieved audiences of between thirteen and fifteen million. Despite this incredible success they were the pariahs of Thames, who according to Mallet never really understood what they were trying to achieve. The signs were there from the start, when the network's executives took against the title. 'You can't call it "Video",' they said. 'Nobody knows the word "video".' And that was only the beginning of the team's troubles. 'We set out to be renegades,' says Mallet. 'And the executives at Thames were so far out of their depth that they just didn't get it, they queued up to cancel the show. But by then we had picked up ridiculous ratings. Then just as they were about to cancel it again, because they hated us so much, it won a BAFTA. That was the same week that we were all getting the sack, because I'd fiddled around with one of the video-tape machines and blown it up – it did an awful lot of damage. Every week there was a memo from somebody trying to knobble us.'

Philip Jones tried to stand by the show. A decent bloke and first-class television executive, he remained in a permanent state of nerves over Kenny and Co. Eric and Ernie, who that year Jones had managed to lure away from the BBC, were much more his cup of tea. 'Kenny and me, he just couldn't hack at all,' reveals Mallet. 'He was very good because he did let us get on with it, but he got a lot of flak from above.'

Mallet was lucky in that he had a staunch crew behind him who would do anything because they loved Kenny and loved the show. For one sketch a television set was required and the props crew ran off and two seconds later came back with a rather nice-looking TV they'd nicked from the managing director's office while he was out at lunch. He came back and found two bare wires sticking out of the wall.

The executives won a small victory when they managed to sack

Mallet after three series. 'I was too much trouble. It didn't help when we had some of the Sex Pistols and Thin Lizzy doing "We Wish You a Merry Christmas" on the New Year show. I had tons and tons and tons of fake snow falling from the top of the studio throughout. Like everything else, we overdid it and this snow was then falling for the next year from the ceiling, through everybody's posh dramas and quiz shows.'

During their two years working together on the *Video Show* Mallet and Kenny developed a close working relationship. Mallet rated Kenny a dream to work with and one of the funniest people ever seen on British television. 'He could make virtually anything funny. He had instant recall for a gag or a joke, he never had to write it down or read a script, he could just do it. Quite often one of the camera crew would come in with a joke he'd heard in the pub at the weekend and say, "I've got one, Kenny." Ev would listen and then go straight on and repeat the joke, just like that. Instant scriptwriting. He was a complete natural, provided he was in his own environment. He was a desperately shy man.'

In all the time they were working together, Mallet and Kenny never mixed socially. It was only when Mallet left the series that they started to meet up occasionally for lunch. 'When we met, Ev would be introspective and quiet but interspersed with thirty-second blasts of sheer genius. In private he was never at all like he was on the show. He would switch that on and switch that off in a matter of seconds.'

Mallet remembers the last lunch he ever had with Kenny, a few weeks before he died. 'In fact I've still got a message on my answering phone from him saying goodbye, literally goodbye.'

Mallet was quickly replaced by Royston Mayoh, who'd earlier spurned the chance to direct the show. When he met with Kenny for the first time Mayoh came away with the distinct impression that Everett considered himself to be a technician rather than an artist. 'He didn't think he was funny, but he did think what he did with technology was funny. For instance, he'd do a funny voice, but to him it wasn't funny until he'd put it through a harmonizer or whatever. Thing is, I had similar interests to him, but from a visual point of view. Anything that enabled me to manipulate a picture interested me. So when we first met I thought it would help to break the ice by telling him I was also interested in visual manipulation. And he said, "Oh, yes, like what?" So I said I'd had an idea of him pushing the television frame all over the place. He said, "How do you mean?" So I said, "We can make it look like you're pushing the TV around the studio." And then I showed him how, and he absolutely loved that.'

Chroma keying was a fairly recent innovation and naturally Kenny was fascinated by the process and what could be achieved by it. Chroma-key compositing is basically a special effects/post-production technique for compositing two images or video streams together based on colour hues, in other words green screen or blue screen. Mayoh recalls that Kenny came up with the idea of putting a picture of the universe on a blue piece of paper, and he'd say, 'I know, I'm going to eat the universe!' and proceed to eat all these planets and solar systems. 'He also used to come in with audio tracks which were out of this world. I remember once we'd had the idea of a huge choir singing the end credits, and he said he'd make a demo. The next day he came in and played this track and it sounded exactly like the real thing. There was no way our people could have bettered it, so we used his track. It was genius really.'

Mayoh also observed at close quarters the dual nature of Kenny: the technically gifted and creative genius, and then the naughty little boy who loved playing pranks. He particularly loved winding Philip Jones up. One day a meeting was called on the studio floor. 'Look, boys,' said Jones, all serious. 'I've had a little bit of trouble from the IBA [Independent Broadcasting Authority]. They'd like you to calm it down a little bit. Some of your language is a bit much really, and they've also complained about Hot Gossip, so I'll also be speaking to Arlene. Anyway, to show we're serious about behaving, I've invited the head of the IBA in for a tour of the studios. We'll probably pop in here at some point, so when we do, please be good.'

Well, that was like a red rag to a bull for Kenny. Mayoh describes what happened next: 'So this IBA chap turned up for the tour and the moment the studio door opened, Kenny started. He looked at me and said, "I can't work in these fucking conditions, you twat. Barry, what kind of shit have you written?" He went round everyone in the studio, one by one, and berated them, using every swear word in the book, and eventually looked behind and pretended he'd only just seen the party. "Oh, so sorry, didn't see you there." Poor Philip Jones! He just stood there and went very, very red. He knew us all well, and knew exactly what was going on. The chap from the IBA just laughed. He thought it was hilarious. It broke the ice though, and we all went on to have a chat with him about the show and tried to explain why we did what we did, and talk about the audience we were playing to. I think it actually put his mind at rest. He realized that we weren't just a load of kids trying to shock. We were making good TV. A bit racy, sure, but that was the audience we were playing to. We weren't playing to senior citizens or five-year-olds.'

In the fourth, and as it turned out final series, the high level of star guests was well maintained, with acts like Dire Straits, the Pretenders and David Essex. Booked to perform his latest single, Essex was approached by Kenny to see if he'd have a go at a few sketches, including playing Sid Snot's mate. 'Well, I'd done theatre and films before, so could act, and I thought, why not?' Essex remembers. 'So after I'd done the song somebody walked into my dressing room and handed me this scrap of paper. Literally just a scrap. And on it were a couple of scribbled-out lines. I was expecting a script followed by a few minutes' rehearsal time. No chance! I was handed the scrap of paper, taken to wardrobe and then shown on set. There was me and Kenny, a couple of writers, a cameraman, a sound man and the director. That was it. And after each little skit, we were handed another scrap of paper and just got on with it. It was all pretty much made up on the spot. Kenny and I developed a rapport quite quickly, though, and it worked. We never knew what we were going to do next. I think that was part of the charm.'

There were comedy guest stars, too. When Mayoh mentioned that he was good friends with Bernard Manning, Kenny's eyes lit up. 'Oh, I love him! Can we get him on?' Mayoh thought it could be arranged, but they might have difficulty getting Philip Jones to agree. 'I'll tell you what,' said Mayoh. 'Let's do it anyway, and then try and get it past Philip.'

Barry and Ray loved the idea too, so everyone sat down to talk about how best to use Manning. Kenny said, 'I should try and kill him really, shouldn't I?' The reply was a resounding, 'Yes, you should.' Barry and Ray went away and turned that idea into a sketch in which Kenny walks on camera to announce, 'And now, Bernard Manning!' On comes Bernard and starts telling gags. Cut to Kenny, hiding behind a piece of scenery; he looks to camera, smiles and shoots the comic. Bernard doesn't flinch and carries on, much to Kenny's frustration. Next, he gets a bow and fires an arrow at him, but Bernard still carries on. This goes on for ages, with Kenny using all manner of weaponry to try and kill him, but it doesn't work, he just keeps on telling gags. Eventually, Kenny comes on set driving a forklift. As he drives by he looks manically into the camera. He then picks up Bernard and drives him out of the studio to the car park and dumps him in a river. 'It took us all bloody day to do it,' recalls Mayoh. 'But it was great.'

After filming, everyone went to the canteen: Bernard, Ev, Jo Gurnett, Ray, Mayoh and Barry. They were all chatting, and there was Bernard, looking, in Kenny's words, 'like a large but sweet lump of suet pudding'. The comic had a couple of gigs to do that night so eventually his manager came to collect him. 'We all say our goodbyes and off he goes,' remembers Cryer. 'When he got to the canteen door he stopped, turned around and boomed, "Everett, I always thought you were a cunt, but you're all right."'

Mayoh edited the sketch the next day and took it in to show Philip Jones. 'We got Bernard Manning on the show.'

'WHAAAT?!' came the reaction.

After watching the sketch, Jones had to admit the whole thing worked brilliantly. 'It was clever of Kenny, though, to come up with that initial idea,' says Mayoh.

By now the trio of Kenny, Barry and Ray was working seamlessly. No one knew Kenny better than those two writers: they got what made him tick as a performer, and the way they worked was totally unique, says Mayoh. 'No rehearsal and on some occasions no pre-prepared material. Kenny would simply come on dressed as Sid Snot or whoever, and Barry and Ray would write gags and put them on the autocue, and we'd just keep rolling. Kenny would act them out, having never even seen them. Some were good and some were shit, but overall it worked. We had a seventeen-second rule though. If we weren't laughing within seventeen seconds, it was out.'

Kenny never liked doing more than one take. Barry and Ray quickly cottoned on to this and devised a crafty way of getting round it. 'We used to lie to him,' admits Cryer. 'We'd give him a gag and say, "Just rehearse this to camera a couple of times, Ev," and all the time we'd keep the cameras rolling, so we always got three or four takes.'

Barry or Ray would also take a basic idea for a joke and 'Everett' it. For instance, there was a joke going around which everyone on the team found hysterically funny. It was based on David Frost interview-ing a toilet attendant. This attendant was about to retire after fifty years' service and was being interviewed about his career. 'Well, it used to be quite wonderful,' says this bloke. 'I had all sorts of regular customers; businessmen, MPs, vicars, workmen. It was a real family atmosphere. These days though, it's awful. You've got punks, junkies, hooligans – and they're all drinking or taking drugs. I tell you, these days, when somebody sits down and just has a shit it's like a breath of fresh air!'

Cryer was convinced there was a sketch in it and managed to persuade Billy Connolly to appear. Kenny was set to play the inter-viewer and Billy the toilet attendant. 'I'd like a Leicester Square lavvy, please,' Mayoh instructed the designer. 'With as much graffiti as you can get away with.'

'When do you want it by?'

'Two p.m. this afternoon,' replied Mayoh.

Off went the designer to the scene dock to see what he could find, and somehow managed to rustle up a convincing bog. 'So we had a toilet, Billy and Kenny, a script (which made a change) but no extras,' recalls Mayoh.

As luck would have it, a variety special was being filmed in the studio next door, so the place was crammed with old circus and variety artists. Mayoh recognized a few that he'd worked with in the past and asked if they'd mind stepping into the breach, as it were. Being old pros, they were only too happy to oblige.

Eventually they were ready to film the sketch, which begins with Billy washing his feet in one of the basins. A cubicle door then opens and Kenny's sitting there. He pulls the chain of the toilet, which comes away in his hand, and he proceeds to use it as a microphone. He then walks over to Billy and starts to interview him. So far so good. 'After a couple of minutes I cue the extras and then chaos ensues,' recalls Mayoh. 'As the boys are doing their stuff, they start to notice the extras on the monitor. We had transvestites, jugglers, the lot – all nonchalantly walking in and out of the cubicles. We even had one chap juggling apples wearing a frock and a bowler hat. Now Billy's a bloody dreadful giggler and this set him off big time. Even Kenny, who wasn't known for corpsing, fell about in fits.'

Mayoh blamed himself for leaving the extras as a surprise. But as the afternoon dragged on it began to look as if they might run out of time. And as funny as it all was, they needed to finish with a completed sketch. 'Anyway,' says Mayoh, 'after God knows how many hours I had an idea. I thought, sod it, we're not going to get this done. So I just edited all the corpses together and that was the sketch. The punchline became secondary. Incidentally, we had to change the punchline to: "I tell you, these days, when somebody sits down and just has a SIT, it's like a breath of fresh air!" But the whole of that sketch came from somebody hearing a joke in a pub.'

The fourth series of the *Video Show* had proved as popular with audiences as its predecessors, and there seemed no reason why a fifth would not be forthcoming. Barry and Ray had even written a sitcom called 'The Snots', based on one of Kenny's characters. 'The dialogue was funny,' recalls Barry. 'And they spent most of the time hitting each other, but it was quite jolly. We almost got Diana Dors to play the mother, but it didn't happen because she had a part in a dinosaur film or something. Anyway, Ray, Ev and I arrived at Thames' studio at Teddington, and there was a very strange atmosphere about the place, like something was wrong. So we went into the studio and it was deserted. It should have been a hive of activity, but there wasn't a soul in the place. The set was in place, but no crew.'

As they all stood around mystified, the tea lady turned up. So everyone had a cuppa and a nice natter. Then it clicked with Ev what was going on. 'His eyes went,' says Cryer. 'That's what always happened when he got angry (which wasn't often), his eyes would go. "We're going to see Philip," he said.'

It turned out that someone had been secretly feeding the scripts upstairs to Philip Jones – an act that went totally against the ethos of the show. Jones had read the script for "The Snots" and found them too vulgar and wouldn't sanction it being filmed.'

'Philip Jones could be extremely straight-laced,' confirms Barry. 'So as soon as he got hold of the scripts, we'd had it. In fact the big joke at Thames was always, "If Philip Jones ever finds out that we're making *The Kenny Everett Show* . . ."'

Kenny was furious. He was already livid over Thames' decision to use the show as part of a ratings war by moving it to Thursday nights, where it clashed with *Top of the Pops* on BBC1, but this was the last straw. Jones tried to defuse the situation: 'Oh, now then, luvvies, we can talk about this. I've booked a table for lunch in the restaurant.'

'What a pity,' said Ev. 'We already have somewhere booked.' Then he, Ray and Barry walked out, never to return.

A few days later Jim Moir, a top-flight BBC producer who'd heard rumblings, rang Cryer. 'Hello, Baz, how are things getting on at Thames?'

'Jim, I'm just a writer.'

'Come on, you can tell me,' urged Moir. Barry spilled the beans. 'OK,' said Moir. 'Next Tuesday. Drop of champagne in my office?'

Within weeks, a deal was done. Kenny was back at the Beeb. As for Philip Jones, he couldn't forgive Kenny for leaving and relations between the two men were never the same.

25

Chemically Altered Kenny

By THE TIME Kenny had begun work on his television series for Thames his marriage to Lee was effectively over. They'd sold the Cotswold house and bought a London flat with a walled garden in Pembridge Villas, Notting Hill. Although they shared a bedroom, they slept in separate beds. They were now man and wife in name only.

Kenny was always unapologetic about the primary reason he married Lee: as a means of 'normalizing' himself, for want of a better word. 'If I could press a button and make myself straight, I would,' he once confessed. By marrying Lee, someone he truly felt comfortable with, Kenny hoped everything would fall suddenly into place, that he'd wake up one glorious morning, look across at her and something would click inside him: 'Oh, I get it, the shape and the lumps and the softness.' Instead, he eventually realized that you are what you are. If you're born gay, then you'll stay that way.

Growing up in Liverpool, Kenny had felt 'totally alone in the world. I did not know any other gays. When I moved to London I discovered I was not the only one, and that helped.' But it had taken him another decade and a half to finally accept who he was and to call a halt to the pretence.

In many respects, Kenny and Lee were made for each other – 'soulmates', in Lee's words. But as Kenny succinctly put it: 'The only thing that was wrong about Lee and I is that we're not physically compatible – she's a chick, and so am I!' In the never published 1983 interview conducted with Lee and John Alkin, Kenny confessed: 'We were never physically compatible for the whole ten years . . . We get along mentally. If we were physically compatible that would be the great romance of our time. If I fancied her as much as I fancy some of the leather-clad, moustachioed creatures in Heaven [a London night-club], then our marriage would have lasted until the end of time. But God said, "Forget it, you're a faggot."'

Had it been a mistake, then, to get married? Lee remains adamant it was anything but. 'We got it out of our system,' she affirms. 'And we had a great time. And we loved each other.'

To the press and the wider public, they carried on the pretence of still being a happily married couple, appearing as husband and wife at premieres and celebrity parties. They even flew to Australia together when Kenny undertook television work there. It was a charade, but only up to a point, since Kenny hadn't really disappeared from Lee's life. Although he had moved out of the Notting Hill flat into new accommodation in Hammersmith (Cate remembers buying her brother a house-warming present of a polished mahogany loo seat, the lid hand-painted and embossed in gold lettering with the legend 'Edith'), he'd kept a key to the marital home and was forever dropping in.

And although he'd 'come out' to himself, Kenny had yet to fully embrace a gay lifestyle, save for regular visits to Heaven. He'd not yet made the bold move of beginning a gay relationship. That all changed one evening when he went out to dinner with Lee at a restaurant in Brompton Road. He was joined by Freddie Mercury and Queen's drummer, Roger Taylor. 'I ended up pulling the waiter for him,' reveals Lee. 'He said to me, "That waiter's dishy." So when he came up to serve us I said, "Are you doing anything afterwards? We're going to a club, do you want to come with us?" And he said he'd love to. And Freddie went, "Oh, your wife's just pulled your first boyfriend." He needed pushing, at first.'

The waiter was called John Pitt. A gentle and reserved Australian, he moved into Kenny's place in Hammersmith. Yet the urge or compulsion to visit Lee remained as strong as ever. It was a strange set-up – and got even stranger when Lee met and fell in love with the actor John Alkin, who'd played the recurring character of Detective Sergeant Tom Daniels in the long-running cult TV series *The*

Sweeney. 'At first I was intimidated by the whole situation,' confesses John. 'I was sitting in the flat late one afternoon, I'd only moved in three days earlier, and Ev walked in with two huge bags of laundry and said, "What's for dinner?"'

During the early stages of the romance with John, Lee says Kenny behaved in much the same way as he'd done with her boyfriends prior to their marriage, pushing things close to the edge, seeing if it was just a fling. 'Ev could see I was settling down with John,' remembers Lee. 'He came round one night and brought an acid tab. We all took it, and I could only look at John. I think that was the day he knew, that was it.'

Kenny and Lee divorced in 1983, leaving Lee free to marry John in 1985. And who was the best man? Kenny. He was quoted in the press as saying, 'Who better to give her away, darlings?'

In the late seventies and early eighties the gay clubs of the world were teeming with cocaine: it was everywhere. Having beaten his addiction to Mandrax, Kenny had developed a coke habit, and although it didn't take him too long to come to his senses, it lasted long enough to make a rather large hole in his wallet. 'I did quite a binge on the stuff,' he once admitted. 'It's also absurdly expensive and, like Maltesers, highly moreish, so that in the course of a heavily cocained evening, it's easy to push a hundred quid's worth up your hooter.'

Friends tried to keep him off the stuff but Kenny wasn't interested. 'When you're on it, everyone who isn't seems like a bore and the last thing you want to hear is nagging reminders about how bad it is for you. Your pusher takes over as your best friend, and he, obviously, isn't going to preach the evils of whatever drug is making him rich.'

Fortunately Kenny's best friend wasn't his dealer but his manager, Jo Gurnett. She remembers many a battle over his drug use. 'I used to go mental when Kenny had been on cocaine. I had a long talk with him one night and tried to persuade him that you could get more joy out of just being with friends and having a nice meal than you could sticking that stuff up your nose. And he'd say, "Oh but, darling, it gives me such a high." I used to beg him not to do it.'

Sometimes Jo and her husband would go for a meal with Kenny and John Pitt; Freddie Mercury would often be there, too, and periodically one of them would go to the loo and then come back a bit perkier. 'That would have been fine if it were just the once,' says Jo. 'But they were constantly getting up. "Shan't be a tick," they'd say. It's actually quite an anti-social drug in that respect!'

It was also making Kenny paranoid. He began to imagine that people were after him, scheming behind his back, plotting to undermine his self-confidence and his career. He'd get irritable, too, and snap at the slightest thing. 'If the temperature was one degree away from perfect, or if the milk was off, I'd become highly argumentative and difficult to live with,' he once remarked. Jo Gurnett agrees. 'Kenny could be a grump sometimes – who couldn't? But when he'd been on cocaine he was a nightmare. Everything you did was wrong.'

Even Cate had begun to notice what was going on and the tell-tale signs. 'I saw that his eyes used to be dilated on television. I saw that his nose wasn't as pretty as it used to be.'

Not surprisingly, Kenny's work began to suffer. All too often he'd ring Jo and say, 'Can I cancel that voice-over? I've got a really bad cold,' and she'd blast down the telephone: 'No you haven't, Ev, you snorted fucking coke last night.' He always tried to deny it, but Jo was too savvy to be hoodwinked and he knew it. 'He eventually came off it, but that period did worry me and I got very upset about it.'

Kenny's habit came to a head towards the end of 1980. 'I really lost interest in doing any work,' he explained. 'And it got to the stage where I was just anxious to get the work over and carry on partying.' Consequently the work suffered – not disastrously, but enough to tarnish Kenny's reputation slightly and cost him a fair amount of professional pride.

The person who really bore the brunt of this lapse was Capital Radio's breakfast DJ, Mike Smith. One of the rising stars of early eighties British radio, Smith went on to enjoy a long career at Radio 1 and on television. He was also a huge fan of Kenny's. 'I loved him for his audio creativity and his waspy gentleness.' Soon, however, that respect was to turn to annoyance and downright resentment.

Kenny had stepped down from his position at Capital in 1980. The break was amicable, he wanted to concentrate more on his TV work for Thames, but his departure was tainted by the fact that he wanted to take all his tapes and cartridges with him. 'All the jingles and things that he'd done,' says Jo Gurnett. 'There were mountains of them. Michael Bukht said, "You can't take all that, it's not your property." And Ev said, "Yes it is, I made it all so it's mine." His work was lying all over the place and he was extraordinarily proud of it all. Why should he leave it all behind? He'd been there a long time though. Seven years, I think. That was a long time for Everett!'

Because of his popularity at Capital, the powers that be were keen to prolong his association with the station and utilize his burgeoning multi-media popularity. 'He was a massive star,' remembered Mike Smith. 'And I was told by the controller at Capital that I must – *must* – carry an Ev creation on the breakfast show every morning.'

In order to keep Ev's name on-board, Capital commissioned new episodes of Captain Kremmen which were to be broadcast after the 8 a.m. news – peak listening time! This was a good deal for Kenny. The money Capital had offered him was not inconsiderable, and it would keep him in the public's consciousness on an almost daily basis.

Kenny may not have been an especially career-minded individual, but even he, under normal circumstances, would have appreciated the merits of maintaining a relationship with Capital. Jo had talked it through with him and he agreed it made perfect sense. The problem was, Kenny wasn't simply burning the candle at both ends, he was burning it in the middle too, and Kremmen quickly became little more than an inconvenience. 'I'd often snort a lot of coke and then go dancing and partying until the small hours,' remembered Kenny. 'When I got home I still had to do the episode of Kremmen for broadcasting only about four hours later at ten past eight.'

Mike Smith recalls, 'I would wait for these new episodes to arrive. These days, you'd wait for them to be recorded, listened to by a room of lawyers and then transmitted, once the pages of compliance forms were signed off. Then, it was different – the eight a.m. news would come, a three-minute bulletin. No sign of Kremmen. Take an early ad break, still no sign of the spaceman – or even a taxi with a tape. Play a record. During record, cab arrives with tape. Tape gets rewound and transmitted without being checked. This was not a rare occurrence. Daily I chewed my nails waiting for bloody Kremmen to arrive.'

Unfortunately the quality of the episodes was even worse than the timekeeping. 'The last thing I wanted to do while I was stoned on coke was to work,' admitted Kenny. 'I'd do a script which went something like: "You remember yesterday's episode . . . you don't? Well, what's the point in doing this one? Stay tuned for more adventures tomorrow." I'd then dash off a quick, very substandard episode which would often only last thirty seconds, and phone a mini-cab to take it to Capital. Really embarrassing in retrospect, and all due to my love affair with little lines of white powder.'

It was a nightmare for the management at Capital. And all the while Mike Smith was losing faith in one of his heroes. Indeed, Kremmen got so bad that sometimes Smith would transmit old episodes instead. 'Nobody really noticed. By this time, Ev was not in a good way inside that head of his. He was being paid stupid amounts by both Capital and the BBC. He was chemically altered – and he simply wasn't delivering on the deal.'

Kenny finally woke up to the fact that he had a problem one weekday morning when he heard Mike Smith broadcast a Kremmen episode and then say: 'How much are we paying for this?'

Fortunately this embarrassment forced Kenny to alter his behaviour. He didn't stop taking the drug – he would carry on taking it occasionally for a few years to come – but he came off the danger list enough to concentrate on the thing that made him truly happy: his work. 'I'm never happy until I'm working. If there's a great steamy affair going on at the same time it's more enjoyable than the work, but it doesn't last as long and there's no future in it.'

26

The Station with the Queen Anne Legs!

WHILST PERHAPS NOT a coup, luring Kenny away from Thames to Television Centre had been a good move for the BBC. They had taken full advantage of his falling out with the channel and had put paid to any hope of reconciliation. That said, they were nervous about the appointment, as they had absolutely no control over what Kenny might get up to when not filming. He was a radio man; everybody knew and appreciated that, but he was without a station. What if he began pining for the airwaves again? And what if he began broadcasting on another commercial radio station? It wouldn't look good, would it? The best thing to do, as he prepared his television show, would be to pre-empt Kenny's inevitable return to radio by offering him a job. But where?

He couldn't go to Radio 1, there was far too much history, and Radios 3 and 4 weren't suitable, not for a regular show. The only place left for Kenny was Radio 2. He'd be fine there, amongst the Jimmy Youngs and the David 'Diddy' Hamiltons – wouldn't he?

In an interview with Paul Gambaccini in 1981, not long after starting at the station, Kenny gave his take on the difference between broadcasting on Radio 1 and 2. In terms of presentation, he felt there was no difference whatsoever. 'It just feels like I'm getting away with a lot more, because it's a sort of straight channel. At Radio 1 they expect you to be outrageous and dreadful. But at Radio 2, all the people around me just step back a little in horror as I hit the microphone, and it gives me that old feeling of outrage.'

This was like sticking a DeLorean between two Morris Minors.

Back then, Radio 2 was a very different station to the one we know today. The only thing that had altered since 1967, when it had changed from being the Light Programme, was the name. Even the ubiquitous David Jacobs and Pete Murray were still there!

Whereas Radios 1, 3 and 4 had evolved, Radio 2 seemed to be stuck in a time warp. Before joining, Kenny used to refer to Radio 2 as 'the station with the Queen Anne legs'. Not a bad description. Its core listenership was dying off though, and as yet the Beeb hadn't pinpointed exactly who the station might target next.

Was putting Kenny on Radio 2 an inspired choice? Well no, it wasn't really. In the early eighties little else was changing at the station and so his show stuck out like a giant, creative beacon. Yes, a lot of people would tune in to listen to him, but they would tune out again as soon as he came off air.

Be that as it may, Kenny was thrilled to be back on the airwaves, and could be heard every Saturday morning from 10 a.m. to 12 p.m. And after almost a decade of regional radio he was at last broadcasting nationally again. His stints on Radio 1 and Radio Luxembourg were a distant memory, and there were now millions of people throughout the UK who had never heard him broadcast. They'd heard of him, of course; after all, he was a huge TV star. But now Kenny's star was shifting sideways instead of ever upwards.

Being back at Broadcasting House excited Kenny. More so than being at Television Centre. That was merely work. This was life. There was no wireless workshop any more, but then he didn't need one. What he did need, however, was another Angela Bond – a producer who could inspire him and excite him by continually raiding the BBC archive on his behalf. Luckily, he came pretty close to getting exactly that – except this particular Angela Bond was called Geoff Mullin.

Geoff had been Terry Wogan's producer at Radio 2 from 1975 until 1979, and it had been Wogan who had recommended Geoff to Kenny, and for a very good reason. 'Terry knew that I'd produced the last few shows for Jack Jackson, so said I'd be perfect for Kenny. The link obviously being that Kenny was one of the first DJs to follow in the footsteps of Jack Jackson. Jack was his inspiration in many ways, so it seemed like a good fit.'

It was indeed an excellent fit, and Geoff was quick to inform Kenny that the admiration he had for Jack was reciprocated. 'Jack was a big, big fan of Kenny's. Kenny had taken what he'd started and lifted it to another level. That pleased Jack enormously. Kenny was keeping it all alive! He was very pleased to have been emulated though. To him, imitation was the sincerest form of flattery. It was also Jack who coined the appellation Auntie when referring to the BBC, and Kenny the Beeb.'

According to Mullin the similarities didn't stop there. 'In the mid-seventies, when Jack was doing his last programmes, he could only do Bank Holiday specials and things like that. He'd run out of steam health-wise, but his enthusiasm for radio was as strong as ever. Jack actually worked in a very similar way to Kenny. He had his own little studio where he'd have his tape recorders and records, etc. And he'd stay in there for hours, creating his skits and talk-backs, so there were a lot of likenesses. I used to go and see him a few days before the show and I'd give him a few dates, a few anniversaries and a few things which he might want to touch on. I'd also give him forty or so records and he'd choose twenty to play on the show. It was pretty much the same with Kenny.'

When it came to format, the shows were similar to what Ev had been doing at Capital, but with one added ingredient. Geoff explains: 'I did all the research for the show. I'd get every date that was pertinent that week and I'd raid the BBC archive. Kenny called it the "treasure trove". It was totally unique. We used a lot of clips for the show. Historical clips, like the outbreak of WWII, the launch of the *Queen Mary*, all sorts of things. Kenny thrived on this sort of stuff and over the years made better use of it than any other DJ. It opened up a whole new world of possibility.'

When it came to the music, carte blanche was once again the order of the day, with not an 'official' playlist in sight. 'Those kind of week-end shows were quite free really,' says Mullin. 'What we played on Kenny's show took it a step further though. We kept completely away from the Radio 2 playlist. I think we were one of the first radio shows to play the Eurythmics in the UK. Kenny loved anything electronic, of course. He also loved disco stuff. I used to go down to a shop in Berwick Street in Soho and they had all the imported twelve-inch singles. They were fantastic the guys in there. They'd give me all sorts of stuff to listen to and I'd take it in on a Saturday morning.'

Kenny was quite happy to hand some of the musical duties over to Mullin, as he had plenty to be getting on with creating jingles and preparing skits, etc. Whereas in the past he'd insisted on choosing or at least vetting the playlist, now the first he knew of what was to be played on his show was when it was handed to him to cue up! Geoff remembers the arrangement working well. 'Even Kenny hadn't heard it when he put it on the turntable. Apart from the golden oldies and the classical stuff, which he picked, he'd just let me get on with the music. I used to sit opposite him in the studio and he'd say, "Right then, what's next?" and I'd just hand him a record. That's why, if any-one ever asks me who the most stimulating person to work with was, I always say him, because I was so involved with the programme. It was really good fun.'

But there was another reason why Kenny stood back from compil-ing the playlist for his shows: he didn't like the music! Paul Gambaccini was well aware of this: 'He loved that whole ELO, 10cc thing – again with the multi-tracked harmonies, showing that there was a lot of work that had gone into the record, as a work of art on which you'd spent a lot of time. Now in contrast punk, for instance, was the three-minute burst of energy, which was just done in one go, and that didn't interest him.'

Nor, it has to be said, did a lot of the New Romantic and electronic music of that era. The late seventies and early eighties was a barren period for Kenny – musically, at least. 'It's not an insult to say that he didn't like it,' claims Gambaccini. 'He wasn't judging it; it just didn't appeal to him. To the career DJ, one of the thoughts always in the back of one's mind was something perfectly articulated by John Peel when I asked, "How long would you like to keep doing this?" and he said, "I want to keep doing it as long as I like the music. When I don't, I'll

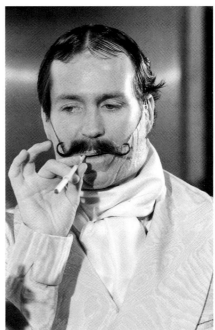

Above: Two of Kenny's most memorable television creations: Sid Snot (*left*), and Marcel Wave (*right*).

Below: A still from *The Kenny Everett Video Show*, given to his parents.

Above right: Kenny re-enacting *Sunday Night at the Palladium* at a Chinese restaurant in London. He used the Lazy Susan as a revolving stage …

Below: Kenny with Geoff Owen, the head of Radio 2 (**left**), and his producer, Geoff Mullin (**right**), at The Belfry Club in 1982.

Bottom: 'Herewith one mighty cheque to settle us up.' A cheque for one million pounds, sent to Geoff Mullin.

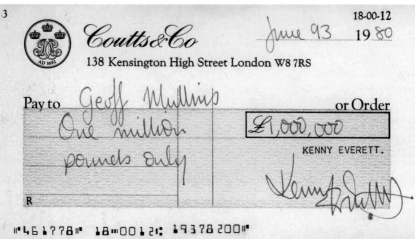

3

Coutts&Co

138 Kensington High Street London W8 7RS

18-00-12

June 93 19 80

Pay to *Geoff Mullins*

or Order

One million pounds only

£1,000,000

KENNY EVERETT.

R

⑆461778⑈ 18⑈0012⑉ 19378200⑈

Greetings from NEW YORK

BROOKLYN BRIDGE This world-famous architectural masterpiece surges over the East River in a stunning display of engineering imagination. Each day it brings thousands from the tree-lined streets of fashionable Brooklyn Heights and Cobble Hill to the concrete canyons of the bustling Lower Manhattan Financial District. Only the magic of Xograph® three-dimensional photography can hint at the majesty of this wonder of the world.

3-D POST CARD

SUPER XOGRAPH ® PRINTED IN USA

© VISUAL PANOGRAPHICS, INC., P. O. BOX 5646, ARLINGTON, TEXAS 76011

Be properly addressed POSTCODE IT

Philip Mazzei
Patriot Remembered

40c

Dear Folks

It's snowing here but having the time of my life. Hawaii next !!!

All the Best 2

" Have a happy day ! "

Mo.

Mr & Mrs T Cole
7 Primrose Close
Freshfield
Nr Formby
LANCS
ENGLAND

Above: A postcard to Mum and Dad, 1982. When writing to his parents, he always signed his name 'Mo'.

Below: Kenny and Cleo Roccos at the top of the Empire State Building. The pair were virtually inseparable for almost fifteen years.

Mike and Julianne Batt
invite you to join them for the First Night party at

25 Store Street, South Crescent, London WC1
immediately following
the Opening Night Performance of

THE HUNTING OF THE

Snark

on Thursday 24 October 1991

RSVP: Carole Beckwith 071- 323 3300 • Admit One • Dress Black Tie

Above: The official invitation to press night of *The Hunting of the Snark*. Although a financial flop, appearing in the musical became one of Kenny's proudest achievements.

Below: Cleo, Lily Cole and Cleo's mum, Audrey, setting off for the opening night of *The Hunting of the Snark*.

On holiday in America in 1989. The first time he'd been clean shaven since the late 1960s!

Looks like Kenny really did eat his heart out!

Above: Kenny became very fond of walking with his bank manager, Eric Gear. 'He was always happiest in a small group,' said Eric of his friend. This photo was taken on a walking holiday in Exmoor in 1990. *Left to right*: Eric's brother, George, Kenny, Eric and George's wife, Betty.

Below: Kenny and Jane Gear taking a bath on a walking holiday in Derbyshire.

Above: Padstow, Cornwall. ***Left to right***: Jane Gear, Betty Gear, Kenny, Pepe, Nikolai and Eric.

Below: Kenny on the rocks!

Outside the Sydney Opera House. Kenny loved Australia and, had he lived, would more than likely have moved there permanently.

Below: The Cole family, together for the last time, having fish and chips in Fremantle, Australia, in 1994.

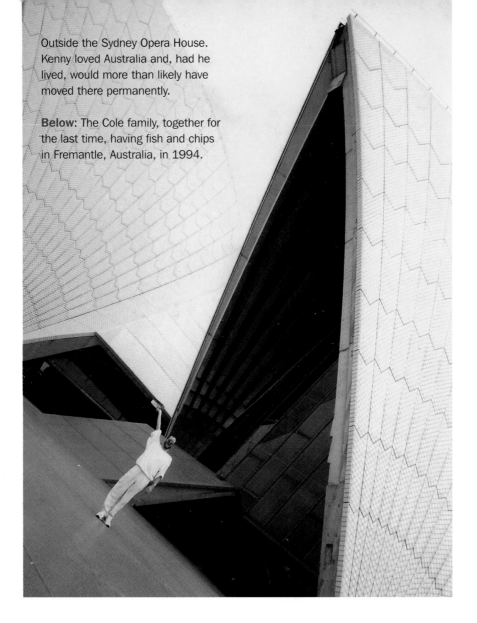

stop." And I thought, oh my God, what a concept, that there might be a day when you don't actually like what's new, and I think that started to happen to Kenny in the eighties.'

Indeed. By the early eighties Kenny had to wade through an awful lot of musical chaff to get to anything that to him even vaguely resembled grain, and in the end he just didn't bother. 'When I put a record on the turntable now, I put the needle into the groove to rehearse the beginning of the song. I'll then play a bit of it off air, and I'll say, "Hey Geoff, this is great, what is it?" And he'll say, "Darling, it's number one!" That's how much I know about it.'

Fortunately Geoff's taste in music mirrored Kenny's nicely, and so almost everything he chose worked with Kenny. On an average show you could hear the likes of Donna Summer, the Stranglers, the Dazz Band, Wham, the Weather Girls, Grace Jones, Human League, Elvis Costello – all pretty standard stuff these days, but on Radio 2 circa 1981, it was almost revolutionary.

One new song Kenny did choose himself was Laurie Anderson's 'O Superman'. A cover of a Jules Massenet aria, Anderson created the song using a voice decoder and lots of looping techniques; all very similar to Kenny really. John Peel had been the first DJ to play the song on air and had also played it to Kenny, knowing full well that he'd fall for it. And he did. In fact it completely mesmerized him and he later cited the song as being the one track he wished he'd made himself.

While unfortunately not receiving the attention or acclaim of his work on Big L, Radio 1 or Capital, the Radio 2 shows are, in terms of ingenuity and entertainment, first class, and were undoubtedly his broadcasting swansong. Perhaps he knew that this would be his last hurrah on national radio and so attempted to crystallize the previous fifteen years by creating a long-running 'showcase'. The icing on the cake is that Kenny genuinely appears to be enjoying every second. Even the start of his first show features a moment of pure, mischievous brilliance. When the newsreader signs off, Kenny says, 'OK, folks, let's get this show on the road,' before playing a jingle for Capital Radio. 'Oooops!' says Kenny. Brilliant!

The show did receive a number of glowing reviews, not least from the

Guardian's Arts correspondent, David Walker: 'Listen to Kenny Everett on his two-hour Saturday programme on Radio 2. He's worth it, for this is a popular cultural performance out of the ordinary.'

Walker argued that Kenny may well have been broadcasting on the right station after all, having listened to the show when he'd played music by the composer, Eric Coates. 'Kenny's simply coming to terms with age,' said Walker. In fact, Kenny had been playing Eric Coates since his early days on Radio 1, after Angela Bond brought him some 78s from the archive.

Forget the station; Kenny was back on national radio and pretty soon attracting weekly audiences of over three million. A few days after the audience figures were released, Geoff received a letter from Radio 2's controller, David Hatch.

> Dear Geoff,
> I'm so pleased Kenny is doing so well. The GEs [general evaluations] are high (70, which is excellent) and the programme is a superb listen.
> This is somewhat overdue but I want you to know that I recognize the hard work and skill you both put in. Your billings are also superb – almost the only thing in the *Radio Times* worth reading.
> Kenny would be embarrassed if I were to write to him personally, so please pass on my applause, but keep a good chunk back for your good self.
> Thank you. I'm grateful and am listening with great pleasure.
> Yours,
> David Hatch

Geoff still has one of the show's original listening panel reports, and the figures are fascinating. One thing that really sticks out is that the over fifties simply didn't get Kenny. The report says: 'It is worth noting that the listeners in the twelve- to nineteen-year-old age range accorded Kenny Everett a very high personal rating of 92. Twenty- to twenty-nine-year-olds, 82. Thirty- to forty-nine-year-olds, 78. And fifty- to sixty-four-year-olds, 59.'

'The first figure is almost unbelievable,' says Geoff. 'Bearing in mind that 70 is an extremely good score. The whole ethos of Radio 2 at the time was very old-fashioned though, and the older crowd did not get him at all. It was all Jimmy Young and stuff like that. He was Radio 2 really – him and Pete Murray. It hadn't really changed since it was the Light Programme.'

The 'billings' David Hatch referred to in his letter are the show billings in the *Radio Times*. It was Geoff's job to write a billing for the show each week, but as it was for Kenny he decided against using the same one week in week out, the way most producers did. People started to notice them and they became rather popular, building a following of their own.

The first one was dated 3 October 1981 and read: 'Cuddly Ken returns to Auntie with an amazing display of Wireless Wizardry. It's wacky, it's fun, it's rubbish. Do not adjust your set. The producer of this show wishes to remain Geoff Mullin.'

David Hatch called Geoff the following day. 'He was enthused. "Your billing was very creative," he said. "Do more like that. Whatever you like." So I went off and wrote a different one every week, and they became more and more surreal. I'd also theme them, say if it was Christmas or Halloween or whatever. Then one day, I decided to write the whole thing backwards. It started EHT YNNEK TTEREVE WOHS (*The Kenny Everett Show*) and finished RECUDORP, FFOEG NILLUM (Producer, Geoff Mullin). After that people started writing to us backwards. Fortunately it didn't last very long though.'

One of the author's favourites, from 27 February 1982, reads: 'Mirror, mirror on the wall who is the fairest of them all? Well, after exposing himself all over the *Radio Times* last week, Kenny thinks he is, and he's developed a rash of love-bites, mostly self-inflicted. And you thought Narcissus was just another Daffodil.'

By 1982 Kenny was one of the highest-earning entertainers in the UK. He had hit shows on both national radio and television – and, if time allowed, would still record the odd voice-over. Jo Gurnett remembers him finding the wealth more puzzling than exciting. 'He was making a lot of money, so he didn't need to worry financially. I think it amazed him sometimes, why people were willing to pay him so much money.'

Geoff remembers asking Kenny to share some of his wealth, albeit jokingly, and got more than he bargained for. 'Just for a laugh one day, I said to him, "Kenny, you must be minted now. How about giving me a few quid?" Anyway, a few days later I received a letter.'

Dear Geoffrey
Herewith one mighty cheque, to settle us all up.
As I said on the phone I'll send you a postcard dipped in stranded Viking, and you can swish it round in a glass of Perrier and relive the taste of the Tropics in your very own living room.
Yours till we meet again,
Edith, Queen of the waves

Enclosed with the letter was a cheque from Coutts & Co for one million pounds, signed by Mr Kenny Everett!

With his annual income fast approaching a figure similar to his weekly audience, Kenny could afford to buy any gadget he wanted. He once bought Jo Gurnett a huge Bang & Olufsen TV, which arrived at her apartment with a big bow around it. 'I think he'd have bought me anything if I'd asked for it. He was so generous.'

Even so, by the end of 1982 Kenny still hadn't invested in a CD player. Neither, would you believe, had dear old Auntie. 'This was typical BBC,' sighs Geoff. 'At the time of Kenny's show CDs had just started to emerge, and Kenny and I had been sent demo copies of the first one. I think it was Billy Joel or Dire Straits. Kenny then said to me, "We should play this, Geoff." And I said, "Yes, Kenny, we should play this, but unfortunately the BBC don't have a CD player."'

Geoff had to go to the acquisitions department and plead with them, 'Can you get me a CD player, please?' Eventually it arrived. 'And from then on at 9.30 a.m. every Saturday this CD player would be ceremoniously brought down to the studio for Kenny, plugged in and set up. Kenny would then use it during the course of the show, and then at the end of the show it went back! Somebody came down and packed it up and took it away again. The Beeb actually had a "Keeper of the CD Player". It's the kind of thing that would happen at a school or something. Hilarious!'

The weekly routine Kenny and Geoff went through in order to bring the show together is almost a book in itself, and offers a fascinating insight into how Kenny operated and what made him tick. The two would meet on the Thursday evening, after Geoff had already spent several days researching – usually via the BBC Archive. 'I'd come out of there with a load of stuff, transfer it to tape and then take it round to Kenny's. I'd also give him a list of what it was and what relevance it had to the week. There was always loads of material – far more than he needed for the show. So he'd take all this stuff into his studio, and turn it all into entertainment. It was that simple!'

It may have been simple to Kenny, but only under the right conditions. It was no good cracking on with it straightaway. In fact he wouldn't even touch Geoff's research until Friday evening at the earliest. This, as we're finding out, was the crux of Kenny's creative process. It gave him adrenalin. Nothing meant more to Kenny than producing a perfect radio show. And the closer he got to deadline the more crucial it all became, which produced even more adrenalin and more creativity.

And arriving at the studio with minutes to spare before he began broadcasting to the nation was all part of the routine. Unfortunately for Geoff, he was the one given the unenviable task of getting him there. 'On Saturday morning around 9.30 a.m. I'd pick him up. Very often he'd still be in his pyjamas in his studio, putting bits of tape together, and we're on the air at ten o'clock! I'd be standing there saying, "Come on, we've got to go," and he'd always say, "I won't be a minute. I've just got to finish one last bit." Every week we'd leave his flat right at the last minute.'

Quite often Kenny would insist on driving to the studio. This was all well and good, but before they could set off, they had to try and locate Kenny's car! 'It was very busy round where he lived and some-times he'd have parked two or three streets away. Kenny always carried a large map of the area with him, and when he eventually found a space to park, he'd put a pin in the map so he'd remember where he'd parked his car. When I turned up to collect him, he'd bring out this map and we'd go looking for his car. Very methodical!'

Once they'd completed the task of finding Kenny's car, they then had to negotiate something far worse – London's notorious Westway flyover. The journey should have taken no longer than ten minutes, but they were forever running into traffic jams. Geoff recalls one particular 'Westway run': 'Kenny was at the wheel and we were already late for the show. There was a horrible jam for some reason and I was really starting to panic. The Westway's a dreadful road to get stuck on as there are no slip roads. Once you're on, you're on! When we eventually got to the traffic lights at the end, a car pulled up alongside us. When I turned to look out of the window I saw Geoff Owen sitting there, the head of Radio 2! When he saw Kenny and me, a smile broke out on his face. He mouthed "hello" and started to wave. Then he suddenly stopped, looked at his watch and then just gazed back at us with a look of complete horror. I gave him a Gallic shrug, Kenny waved, the lights changed to green and we sped off. That was about five to eleven!'

Once at Broadcasting House they were on the final leg of the journey, but this was invariably just as dramatic. 'We very often didn't make it on time,' remembers Geoff. 'More often than not, in fact. We'd be running down the corridors of Broadcasting House while the ten o'clock news is on the air, and we've got to be on at three minutes past the hour. There were several occasions when the newsreader had to cover for us. I always left him or her three records every week, in case we didn't turn up. Kenny hated being there on time. He didn't want to have any down time or any wasted time in the studio. It took him very little time to set up. He had everything on tape ready, and I had all the records, so the moment he entered the studio he was good to go.'

Far from the Westway being Kenny's nemesis, it simply became his excuse for being late, although the way he used to complain about it you'd have thought it was always the road's fault, not the fact that he left home five minutes before he was due on air! 'I remember once he rang me on the car phone just before he was due on air,' remembers David Briggs, one of Kenny's producers back on Capital. 'He said, "Darling, the traffic on the Westway is awful. You'll have to start without me. Just put me through on this line and I'll do a link." So I pressed a jingle, put a record on and said, "Right, Ev, we've got to come to you now," and he just did something brilliant down the phone line and for the next link he was in the studio complaining about the traffic.'

About ten years later Kenny would trump this by becoming the first DJ ever to present an entire radio show from his car – stuck in traffic on the Westway, of course! This time he could blame the traffic with genuine conviction, as he was stuck in the middle of an eight-mile tailback. The DJ who had been on before him, David Symonds, had agreed to stick around for a couple of hours and play the records for Kenny while he provided the links and chat from his car. The sound quality of the presenter may have been questionable, but the show delivered a strange sense of occasion and was reported throughout the UK and beyond, even making it on to page 26 of the *Sydney Morning Herald*!

On another memorable occasion Kenny was so late for a television appearance that he missed it altogether. He was supposed to be doing the Mavis Nicholson lunchtime show at Thames, which went out live. It got to noon and he hadn't shown up. Jo Gurnett received a call from the panic-stricken producer and phoned Kenny's flat. 'Why aren't you at Thames? You're supposed to be doing the Mavis Nicholson show NOW!'

'That's not today,' he said. A quick scan through his diary revealed he'd put it down as the following week. 'Don't worry. I can be there in ten minutes.'

Kenny drove frantically to the studios. Then, just as Mavis Nicholson was closing the show, 'I'm sorry Kenny Everett couldn't join us today,' he came bounding on to the set. 'Darlings, I'm so sorry I'm late. Please tune in tomorrow and I'll see you then.' He did the show the next day.

Although Kenny hated arriving with time to spare, when he did, it would provide Geoff Mullin with an interesting spectacle. 'If we ever did get there on time, or even during the news, he used to lie on his back in the studio, kick his legs in the air like he was riding a bike and scream at the top of his voice. That was his preparation before the show. That was his warm-up. He basically wanted to get out of breath. If you listen to the beginning of any of those shows it was always a breathless start. Sometimes all he could manage was, "Hello, darlings," and then he'd have to play a record because he didn't have the breath to talk.'

Once settled, Kenny would begin that most important of broadcasting rituals – cleaning! 'I like everything to be spotless, darling. Do you think that's strange?' Strange or not, it was one way of getting the studio cleaned. 'We used to use Jimmy Young's studio at Radio 2,' remembers Geoff. 'He was in it Monday through Friday and we were in it Saturday. There'd be coffee stains all over the place and Kenny would whiz round and make them all disappear!' As funny as it sounds, cleaning the studio was an essential task before Kenny could finally settle down and present his show. 'He'd been like this ever since he was a child,' remembers Cate. 'His room was always spotless at home. I think he needed to have order. I think it helped him to function.' Cate's probably right. In order to create, Kenny needed a fast approaching deadline and lots of adrenalin. But when it came to broadcasting his creations, he needed order.

Kenny's fastidiousness (domestic and personal) was well known, with around half the people interviewed for the book mentioning it. Many believe he bordered on OCD, but that's probably exaggerating things slightly. Geoff's not so sure though. 'He said to me one day, "Geoff, you're not doing anything after the show today, are you?" And I said, "No, I'm not actually." And he said, "Good, because we've got a special mission on today. It's really important." Naturally I was intrigued. So eventually we leave Broadcasting House and he leads me straight to John Lewis on Oxford Street. It turns out he only wanted me to help him to buy some black bin liners. He made it all sound like there was something special going on – like it was just between him and me – and we end up buying bloody bin liners! That was the kind of company he was though; obsessive but totally unique!'

Things had been no different at Capital. Back at Euston Tower, timekeeping and cleanliness had enjoyed the same differing positions on Kenny's priority list as they did at Radio 2 – much to the irritation of his old friend, Alan Freeman. 'I remember Fluff used to do the Capital Countdown from nine till twelve on a Saturday,' explains Kenny's producer at the time, Simon Booker. 'Alan would always get very anxious when Ev wasn't there when the twelve o'clock news started. He'd start saying, "Where's Kenny? He should be here!" When he did arrive, Fluff would go and Ev would get out his J-cloths and dusters and start clearing up Fluff's cigarette ash. I honestly don't know how the non-smoking DJs put up with it. The majority smoked and the studios were tiny. There was no air conditioning either. Cleaning up the studio only took a few seconds, but it was definitely an important part of the ritual to Kenny.'

When Kenny returned to Capital in 1984, everything had started to become a bit less frantic. For a start, he began getting to work on time; sometimes arriving up to an hour before his show! Things were still ritualistic, but the studio would now be cleaned before he went on air, and the frantic dash from his flat to Capital had been replaced by a trip to the loo and a cuppa. Kenny's then producer, Annie O'Neill explains. 'After he'd cleaned the studio we'd join hands and walk to the loo (he'd go, I wouldn't). When he came out we'd join hands again and go off to the kitchen and make a cup of tea. Then we'd go back to the studio and off we'd go. None of it felt contrived though. It was just what we did. You hear about people like Madonna saying her prayers before a concert. Well, that was Kenny's version. Once he'd done that, he was ready to go on air. But it all had to be done first.'

Kenny was well aware of his foibles. Sheila Steafel, a guest star several times on his TV shows, remembers him saying to her once, 'Sheila, I've gone too far. I found myself actually cleaning the Hoover! I must stop!' Lee remembers when they were married Kenny was constantly cleaning. 'He'd scrub the house, which was great. He'd clean things like mad. After we split up, he'd come round for a chat and while he was there he'd clean the whole kitchen.'

His behaviour often puzzled even himself. His friend and former colleague David Jensen remembers one such occasion. 'We were in his kitchen one night and he suddenly opened a cupboard door. It was absolutely full of rolls of kitchen towel. There must have been fifty. He then looked at me and said, "Do you think that's crazy?" And I replied, "Well, no. It's going to be a long time before you have to buy any."'

David Symonds, who worked with Kenny at Radio 1, Capital and Capital Gold, remembers a similar experience. 'I had to help him back home one day when he'd bought this enormous television, and when we got to his flat I saw this pile of toilet rolls. There must have been at least a hundred. I asked him why he'd bought them all and he said, "Oh, I'm a compulsive hoarder. I buy something and I think, shit, I'd better get some more of that in case I run out." He also had dozens of cans of baked beans, too. He could have survived for weeks in that flat, without ever having to go out.'

In a home video made in 1992, Kenny can be seen going on a tour of his flat, stopping first at his cleaning cupboard. In actual fact it's a room! 'There you are,' he says, 'enough to keep me going through a nuclear war.' And he's not kidding. There are shelves upon shelves full of toilet rolls, shampoos and cleaning products – a real Aladdin's Cave.

Kenny might have been 'obsessive compulsive', but it was never a disorder. It puzzled him, but never worried him. Friends were amused, generally, and on occasion touched by their ultra-clean but ultra-caring friend. Geoff Mullin is one of many who will testify to this.

'I was leaving his house. He came outside to say goodbye to me and he suddenly said, "Don't drive away. Stay right where you are." He ran back inside and he came back out with a dishcloth and started washing my headlights because they were dirty. "You can't drive around like that. It's very dangerous, Geoffrey!" What a very, very sweet thing to do.'

One slightly more understandable foible of Kenny's had him collecting TV and radio shows that he considered either enjoyable or important. When David Jensen was invited to his flat once for dinner,

Kenny took him into a room that was full of huge cupboards. 'He opened one up and it was just full of cassettes, and he looked at me and said, "Do you know what all that is? That's your *Network Chart Show*. Every one you've ever done."'

In 1984 Jensen had left the BBC in order to do *The Network Chart Show*, commercial radio's answer to the BBC's Top 40. 'For some reason Kenny had catalogued every show. I was so taken aback and flattered. He was definitely a hoarder, but paradoxically he couldn't stand mess or clutter. I think he only kept things which were truly important to him, but he kept all of them!'

Something else Kenny considered important enough to archive was the cult Saturday-morning kids' TV show, *Tiswas*. The antithesis of Noel Edmonds' *Multi-Coloured Swap Shop*, *Tiswas* dished out custard pies and anarchy-for-kids from 1974 to 1981. Kenny revelled in the chaotic spontaneity of it all. It was exactly how many had described his own work over the years, and so in 1976, when he was asked if he'd like to appear as a guest, he agreed immediately. 'It was right up Ev's street,' explains Jo Gurnett. 'Chris Tarrant was one of the presenters and personally asked him to go on. I think Kenny was quite flattered.'

Tarrant lived in Stratford-upon-Avon when Kenny and Lee lived not too far away in the Cotswolds, and they met up the night before the show was due to go out. 'That was about as much planning as we ever did on *Tiswas*,' says Tarrant. 'Kenny and I met in a Greek restaurant in Stratford. It was basically the two of us sitting there with our then wives crying with laughter, much to the bewilderment of the staff, who kept saying things like, "We really do need to close up now, sir." It was about one a.m. when we left the restaurant and we were doing the show that morning. I can't remember exactly what he did, but he joined in on a few silly sketches.'

Kenny and Chris Tarrant became quite pally during this period, with Chris occasionally visiting Kenny's home where they'd drink coke and brandy, one of Ev's favourite drinks. 'And then after a bit Ken would go, "Darling, I've got to go and do the show." And he would just disappear. And the thing I loved about it was he'd go into his studio and emerge two hours later with this great big lump of tape, which he would put in a padded envelope and take to the postbox at the end of the road in Cherington and send to Capital Radio, and that would be the show. He would literally say, "There it goes, darling, on its way to London, God speed." Then we'd go back and have more brandy; it was quite bizarre.'

Sometimes Tarrant would pop his head round the door and watch the man at work; quite a spectacle and totally unique. 'He was mad, and he was the only person who understood it. There didn't seem to be any hint of a filing system, so he'd go, "Oh, that's Captain Kremmen, that's the intro and that's the music for the bit at the end." You'd just look at this blank wall of tape and Kenny would be the only person who understood what the hell he was doing. So if anybody moved anything, it would be chaos.'

Like many in Everett's orbit around this time, Tarrant knew that he was abusing drugs. 'But he was never unpleasant, he was just odd. And sometimes he'd go very quiet. He wasn't always a barrel of laughs. He was very rarely grumpy, though, but he could sometimes go very quiet.'

One bizarre conversation Tarrant remembers having with Kenny occurred some time in the seventies and is today horribly relevant, and that was an admission that he loathed Jimmy Savile. Coming from Kenny, who Tarrant had never heard being unkind about any-body, it was something of a revelation. 'But he really genuinely disliked Savile. Now, the trouble was with Ken you could never take him seriously, you didn't know if he was pulling your leg or not. Anyway, this one time he said to me, "You know why Savile hangs around Leeds Infirmary at night?" I said, "No, Kenny, why does he do that?" And Kenny said, "Dead bodies." I went, "Oh come on, don't be so daft. Kenny Everett, you're being even sillier than normal." But actually he meant it. And now you think, my God. I remember Kenny saying this and for once he wasn't being funny.'

Strange thing was, Savile was an early admirer and supporter of Kenny. 'When he first started on Radio 1, Savile recognized Kenny's talent,' reveals Lee. 'He took him out in his car one day and said, "Look, can I give you some advice . . ." and he guided Kenny about what he should do, which direction he should pursue, that kind of thing; Savile gave him masses of fabulous advice.'

Unfortunately Ev's appearance on *Tiswas* was wiped in the eighties, along with many of the other episodes. And, when an appeal was made to retrieve some of them, Tarrant was contacted by two surprising but welcome donors. 'When we tried to put together the first *Best of Tiswas* video, we discovered that some idiot at what later became Central Television had actually wiped about two hundred and seventy of the three hundred or so episodes. I think I had about one at the time. Anyway, we started asking around to see if anyone had copies of any of them, and it turned out that the only two people who did were Tommy Vance and Kenny Everett. They had dozens and dozens! I had no idea they were such huge fans.'

Kenny most certainly was, and in the late seventies even started to 'borrow' the odd idea. 'This was in the days before *Tiswas* was broadcast nationally,' explains Tarrant. 'It could only be seen in the Midlands and a few other areas, but was yet to reach London. Kenny obviously thought, they'll never see it in London, darling, so what does it matter? And so he used to nick bits off *Tiswas* and do them on his show.'

Although it was a bit cheeky, Chris didn't mind Kenny lifting the odd skit; in fact he was quite flattered. Not everybody felt the same though. 'I'd go, "Hang on, did you see what Kenny did on his *Video Show* last night? That came from us last Saturday!" And Lenny Henry used to get very upset about that, but it was kind of amiable. We would never have said, "How dare you, Kenny?" and slapped a writ on him. It was just Kenny being silly. Sometimes he'd take a silly idea that we did and actually take it to a whole new comedy height. He just loved tricks, like walking through walls. We once got hold of a pair of shoes that you could wear and literally fall forwards without actually breaking your nose. He loved that. And there was an upside-down thing we used to do where you reversed the camera, so when you poured a cup of coffee it went straight up into the air. One of the directors showed us how to do that on *Tiswas* and we loved it. About a week later, I saw Kenny Everett do it!'

*

Kenny's departure from Radio 2 in December 1983 had followed the same pattern as his departure from Radio 1 thirteen years previously, in that the public had been misled on both occasions as to what actually occurred. At Radio 1 he had been sacked, but for a different reason to what was initially, and often still is, reported by the press. At Radio 2, they got it wrong completely. According to the press, Kenny was sacked again, this time for making a joke about Margaret Thatcher. In actual fact, by the time Kenny had told the gag in question he had already decided he wasn't going to return after his forthcoming break. That's not to say he wouldn't have been sacked if he hadn't, as the gag in question would probably have caused consternation at 11 p.m. on Channel 4, let alone 1 p.m. on Radio 2, the station with the Queen Anne legs.

For those not familiar with the joke Kenny told, here it is: 'When England was a kingdom, we had a king. When we were an empire, we had an emperor. Now we're a country, we've got Margaret Thatcher.'

Geoff Mullin remembers it all vividly: 'We used to have a copy of one of Nigel Rees's famous Graffiti books in the studio. It was full of humorous stuff so if we saw something we found funny, we'd use it. Right at the end of his show I handed him the book. I'd marked a particular gag I thought he should read out, but he saw the Thatcher one, thought it was funnier so read that out instead. His microphone's live and he starts reading it out, and I remember thinking NO! You can't do that one. By then of course it was too late, and it was right at the end of the show. The moment he said the last word we went straight to the news and that was that. That was his second or third to last show, which is possibly why people thought he was sacked, but we already knew then that he wasn't coming back.'

27

Cupid Stunt

DURING THE EARLY months of Kenny's reign at Radio 2, over at Television Centre he was putting the finishing touches to his assault on BBC1. Both Barry Cryer and Ray Cameron had defected with Kenny from Thames and were complemented by top-class creative talent: producer Jim Moir, who'd worked with Mike Yarwood and produced *The Generation Game*, and director Bill Wilson, who'd previously worked for Moir on the first two series of *Not the Nine O'Clock News*. Within days they'd all bonded as a team. 'I recall a sequence in the first programme where Kenny was kidnapped,' says Moir. 'He was bundled into a car, supposedly from Thames, and brought to the BBC. It was a marvellous way to kick things off. Very creative.' Indeed Moir recalls that first episode was considered a huge success. 'It all got off to a cracking start and was well noticed within the BBC. It was a distinguished piece of work.'

Wilson hadn't seen much of the Thames material, since he didn't want to be too influenced by what David Mallet had done. After all, the BBC was a very different place to work in. 'Even if we'd wanted to replicate what they'd done there, we couldn't. The way they did things at Thames suited Everett though. He was very much an "instant" person. At the BBC he'd come in, sit and talk with Ray and Barry, then I'd come down with the script and we'd chat about the direction and we'd go from there. It certainly wasn't instant, but I think he was happy.'

Mallet isn't too sure and it's his belief that when Kenny moved to the BBC the show lost a vital edge, it wasn't a renegade show any more, it became establishment. Mallet remembers Kenny telling him a story about the first day he arrived at Television Centre. 'He was a bit nervous and this BBC executive came thumping down the steps from the control room saying, "We just want to tell you how very pleased we are to have you in the corporation." And Kenny said to me, "From that moment on I knew I was fucked."'

The show's format was much the same as before, with musical guests and comedy sketches featuring some of Kenny's old Thames characters like Sid Snot and Marcel Wave. Over time new characters developed, such as Reg Prescott, the hapless DIY expert forever chopping off limbs, and General Norm Bombthebastards, with guns sticking out of his enormous shoulder pads, who'd holler his catchphrase, 'I'm gonna line 'em up, put 'em in a field and BOMB THE BASTARDS!' However, one character was to eclipse them all and become arguably Kenny's most popular creation – Cupid Stunt, the bearded actress with breasts the size of Belgium.

Then there was her famous catchphrase. Cryer was watching television one night and saw some young actors plugging a new horror movie. They were talking about a scene where somebody gets murdered with an axe and one of them said, quite seriously, 'It's all done in the best possible taste.' 'I told Ray and Ev this and they laughed a lot so we stored it for later. And then, typical Ev, we were working on this character Cupid Stunt and he suddenly started laughing. We just looked at him and he came out with it, in character, "It's all done in the best pAAASIBLE taste," and that was it. Brilliant. And he immediately had an idea of what she'd look like. It was his idea to keep the beard, too.' And the famous exaggerated crossing of the legs? 'Ev told me that he got that from Old Mother Riley,' recalls Cryer. 'Arthur Lucan, who played Old Mother Riley, used to do almost exactly the same thing. His was slightly less exaggerated though. Ev took it to the next level. Knickers and all!'

Cupid was a great comic invention and to a large extent epitomized Kenny's working method on his TV shows – that there wasn't one. Essentially, he worked on pure comic instinct. 'I'm absolutely certain that it was entirely and utterly natural to him,' says Moir. 'I don't think it was a strain for him at all. He just intuitively and instinctively knew which voice and which actions were going to make a character work.'

Looking back, it is amazing how they got away with the name, though, considering this was a show going out at primetime and a large percentage of its audience would be families. 'I do remember there was a lot of hoo-ha about the name,' recalls Kevin Bishop, the assistant floor manager on that first BBC series. 'The hierarchy were very nervous, but I'm astonished that in the end they just said OK. I was really quite surprised because, knowing the BBC as I do, I thought they'd say, "You can't do that!" Kenny loved playing that character, as you can imagine.'

Right from the outset Cupid Stunt caught on with the public in a major way. When Kenny went on the *Parkinson* chat show, he planned to come on as Cupid, in full drag, and then get changed and come back on as himself. The team were standing backstage and Parky saw Barry Cryer and came over. 'Baz, I want to introduce Kenny properly. What's Cupid's surname?' Cryer looked at him and said, 'Stunt.' Parky's face fell away. 'Thank you very bloody much. I'd better go off and rehearse.'

There was another new addition to the cast, not a character this time, although she was as equally larger than life, but a real person who made just as much of an impact on viewers. The call had gone out for someone sultry to play a dominatrix type in a sketch, and the usual casting-agency girls duly turned up for the audition. 'I went down to the room where they'd gathered and almost killed myself auditioning them all,' recalls Moir. 'My recollection is coming away thinking, Well they're all very talented and attractive, but I haven't seen The One, if you know what I mean.'

One particular girl had failed to turn up for the audition but Moir agreed to see her in his seventh-floor office. When she walked in Moir recalls that everyone in that room nearly passed out. The girl in question was Cleo Rocos, of course. 'I think she was wearing a fur coat, but she was such an image. Breathtaking! There was no contest. None of the other girls could compete with the image that Cleo gave out, as a kind of urbane, sophisticated international beauty. Which, of course, she actually was. She most certainly didn't have to act. She also had gorgeous naivety about her. You couldn't take your eyes off her and she had all the charm of somebody who'd be perfectly happy chatting with the ambassador at the embassy. She had that kind of class.'

Born in Brazil, but of Greek and English descent, Cleo was to form an incredibly close bond with Kenny. Cate even refers to them as having been, 'Real soulmates. They had tremendous fun together. They were always doing Spanish dancing and going off to some night-club to dance the night away to the Gypsy Kings. I went with them once and ended up doing the floor show, the three of us doing Spanish dancing and the whole audience just gawping.'

Even before the series was transmitted it had a dilemma to deal with. While they were planning the first show, due for broadcast on Christmas Eve 1981, Moir was called down to see Alistair Milne, the Director-General, and told he wouldn't be working with Kenny Everett any more because he was about to be made head of Variety. Returning to the studio floor Moir was sworn to secrecy but the dis-appointment he was feeling showed only too blatantly on his face. 'I felt very frustrated at being promoted away from it, to tell the truth, because I'd enjoyed working on the show. If you go to any dictionary and look up the word genius, you should find a picture of Everett cre-ating one of his characters. His genius of bringing all of them to life was astonishing. I thought very, very highly of him. He wasn't a diva in any way. He was straightforward – let's just get it done. He could see the obvious enjoyment people working with him had from helping realize the material. The crew absolutely loved it and were always having to bite their lips so as not to laugh. I recall it as being a hard-working time, but it was a very happy time because everyone was confident in one another.'

Beginning its run in earnest in April 1982, *The Kenny Everett Television Show* went from strength to strength as the BBC backed their latest acquisition. For example, in one sketch Kenny was given a tank to drive over a row of parked cars. In another, Kenny plays a husband returning home to see his wife in bed with a strange man hiding in the wardrobe. 'What are you doing here?' asks Kenny, rather innocently. 'Waiting for a bus,' the man replies and with that a double-decker bus comes crashing through the bedroom wall.

One of the main differences between the BBC shows and those on Thames was the corporation's insistence they be recorded in front of a live studio audience. At Thames it was just the crew you could hear laughing in the background, 'but when we went to the BBC they tried to turn Ev into a BBC comedian,' recalls Cryer. 'Rehearse all week, audience comes in, do the show, always on a Friday. And when it got to Friday we'd be there and Ev would say, "Oooh, I can hear them coming." But eventually he became brilliant with a studio audience, and they loved him.'

According to Kevin Bishop, Kenny would always welcome the audience to the show and even engage in conversation with them during the two hours or so it took to record an episode. It was a world away from the timid creature petrified in his dressing room during his nightclub DJ days, dreading having to come out and face his public. 'I think that was very important, to keep the audience on side, as it were. I'm not sure everybody does it. The Two Ronnies were very good at keeping the audience "alive" during all the breaks in between sketches and costume changes, and Kenny was the same, he'd have a bit of banter with the audience.'

Considering that Kenny would cower in front of ten people, let alone five hundred, it was a very brave thing to do. He just decided to face his demons. He was also very well protected by Barry and Ray, who saw their role on the show as not solely writers but to look out for Kenny. Ev knew this and as a consequence felt secure and safe in that environment. 'Ray and Barry were brilliant and really supportive of Kenny,' recalls Kevin Bishop. 'And they spent all the time they were in the studio huddled in a corner writing, so they were always firing off each other. They were always being creative.'

Even when the show was being recorded, Barry and Ray were still in conference, coming up with new gags and ideas they'd pass on to Kenny and he'd try them out on the next take. 'And what was good about Kenny was he could pick things up really quickly,' says Bishop.

'If you threw him an idea he could make up dialogue from that idea, he didn't need anything written down. That was unusual for the BBC, where things are much more planned. Take *The Two Ronnies*, which I also worked on: that was very carefully scripted, hardly any improvisation. So this was exciting and new for us, because it was so different, especially within the BBC where there was very much a correct way of doing things. Then suddenly this show came along that was off the wall, so to be working on it was really exciting.'

Kenny, Ray and Barry had also fallen into a regular routine of heading straight to a Chinese restaurant on the Goldhawk Road the moment they finished recording the show. 'It was a nice little restaurant,' recalls Barry. 'And I remember that Ev was enchanted by the sign on the Gents' door which had a stick man on it with a top hat and cane. Anyway, one night after the show the three of us piled into the restaurant and Ev had a carrier bag with him. About halfway through the meal he stood up and said, "Ooooh, Baah, I must go for a pee!" He then took out a top hat from this carrier bag, put it on, pulled out a cane and danced down the restaurant to the Gents – just for us and him. Wonderful!'

28

Nikolai

THAT FIRST BBC series had got off to a roaring start and Kenny was now operating at perhaps the peak of his fame, but he still closely guarded his homosexuality. Everyone who knew or worked with him was fully aware he was gay and didn't care a hoot, but Kenny had still not publicly come out; he was too afraid of the consequences, that it might damage his image and repel his fans. 'This adoration that he got from the fans and listeners, I think he felt that was the kind of love that he'd never really had before,' believes Nicky Horne. 'I think he felt that if he were to come out, somehow the listeners would desert him and think badly of him, think that he was a lesser person. That's a lot to do with his religious upbringing, and how the Catholic religion looked on gay people.'

Ironically, he'd already come out to his parents, in a bizarre episode on Christmas Eve 1981. Lily and Tom were staying with Cate in Wimbledon and one evening before Christmas she'd thrown a house party. Kenny arrived with John Pitt, Lee and John Alkin in tow. Strange as it may seem, they'd often all go out together as a foursome. On a couple of occasions Billy Fury would join them. 'We all went to this club once,' remembers Lee. 'And this queen in a corner said, "Does she go everywhere with her old husbands?" And I said, "Shut up, you're only jealous."'

After a couple of glasses of wine Kenny began extolling the virtues of John Pitt: 'His eyes are limpid pools of love. They are Gina Lollobrigida eyes.' He then nudged Pitt closer to Lily and said, 'Hasn't he got beautiful eyes, Mother?' Still, she didn't twig, or perhaps thought it best to keep her own counsel.

She was left in no doubt whatsoever come Christmas Eve when just Kenny and John Pitt arrived at the house. 'Where's Lee?' asked Lily. As blunt as you like, Kenny replied, 'Lee's not here. This is my new wife.' If Kenny had designed this remark to be shock therapy for his poor innocent mother, then it worked spectacularly. Cate, of course, had known for years, but Lily was duly knocked back by the revelation. 'My poor mother didn't know what to think or say,' says Cate. 'We had never told her. She looked a bit upset and rather confused. She turned to my father and said, "What do you think, Tom?" After thinking about it for some time, he said in his slow voice, and reflecting continually as he spoke with plenty of pauses, "Well . . . I suppose . . . if it makes him happy . . . why not?"'

That night Mrs Cole could barely eat or sleep. In the morning things were no better, but nothing was said, it was Christmas Day and also Kenny's birthday, but the atmosphere remained somewhat strained.

Convinced that his career would be in jeopardy if he publicly came out, Kenny continued to fiercely guard his homosexuality. Mike Quinn, his old DJ friend from the sixties, remembers catching up with Kenny one night around 1983 at the opening night of the Hippodrome in London's West End. Peter Stringfellow had transformed the old Talk of the Town venue into a nightclub and restaurant. Quinn went along with Terry Doran, John Lennon's former personal assistant. 'He was a real character, Terry,' says Quinn. 'Very camp, very gay – openly gay. Didn't really give a shit, Terry, but a helluva nice guy.' As gala openings tend to be, the place was packed with rock stars and assorted celebrities. 'I'm not kidding you,' recalls Quinn. 'Everyone in that place was a star, a face. The moment we walked in I saw Eric Clapton and Roger Waters standing together in reception and Terry went up to them, "Hello, darlings." He knew everyone, Terry.'

Later in the evening Quinn noticed Kenny walking across the foyer. The pair of them had lost touch over the years and Quinn was delighted to see him again. 'I went, "Hi, Kenny!" but before I could do anything Terry put his arms round Kenny and kissed him. Kenny went mad, he said, "Don't do that!" And he wasn't kidding, he got very angry with Terry. I'd not seen Kenny like that before. I thought he was going to hit Terry, he was that angry. It was because there were a lot of stars around him, everybody on show. Kenny was furious.'

It was a strange reaction, considering that by the early eighties Kenny had begun to embrace the burgeoning gay club scene in London. Paul Gambaccini recalls that Kenny would often call him up and say, Oh, I really love this club, you've got to go to it. I'll meet you there at such and such a time. Unbeknown to Gambaccini, these were the hardest, most full-on gay bars in London. And you've guessed it, Kenny would never show up. 'I remember he did this to me with a place called Subway in Leicester Square, a place called the London Apprentice in Hoxton and the Coleherne pub in Earls Court. He would say, I'll see you there at a certain time, and he just wouldn't show up, leaving me to cope on my own in a world not of my own making. And I remember thinking, particularly at the Coleherne, I really don't want to be here. But somehow, even though Kenny would strand me in these places, I always forgave him.' Little did Gambaccini realize, but he was standing in what turned out to be one of the thriving hubs of the London AIDS epidemic.

Around this time Kenny read a book that was to have the most profound effect on him. First published in 1976, *Your Erroneous Zones* by American psychologist Dr Wayne Dyer was a self-help book for those plagued by guilt or worry who found themselves unwittingly falling into the same old self-destructive patterns. These, according to Dyer, were 'erroneous zones' – infuriating little quirks of personality that were barriers to a fuller, richer life, and people could learn to overcome and eliminate them, with the help of the book, of course. Only too aware of her brother's guilt complex about his homosexuality, Cate had given Kenny the book as a present and he'd devoured it. It's something she's always looked back on with mixed feelings, because while it did help Kenny purge the guilt-trip he'd been on for most of his adult life, it was also the cause, in Cate's words, 'of him going off the rails a bit'. And the man he went off the rails with more than anyone else was Nikolai Grishanovich.

Kenny met Nikolai, a former Red Army soldier, in a nightclub. The attraction, for Kenny at least, was instantaneous. 'He was a big, butch Russian,' recalls Jo Gurnett. 'Moustache, muscles. That was what did it for Ev. He never went for little effeminate men. That was him to some extent. He was quite delicate. He was the wife, if you see what I mean – and I suppose Nikolai became the husband. He was always attracted to these strong types, which is probably why he sometimes made a pass at somebody who was straight.'

There were all kinds of stories floating around about Nikolai and nobody ever knew if they were true or not, which contributed to the air of exoticism that surrounded him. He bragged that back in Cold War Russia he'd traded currency on the black market and when the police were closing in made an arrangement with a female English tourist to get married. That was Nikolai's ticket to London where, because of his IT skills, he found work as a computer programmer. 'He was a very competent computer analyst,' remembers Geoff Mullin. 'And, like Kenny, was very up to date with new technology.' So good in fact, that when he left his IT firm he managed to hack into their payroll system and carried on receiving his wages for almost two years. When the company twigged what was happening they were too embarrassed by their hopeless security to take any action.

Nikolai was undeniably a charmer, with an abundance of charisma. Cate liked him, thought he was great company, as many of Ev's friends did; he was easy to get on with and his love of life was contagious. 'You couldn't dislike Nikolai. He was very boyish, very charming. He was a lovable, roguish child. And you could take Nikolai anywhere, he was very sophisticated, he knew how to behave. And he used to bring big tins of caviar wherever he went, from some Russian connection, so he was very popular. I remember when my mother was around, whenever we were out together, he always behaved impeccably.'

But for others who were close to Kenny alarm bells sounded almost immediately. Jo Gurnett was not impressed. 'I found him very arrogant. It was Nikolai who wanted to go to all the showbiz parties, not Ev. He hated them. Nikolai wanted all the glitz and the glamour. Ev rang me one day and said Nikolai wanted to go to the Savoy Grill.

I said, OK then, we'll go there. But Nikolai always used to order by price, if you know what I mean. Not by what he actually wanted to eat or drink. He just picked whatever cost the most. Ev always excused him on the grounds that he'd come from a poor background.'

As for Lee, she took an immediate dislike to Nikolai. Actually, that's far too polite: it was an instant loathing. Lee wanted nothing more than for Kenny to acknowledge his homosexuality and settle down contentedly with a partner, as many of her gay friends had done. His relationship with John Pitt had been rather too twee; while it lasted it was a nice little relationship, but Pitt wasn't the most stimulating of company. 'I think he bored Ev to death,' admits Lee. But with Nikolai, Kenny had gone to the other extreme. At play here was a strange dichotomy that his friend Eric Gear understood: 'Ideally, Kenny wanted the carpet-slippers life with someone who doted on him, but when he got it, he got bored. Then when he got the high life, he wanted domesticity.'

So Nikolai was bad news as far as both Jo and Lee were concerned. Especially Lee, who still firmly believes that Nikolai was the cause of Everett's untimely death. She warned him of it too, telling Ev to his face that he was literally playing Russian roulette with Nikolai. And the reason was simple: he was a sex maniac. 'He would go after any-thing that moved,' reveals Eric Gear. 'But in a most childlike way. He had a naivety about him that was completely appealing. He never wilfully hurt anybody. But he would trample over people's feelings. He would enrage Ken because he would go off with somebody else and see nothing wrong in what he was doing.'

Kenny was also infuriated by Nikolai's bisexuality, and an un-palatable habit of making passes at his friends. 'Kenny knew I was straight and never once suggested anything,' says Geoff Mullin. 'Nikolai did though. He'd have been happy to have a threesome. Kenny was no angel, but Nikolai was just the limit. I do hate to think of the amount of people he might have infected.'

There was another man in the background: Pepe Flores, a Spanish university graduate and sculptor working as a waiter in a London restaurant. It wasn't long before Pepe moved into Kenny's flat with

Nikolai. This wasn't a ménage à trois, as the press later luridly portrayed it to be, not helped by Kenny teasingly calling the pair of them his husbands. 'The way I heard it, Pepe didn't have anywhere to live, so Ev let him stay in the apartment,' says Cate. 'I think he outstayed his welcome though, and Ev had to force him out in the end. But I don't believe that they had an ongoing ménage à trois. In fact I know they didn't, even though they might have had dalliances. I remember speaking to Pepe before he died and the press was full of it at the time, and I said, "Is it true, Pepe?" He looked at me and he said, "Honestly I can tell you, it's not true."'

For many, what was going on with that whole relationship with Nikolai and Pepe had the appearance of something rather seedy and sordid. Others, however, saw things rather differently. Annie O'Neill was Kenny's producer at Capital Radio when he returned for a second stint in 1984. 'A lot of people have pointed the finger at Nikolai, but I take as I find and they were always charming and great company. There was certainly a real arrogance about Nikolai though. He was definitely a man who got what he wanted. But for all that I think he always treated Kenny with respect and he certainly loved him very much.'

After his Capital show Kenny always took Annie out to an Indian restaurant across the road from Euston Tower. It was on one of these evenings that she was introduced to Nikolai and Pepe. 'Kenny was so generous. He would never ever let me pay for a thing. Never! But he was also extremely generous of spirit. He also used to invite me to all these Mirrorball parties at the gay clubs. I used to absolutely love it. I could dance my backside off and never had to worry about being chatted up or bothered. They were some of the best nights of my life.'

Kenny and Nikolai also made a habit of going on clubbing weekends round the world – Sydney, New York, San Francisco, anywhere there was a thriving gay club scene, they'd be off, first class all the way and spending an absolute fortune. Geoff Mullin recalls receiving a card from Kenny from San Francisco. 'It features a guy lying on a beach on his back. He's got sunglasses and trousers on, but sticking out of his trousers is an erect penis. On the inside of the card it reads:

"It's so hard without you." It's signed with love from Edith and Boris and he's drawn a picture of a Russian flag and the Union Jack.'

Chris Peers, the man who helped Kenny land his big break on radio at Big L, recalls that the last time he ever saw him was on one of those mad trips. Peers had watched Kenny's ascent to stardom but hadn't seen him since the mid-sixties. In the early eighties he was working for an international television company and making regular trips to the Soviet Union. 'Getting on the plane to Moscow one Sunday morning, I looked at the bloke next to me. It was Kenny. "Jesus Christ," he said. "Good God, it's you!" I said. "What are you up to?" And we had a lovely chat. He had at that time the Russian boyfriend, Nikolai. As I recall, they were going off to a party with all the guardsmen in Red Square.'

Setting this in the context of the time, things had changed within society, the public's perception of being gay had changed, people could now be openly gay and proud of it. This was all mixed up with the hedonism of the new drugs that were coming in, and so the club scene and the gay scene merged into one, and for a brief period there was this huge explosion of total hedonism.

It wasn't only Nikolai who exposed Kenny to this new world. According to John Alkin, Freddie Mercury was something of a mentor to Ev, the person who said, you need to go to this club or that club, come with me, I'll show you. He was also instrumental in introducing Kenny to the hardcore New York gay scene. 'Ev totally looked up to Freddie,' says John, 'because he was a great artist and he'd always liked him. So when Kenny took the next step into being outrageously camp, then Freddie held his hand and took him off to where that scene was happening. Freddie was his finishing school, really. He was the gentleman of rock, Freddie, he was a lovely guy. He'd such great taste, too, his house was full of the most incredible art, and Everett lapped it up.'

Sadly their friendship soured towards the end, and over the most trivial of matters. 'It was all to do with drugs,' reveals Lee. 'Ev had a load of stuff and he hadn't contributed, it was something really stupid like that. But it was a very nasty falling out. Freddie told me that he wouldn't cross the road and pee on Ev if he was on fire.'

According to Eric Gear, however, the pair of them did get back in touch a few days before Freddie's death from AIDS in 1991. 'What isn't known is that Kenny went round to Freddie's just before he died and they made their peace. Kenny told me not long before he died.'

It was 1983 when Paul Gambaccini first stumbled upon what people were calling 'the new disease'. He was in New York walking down Eighth Avenue with his best friend from college when some people came over. 'They started chatting to my friend and then in parting they mentioned, "I guess we'll see you on Wednesday." My friend said, "Wednesday?" They said, "Mr X's funeral." And he went, "What!" They said, "The new disease." When they left my friend said to me, "Will you excuse me for a moment." And he retreated to a side street to sit on a porch and weep, because this Mr X had been the person he'd loved most in the seventies. And I thought at the time that he was crying for Mr X, but I now realize he was probably crying for himself, because that was probably the moment when he realized he might die, which in fact he did – my darling friend David.'

David Carroll was a well loved and respected television and stage actor, earning two Tony nominations for his last performances on Broadway, in *Chess* and *Grand Hotel*. 'I was pretty traumatized, to say the least, by this moment,' says Gambaccini. 'I came back to England and said to a couple of my gay friends, "Are you altering your behaviour in face of the new disease?" Freddie was one of them. He outstretched his arms and said, "Darling, my attitude is, fuck it. I'm doing everything with everybody." And I literally had that sinking feeling – and there is a sinking feeling. I just thought, Oh my God, we're going to lose Freddie. But Kenny I encountered at a show-business event, and when I mentioned it to him he said, "I think I'm pretty safe because recently I've been into bondage." Which was safe sex – whatever else it may be, it was safe sex.'

As usual with Kenny, the weird and the wacky was never far away. Gambaccini remembers Kenny telling him he had some American guy come over to his flat to tie him up one night. Nikolai had gone out to a party and left the phone number of the house he was at.

'Unfortunately the guy who tied Kenny up also went out, leaving Kenny indisposed,' relates Gambaccini. 'And so he thought, I've got to call Nikolai at this party to come home and untie me. And Nikolai says, "I'm not going to come back, I'm having fun, wait till I get home."'

The next person Kenny called was Jo Gurnett, who was at home relaxing with her husband. Over the years she'd come to expect the unexpected when it came to Kenny, but what she was hearing down the phone this time would take some beating. Ev explained the situation and after a few seconds for it all to sink in, Jo asked, 'If you're tied up, how are you able to call me?'

'With my nose,' he replied. 'I've got one of those push-button phones.'

Jo offered to come over and help but in the end Kenny said he thought he'd be OK. 'He sailed quite close to the wind sometimes,' says Jo. 'He really did!'

The story ends with Kenny rolling down the stairs into the street, where he asked an incredulous passer-by to untie him. 'And the moral of the story is,' said Kenny as he finished the tale to Gambaccini, who sat there waiting for some kind of life lesson, 'always use a push-button phone.'

29

Traipsing and Tapestry

THE OXFORD ENGLISH Dictionary's definition of the word hobby is: 'An activity done regularly in one's leisure time for pleasure.' Outside the studio Kenny had few. In fact before the mid-seventies he didn't have any at all, save for nightclubbing and cleaning.

Kenny's hobbies in the true sense of the word are both, on the face of it, quite surprising. But on reflection it doesn't take long to appreciate their appeal. The first was weaving tapestries. This was something Kenny had practised since marrying Lee, who still weaves to this day. Kenny found the whole process of weaving cathartic and rewarding. It bore many similarities to the process of making a jingle. For a start it was creative. You began with a blank tape, or in this case a tapestry canvas, and you finish with something which is unique to yourself. That was certainly part of the attraction to Kenny. If he was creating, he was happy. Secondly there was technique. Weaving a tapestry can be an extraordinarily fiddly affair, as can making a jingle. Everything must be precise and you need reasonable technique if you're going to do it well.

But what really attracted Kenny to the art of tapestry weaving was good old peace and quiet. It offered him an escape from real life. Whether it was depression, insomnia or just stresses of work, tapestry took him away from all that and allowed him to concentrate on something positive and calming. It was one of the few times when he was good to himself – when he did something completely for him, and which didn't involve other people or any harmful substances!

The vast majority of Kenny's tapestries were given away to friends and family members. There are around twenty 'Everetts' adorning kitchen and living-room walls around the world. He'd give them as gifts on special occasions. His good friend and former producer at Capital, David Briggs, was one such recipient. 'When my son was born, completely out of the blue, he made us a tapestry with my son's name on it over a big heart. I don't know why he did it but we were so grateful. It was such a beautiful thing to do.'

Kenny wasn't an expert weaver by any stretch of the imagination. But that was part of the appeal. Being the best wasn't his motive. His motive was to relax, enjoy himself and create something he could give away, forget about and then start again. He adopted a similar philosophy when it came to broadcasting, of course. He just happened to be slightly better at it.

Kenny's second and most beloved hobby was hill walking. Try to imagine Kenny Everett traipsing over hill and dale, complete with a backpack, walking stick and binoculars. Not easy, is it? But as with the tapestries, it doesn't take long to appreciate the attraction.

Since 1965 Kenny had spent the vast majority of his waking hours locked inside a small, soundproofed room, and usually with no natural light. Unlike the majority of DJs, who would finish their show and then be on their way, Kenny would be back in the studio, preparing for the following day or making jingles and voice-overs. Paul Gambaccini sums this up perfectly: 'Most of us just tolerated the studio. After all, we had to work in some sort of environment. Kenny used the studio as an instrument in his product.'

Being cooped up for so long can't be good for you though, regardless what you're doing. This was one of the few negatives of life in the studio, but one which Kenny became happy to put right, thus beginning a hobby which would provide him with many weeks of enjoyment during the latter part of his adult life.

Kenny first got the bug for walking in the mid-seventies, when he was invited to go hiking by Lee's sister's husband, Ken. Kenny had always admired the countryside, of course. He and Lee had enjoyed many a trundle when they'd lived on their farms and in the Cotswolds, but his constant pull back to the studio and to the bright lights of London meant that he was always quick to forget it all.

Kenny's first dedicated hike was like an epiphany, and he came home brimming with enthusiasm about the sights he'd seen. Kenny was a man who lived for 'highlights'. This came across throughout his life, both in the way he behaved and in the things he enjoyed and indulged in. As we know, he rarely read books. 'I think I've read two books in my entire life,' he once said. '*The Wind in the Willows*, and *How to Escape a Russian Concentration Camp* by Vladimir Impossible. I lose interest very quickly. Why can't they just publish the good bits?' And the music he listened to was melodic and usually quite anthemic. 'Sod the verses, let's go straight to the chorus!' His intake of alcohol and recreational drugs showed similar trends. Kenny wouldn't limit himself to one line of cocaine or one brandy and coke, he'd have to have four or five. He was always drawn to things that had a genuine 'effect' on the way he felt or the way he thought. He could become bored in seconds and needed to be stimulated. Pretty much like a toddler!

It had been the same when Simon Booker was attempting to gather information for Kenny's autobiography. 'He wouldn't stop whingeing,' says Simon. 'He kept saying, "It's all in the past. I know what happens and I'm not interested. This is boring. I'm bored, Simon, I'm bored!"'

Kenny never cared for the past. To him it represented a straight line; something which held no mystery or fascination – and Kenny didn't do straight lines. Only corners were worth looking at, and he wanted to see around as many as was humanly possible.

What changed for Kenny with regards to the countryside was simple. 'It had always been there,' he later said. 'I'd just never really looked before.' On his first hike there had been no distractions. Everywhere he looked he saw something beautiful and unique, which was perfect for somebody who had the attention span and the boredom threshold of a three-year-old. It was very much a 'rural awakening'.

Kenny continued walking until his brother-in-law sadly passed away in the early eighties. As he didn't know any other walkers, his boots and stick were stored away in the boot of his car, where they would remain untouched, but not for long.

If Kenny Everett taking up walking came as a surprise, we can probably match that by divulging who his next companion would be. Eric Gear was the manager of the Bond Street branch of the Royal Bank of Scotland. As the branch was situated in one of the most affluent areas in the country, its clientele could be quite 'starry'. So much so that the staff there wouldn't blink at seeing the likes of Audrey Hepburn breeze through the doors.

Despite being used to dealing with celebrities, Eric was still rather taken by surprise one Friday afternoon when into his office walked Kenny. 'He came in to see me with a couple of financial people he knew. He wanted a mortgage, and although I was a bank manager I couldn't actually lend money over a twenty-five-year period, as I would have been retired when it finished. I used to lend money over one year mainly.'

In order to be able to lend money over twenty-five years, Eric would have to write to his head office, and he explained this to Kenny and his financial cohorts. 'I said I'd write the letter today and he'd probably hear back next week. Well, one of these advisers got a bit stroppy and said he wanted to know now. I think he was probably trying to impress Kenny. I explained carefully why I couldn't do that, but he was insistent. So in the end I said, "OK, the answer's no. Now off you go, you're wasting my time."'

Kenny, who'd barely said a word until then, piped up: 'Look, if we waited until next week, what do you think the answer would be?' Eric explained that the answer would probably be yes, but if he really didn't want to wait then they should say goodbye now. At this point Kenny told both his advisers to leave and he and Eric began chatting. 'After a while Kenny uttered those magic words, "Do you ever go for a drink at lunchtime?" and that's how it all started. We didn't go for a big lash up, but we had a nice glass of wine and started to get to know each other. I obviously knew of him, and I was quite a big fan, but I found him somewhat shy to start off with.'

At the end of the drink Kenny suggested to Eric that they have lunch the following week. 'I said I was sorry but I couldn't, as I was going on a walking holiday.' The moment Eric said the words 'walking holiday', Kenny's eyes lit up! 'He seemed to get quite excited by that,' remembers Eric. 'He then started telling me this story about how he used to go walking with his late brother-in-law. I was sure he was spinning me a line.' Kenny, sensing Eric's doubt, said, 'You don't believe me, do you?' Eric claimed he did but Kenny wasn't having it. 'He then took me outside to his car,' says Eric, 'opened the boot, and there were his walking boots and walking stick! It turns out he did used to go walking with his brother-in-law. I thought he'd just killed him off in order to get an invitation! He then looked at me and said, "I've got nobody to go with any more." He joined us on our next trip.'

Between 1980 and 1994, Kenny, Eric and Eric's wife Jane went walking two or three times every year, and were usually joined by Eric's brother and his wife, Betty. The five became an unlikely but extremely happy band, and Kenny developed a close friendship with all four. 'He was always happiest in a small group,' says Eric. 'With strangers he became shy and embarrassed very quickly. He didn't like the world coming to him, if you see what I mean.'

To Kenny this was more than just walking with friends and taking in the view. It was escapism in its purest form. He'd found four new friends, all of whom enjoyed walking, and they couldn't care less that he was gay or famous. They were, in Eric's own words, 'Normal suburban folk who were more interested in Maurice Cole than Kenny Everett.' Things couldn't have been less starry. He hadn't felt this unfettered since he started going to Heaven, but even there he was still 'Kenny Everett' and had to be vigilant. For perhaps the first time in his life he could relax completely. 'I think he felt very comfortable at our place, which was nice,' says Eric. 'Whenever he arrived he'd just walk straight into the kitchen and make himself a cup of Oxo. We didn't fuss and there was no ceremony. He just made himself at home.'

The Gears were probably the only people Kenny knew whose sole connection to him was friendship rather than work. This in turn allowed him to become Maurice Cole again, something he quite obviously enjoyed. The Gears were also among the first to receive an Everett tapestry. 'My wife and I have got one which he made especially for us. We were once having a chat and he said, "You two remind me of a teapot. You're all warm and cosy." At the time I didn't know whether to feel insulted or congratulated. But a few weeks later he presented us with a tapestry of a teapot, with our names underneath. It still hangs on our living-room wall. He also did one for my late brother and his wife. That one was a banana!'

Kenny once claimed that walking with the Gears gave him some of the happiest times he ever had. And after looking through Eric's collection of photographs you can see why. Of the fifty or so we've seen, you'll be hard pushed to find one that doesn't feature Everett laughing or grinning ear to ear. 'The holidays were wonderful,' remembers Eric. 'It wasn't just Kenny who enjoyed them though. We all had an absolute ball. They were the best of times for all of us.' As were the locations, it seems. 'We'd normally go to the Yorkshire or Derbyshire Dales – both stunning parts of the world. I remember one holiday in Derbyshire. Michael Winner had put Kenny on to a place for us to stay. It was somewhere he'd used for his film *The Wicked Lady*, and they didn't usually allow guests. They only took people on recommendation, so Michael Winner recommended us. When we got there the chap who owned the place turned out to be a farmer and a concert pianist, which we all thought quite strange. He was very eccentric but very welcoming.'

The party didn't always enjoy such luxury. But then again they didn't need it. 'It's not about where you stay,' says Eric. 'That place was a one-off. It's about what you see and who you're with. It was usually B&Bs and inns.'

The thing you do most on a walking holiday, if you're not on your own, is chat. And when comfortable, Kenny could chat the hind legs off a donkey. Eric has proof of this. 'I've got some film of him talking to a donkey. If he saw an animal in a field he'd go up and stroke it and start talking to it. He loved animals. We'd have a go at any subject really though, except showbusiness. It's not that we were afraid to mention it. It just never came up.'

Every other subject was covered though, and in order to jolly things up they always stashed a few bottles of wine away in their rucksacks. On the whole Kenny behaved himself, but he did have to be pulled back into line once or twice. 'It was usually all laughs but I had to tell him off occasionally, as did my wife,' remembers Eric. 'My wife is Irish, and one day Kenny was making a lot of Irish jokes, and some of them got a bit near the knuckle. In the end she bit and told him that he really had to straighten himself out and be a bit more diplomatic. Kenny was extremely contrite and it all blew over in a minute or so. He hated upsetting people.'

Being famous meant that there were precious few people willing to tell Kenny when to stop. 'I think it was partly because he was famous and partly because there were some who'd like to see how far he'd actually go,' says Eric. 'But to us he wasn't a star, he was a friend. I once asked him if he considered himself a star, and he said he didn't. He'd love nothing more than coming down to stay with us, and we'd sit in and play cards or we'd go up the pub for a drink. But we always had fun, and he was treated like one of the family. When he came down to see us he was Maurice Cole. Kenny Everett was left in London.'

Eric soon caught on that although Kenny was extraordinarily good at what he did, he could also be very naive, especially when it came to money. People would take advantage, and always expected him to foot the bill for lunches and the like. 'I always insisted otherwise,' says Eric, 'and made sure that we went Dutch. One thing I made clear to him very early on in our relationship was that regardless of how long he was with the bank, he would never affect my salary one iota. If he went to another bank, I wouldn't lose a penny and if he stayed I wouldn't gain a penny.'

This meant that any advice Eric offered Kenny would always be totally impartial. 'I made a point of doing this because, as I said, I could see that his naivety left him open to exploitation, and I wanted to ensure as much as I could that it didn't happen. I also persuaded him to make a will, which, not surprisingly, he hadn't done. I think he appreciated it though, and he told my wife and his sister that he trusted me totally, and that was really good to hear.'

Jo Gurnett, who had to talk money with Kenny on an almost daily basis, makes the point that Kenny's financial naivety was partly born of simply not being interested in the stuff. 'He was one of those people that, if you gave him a contract to sign, he'd say, "What's this for, darling?" and I'd say, "It's for a clip, they're paying a hundred pounds," and he'd say, "Oooh, that's enough for a good dinner." He was always just so grateful, but ultimately he couldn't care less about money. As long as he could get by, he was happy.'

Hill walking truly became one of the great joys of Kenny's life, and he never turned down the chance of a stroll. He even roped in colleagues whenever he could, but these occasions were rarely repeated. 'My wife and I invited him down to our place one day,' remembers Paul Burnett, 'which was near Virginia Water in Surrey. After he arrived I suggested we all go for a quick walk. Ken was ecstatic about this, so off we went. Seven bloody miles he made us do!! We walked all the way around the lake and God knows where else. He insisted though. It was a beautiful day and every so often he'd stop, throw his arms up in the air and say, "Look at this fantastic view!" While he was doing this I'd be in the background wheezing!'

As the walks went on, Kenny's love affair with nature became more and more apparent. 'I think he got a genuine thrill from exploring nature,' says Eric. 'Especially towards the end of his life, when he sort of found religion again. He began to link the two together. I've got a video of him on one of our holidays. He's looking up at the sky, and when the sun comes out he says, "Oh look, God's come out." Then he looks across a valley and says, "God made this, didn't he do well!" or, "Seven out of ten for that, God!"'

By this time Kenny was looking to rebuild his relationship with the Catholic Church. His personal relationship with God had never really gone away, but it had certainly been stained and indeed strained by his ecclesiastical experiences.

Kenny and the Catholic Church always had a love–hate relationship. Hate should perhaps have been the prevalent emotion, given the way it had made him feel about himself, but for some reason it continued to have a hold on him his entire life. You know what they say, once a Catholic, always a Catholic. But that was merely a label. When it came to actual faith, Kenny remained for the majority of his adult life a reluctant agnostic. Sometimes he'd decide there was a God, and sometimes he'd convince himself there couldn't be. It all came in fits and starts. His initial belief in God, or a God, had started around the time he picked up his application form to attend the seminary. But this was a loving, benevolent God, full of wonder and invention, like the one he'd sung about in hymns such as 'All Things Bright and Beautiful'. It was a fairly innocent but burgeoning relationship and full of good intentions. Unfortunately that particular God was usurped as Kenny became more familiar with the teachings of the Catholic Church and creation and benevolence were replaced by vengeance and wrath. This must have been both confusing and disappointing to Kenny, but the real hammer blow came when he started to become aware of his sexuality.

John Birt remembers discussing this with Kenny in about 1967. 'I do remember sharing with him, early on in our relationship, this sense of not really knowing what homosexuality was. I remember Kenny saying that sometimes when there was a good-looking man around him (this was when he was young) he felt a sense of interest and excitement, but he didn't know how to interpret it because he had no paradigm in his life which told him he was homosexual. So the realization was slow coming.'

When this realization did start to materialize it brought with it an inner conflict which would plague Kenny for the rest of his days. The feelings themselves were of course confusing, but when the Church had finished with him he was left demoralized. God didn't love him after all. In fact God loathed and despised him, and it was entirely Kenny's fault.

There was no counsel. No love. As far as the Church was concerned, Kenny was the lowest of the low. His feelings towards men were wrong and evil. And, should he ever make the unwise decision to act on any of these disgusting desires, he would burn in the fires of hell for all eternity.

For somebody so vulnerable and sensitive, this was a hard cross to bear, and the result was twenty years of depression, self-loathing and sexual repression – followed by five years of excess and full-on self-destruction.

But even when he came out Kenny still longed to be accepted by the Church. His friends and family loved and accepted him for who he was, as did the general public. The only place he was still persona non grata was the Church. It was a classic 'Catholic hold', using the stock-in-trade weapons of guilt and fear. Do exactly as we say and we might, just might, be able to get you on the right side of God and into heaven. Don't, and you're screwed.

Kenny talked a lot about religion, but not in the way you'd expect. 'He and my wife had very long discussions about it,' remembers Eric. 'Jane herself is a Catholic, and sometimes they'd go on for hours. But you didn't really argue about religion with Kenny. He'd rant occasionally, but usually he'd just want to talk about it and discuss it with people, its good and bad parts. It was like he was trying to come to some kind of conclusion.'

Eric is exactly right. The conclusion Kenny sought was simply that God loved and forgave him, but the Church held all the aces. It was they who had made him believe that God couldn't stand him in the first place, and only they could tell him that God had changed his mind. It's hardly surprising then that at the end of his life Kenny went back to the Church. 'I always knew he'd go back to it in the end,' says Eric. 'I once told him that, but he always denied it. He said, "I'll never go back, never." But he did, of course, at the very end.'

30

Bloodbath at Auntie's

APPEARING ON *The Kenny Everett Show* had become almost the eighties equivalent of being on the *Morecambe & Wise Show*. Stars were lining up to appear in sketches and bands of the quality of Duran Duran and U2 would perform their latest hit record. Unlike Morecambe and Wise though, Kenny still regarded rehearsal as something of a dirty word. For him, it killed creativity. Guests were simply required to turn up on the day of shooting, run through the sketch quickly, do the take and that was it.

This air of creativity, of instant TV almost, made for a fun atmosphere in the studio. And because Kenny was given as much freedom as possible the shows retained an air of spontaneity. 'The Thames shows were almost totally spontaneous,' says director Bill Wilson. 'But the format was less complicated there. When he came to the BBC we did a lot more sketches. These things need to be rehearsed for cameras and things like that. All in all I think he did find working at the BBC slightly restricting, but we did what we could. To get the best out of Everett you had to catch whatever he did totally live. He knew that better than anyone else, which is why he insisted on no rehearsals. He would lose interest very quickly, so if you didn't catch something first time, there was almost no point going again because he'd lost momentum. The time had passed. In that respect it was very different working with Ev because he wasn't a typical comedy actor or comedian. It's difficult to categorize him.'

Some guests took to this unorthodox way of working, others didn't. For the 1985 Christmas special, Kenny did his own version of

A Christmas Carol with guest stars Peter Cook, Willie Rushton, Rory Bremner and Michael Barrymore. There was also Spike Milligan, one of Kenny's heroes, playing Marley's ghost. They'd worked together before when Spike was a guest on Kenny's radio show and according to Jo Gurnett it was a complete disaster. 'Spike was obviously a depressive, and when he was having a bad day would just sit there and gaze. Anyway, on this particular day he was obviously having a bad one, as all the way through the interview he just sat there and gazed over at Ev. Ev did his best to bring him round but it was impossible. He got a couple of yes's and no's, but that was about it. Poor old Spike.'

For the Christmas show Spike arrived early and Barry Cryer was asked to go and greet him and bring him into the studio. 'So I went down to reception,' recalls Barry, 'and called over to him. "Hello, Cryer," he said, which was his usual greeting for me. I took him up to the studio for a look round, and as we're wandering he sees autocues everywhere. "What the hell are these?" he said. "Oh, don't worry, Spike. Kenny sometimes needs a refresher but he'll be brilliant. Always is." "Rubbish. I've been up all fucking night learning my lines," he said. So anyway, we carry on wandering round the studio and eventually Ev joins us. "Hello, Spike," he says, and Spike stopped, glared at him and said, "Everett, remind me to send you an assassin for Christmas."'

Occasionally, a guest would want more involvement in the creative process. The best example of this is probably Julian Lloyd Webber. The producers had called him up with the idea of a sort of TV masterclass with Gizzard Puke, a punk-rock character played by Kenny. As written, Webber was to perform a virtuoso piece on the cello, after which Gizzard simply gives up even attempting to play it. Webber thought it would be much funnier if Kenny at least attempted to play something. 'So I had this idea of "The Swan", being the most famous piece of cello music ever, that I would play one version but then pre-record a dreadful version of Kenny trying to play it. Where his genius comes into play is that he completely got what I was trying to do, and you can see from the clip that he really plays along with it and at the end when I do that dreadful coming off of strings on to an open A string, he absolutely got that and collapsed on to the floor at that point. I think it's one of the funniest things I've ever seen.'

Webber was also required to smash Kenny over the head with the cello. The prop was made of papier-mâché, and not his own personal cello as many people thought it was, but even so it was quite a big piece of equipment. 'And it did hurt him slightly,' recalls Webber. 'But he went along with those things, he wanted to make things work. I think we did two takes of that, there was another one where the cello didn't break, I hit him and it wasn't hard enough, and then they wanted me to do it again and then I really hit him. But the funny thing is, if you notice, they wanted me to be very serious, obviously I'm supposed to be cross, but the way he did it was so funny, you can see this grin breaking out on my face.'

Webber had done the show partly because of his philosophy of bringing classical music to the people. He'd always considered classical music as something that was for everyone, so doing *The Kenny Everett Show* totally fitted in with everything that he believed in. He was also a fan. 'And it was a pleasure to work with him, he was fantastic. I just thought he was someone who was open to ideas and naturally very funny. And it was great fun to do, one of those funny moments that will stand the test of time.'

Sheila Steafel, a popular comedy actress, appeared in several sketches during the eighties series and liked Kenny enormously. She was there that famous occasion when he failed to show up at Television Centre. It was the day of the recording and with each passing hour the production team grew more and more anxious. As thoughts turned to whether or not the show could go ahead, a call was put through to Jo Gurnett. She immediately rang his flat. Kenny answered. 'Where are you?' she yelled. 'What's happened?' There was a pause. 'I'm watching telly,' he said. 'They wouldn't let me in, so I came home.' For once he'd actually turned up on time but forgotten his pass and the security guard wouldn't let him in. Jo rang Jim Moir at the BBC and explained the situation and that she'd have him there in half an hour. 'Absolutely anyone else would have caused a fuss or demanded to see somebody,' says Jo. 'Not Ev. He just shuffled off home and put the telly on.'

For Sheila Steafel this was pure Kenny. 'He was extraordinary, a lovely, lovely guy, but very shy.' Although she frequently worked with him, Sheila found Kenny a person that you couldn't really get close to, he wouldn't allow it. 'That's why he hid behind this persona of his and he was never out of the Kenny character. I don't know who Kenny was underneath all that. He was always joking. He didn't answer questions. If you said, "How are you today?" he wouldn't say fine or I've got a headache, he'd make a joke in a funny voice. That was very much what he was about. That's why he was so good at what he did because he'd been pretending to be somebody, not himself, for years and years. I'm sure it was some kind of self-defensive mechanism. I mean he married, which was daft, that's kind of a clue isn't it, the fact that he didn't like what he was so he hid and went as far as marrying somebody. Very strange.'

Sheila once invited him to a dinner party and he never showed. The next morning he gave Sheila a gift of a small tape recorder; it was his apology for not turning up and not letting her know.

He'd do this quite often: get ready to go out, buy the wine, but halfway to the house or even outside the door have a sudden change of heart, perhaps unable to face lots of people, many of them strangers. He once missed a dinner party thrown by Jo Gurnett, claiming he went to the wrong flat – despite the fact he'd been there countless times before. 'I told him to come round about seven thirty. It got to eight and he didn't arrive so I thought, Oh well, and just served dinner. He rang me about ten p.m. and said, "I came round but you weren't in." We were on the seventh floor. He went to the sixth floor, rang this bell, nobody answered, so he went home. This is what he did sometimes.'

It was this vulnerability and crippling shyness that was such an endearment. Nicky Horne had a flat near Kenny when he lived in Notting Hill and they used to have dinner occasionally at a Russian restaurant that he always liked going to in Fulham. 'In the basement there were booths built into the arches and there were curtains so you could sit in this alcove and just pull the curtain and no one could see you. And he always wanted to sit there, so we could just sit and chat and eat and no one would bother him.'

It wasn't that he didn't like people approaching him, but when he was out in public he did cherish his privacy. Lee remembers one awful time when she and John were out for the day with Kenny. 'We were in this small supermarket and me and Ev were in the freezer section, looking at what we wanted for dinner, and a woman came up to him and got hold of his sideburns, pulled him up and went, "Oi, will you sign that?" I got so angry. I tell you what used to upset him, it was the proprietorial attitude some of the public had towards him – *I own this guy.*'

The huge success of *The Kenny Everett Show* had an interesting impact on Ray Cameron's son, then seven or eight years old, the future stand-up comedian Michael McIntyre. In an interview for the *Daily Mail* in 2008, McIntyre revealed that all the children at his school asked him if Kenny Everett was his dad. 'I told them he was – and that his TV sidekick, Cleo Rocos, was my real mum. They all believed me, so it took some explaining a few years later when it emerged that Kenny was gay.'

According to McIntyre, Kenny remained one of his mother's best friends and right up until the week before his death was still ringing her up and making her laugh. 'He was the kindest and sweetest man I had ever met. And when I heard the news on the radio about his death, it was so gut-wrenchingly sad.'

Taking a well-deserved break from the TV series, the dream team of Kenny, Barry Cryer and Ray Cameron turned their attentions to the big screen. For a couple of years now Kenny had harboured ambitions to move into feature films, either as a writer or a director. An earlier attempt to make a movie with Kenny had almost come to fruition involving one of the biggest names in world cinema. Ray and Barry had written a black comedy called *Suicide: The Movie*, about a brilliant man who, whenever there was a crisis, would threaten to kill himself. They'd even gone so far as to shoot a test reel at Elstree Studios with Ev and Joanna Lumley, cast as the female lead.

At the time *The Shining* was about to hit British cinemas and Stanley Kubrick was heavily involved in organizing the film's promotion. When it came to choosing a voice for the radio ads Kubrick told his marketing people, 'Look, I don't want a clichéd voice, all slow and deep, I want something different.' Later that day he heard Ev on the radio and said, 'That's the one! I want him. I want Kenny Everett to do it.' His people said, 'What, really?' But he was adamant, so Kenny was invited to meet the great man. 'Well, they chatted for a while,' recalls Cryer, who got the whole low-down later from Kenny. 'And Ev said to me that Kubrick wasn't at all quiet or reclusive or anything, he was just really good company and they ended up talking for ages. Anyway, during their conversation Kubrick asked Kenny what he was doing at the moment, and Kenny said that some chums had written a film for him and that he'd just shot a test reel. "What's it called?" asked Kubrick. "*Suicide: The Movie*," replied Ev. "I want to do it," replied Kubrick. "WHAAAAT?" replied Ev. "I do," said Kubrick. "On the title alone, I want to make this film. Send me the script." So Ev came back to us turning cartwheels, saying that Mr Kubrick wanted to make our film, and Ray Cameron turned round and said, "No, he's not having it." And we said, "Are you mad? This is Stanley Kubrick." Ray said that it wouldn't be our film any more once Kubrick had got hold of it. I remember saying, "Who bloody cares!!" But Ray put a block on it and Kubrick never even got a copy of the script. I'm not saying he definitely would have made the film, but it's certainly one of the great If Onlys.'

In the end Kenny did get to voice the UK radio ads for *The Shining*. It turned out to be quite an inspired choice.

So, narrowly missing out on a partnership with Kubrick, the team came up instead with the idea of making a pastiche of the recent spate of slasher films like *Friday the Thirteenth* and *Halloween*. A huge film fan, Kenny particularly liked the fantasy and horror genre and always managed to get hold of copies of new films long before they publically came out. His Radio 2 producer Geoff Mullin recalls being invited one night to come over to Kenny's flat to watch the latest John Carpenter film, *The Thing*. 'I turned up and we sat down to watch it, but when the film started it was just a continuous run of blood and gore. It turns out he'd actually edited out all the dialogue and just left the gory bits! He used to do that with a lot of things though. He was only interested in the highlights – always looking for the magnificent part of something. It was an education, being around him. He was so inventive. And he'd always give you a totally unique perspective on something.'

With a script courtesy of Barry and Ray, *Bloodbath at the House of Death* went before the cameras. Its rather unoriginal storyline saw Kenny as the head of a group of scientists investigating strange phenomena at a manor house that years before had been the scene of a series of gruesome murders. Along with Kenny, the film was bolstered by a number of familiar British TV faces like Pamela Stephenson, Gareth Hunt and Cleo Rocos. By far the biggest coup was hiring horror film legend and Kenny's friend, Vincent Price, in what turned out to be his last ever appearance in a British film.

However, it rapidly became clear to everyone that there wasn't enough money to finish the picture. Luckily Ray Cameron knew someone in the film distribution business. After work one day Laurence Myers returned home to find a rather frantic message on his answerphone. 'I called Ray back and said, "How much?" because I knew he was after money. I can't remember how much cash they needed but it was quite a lot.' Myers was in, and installed as an executive producer. A regular visitor to the set, Myers found Kenny enormous fun, always joking and mucking around. 'But he was the same on screen as he was off. I never saw any other side of him.'

Released in 1984, *Bloodbath at the House of Death* is a classic example of the old adage that sketch comics struggle when it comes to full-length feature films. 'I'm sure a movie of a hundred minutes of Kenny Everett's best routines would have done very well,' says Paul Gambaccini. 'But that's not what that film tried to be. I remember coming out of a preview screening thinking, when are we going to laugh?'

Not surprisingly the film did poor business and received foul reviews – totally deserved, according to Myers. 'It's a fairly terrible film,' he admits, 'and there's probably a good reason for that. Myers was distributing the film through his own company and it suddenly occurred to him that there might be a censorship issue because of all the blood and gore. 'I had quite a good relationship with the then chief censor James Ferman. I said to him, "Would you mind coming along to see it, to talk about certification, see what your view is?" So he came to see it and he laughed a lot and he said, "Don't worry, Laurence, it's all fine. But by the way, next time you show it to anyone, if I were you I'd get them to put the reels the right way round." I said, "What do you mean?" He said, "Well, obviously the reels are the wrong way round, the story made no sense." I said, "Oh, thank you very much." And I went into the projection booth and said to the projectionist, "You idiot, what have you done? This is very important and you got the reels the wrong way round." The projectionist said, "No, I didn't."'

The film just didn't make any sense and the blame, as Myers sees it, rests on the script and the direction by Ray Cameron. 'Ray, bless him, thought he was the funniest guy in the world, so he would laugh hysterically after every take, enjoying every take. He'd say, "Isn't that the funniest thing!" Ray was totally out of his depth. He was a gag man. He'd never directed a film before and he was totally out of his depth. It's very sad.'

Kenny took the criticism on the chin. By then everyone knew it hadn't worked and nobody pretended that it was good. 'But nobody thought less of Kenny because of it,' says Gambaccini. 'They just thought Kenny's particular brand of comedy was not made for film, but it wouldn't mean that they wouldn't tune in the next day to watch his TV show.'

Curiously, *Bloodbath at the House of Death* has become something of a minor cult movie and in hindsight looks pioneering in that the recent *Scary Movie* franchise treads almost identical ground. Kenny would have enjoyed the irony of that.

31

Coming Out

IN THE EARLY eighties Earls Court was one of the main gay areas of London, and Harpies & Louies had the distinction of being one of the most popular gay bars in the area. It was here one night that Kenny met eighteen-year-old David Smith. 'He was always trying to come on to me and at first I wasn't really interested,' David says today. 'But he made me laugh so much that in the end I relented. That's what made me go for him, really. He just made me laugh so much. To me he was a lot funnier off screen than he was on.'

Kenny and Nikolai had not long broken up and Nikolai had begun to see Pepe. 'Kenny just seemed to accept that, though, and left them to get on with it,' remembers David. 'I think Nikolai and Pepe was more about sex though. Kenny and Nikolai were in love. But Nikolai was humping everything in sight. He was very much the active one. I think he enjoyed the openness of London, after being in Russia for so long. I think he probably had a sex addiction, really.'

Desperate as he was for affection, Kenny's relationship with David became very intense and close in a relatively short space of time. Within four days, Kenny had put David on the insurance for his car. He'd also been introduced to David's parents and the pair of them went on holiday to Key West in Florida, flying first class with Pan Am. Kenny had recently done some work for the company and they'd paid him with flights. 'We had a really nice time. Kenny was just mad and was always looking for the funny side of life. We'd go to discos and run around the dance floor.'

David also recalls a party he attended with Kenny given by Elton

John at his private suite at the Dorchester. Lee was there with John and, as David remembers it, quite a lot of people were sniffing cocaine, Kenny included. 'I was only eighteen at the time and wasn't really in to that kind of thing, but I remember soon after it started, everybody began talking very, very quickly! We also used to go to Heaven, which was like a huge drug haze. But it was all very upbeat and fun. It wasn't seedy.'

After three months the affair was over. David had realized that he wasn't truly in love with Kenny and he couldn't commit, so he called time on the relationship. 'That was the only time that I saw him upset. He became quite distressed. I never saw him again after we split up. I think he just wanted to move on, which was fine. Kenny needed to fall in love though. That was what he wanted to do, to fall in love and be happy. He was very loyal. A lot of people, especially back then, when they were told somebody was gay, could only think about the sexual side of things. They didn't realize that gay men and women also aspired to fall in love. People couldn't, or wouldn't, see beyond the sex. People were becoming liberated and enjoying themselves, but that wasn't just what it was about. And I think that was the main thing for Kenny. He wanted to fall in love more than anything else.'

Over the years Kenny had spoken many times to close friends about his desire to come out publicly as a gay man. 'He hated being in the closet,' says Jo Gurnett. 'But he was terrified about what would happen and always thought he'd lose his audience and then his career. I always had the firm belief that if people respected you and admired you for your work, it wouldn't make any difference.' Still that fear remained. Was it a fear that people might judge him? Or that people might fail to understand the true nature of his homosexuality? The public in general had in recent years become a little more tolerant of gays, but remained mostly confused about how people came to be that way. An incident with his sister only reinforced this view for Kenny. In 1983, a couple of days before emigrating with her family to Australia, Cate met up with Kenny and Nikolai for a farewell dinner. During the conversation Cate mentioned a friend of hers who worked in the fashion industry and to her mind was gay but was married with three children. 'And I said, without really thinking, "He's obviously made a choice, hasn't he?" That was the wrong thing to say, because Ev did not enjoy being gay, and he was mad that anyone would think that people choose to be gay or choose to be straight. If you're born gay, you're gay. It's a genes thing. That's how you're programmed. But that wasn't really talked about in the early eighties. So I think I put my foot in it and he was really, really upset and mad and we didn't communicate for about six months. He got upset and I can see now why. From his point of view, I was telling him that he could have made a different choice, and really he couldn't. And he tried. Even when I was looking after him in the last few weeks of his life, he was saying to me, "God, you're so lucky to have a family, I would have loved a family." He would just have loved to have lived a normal family life, in inverted commas.'

In October 1985, Jo's words that it didn't matter what he did, the public would never fall out of love with him, had finally given Kenny the courage to come out. The fact that several other celebrities had recently come out and it hadn't adversely affected how the public viewed them also gave him the confidence he needed.

Kenny's 'coming out' was typically flamboyant and unique, involving him posing outside his flat with Nikolai and Pepe and telling the ranks of reporters that, 'Two husbands are better than one.' He then went back inside and telephoned Lee. 'I've just told the press I'm gay. What shall I do? I'm dreading tomorrow.' Lee told him not to worry and that she was going to organize a coming-out party.

Amidst all the confusion and ballyhoo, Kenny plain forgot to tell his parents he was going public and their house was besieged by reporters. Later on there were some rather nasty insinuations in the press that Tom and Lily had left the UK to join Cate in Australia because of the shame they felt about their son being gay. Even Kenny himself revealed in an interview that his mother contemplated suicide after the revelation. All wrong, says Cate. It was her idea that her parents should come to live in Australia so they could be near their grandchildren. And any angst her mother endured over her son's homosexuality related more to concern about the hurt he might be suffering than her own sense of shame. 'There was never any sort of estrangement,' insists Cate. 'My mother adored him. She worried about him all his life. She went through agonies over his gayness but never criticized him. She adored him.'

Many friends believe that Kenny found life easier once he'd discovered the strength to be able to say, This is what I am, take it or leave it. 'I think that coming out and being public about it helped him just be him,' says Nicky Horne. 'It was enormously helpful for him.' And yet, the ignorance and prejudice of people was never far away, especially after he came out. 'Every morning Kenny walked from his flat to Capital Radio,' recalls Chris Tarrant. 'And he'd pass this building site with all big lads on scaffolding, and every morning it was, "Hello, Kenny, you all right, mate?", "Captain Kremmen!", and all this stuff for months. And then suddenly, after he'd made this announcement, these builders became extremely abusive to him – "You poofter, you dirty bastard," all this – and Kenny used to come into the studio really upset.'

Just as a blind person who can suddenly see might want to fly around the world visiting all the great art galleries, Kenny was determined to make up for those years of repression. 'When he first came out he did go a bit wild,' admits Jo Gurnett. 'He was down at Heaven all the time, doing God knows what with God knows who. But he'd been living a lie for so many years. He kind of just exploded really. It's a pity he didn't come out earlier though, because he might have got it out of his system before the AIDS epidemic took hold. I don't know. Heaven was a bit racy, back in the early to mid-eighties. A lot of people who were going there at that time are unfortunately no longer with us.'

It was definitely a case of, 'I've come out, so I'm going to be outrageous.' All that pent-up Catholic guilt erupted like a volcano. It was undiluted hedonism. 'It was that childlike thing that Kenny had,' says John Alkin. 'If there's more, let me see it. If there's more, let me experience it.'

John and Lee saw a lot of Kenny, Nikolai and Pepe during this period, whether they liked it or not. The trio even showed up when

Lee and John were on holiday. The couple had an apartment in Lanzarote and Ev, Nikolai and Pepe arrived with their bags out of the blue one day; they'd been skiing in Spain or something and got bored. 'So suddenly, they'd all moved in,' recalls Lee. 'And one night Ev came to me and said, "Nikolai's in a dreadful state." I said, "How sad." He went, "You must come and have a look. You've got to look at his ball." I said, "I do not want to see Nikolai's ball, thank you very much." This went on for a little while until Ev started pleading, "You've got to go. It's serious." And it was, his testicle was the size of a football.'

Apparently while they'd been skiing, Nikolai had managed to impale his testicle with his ski stick – a very nasty accident in itself, compounded by the fact he was already ill, dying essentially, as he had full-blown AIDS by this stage. Fast forward a couple of days and Lee and John were woken in the middle of the night by screams. Nikolai's ball had burst. 'Ev ran into my bedroom,' recounts Lee, 'yelling at the top of his voice: "You've got to see Nikolai's ball again, it's really serious this time." It was actually, it had burst. So I put some disinfectant on it, the stuff that really stings, and he went – "Argghhh!" The whole bloody block heard him screaming. I had him. It didn't go septic, put it that way, but I enjoyed it. It was virtually cauterized. I never wanted to see his ball, but I was very happy to abuse it.'

There's little doubt that Kenny was pushing it to the edge. It was a case of having all these sexual fantasies and being rich enough to indulge them – and that's exactly what he did. 'When Kenny did come out, he was extremely flamboyant about it,' says John Birt. 'I can remember having lunch with him and him showing me a picture of his Russian boyfriend on the toilet, which in the early eighties was quite a shocking thing to be exposed to, really. I think he'd reached the point where he was extremely forthcoming and comfortable, and of course he was a big star, so I suppose all those things gave him sufficient comfort to be open about his true sexuality.'

32

Bye Bye, Beeb – Again

B Y 1988 KENNY had been doing his TV show for Thames and the BBC for ten years and had reached the point where it simply wasn't fun any more, getting into ridiculous costumes, sitting through time-consuming make-up sessions and performing every possible variation of comedy sketch. He had not found the same level of satisfaction at the BBC that he'd had at Thames, and despite everyone's best efforts he felt he'd never been allowed to display the same spontaneity. In a letter to Ray Gearing, a cameraman at Thames, Kenny wrote that his switch from Thames to the BBC 'was like stepping out of a Rolls-Royce into a heap of gorilla shit'.

The catalyst was a particularly wretched day of filming. Dressed as Quasimodo, Kenny was suspended in the air on an uncomfortable harness. When the machinery broke down or there were technical problems, he was left up there, twirling around, gently frying near the blazing studio lights. That evening he met Eric Gear for dinner and Eric sensed something was wrong. 'He seemed very down, so I asked him what was wrong and he said, "This is no career for a grown man. This isn't right." He didn't often say things like that. He rarely complained, but this had got him down.'

But there was another reason, much more personal, why Kenny had decided to call a halt to the series. He and Ray Cameron had fallen out to such an extent they could no longer work together.

Jim Moir, BBC's head of Variety, was keen for the series to continue and had heard rumours about Kenny and Ray falling out. His solution was to hold a meeting in an effort to patch things up.

These were professionals, after all, and he believed the show was something everyone could take pride in. The meeting took place at Television Centre and was chaired by Moir himself. 'Ken arrived first by about twenty minutes and I explained how it would be absolutely wonderful if we could return everything to an even keel and overcome any difficulties. Then Ray and Barry came in. Unfortunately the meeting did not go well. There were hidden tensions. Actually that's incorrect. There weren't hidden tensions, there were tensions which became very apparent. In a way, not much was said, but nothing was said that would improve the situation. I remember sitting there thinking, This ain't going nowhere. Then after about half an hour the meeting split up and it was evident that Ray had a very large bee in his bonnet. Barry had a kind of "dark" face on, but the tensions were really between Kenny and Ray. I knew as the two boys left that that was it. I remember feeling extremely down because as a trio they had been a superbly creative team. I blame nobody, though, because I've seen it happen so many times before. It's the same with any kind of "marriage". This one had just run its course, and no third party, however persuasive, was going to alter the situation.'

For writers to maintain a relationship with their star for so long, ten years at the top in this case, is something quite rare. If you look at Galton and Simpson and Tony Hancock, there were always tensions between them and their star. Not to say Everett ever acted in a 'starry' way. He was probably the least 'starry' of any television personality. 'Honestly, you will not find a single member of staff at Thames or the BBC who has a bad word to say about Ev,' confirms Jo Gurnett. 'He'd talk to everyone and anyone. There weren't many other stars that'd stop for fifteen minutes to have a chat with one of the riggers or carpenters. Everett talked to everybody though, and not because he thought he should. He did it because he was interested.'

Kenny relied totally on Ray and Barry, he needed them in the studio at all times, even if it was only to validate what he was doing or to allow him the freedom to express himself, he needed that confirmation. Barry was almost a father figure for Kenny. The comic had lots of gay friends and Ev used to refer to him as an honorary gay, whispering to him, 'Married thirty years and four children. What a brilliant smokescreen.' Kenny also respected him and his legacy in comedy. Ray, although a bit older than Kenny, was practically his contemporary, and edgier in his comedy. Barry was more traditional, although still capable of flights of comedic fantasy. 'That's why Barry and Ray were such a good combination,' says Kevin Bishop, who'd started his career at the BBC as an assistant floor manager on Kenny's show and had ended up producing and directing the final series. 'Because they were coming from slightly different fields of comedy, and they just gelled.'

This made it all the more tragic when Kenny's relationship with Ray irretrievably broke down. But what Moir didn't know was that Ray and Kenny had fallen out over matters surrounding Ray's marriage and subsequently the two of them never spoke again. An amazing friendship and working relationship was over.

Ray and his wife eventually divorced and he moved to America, hoping to make it big in comedy over there, but things didn't go right for him. In 1993 he died, penniless, in Los Angeles; he was just fifty-three. 'I got a call from him once,' remembers Laurence Myers, one of the producers on the *Bloodbath* film. 'I hadn't spoken to him for years and he said, "I just want to let you know I'm working through my address book. Will you lend me some money?" It's sad because we weren't very close at all. He was obviously desperate.'

When the BBC series finished, Bruce Gowers had the idea of trying to bring Kenny over to the USA. Since turning down the chance to direct the Thames shows, when Kenny told him to take a job in New York instead, Gowers had worked extensively in American television, directing and producing the likes of Eddie Murphy, Billy Crystal and Jerry Seinfeld. He knew all the networks and the right people and talked Kenny into flying over to LA and giving it a go. 'We saw all the networks,' recalls Gowers. 'There was certainly some interest, but like a lot of these things it never really came to anything. Back then it was difficult to get a new show for an established star, let alone a complete unknown. Eventually Kenny got bored and flew back home. It was such a shame, because had they given him a chance, I honestly think he would have become huge.'

33

Capital Old

PROFESSIONALLY, KENNY WAS starting to get bored. Television sent him to sleep. He hadn't fallen out of love with it, for the simple reason he'd never been in love with it. It had lost its lustre, though, and he was glad to be out. And, although he did carry on making a few quiz shows (which involved neither costumes nor rehearsals), this was done solely for the money – something he would soon have to think seriously about.

What is even more surprising is that Kenny was falling out of love with radio – professionally at least. Everything had become quite staid and predictable and there were precious few 'highlights' left to be had. The launches of the pirates, Radio 1 and commercial radio had been the medium's three most important inceptions, but these were now distant memories.

It had been a fantastic way to start a new career, but surely everything thereafter would be slightly anti-climactic? This hadn't been so noticeable in the late sixties or seventies, as Kenny had been busy helping launch Radio 1 and Capital, and there was no shortage of inspiration. But by the late eighties the BBC and commercial radio had found their equilibrium and were chipping away at each other nicely. That would be the status quo for a long time to come, and as a result, Kenny was losing interest. He and his beloved wireless had extracted almost as much interest, imagination and creativity from each other as was possible. It was sad that things were coming to an end, but that's the way it goes.

The slow demise of Kenny as a creative entity on the radio was to be hastened slightly when, in 1988, he was asked to switch to Capital's all new 'Oldies' sister station, Capital Gold. These 'Gold' stations became huge in the late eighties and nineties, and are still popular to this day. They came into being courtesy of a government directive prohibiting the UK's commercial stations from broadcasting simultaneously on their AM and FM frequencies. As the majority of these were targeting the Radio 1 listeners, it seemed natural for the new stations to target Radio 2.

One of the downsides to this new network of stations was the fact that they would be broadcasting on the AM frequency, something Kenny loathed. 'Listening to music on AM is like listening to a mud factory,' he once said. Worse still, for Kenny at least, he would be broadcasting in mono – something he hadn't had to endure since his Radio 1 days. Nobody had been more excited about the advent of stereo than Kenny, and when he joined Capital in 1973, he talked about little else. Everything there was 'groovy and stereophonic'. Now, things were 'crappy and monophonic'.

Peter Young remembers speaking to Kenny not long after he was given the news about his switch. 'All the new Gold DJs were asked to turn up for a group photograph in order to publicize the station and I saw Kenny on the staircase in the Euston Tower. There used to be a huge Busby Berkeley staircase there and he just looked at me and said, "You too, huh?" He really wasn't happy about it. He got used to it in the end, but I don't think the station did him justice. He loathed presenting in mono and on AM.' Kenny had done the same thing in his pirates days, but that was before FM and stereo had been invented. 'By now he'd progressed tremendously and I think putting him on Capital Gold did him a great disservice.'

When Kenny rejoined Capital in 1984, taking the same slot that he'd had on Radio 2, he would spend hours preparing his shows. The conveyor belt of jingles was still moving, and he even created a new weekly serial entitled 'The Adventures of Lord Elpas'. It wasn't a patch on his earlier work, but it was streets ahead of anything you'd hear anywhere else, including Radio 1. Even Kenny Lite was still 'the Benchmark'.

Now his interest and motivation had dissipated, and despite his apathy for what had passed, he did occasionally yearn for the buzz of being a pirate. But even when he was denied a free hand, Kenny remained a radio man and he was determined to carry on producing shows that were above average and in some way unique. He simply had to change tack. What had originally made him tick was no longer there. All he had left now were his listeners. They would have to become his material and his inspiration. David Jensen believes this suited Kenny just fine. 'He took inspiration from all over the place. He didn't need one element in particular. But he was his own mentor. He taught himself everything, and along the way covered every base.'

Kenny's colleague and closest friend at Capital Gold was Paul Burnett. He remembers there being a bit of a backlash to the new Kenny. 'Steve Wright said something when he was asked who his favourite broadcaster was,' remembers Paul. 'He said, "Kenny used to be my favourite, but now he's on Capital Gold he's not the same." What he meant was that when Kenny was on Capital Gold there were fewer jingles and no Captain Kremmen. It was just Kenny, some records and a microphone. But to me "Spontaneous chatty Everett" was equally as funny as "Spending-hours-in-a-studio-preparing Everett".'

Kenny always had been spontaneous, but he was also pressing lots of buttons and running tapes, etc. 'At Gold, there was a lot of inter-action with listeners,' says Paul, 'something he'd never really done before or had time for. And he was wonderful. He turned it into an art form. A far more understated art form than before, but an art form all the same.'

What Steve Wright and others like him didn't get was that Kenny was simply cutting his cloth accordingly. 'You couldn't do all that Captain Kremmen stuff on a daily show,' says Paul. 'It wasn't possible. It also wasn't in his remit. Even though he was on a different station, playing to a different audience, he was still for my money the best broadcaster in the UK.'

Despite all the changes, Kenny did continue to make jingles at Capital Gold, and would even produce them for his fellow presenters.

These were rarely done by request though. 'I never asked for any,' remembers Peter Young. 'But he made them anyway. They'd just suddenly turn up. I remember one time I was doing the *Drive Time* show on Capital, and somebody said there was a package for me downstairs. So I went to see what it was, and there was a tape for me with about five or six jingles on it. Everett had just made them for me. I was completely bowled over by it.'

Young was amazed that anyone, let alone somebody as popular as Kenny, could be bothered to do things like that. 'The next time I saw him I thanked him and he said, "Oh, don't worry about it. They only took me five minutes." He did some jingles for me on my Capital Gold show, again completely unexpected.'

Kenny was also happy to do demos, and would often spend hours creating jingles that might never be used. Paul Burnett remembers one such occasion. 'I had an idea for an on-air competition once called "Jukebox Jackpot". Unfortunately it didn't go ahead, but I remember coming up with the initial idea and then writing a kind of jingle for it. Kenny had always said to me, "If you ever want any jingles making, just give me a call." So I rang him up and explained what I'd come up with and sang this idea down the phone to him. The very next day he walked in and said, "I've thrown something together, would you like to come and listen to it?" Well, first I was amazed that he'd actually done something for me, but when I heard it I was completely blown away. He'd recorded it with a four-part harmony and it was sung to perfection. It was amazing. He honestly must have spent hours on it.'

The whole concept of oldies radio lacks imagination, but then there really isn't any required. 'There can be nothing imaginative about oldies radio,' says Dave Symonds. 'It's gone, it's past. What's the old saying? "The past is a very nice place to visit but I wouldn't want to live there." That's exactly how I felt, and I know it was how Kenny felt too. The beauty of contemporary radio is that you never know what's going to happen tomorrow. Somebody could release a piece of work that could astonish you, and that's going to make you excited. Playing stuff that we were playing back in 1966 isn't going to excite us. We've done it, we've been there.'

Ironically, the people who Kenny and Dave were broadcasting to on

Capital Gold would have been the same people who were listening to them on the pirates and Radio 1. It was also the same music, of course. The difference being that back then the music was new, as were Kenny and Dave! Now, they were all part of the burgeoning nostalgia circuit and would have to get used to the idea.

One of the things that frustrated Gold's DJs the most was the station's refusal to utilize the catalogue it had at its disposal. There were thousands of good records released in the sixties, but very few made it on to the Capital Gold playlists. Geoff Mullin remembers bearing the brunt of Kenny's frustration on several occasions. 'I remember he rang me up once when he was on Gold, and he said, "Geoffrey, do you know how many hit records Otis Redding made?" And I said, "Wow, quite a few. There's 'Mr Pitiful', 'Respect', 'Just One More Day', 'My Girl'. There's loads." And he said, "Do you know how many we've got on the Capital Gold playlist? We've got one – 'Dock of the Bay'. That's all we're allowed to play." I said, "You're joking! What about 'Hard to Handle'?" And we started going through all the wonderful records Otis Redding had made, but he wasn't allowed to play them, and that infuriated him.'

Dave Symonds suffered similar frustrations. 'The playlists never seemed to change. I remember on my Monday-morning show, I'd come in and Richard Park, our boss, would come bounding up to me all excited and say, "Morning, David, it's a Motown Monday!" What he should have said was it was *the* Motown Monday. It never differed. There were only so many good Motown records and I had to play the same ones every week: the Supremes and the Four Tops, etc. I had to come in and try and sound excited about it.'

Away from Euston Tower, Kenny could obviously listen to whatever he liked. The eighties had been a fairly barren period for him musically, and he'd failed to latch on to anything in a big way. Singles such as Talk Talk's 'It's My Life' became favourites, but it was a far cry from the glory days of the late sixties and seventies. But by the early nineties, Kenny's toes were beginning to tap once again, and his resurgent interest in 'modern music' would bring with it an unlikely but welcome friendship.

When Kenny had moved from Capital to Capital Gold he'd been assigned a new studio assistant named Russ Evans. Russ was a nineteen-year-old college-leaver who had been desperate to work in radio since he was a child. As excited as he undoubtedly was about working with Kenny, Russ remembers being flabbergasted when he found out what his new boss was listening to. 'Kenny absolutely loved Italian House music. Not many people know this about him, but around 1991 that was all he was listening to. I was listening to the same stuff. I was so impressed!'

It was a strange situation though. Here was the great Kenny Everett bonding with a nineteen-year-old 'youth' wearing a ponytail and KLF T-shirt over a shared love of Italian House. 'I was running back and forth from the Capital Gold music library, fetching him all these different records from the sixties that neither of us wanted to listen to. All we ever talked about was House! That was our connection. Not long after that we started doing mix tapes for each other. Imagine swapping mix tapes with Kenny Everett. The whole thing was quite surreal.'

Kenny's love of Italian House had started, not surprisingly, in his favourite nightclub, Heaven. Under normal circumstances what he listened to there, stayed there. It was enjoyable but disposable. This was one of the few occasions when he had taken the music home with him. 'I used to go clubbing and do my thing on a Saturday,' says Russ. 'And Kenny would go off and do his thing at Heaven. Then on a Monday morning, he'd come in, put the first track on, turn the speakers down, look at me and then hum the tune of the weekend. Then he'd say, "Right, what was that song?" And, if I didn't know it, it'd be my job to go off and find out what it was and get a copy. I was a real clubber at the time and heavily into that kind of music, but Kenny was as contemporary as anybody I knew.'

Not long after this Kenny suggested they go clubbing together. 'I was really pleased when he asked me,' says Russ. 'We ended up going out almost every Saturday night for a good couple of years. It was fantastic. We always went to Heaven. That was the club of choice, and there was always a small group of us. There was Kenny's new partner, he was usually there, and Cleo, occasionally. Sometimes it was just the two of us.'

Despite it not being his natural habitat, Heaven had a positive effect on Russ. 'It had such a superb atmosphere. I absolutely loved it. I was so lucky too. Here was this young guy from deepest Surrey, who suddenly gets this job at the Euston Tower, where he'd always wanted to work. Then, he's out clubbing with Kenny Everett at this awesome club listening to amazing music! I couldn't comprehend it at the time. I just couldn't wait for Saturday!'

Heaven was one of London's most popular clubs back then and there were always queues around the block. 'Kenny used to just walk straight up to the front though,' remembers Russ, 'and we'd be straight in. No queuing for us.' Once in, Kenny and Russ would make a beeline for the dance floor, and according to Russ, his new clubbing partner was a good little mover. 'Kenny was a great dancer. He was a fit guy for a start and had a lot of experience. He'd danced in clubs all over the world and even then would still go clubbing when he went abroad. I remember when he was about to go to Italy once. As he walked out of the studio he said, "I'll give them a twirl for you, Russ."'

Kenny and Russ would dance for hours at Heaven, and usually had a little assistance. 'It was never boozy,' says Russ. 'This was the early nineties and London clubs were awash with ecstasy pills. That was what you did back then. And it was what we did. Just the one though! After that it was always back to Kenny's place to chill out. We'd usually listen to something like Puccini and then just fall asleep.'

Like many other people we've spoken to, Russ says that Kenny's apathy for the past was apparent, particularly when it came to his own role in events: 'He loved the Beatles and Queen, and we talked about their music quite a bit. But he never told me he'd been on tour with the Beatles, or that he'd helped make 'Bohemian Rhapsody' a hit. He never referred to them as people he knew or had known. He didn't seem interested. If you went to his flat, there were no gold discs or anything like that. No acknowledgements to the past.'

What impressed Russ most about Kenny wasn't his illustrious past or his taste in nightclubs and music – it was his kindness and generosity of spirit, something Russ admits he wasn't expecting from a DJ. 'He was such a kind, gentle and generous man. Can you imagine, I'd been listening to radio all of my young life, and I start this job at Gold and have all kinds of preconceived ideas as to what DJs are like. I thought it would all be fast cars and fame, etc. – and there are elements of that. But what I got was this man who used to buy me lunch from the sandwich shop every day, and ask how I was. "Have you got a girlfriend yet?" Media can be such an aggressive culture and can be seen to be very egocentric, but Kenny was the complete polar opposite of that. He gave me the perfect introduction to radio and media. I knew the egocentric stuff existed, but I wasn't necessarily aware that there was a different side, and he gave me that. He taught me how to behave, really. He didn't have to sit me down and instruct me. I just learned by watching how he behaved. The way he was as an individual. He was like that with everyone though. It didn't matter if you were the boss or the studio assistant. I used to think, You don't have to be like this. The fact that someone took such an interest in my life so early on in my career made a big difference, and that kindness has stayed with me.'

Despite a distinct lack of enthusiasm for the station's output and frequency, Kenny still adored his job at Capital Gold. Everything he needed was there for him in spades; love, respect, friendship, camaraderie. He'd been working for what was by then known as the Capital Group on and off since 1973, and had been truly instrumental in helping it become one of the most successful radio groups in the world. His position there now was almost that of honorary Queen Mother!

Dave Symonds agrees. 'That's about right. Kenny was definitely broadcasting royalty. You couldn't get any higher really. He may not have been the most popular when it came to listening figures. He didn't have the right show for that. But he was still the best there was, or had ever been. Everybody loved him.'

These feelings of love for Cuddly Ken were not held by everyone in the radio industry. Over the years he, like most people, had made enemies. And when one such adversary was offered a job on Capital

Gold, Kenny took quick and evasive action. 'Richard Park [the station's controller] used to give a guided tour for the people he was thinking of hiring,' remembers Dave Symonds. 'So whenever we saw somebody being shown round, we always assumed he or she would be our next new colleague. One day Richard was spotted giving the tour to Ed Stewart, and when Kenny found out he went to see Richard and said, "If you hire that man, I'm out." I think it went back to an incident on Radio London. Kenny certainly didn't like him.'

Kenny's exalted position at Capital was threatened on occasion; usually when he'd had a run-in with Richard Park. One of their earliest spats came about when Park made the extremely unwise decision of reprimanding Kenny mid-show. Dave Symonds was in Kenny's studio at the time and watched it all unfold. 'Depending on who you were and how much he trusted you, Park would give you one or two free plays an hour. Kenny would quite often do something unexpected with his, like play a piece of Brahms. Occasionally, though, he'd go so far off format it wasn't true! Now Richard Park had one habit which I thought was an absolute no-no. If he was listening to you and he thought you'd played or said something unsuitable, he wouldn't wait until you came off air, he would appear in the bloody studio and stand there with his hands on his hips saying, "What the fuck was that?" He did that once to Kenny, who must have used his free-play slot to play something Richard didn't like. So he came bounding down from his office, came into the studio and blasted, "What the fuck do you think you're doing?" Kenny waited a few moments, and then very calmly looked at him and said, "OK, Richard. You obviously know much more about this than I do, so I'll leave you to get on with it." And he just got up and left. Park was gobsmacked. You didn't mess with Kenny though. By the time Capital Gold came along, he'd done it all, and he certainly wasn't going to take behaviour like that. I think Richard knew he'd crossed the line. When they eventually got Kenny back, Park said, "Sorry about that, Kenny," and off he went.'

On a subsequent occasion, the boot was on the other foot and Richard Park had every right to blow his top. And this time it was done in the privacy of his office. 'Kenny came into my studio one day,' remembers Paul Burnett, 'and I told him a joke I'd heard. It wasn't in the best of taste I'm afraid. The joke was, "What were Laura Ashley's last words? 'Well, I'll go to the foot of our stairs!'" Laura Ashley had died a few years previously after falling down some stairs. As I said, it wasn't in the best of taste. Anyway, Kenny absolutely wet himself. He was falling about all over the place. I was a bit embarrassed by his reaction really, as it wasn't that funny. He then, to my absolute horror went on air and said, "Paul Burnett's just told me this very funny gag" – and he repeated the joke. I have to say I could have done without the name-check!'

As with the Monty Python funeral sketch debacle fifteen years previously, the bank of lights on Capital's telephone system lit up like Blackpool illuminations. 'Kenny turned round and just gawped at me with a mixture of horror and confusion,' remembers Paul. 'What had he done? I said to him, "Please tell me you didn't do that on air," but of course he had. Then it dawned on me. He didn't actually know she was dead! So I told him she was, and he said, "Oh no. How did she die?" And I said, "How do you think?" I then proceeded to watch every drop of blood drain from his face. You could see his life flashing before his eyes. The shit really hit the fan, too. The family complained, as did several hundred listeners. We weren't suspended or anything, but Richard Park gave us a right telling off. Later on though I said to Kenny, "If you didn't know she'd died, what did you think the joke was?" And his reply was typical Everett, because NOBODY had a sense of humour like Everett. He said, "Well, you know, a flouncy blouse flying down the stairs." I thought I'd better leave it there.'

A month before Kenny left Capital Gold the Radio Academy presented him with their Lifetime Achievement Award, the highest accolade the industry can bestow. This was a fitting decision, and ensured that the very end of Kenny's career was marked not by sadness, but by celebration.

34

West End Star

J O GURNETT WAS used to receiving strange telephone calls at unearthly hours from Kenny. It's par for the course when you look after celebrities. But one night in June 1991, just after 10 p.m., Jo received one of the strangest telephone calls yet.

'Jo! Hello, darling, it's Ev. How are you? Look, I'm out with Mike Batt. Yes, yes, we've had a few. Anyway, he's asked me to appear in his new musical, *The Hunting of the Snark*, and I've said yes!! Jo? Are you still there? Oh good. Anyway, I'll put him on. Here's Mike. BYYEEEEEEEEEE.'

As Jo began to contemplate the numerous pitfalls of Kenny appearing in the West End, Mike Batt came on the phone. 'Honestly, Jo, I think he's going to be brilliant. It'll work, trust me.'

'Mike, I think he'd be brilliant too,' said Jo, trying to sound reassured. 'But he's not a stayer. He's got a very short attention span.' As we've already seen, it equalled that of a four-year-old. So how on earth would he cope, repeating the same thing day in day out for potentially months on end? Every single radio show Ev had ever presented had been a unique entity, featuring different records, jingles, gags, competitions and much more. This was part of the attraction to Kenny. Things changed by the second.

When Kenny came back on the line, Jo tried her best to articulate her concerns. 'Look, Ev, I'm a real fan of the music of *The Hunting of the Snark* and of Mike, but you, doing the same thing night after night, eight shows a week? You get bored after an hour! It'll never work.'

In addition, it would be exhausting for him. Kenny had never been the strongest of individuals, and had played on his weediness for aeons. On top of this, he hadn't long been officially diagnosed as infected with the HIV virus. It was a potential disaster, surely? Unfortunately, the only person who could really see it was Jo, and it would be her who would have to pick up the pieces. Or would it?

When the call came to an end around thirty minutes later, after much toing and froing, Kenny and Mike had made up their minds, leaving Jo genuinely lost for words. She poured herself a large brandy, sat down and thought: Oh God, Everett, what the hell have you done?

Ev's friendship with Mike Batt had begun back in the late seventies when, ironically enough, he had contacted Kenny with a view to turning Captain Kremmen into a musical. 'I was a huge fan of Kenny's, and especially Captain Kremmen. I listened to his show every week on Capital and Captain Kremmen was always the bit I looked forward to most. After listening to one of these shows one day, I thought to myself, I've got to make this into a musical. So, as opposed to just thinking about it I rang him up and suggested the possibility. Kenny was really enthusiastic about the idea and so we met up for an initial chat. I then listened to the episodes again and started writing a treatment.'

Over the following months Kenny and Mike met several times to discuss the project and it became a genuine work-in-progress. Unfortunately, due to work commitments, they never found an opportunity to see it through to fruition. 'It's a pity really,' says Batt. 'I'd just written "Bright Eyes" and Kenny was moving into TV, so we both had a hell of a lot on. Had all that not been happening, who knows?'

Who knows indeed? The stage was about the only medium Captain Kremmen hadn't conquered, and you get the feeling that it could have worked as, bizarrely enough, sci-fi musicals had a habit of doing well, one prime example being Bob Carlton's jukebox musical, *Return to the Forbidden Planet*, which enjoyed a long run in the West End in the late eighties.

Despite Captain Kremmen not taking off as a musical, a friendship was formed and the two men stayed in touch. Batt adored Kenny's work on the radio and had been listening to him since his days on wonderful Radio London. The respect and admiration was very much reciprocated – to Kenny, Batt was another one of those melodic magicians like Jeff Lynne, Paul McCartney or Chris Rainbow.

Starting his career in the late sixties, Batt had written and produced a string of hits for a variety of groups and artists, including Elkie Brooks ('Lilac Wine'), Steeleye Span ('All Around My Hat') and Art Garfunkel ('Bright Eyes'). His most high-profile success came in 1972, when he had the unusual, but as it turned out genius idea of turning Elisabeth Beresford's burrowing litter addicts, the Wombles, into pop stars. Several gold records later, Batt was established as one of the most influential names in popular music.

By the early eighties Mike had begun writing a concept album based around Lewis Carroll's nonsense poem, *The Hunting of the Snark*, which tells of, 'The impossible voyage of an improbable crew to find an inconceivable creature.' It wasn't a musical at this stage, simply a collection of songs. A Carroll fanatic since childhood, Batt had always loved *The Hunting of the Snark*. It fed his imagination, leading him off to all kinds of amazing places.

By 1986 Batt had finished writing the album and it was ready to be recorded, utilizing the vocal talents of Roger Daltry, Sir John Gielgud, Cliff Richard, John Hurt, Art Garfunkel and Julian Lennon. Two fully costumed concerts of the album took place at the Barbican and the Royal Albert Hall, by which time Batt was convinced that a full musical theatre adaptation was possible.

The biggest doubt hanging over *Snark*'s suitability as a musical was its storyline – or lack of it. The characters were strong but apart from that, there wasn't much there. Batt wasn't to be deterred. 'If you compare Carroll to other nonsense writers like Edward Lear, he's absolutely streets ahead. He's not really a writer of stories though, and that was one thing the musical was criticized for – not having much of a story to it. *Snark*, like *Alice in Wonderland*, is just a series of tableaux, and very little more. It nevertheless possesses huge potential for music, character, atmosphere and dance development. Other shows have managed with little or no plot. Take *Cats*, for instance, which is also based on poetry. Nothing really happens; it's just a chain of characters introducing themselves. Then you've got *The Nutcracker*, which is basically just an excuse for a chain of dances by different characters. Compared to these two, *Snark* was an edge-of-the-seat thriller!'

Driven on by a belief that imagination and a damn good score would win the day, Batt began finding the £2.1 million he'd need to make his dreams a reality. The money came from various sources, including his own coffers, so there was an awful lot at stake. That said, confidence was high. The reception at the two concerts had been superb and, as far as Batt was concerned, the songs he'd written were among his best to date.

Next up, Batt would have the difficult task of casting the show. As *Snark* was an ensemble piece featuring ten lead characters, he wasn't looking for one star or one fantastic singer. 'I wanted a group of strong professionals. I wanted characters with decent voices!'

After several casting sessions, *Man from U.N.C.L.E.* star David McCallum was chosen, along with seasoned TV performer Mark McGann and West End leading man, Philip Quast. There was one role, however, that didn't require any auditioning. 'I had Kenny in mind for the role of the Billiard Marker from the off,' explains Batt. 'The reason for this was his affinity with the works of Lewis Carroll. There was a certain "wackiness" to what Kenny did, but it went a lot deeper than that. Kenny understood nonsense immediately – as did his hero, John Lennon. They were both huge fans of Carroll and could relate to his works very easily. That was so, so important.'

Lennon often said about his song lyrics, 'Isn't it funny that people think we mean this, or we mean that? It's just a piece of nonsense!' Songs like 'I Am the Walrus' and 'Lucy in the Sky with Diamonds' have been analysed to death by music scholars when all they were supposed to be were bits of wonderful nonsense. But then, not everyone 'gets' nonsense. 'Kenny did though,' says Batt. 'He had it running through his veins. Look at his musicality, for a start. He produced loads of beautiful music for his jingles and his radio shows, yet he never once thought of making a record and releasing them commercially. They were simply his pieces of nonsense.'

Kenny was also drawn to music with a whimsical air; it was one of the reasons why he so loved the Beatles, and also Queen. 'Kenny was a very whimsical man,' says Batt. 'And that was perfect for the role he was playing in *Snark*.'

Rehearsals, when they got under way, proved long, arduous and at times frustrating. It wasn't long before Jo received her first SOS, arriving even sooner than she'd imagined. 'I think you were right,' Kenny announced. 'I'm bored!'

'I said you would be,' replied Jo, doing little to hide the anger in her voice. 'But you can't let everybody down. You're going to have to go through with this.' And to his credit, Kenny got his head down and carried on. 'I know he found it extremely hard going though,' Jo remembers. 'He wasn't used to rehearsing, for one thing. The very nature of a rehearsal is to practise something again and again until you get it right. And for somebody who never rehearsed, and whose entire act was based on spontaneity, this was always going to be a problem. Ev had no choice other than to knuckle down and make the best of it.'

The situation wasn't all bad, and it didn't take long for Kenny to find his feet and start making mischief. His favourite way was to mess around a bit with the lyrics. Fortunately, Mike Batt saw the funny side. 'He'd change the lyrics every day. I remember at the end of one particular song he'd always change the very last line to something totally nonsensical – something that only I would really notice. If anyone else had done that I would have probably said, "Would you mind not changing my lyrics!" But with Kenny it was great and it showed that he was enjoying himself, which was important to me.'

It wasn't just the lyrics, Kenny also ended up altering some of his dialogue and bits of choreography. But as always with Kenny, not in the conventional way – as Batt recalls: 'He didn't ask you first. He'd just do it, and you'd decide if it was any good. Anybody else would have a quiet word with the writer or director – and with a lot of actors that quiet word would have something to do with building up their part. That wasn't Kenny's way. He was just happy to be there. He loved being surrounded by showbiz people and he loved performing.'

And having Kenny in the show stimulated Batt into doing Everettesque things, which he loved. For instance, at one point during the show Batt had Kenny throw a fishing line into the orchestra and pull out a real-life viola player; little touches like that.

There's no doubt that Kenny was way outside his comfort zone doing musical theatre, but as rehearsals drew to a close a camaraderie had developed among the cast and crew that energized Kenny, giving him the strength to carry on and enjoy himself. It was perhaps a blessing that there were no 'leading roles', so to speak. If it had been *The Hunting of the Snark* starring Kenny Everett and about thirty also-rans it wouldn't have worked, that would have placed far too much pressure on him. 'He was probably the most famous person in the cast, but he wasn't presented that way and we didn't sell the show on his name,' says Batt. 'It was a real mixture but there were no stars and I think Kenny felt protected by the fact that he was surrounded by a great bunch of professionals who were all on the same level as him.'

Ironically, Batt was criticized by the press for not using Kenny enough, but it simply wasn't practical or fair to burden him with more time on stage. At the end of every performance Batt would call on Kenny in his dressing room and see a man physically exhausted, quite unable to give any more. 'Had the role of the Billiard Marker (and it wasn't one of the bigger roles) gone to anyone else, the show would have lost a wonderful edge.'

The Hunting of the Snark opened at the Prince Edward Theatre on 24 October 1991. Unfortunately, despite all the investment, hard work, excellent score and happy cast, it was universally panned by the critics and closed seven weeks later on 12 December.

As is so often the way, the audiences themselves held opposing views to the critics, and many who saw the show enjoyed it. James Hogg, one of the co-authors, can testify to this, having seen the musical twice during its short run. He also recalls that Kenny was terrific in his role as the Billiard Marker and appeared to enjoy every second he spent on that stage. He most certainly did not appear like a man who was dying.

Fortunately, theatregoers today pay far less attention to the once all-powerful critics, choosing instead to go more by word of mouth or recommendation. Unfortunately for *Snark*, this particular culture had yet to become prevalent in Theatreland, and so it sank without trace.

Kenny, like everyone else involved in the show, was deeply upset by the closure and found it hard not to take the critical mauling personally. Mike Batt was just glad to have him around. 'We held each other up. There were times when I'd pop in and see him after a show and he'd say, "Come on, let's go and have a Chinese," and we'd go down to Chinatown. It was nice to have a mate there who you could have a laugh with, or just sit there and be quiet with. We didn't have to make conversation all the time. He was an extraordinarily stoical person. When he was in hospital some time later he used to send me postcards letting me know what was going on. I remember reading one which said something like, "I'm on drips now and in quite a lot of pain. Never mind, eh!" I think he took life like that. Once he knew that he had HIV, that was it. He altered his attitude accordingly and ploughed on. He was an amazing man.'

Despite the early closure of *Snark*, Kenny had enjoyed his experience on the West End stage immensely. And notwithstanding what the critics said about the show, Kenny himself had received encouraging reviews. He could (and did) walk away from the Prince Edward Theatre with his head held high, having accomplished something that perhaps even he believed himself incapable of doing, as he explained during his appearance on *Desert Island Discs* in 1994. 'If you forget your lines or you land in the wrong place and fall over a dancer, the orchestra will have to stop and start again. It'll be a nightmare! You've got to get it right. You've just got to concentrate – and I did. I told myself to behave and I got it right. I remembered all my lines and twirled in the right places.' In terms of responsibility, it must have been terrifying. And for somebody with Everett's temperament and tendency to 'wander off', it was a masterclass in willpower.

He later went on to cite the musical as one of his proudest ever achievements. And it's not difficult to see why. Working on the radio was second nature to him, and had been since the mid-sixties. Even TV, despite some early wobbles, had become something he could do standing on his head. He felt comfortable. He was sure of his talent and ability and had complete confidence in those around him. These shows weren't 'achievements' in the true sense of the word. To us they are. To us they're towering achievements, littered with creative and comic genius. But to Kenny, they were work. They were his job. He was certainly proud of what he did for a living, but it all came naturally to him. With *Hunting of the Snark* he'd had to face every one of his personal and professional demons simultaneously, and all in the knowledge that he was living with (what was at that time) a terminal disease. Then again, maybe that was what spurred him on.

Kenny's affinity and association with *Hunting of the Snark* went with him to the grave. Mike Batt explains: 'Unfortunately I couldn't get to his funeral as I was in New York, but somebody told me that "Children of the Sky", which was the opening track from *Snark*, was played as his coffin was brought into the crematorium. It was his favourite song from the show and I think it was even one of his choices on *Desert Island Discs*. I was so honoured by all this though – honoured but extremely sad.'

For the opening night of *Hunting of the Snark* Kenny had flown his parents over from Australia first class. In spite of the huge distance between them, Kenny had made every effort to visit his mum and dad, and Cate, as often as he could, especially since discovering a great knack for surviving long plane journeys: 'Get very drunk and pass out quick.' One particular long-haul flight, however, he'd never forget. Kenny made a habit of bringing along with him a little radio. Listening by the porthole he could quite often pick up the local FM band down below, so he'd hear something like, 'This is WXYZ Kansas . . .' and know he was over Kansas and think, How interesting, Kansas. This one time he was listening away when the captain's voice intruded on his waveband and in a solemn tone said, 'Ground Control, we've just found a note in the loo saying that the bomb is going to go off at twelve o'clock.' Seconds later one of the cabin crew burst out of the cockpit and walked purposely down the aisle. Kenny managed to grab him and whispered, 'I know what's going on.' The man looked back sternly, 'Don't tell anybody!'

Fortunately it turned out to be a hoax. When they landed and the tannoy came on, instead of the usual 'Please stay in your seats until the plane has come to complete standstill', the pilot's announcement was simply: 'Get off!'

For this trip, Kenny was accompanied to Australia by Cleo Rocos. Another time he and Cate went over to Sydney for the gay Mardi Gras. 'He loved Australia,' says Cate. 'We used to go for long walks along the beach at Perth and he'd say to me, "What does it feel like, living in paradise?" I'd say, "Why don't you come and live here?" We were always trying to get him to move here. He really did like it. He loved the fact that he could walk around in Australia and people never bothered him.'

35

HIV Positivity

DESPITE HAVING BEEN tested positive for HIV in 1987, the press couldn't get a confession out of Kenny until 4 April 1993, exactly two years to the day before he died. Rumours had been circulating since 1991, when both Nikolai and Freddie Mercury died within a few months of each other, and had culminated in the Sunday newspaper, the *People*, printing a photo of Kenny, stating: 'Comic Kenny Everett looks pale and gaunt in this amazing photograph which shows why friends are so concerned about his health ... two years ago, his gay lover Nikolai Grishanovich died of AIDS.'

The photo in question had been taken outside the Chelsea and Westminster Hospital where Kenny had been receiving treatment for HIV. 'I'd been spotted by a press cameraman,' he said. 'He took lots of photographs of me walking with an umbrella and I was looking a little annoyed about the rain. The next day there was this huge colour photograph in the newspaper of me looking annoyed!'

It wasn't so much how he looked as where he was going. Had Kenny been wandering down Oxford Street looking annoyed, it would have been too tenuous, even for them! The press knew full well that it was likely Kenny was HIV positive, but in order to run a story and squeeze out a confession they needed more than just a look of slight displeasure. A trip to the Chelsea and Westminster Hospital, home to Europe's largest HIV unit, was exactly what they needed.

Now that the rumours had been printed, their substance could be confirmed or denied. Kenny had been on a short break in Italy and was due back in London in the afternoon. When he got out of his taxi at Lexham Gardens, the journalists were waiting for him. 'There were four of us outside the house,' said Chris Pharo of the *Sun*. 'We said, "Well, Kenny, you've obviously seen today's papers. We have to ask the question: Are you HIV positive?" To which he replied, "Yes."'

Kenny had never hidden the fact he was HIV positive. 'I just chose not to broadcast it on my show,' he said. 'If people had said to me, "Nikolai died of AIDS, do you worry about catching it?" I would have said no, because I already have it.'

As far as Paul Gambaccini is concerned, Kenny's forced confession was a watershed moment which signalled the end of what had been a prolonged and unscrupulous attack on the gay community. 'I think Kenny's exposure in the tabloids for being HIV positive was the last attempt by the tabloid press to stigmatize gay people. The eighties was really the Murdoch reign of terror – the dark ages – and they were trying to either expose, invent or seduce every gay person they knew, every gay celebrity, but they came a cropper because they had so little respect for gay people that they thought that almost every famous gay person must patronize rent boys.'

Up until a few years before Kenny came out as being gay he'd enjoyed a cordial relationship with the gentlemen of the press. In 1975 when there were allegations of an attempted suicide, the press knew full well that there was more to the story than they were being told, but they didn't push it. Also, Kenny's friends weren't the only ones who knew he was gay. Several reporters were aware, and those who didn't had a very good idea, but again, they refrained from going for the jugular. They knew that it could have destroyed Kenny's career, and they quite liked him. Back then Kenny sold papers because he ruffled feathers, and in the most original of ways.

By 1982 the moral paradigm to which the press usually adhered seemed no longer to be valid. A new breed of editor had been created; one that would change the face of tabloid journalism for ever. Ruthless as orcs, these people had one lesson drilled into them from the off: Profit at any cost – human included. Stylistically, things would also change. From now on it would be ignominy and loathing 'masked' as consideration for the 'Great British Public'.

Kenny noticed the shift almost immediately. All of a sudden photographers began loitering outside his flat and reporters would appear as he was arriving home after a night out. Kenny was now high on a list of gay celebrity targets (not all of them openly gay at the time), who would be hounded for as long as the tabloids could keep the public fearful of what they'd christened the 'Gay Plague'.

In 1987, the media assault on the gay community went nuclear when the *Sun* ran a completely untrue story accusing Elton John of sleeping with under-age rent boys. 'That cost them a million quid,' remembers Paul Gambaccini. 'Because Elton actually had eighteen thousand witnesses who said he was in Madison Square Garden at the time it was supposed to have happened.'

Despite the record pay-out, McKenzie was unrepentant about running the story. 'I think the *Sun* should have its million quid back,' he later said. 'It hasn't damaged him at all, has it? Libel can only have a value if there has been some kind of damage, right? Where is the damage? Where? There's nothing wrong with him. So no, I don't feel bad about him, not at all.'

So the 'story' being absolute codswallop counted for nothing then? This wasn't journalism; it was an attempt to stigmatize all homo-sexuals, thus creating mass prejudice, hundreds of pages of copy and a huge profit.

On the tabloids' hit-list were Freddie Mercury, Holly Johnson and Kenny – and my word did they go to town. Many reading this will remember only too well the incessant bile that was printed about the three stars. Yet once again the attempt to turn the British public into narrow-minded idiots failed. 'The public wouldn't buy the *Sun*'s attempt to discredit Freddie,' says Gambaccini. 'And with Kenny, the attempt to discredit him for being HIV positive failed too – the public supported him. After that, they all gave it up. They realized that there was no money to be made. In my opinion, Kenny performed a tremendous public service, without intending to or knowing it.'

It was perhaps naive of the *Sun* to have another go at Ev. Eight years previously, right at the very start of the AIDS epidemic, Kenny had walked nervously out of his flat and had declared to the world that, 'Two husbands are better than one'. In those days the media was awash with anti-gay sentiment and the ménage à trois story made front-page news – not only here in the UK, but also in Australia. Yes, he received some verbal abuse from a few builders, which did upset him, but did it affect his career? Not in the slightest.

'Kenny was breathtakingly naive,' says Chris Tarrant. 'He could not get his very intelligent head around the fact that he may not have chosen the best time to come out. Thank God the public loved him!'

The one thing that did change when Kenny confessed to being gay and HIV positive was his celebrity. From then on it would take on a new tone: he would be a gay/HIV celebrity, someone famous for being famous and for being gay, then HIV positive. This labelling has without doubt hindered Kenny's 'legend', if you like, as he is still often remembered as being, 'The funny poof who died of AIDS.'

Despite the public not giving two hoots about the tabloid muck, the fact that it appeared in the first place upset Kenny deeply, as did the methods the press resorted to in extracting their information. As far as we know, he only ever once vented his hatred for the press, or those elements responsible.

In September 1987 he was interviewed by the journalist Tom Hibbert for a long-running feature in *Q Magazine* entitled 'Who the Hell . . .' This was devised around Hibbert's withering and acerbic wit, as well as his extraordinary ability to get public figures to make idiots of themselves. While Kenny doesn't oblige in that respect, the interview was obviously an awkward and at times ill-tempered affair and the feature itself makes for uncomfortable reading.

After Hibbert's preamble regarding Kenny's coverage since coming out, they move on to his opinion of the press. 'I think they should all be lined up and shot,' said Kenny. 'They are all Fleet Street Shits. I really mean this. They should be tortured before being shot. For about three months – three months of torture. They came to my front door once and they said, "Hello, it's the *Sunday Mirror*, do you have AIDS?" I said, "No, I don't." And they said, "Well, what would you do if you did?" And I said, "I'd go round the world and have a good time." The next day the headline was: "Kenny Everett in Amazing AIDS Pact". They're all shits. I've had enough. I really have had enough.'

So, Kenny may well have been immune from a public backlash, but he was not immune from the effects of press harassment and gutter journalism. How could he have been? But the fact that the public's love for him was of the unconditional variety must have helped him enormously.

This was demonstrated in glorious fashion the day after Kenny admitted he was HIV positive. He had no idea what to expect when he arrived at work on the Monday. Lots of people asking, 'Are you OK?' probably.

One of the first DJs he met that morning was Chris Tarrant. 'Nobody quite knew what to say, because I'd never actually met anyone who was HIV positive before, and I remember him coming into the studio and I went, "Hello, Kenny, how are you?" which was a stupid thing to say, and he went, "Darling, I'm doomed. I'm doomed." And that became a release for everybody, it made it easier for us, because every time we saw him it was, "You're doomed, Everett, you're doomed." He always made light of things.'

One thing he most certainly wasn't expecting were the hundred or so well-wishers who were waiting for him as he arrived at Euston Tower. 'It really, really touched him,' says Jo Gurnett. 'There was still a great deal of ignorance surrounding HIV and AIDS, and a lot of people believed you could catch it from shaking hands and things. But when Kenny arrived at work, all anybody wanted to do was hug him.'

Kenny was mobbed when he arrived at Euston Tower, and by the time he made it inside he'd been squeezed half to death. Paul Burnett recalls: 'He fell through the door, looked at me and said, "Paul, I'm black and blue. Everywhere I go, people keep coming up and hugging me." He certainly wasn't complaining. In fact he was extraordinarily touched by it. I don't think he knew what reaction he was going to get from the public and he was naturally quite nervous. He was very pleasantly surprised though.'

This hugging lark would continue for the rest of his life. 'People would stop him in the street,' remembers Jo, 'and as opposed to just asking for an autograph they'd give him a hug. They were letting him know how much they loved him, and that they didn't care what he was suffering from. How could that not touch you?'

Kenny continued arriving at Euston Tower (although not always to a mob of screaming fans) for just over a year after going public, and presented his last ever show for Capital Gold on Tuesday, 31 May 1994. The courage which Kenny displayed during this period does at times beggar belief, and discussions on the subject have produced smiles and tears from many an interviewee.

Although sympathetic, few of Kenny's friends and colleagues had any idea how to treat a dying man, especially one who was, or would be, dying of AIDS. It was a new and at times extremely uncomfortable experience. Yes, he was the one who was ill, but the prospect of having to deal with hundreds of long silences for months on end soon forced him to take action. 'I think he thought the best way to deal with what was happening was to just go with the flow and laugh about it,' says Paul Burnett. 'That helped him, of course, but as importantly it helped everyone else around him. It was a very brave road to take.'

Kenny always claimed that, regardless of what happened with the disease, his sense of humour would be the last thing to go. Indeed it was, and during his final months at Capital Gold he came out with some absolute corkers. 'The day he went public about having full-blown AIDS I remember meeting him in the studio,' says Paul Burnett. 'He was on directly after me and during the news he said, "Paul, when I first go on air and say, 'Hi, folks, it's Cuddly Ken here,' I want you to shout, 'You're still here then?'" And I said, "I can't do that, Ken. It'll sound awful. I'll tell you what, let's get everybody in and we'll all do it as a chorus." There were so many well-wishers in the place, it seemed to make sense. Kenny said, "OK, that'll be great." Sure enough, he went on air, played the first record and then straight afterwards said, "Hello, folks, it's Cuddly Ken here!" and we all shouted, "You're still here then?" And he said something like, "How dare you! They just don't care!" And that was that. It was an extremely bittersweet moment.'

This macabre theme quickly became the norm, and despite his

undoubted suffering, and the underlying sadness of the situation, from a comedic point of view Kenny was in his element. The more ill he became, the more material he had! 'In that period before the mid-nineties, it meant that your friends who were HIV positive were going to have a short and brutish existence,' explains Paul Gambaccini. 'And I thought Kenny was one of the most courageous people I ever knew because he met the challenge with humour. Towards the end, he said, "It's a good thing I'm on Capital Gold – I've gone deaf in one ear and it's in mono."'

'His sense of humour never left him,' says David Jensen. 'I remember not long before he finished broadcasting, I popped into his studio to say hi. He was sitting in one of those big office chairs. The ones that, when you lean back on them, you almost go into a horizontal position. He looked at me and said, "Hey, David, look at this—' and he kicked back the chair into a horizontal position, crossed his arms over his chest and closed his eyes. I remember looking at him and saying, "What the heck are you doing?" And he said, "Just practising, dear."'

When Kenny's condition became full-blown, he once again spoke to the press – this time voluntarily. 'Everyone at the station was unsure as to whether he'd carry on broadcasting,' says Paul Burnett. 'But he did. He came bouncing in the day after the press release like nothing had happened, and he wasn't putting it on. His philosophy was, Right, it's out there. Everybody knows so let's just get on with things.' And from a health point of view, Kenny's attitude followed suit. 'It's not affecting my work,' he said. 'How healthy do you have to be to play "Da Doo Ron Ron"?'

Not long after this Kenny came face to face with a situation that could well have finished him mentally. He now had full-blown AIDS and was, in his own words, 'About to take a seat in God's waiting room.' But his reaction to the situation surprised even Paul Burnett.

Every so often the National Blood Service would set up shop for the day at Euston Tower, and the Capital and Capital Gold DJs would go on the air and encourage people to come in and give blood. 'There used to be an enormous reception area on the ground floor of the Euston Tower,' remembers Paul. 'And the whole area would be chocka-block with beds and nurses. Given what Kenny had just announced, it could have been very, very awkward for him. Really upsetting. He was having absolutely none of it though. I remember him walking into reception, in amongst all these nurses and donors and bottles of blood, etc., and he lay down on a bed, rolled up his sleeves and said, "Right then. Who wants mine?" He had full-blown AIDS! It was unbelievable. Everybody there, without exception, just cracked up. It was hilarious. It wasn't really up to him to break the ice with people, but that's exactly what he did. It wasn't as bad as the mid- to late eighties, when people wouldn't breathe the same air or use the same toilet seat as somebody with HIV, but there was still a lot of ignorance around and he certainly helped break down barriers. I've never seen courage like it. Astonishing really, when you consider what he was going through.'

It wasn't all guffaws, however, and there were times when even a shedload of courage and an unparalleled sense of humour simply weren't enough. While broadcasting he'd occasionally forget about his fate, and then it would hit him again: the enormous psychological toll of knowing that you're going to die, but not quite when. That said, working was still preferable to being stuck at home. But as the disease progressed, so did his ability to maintain his by now legendary courage and sense of humour. One of Kenny's fellow presenters at Capital Gold, David Hamilton, witnessed the other side of the coin first-hand. 'I remember once he just got up and walked out. This was mid-show. He just took off his earphones, walked out of the studio and left the building. He'd obviously had enough. He came back in the next day, I think, but at that moment he had to get out. It was amazing he carried on as long as he did.'

Kenny had an inkling that he might be HIV positive as early as 1983. His reaction to the initial warnings from people like Paul Gambaccini hadn't fallen totally on deaf ears, but they certainly hadn't had the desired effect. 'He knew it could happen,' says Jo Gurnett. 'In fact he knew it probably would, given what Nikolai had got up to. He was a fool for not practising safe sex, but he wasn't stupid, if you see what I mean. It was a choice he made. Of course he was in danger, but he kind of just accepted it and got on with things.'

Before those famous doom-laden TV commercials of the late eighties warning against the spread of AIDS, there were three radio commercials. One of them had Ian Dury saying, 'I used to sing about sex, drugs and rock'n'roll. Now only one of them is safe.' Then there was a generic woman pointing out that it didn't just affect men, and then there was Paul Gambaccini. 'Remarkably, they let me write my own copy – amazing,' says Paul. 'Which I did and they accepted it. I thought, this is a very progressive attitude. And of course the United Kingdom did have a progressive attitude towards the disease, particularly with reference to the United States, where Reagan didn't even mention it until 1987.'

Since Gambaccini was doing this public information announcement he thought he'd better make sure he was negative first. It turned out he was fine. That week, Gambaccini had arranged to have lunch with Kenny and Nikolai, and called Ev the day before to finalize details. 'By the way,' Paul closed with. 'I've had an HIV test.' There was silence on the other end of the line. 'Oh,' a voice said finally. 'I've had an HIV test, too. I'll give you the result on a piece of paper over lunch.' Kenny never gave Gambaccini that piece of paper. 'That was his way of telling me. Now I knew at that point that Nikolai was positive, and as a matter of fact, that was my social tolerance moment. You know how Diana was acclaimed for going into the hospitals and touching people with AIDS? Well, it came time for dessert in this restaurant and we ordered a bowl of ice cream, which we would share. I got my spoon to dip into the ice cream, and I suddenly thought, oh my God, this is where you are testing what you are saying in public, because obviously Nikolai was also dipping into this ice cream. I had to put up or shut up. And I did put up and, of course, as we know, it was all safe. But that was a landmark moment in my personal experience with AIDS.'

When Kenny's condition was confirmed in 1987, it served as a catalyst for him making some pretty important changes. Kenny's outlook on life was shifting, in that he now had an outlook. From a personal point of view, he knew that he would have to modify his behaviour. It was about ten years too late, of course, but he was where he was. Little was known about HIV/AIDS and for all he knew, a cure might be found before he became full-blown. There were also a very small percentage of sufferers who didn't become full-blown. To give himself the best possible chance, Kenny decided to take action. 'When he found out he was HIV positive he went on a fitness regime,' remembers Jo Gurnett. 'He had his walking, of course, but he began going to the gym three times a week, doing weights and things. He looked fantastic. What an irony though. He became fitter when he was HIV positive than he'd ever been in his life!'

And it has to be said he looked it. In June 1993 Kenny was asked to do an interview for *Hello!* magazine, which would feature a series of photographs taken at his flat with his niece Joanna accompanying him. He wasn't keen at first, but the money was good and it also gave him the opportunity to dispel a few myths. Even then people assumed that anyone with HIV would weigh six stone and look as if they were at death's door. Kenny was the antithesis of this description, and it did help to educate people about the disease.

Kenny enjoyed keeping fit; it all came quite naturally to him, although perhaps not to us! Kenny Everett the hill walker was hard enough to comprehend, as was Kenny Everett the body builder. But the one that really makes the mind boggle is Kenny Everett the squash enthusiast. Geoff Mullin was his partner in this most unlikely of pastimes. 'Ev was a terrible squash player, but he loved it. He used to enjoy going berserk around the court, running himself mental. God, he was awful though. Just the thought of Everett playing squash still makes me smile.'

The last note Kenny ever wrote to Geoff mentioned squash. It was written when he was at Capital Gold. Geoff hadn't spoken to him in a while and this suddenly arrived one day. It reads:

Dear Geoffrey
How the devil are you? Why don't you ring? Don't you love me any more? Is it true what they say about Dixie?
　Yours,
　Edith
　PS: Squash?

Becoming super-fit more than likely helped prolong Kenny's life, but it was never going to save it. As his immune system began to fail, his need for treatment gradually increased, and by the end of 1994 he summed up his condition in the *Daily Mail* as, 'Very delicate. I feel like a Kleenex for men.' Yet another brave statement, but by now the jokes were becoming more elusive. Skin cancer had begun to blemish his face and he had contracted a violent dose of tuberculosis. He was also now suffering from regular bouts of pneumonia, something which ultimately kills around 16 per cent of all AIDS sufferers.

In his final interview, which took place in January 1995, Kenny described a world of both physical and mental devastation, and you don't necessarily have to be an admirer of Kenny's to find it hard going. By this point he had lost his sense of taste and was deaf in one ear. His eyesight was also deteriorating. 'I think I've had everything now,' he said. 'Last week one lung filled with fluid and I had to take pills the size of fists. I don't know what's lined up next.'

As upsetting as this interview undoubtedly is, it was also hugely significant, as it was the first time a major UK star had spoken publicly about what it was like living through the advanced stages of HIV/AIDS. This was another public service then, as although many people had an idea of what happened, the detail Kenny goes into makes it all extraordinarily real.

In addition to this, there was an 'It'll never happen to me' attitude which was as prevalent then as it unfortunately is today. The effects of the disease needed to, ironically, be brought to life. The paparazzi photos of Freddie Mercury, taken when he too was dying of full-blown AIDS, had been billed as 'shocking', but were they really? In relation to how we were used to seeing him, then yes, they probably were. But ultimately they were just pictures of an extremely 'gaunt' (the media's favourite HIV/AIDS description) rock star, and by no means told the full story. Unless you knew somebody who had the disease, it would remain intangible. Although Kenny was also a star, he was our star. He was Cuddly Ken, and people felt close to him without knowing him. But the significance of the interview, or perhaps just the interview itself, was missed by those fighting the disease and would ultimately be a lost opportunity.

Kenny's testimony had gone beyond shocking. As we have said, not only did he detail what the disease was doing to his body, but also to his mind and indeed his spirit. It was one of the most important pieces of 'AIDS awareness' propaganda since the start of the epidemic and should have been seen wherever Kenny had an audience. Unfortunately, after appearing in one edition of the *Daily Mail*, it became history.

36

Goodbye, Darlings!

K ENNY WASN'T AFRAID of dying, and he wasn't particularly scared
of pain. In fact, for somebody who once described himself as
being, 'short, wiry and occasionally a bit sensitive', he was extraordinarily resilient. Brave, courageous, stoic: some of the many
adjectives both we and our interviewees have used when describing
Kenny in his final months. But the other adjective prevalent towards
the end of his life is 'reclusive'.

Although he wasn't a particularly vain individual, Kenny hated
what AIDS was doing to him aesthetically. He'd never enjoyed people
staring at him in the street, but usually it had been because they'd seen
'Kenny Everett' or 'that funny bugger off the telly'. Now that funny
bugger off the telly was beginning to change physically and was
becoming even more self-conscious. He didn't need to put himself
through this, and from the start of 1995 he withdrew completely, not
just from public life, but from his social life. His last hurrah had been
his fiftieth birthday party, which had taken place at Heaven (where
else?) just before Christmas. He wasn't drinking at the time and had
only recently returned from a trip to Australia. At first he hadn't been
keen on having a party, but friends had persuaded him. 'I thought it
might be jolly,' he said, 'being an ex-disco bunny.'

Heaven had been a home-from-home for Kenny since 1979. He'd
enjoyed hundreds of nights out there, and had spent the vast
majority of his time on the dance floor. Now, for the first time ever, he
was a spectator. 'I managed a couple of twirls, but then just sat down
and watched the others,' he said. 'Then some friends tried to push

some drinks into me, but I thought I'd better go home.' This was a big change for Kenny, and brought with it an upsetting realization. If all he could do at his favourite nightclub was watch other people have a good time, what was the point in going? His retirement as a 'disco bunny' was now official.

A couple of weeks earlier, whilst visiting Cate and his parents in Australia, Kenny had been taken ill. Up until then he'd had a wonderful time, as had Cate. 'He was in great form, and he seemed to be in good health. Then, towards the end of his trip, Kenny began to get stomach pains.' All of a sudden Kenny was in a bad way. 'He was very uncomfortable,' says Cate. 'I thought it may have been something he'd eaten, but it wasn't.' Kenny hated being ill in front of people. 'I find it unbearable to bring other people down. All I want to do when I feel unwell is crawl into a hole.' And this is precisely what Kenny did. He knew the stomach pains weren't food poisoning. He'd had that before. These were probably AIDS-related. The sooner he was back in London, the better.

Returning home had been a bittersweet experience. Much as he was looking forward to being back in Kensington, Kenny was aware that he would probably never see his parents again. They were too old to travel to England, and pretty soon he'd probably be too ill to travel back to Australia. His parents knew it too. Kenny may never have been especially close to them, but Tom and Lily Cole were incredibly proud of their son and of course loved him deeply. They never once voiced disapproval of Kenny's lifestyle or sexuality, and whatever they thought privately always remained exactly that: private. Maurice was their son and had done far more good in the world than bad. In fact, he'd done more good than most. How many other people had brought happiness into the lives of tens of millions of people? This may have been at the expense of a close relationship, but he would always be their Mo, and nobody could ever take that away from them.

One member of the family who Kenny was confident of seeing again was his sister Cate. The Cole children were both resilient, but the elder of the two undoubtedly more so. Cate was his big sister, and if the stomach pains were perhaps signalling the beginning of the end, Kenny couldn't think of anyone else he'd rather have with him.

But what Kenny wanted and what Kenny asked for usually took some reconciling. 'I was in constant touch with him by telephone from Australia,' remembers Cate. 'And then suddenly the calls stopped and I couldn't reach him.' Cate was aware that the stomach pains had continued after his return from Australia, and she knew that he'd been hammering the booze a bit around Christmas and his fiftieth. But what she didn't know was that the pains had worsened, and that he was due in hospital at the end of January for tests. 'When I eventually got hold of Ev, I discovered that he had to go into hospital for a colonoscopy and some other tests. It appears that after he'd got back, his boyfriend Freddie had been feeding him milkshakes with raw eggs in them and at the time it wasn't good to be eating anything with raw eggs! Freddie wasn't to know, bless him. He thought he was feeding him some sort of health drink. But Ev had caught a really bad tummy bug and this was on top of the pains he already had. He was so susceptible.'

In addition to the colonoscopy, Kenny was then informed that an endoscopy would also be in order. 'He was bothered because there wasn't anybody available to take him in,' recalls Cate. 'Jo Gurnett was very busy working, I think, and Freddie had gone to Italy. I just felt like he was ready.' As we've already stated, reconciling 'want' and 'ask' was a difficult one for Kenny, and even if you knew he wanted something, you had to bide your time. 'It could only happen when he was absolutely ready,' says Cate. 'You always had to wait and you could never push him. In the end I said, "Look, Ev, would you like me to come over?" And he said, "But it's a lot of trouble for you, you can't just leave Conor." And I said, "No, it's absolutely no problem."'

When Cate arrived at Kenny's flat a few days later, she was shocked on first seeing him. 'When I walked through the door he was lying on a yellow sofa eating a bowl of cereal, but you could hardly see his face, the poor thing. He was almost the same colour as the sofa. He looked so ill and I was so relieved to be with him.'

Cate stayed at her flat in Abingdon Road five minutes from Kenny's in order to give Kenny and his boyfriend Freddie the space they might need. After a few days she accompanied Kenny to the Chelsea and Westminster Hospital where he was to have the tests he'd been so dreading. Kenny was now a familiar face at the Chelsea and Westminster AIDS Unit and was on first-name terms with the majority of the staff. He'd been receiving treatment there since 1987, and had been a visitor even before that, while accompanying Nikolai. But whenever he had to go in, regardless of what he was having done to him, Kenny always did his best to make everybody laugh. 'I have to say they were fantastic in the hospital, absolutely fantastic,' says Cate. 'And they loved Ev. It always felt like they were doing more than they could. They didn't have the drugs they do now, of course, and they tried everything.' Had Kenny not become full-blown for another few years, who knows? His ex-boyfriend Pepe lived for two years after Kenny. 'Just like Ev, Pepe went downhill very quickly,' remembers Cate. 'I visited him in hospital quite a few times before he died. He was such a beautiful man, and then suddenly he got ill and was dead within weeks. I think the combination of drugs he was taking had eventually induced cancer. It was all so experimental in those days. The doctors tried everything, as they had done with Ev. I don't know when they discovered the combination drugs they use now, and I kind of don't want to.'

When the tests were over, Cate took her weary brother back to the flat and got him comfortable. Now she was here, it was time they had a chat about the future. This would be a new experience for Kenny! 'The whole thing is tedious,' he once said. 'I'm used to bouncing around and not giving a damn. But suddenly I really have to give a damn.' Kenny had never wanted to discuss the future. 'This time he had no choice,' says Cate. 'But rather than bombard him with a whole list of questions, I thought it best to drop the odd one in during conversations, that way he wouldn't feel like he was decision making!' One of the first questions Kenny asked Cate after she arrived was how long she thought she might stay. 'I had to be very careful how I answered that question,' recalls Cate. 'I didn't want to use words like "the end" so I just promised him that I would only go back to Australia when he was sure he didn't need me any more.' There was of course no way of knowing how long that would be: 'We were still quite optimistic at the time so I was initially thinking about a month until he was well enough.' In all Cate would spend four months looking after Kenny before he died.

Kenny's relief on being reunited with his sister was apparent, as he was finding the unpredictable nature of his condition more and more difficult to handle. 'At present I can still feel all right for a few days at a time, and just get used to it when, wallop! It's an up-and-down illness. Very exhausting, and everything hurts a lot. Even showering is painful.' Illnesses arising from full-blown AIDS can vary enormously in both number and severity. Kenny could be stubborn in many ways, but he knew that he couldn't do this alone. Cate prepared the ground perfectly though, and made sure that her little brother didn't feel like he was losing control. It had been thirty-five years since Cate had left home, leaving her brother back in Liverpool with his two tape recorders and dreams of one day usurping David Jacobs. Yet despite the circumstances and eventual outcome, the Cole children living under the same roof again after such a long time would provoke far more smiles than it would tears.

After a couple of weeks Kenny asked Cate to move in so she could better care for him without having to walk to and from her flat late at night. Then there were three of them living in the flat. Kenny had been living with his partner Freddie for a number of years, but over the past few months things hadn't been going well between the two. 'By the time I arrived in London the relationship with Freddie was becoming a bit difficult. I think it was hard for Freddie to see the man he loved becoming so unwell. Ev was living on the top floor of the flat, and Freddie on the bottom. That's another reason why he needed a bit of TLC, I think.'

Cate's arrival did help bring Kenny and Freddie closer for a while, and they both moved back into the same bedroom. 'The three of us lived very harmoniously for a good period' says Cate. 'We had little dinner parties for the three of us and would all go to the hospital together, often myself and Freddie riding there in tandem on Freddie's Lambretta moped. Ultimately, I think Freddie found it very hard to cope and it wasn't long before he and Kenny began to drift apart again.

'Freddie was a busy man and had to travel a lot with work, and there was no way he could put his life on hold indefinitely. He wanted to look after Ev but life had to go on. There were frustrations on both sides, I think, but not enough communication.' Eventually, Freddie thought it best that he move out of the flat. He'd been offered a good job in Italy and so asked Kenny and Cate if they were OK with him taking it. He'd come back at weekends, but during the week they'd be apart. 'We both said yes,' says Cate. 'It was a really good idea and I think it saved them from falling out badly. But we both missed him.'

After Freddie moved out it was just Kenny and Cate, which is how it would remain until he died. Kenny wanted few visitors and he screened every phone call he received. 'It was like he was in a bubble,' remembers Cate. 'He became very reclusive and didn't want to speak to anybody really, apart from myself, Jo Gurnett and Eric Gear. When the phone rang I'd answer it, and tell him who it was. Nine times out of ten he'd just say, "Tell them I'm asleep." I tried to persuade him to take calls. I didn't want him to become so reclusive, but he was adamant. Cleo used to call and ask if she could bring round some soup, and I'd say "Please let me agree, Ev," but he always said no.'

Kenny's reason for not wanting to see Cleo was simple. She had been his friend and constant companion for the best part of fifteen years and their time together had been glamorous, exhilarating and filled with laughter. The last thing he wanted was for Cleo to see his deterioration. It would tarnish everything, all those wonderful memories. 'In the fifteen years we've been together, I've never once seen you without your make-up on,' he'd said to her. 'But the thing is ... I don't want you to see me without my make-up on. Do you understand? That wouldn't be right either. You realize what I'm saying, don't you, Clee?' Of course Cleo understood. Over the past year or so she had come to terms with Kenny's departure, but cutting the cord and having no contact with her friend was always going to be an impossible task.

Apart from Cate and Eric, one of the people Kenny did see during his final weeks was Barry Cryer. Few of the people Kenny worked with over the years were what you would call an 'influence'. Many became friends and many made him laugh, but the one person Kenny would quote on a regular basis was Barry. 'Kenny used to reference Barry a lot,' remembers Russ Evans. 'I don't think anybody made Kenny laugh like Barry, and he talked about him all the time. I never met him, unfortunately, but Kenny was obviously very, very fond of him.'

Barry's final meeting with his old friend was to be an emotional occasion, but it did Kenny the power of good – not to mention Cate. 'I was getting really worried about him,' says Cate. 'He'd sit there and stare at the wall for hours and hours, and you couldn't get through to him. I always felt that if I pressed him too hard it might open some kind of Pandora's Box, so I just floated around really and tried to remain cheerful.' In an effort to bring Kenny back out of his shell, Cate one day suggested inviting Barry round. 'I said, "Come on, why don't we invite Barry round for a proper cream tea!" And the moment he heard Barry's name he perked up and said yes.'

We've spoken to Barry on numerous occasions about Kenny and this was the one experience he found difficult to describe. 'I went to the flat and Cate greeted me at the door. That was the first and only time Ev hadn't, which felt really strange. Whenever I'd visited previously he'd open the door and say, "Oooh, where's Mrs Ashtray?" and he'd run off and grab one and we'd sit down, have a coffee and start laughing. This time I went in and he was lying on the settee and he was obviously very ill. So I sat down next to him and we laughed and joked for a bit. I was just heartbroken though. As we were talking I was aching inside. I just thought, No. Why is this happening to such a lovely, gentle man?' But for those few hours it was like Kenny had been reborn. 'They sat there and just laughed and laughed,' remembers Cate. 'It was so wonderful to watch, it was like they were creating a new TV show!'

As with Cleo, Kenny and Barry had had a friendship based almost entirely around laughter. They made each other laugh and for ten years had been paid to make the public laugh. As Barry once said, 'Not a bad life, is it?'

Before he died, Kenny paid Barry the ultimate tribute. Asked what he'd like to have written on his tombstone, he said, 'I've been wondering about that. I think it would have to be, "No punchline – ring Barry Cryer!"'

Even though he was withdrawing socially, Kenny was still keen to get out of the flat and harboured hopes, however slim, that one day he might be able to go walking again with the Gears. As it was, he would have to make do with strolls in Richmond Park, where he and Cate would walk arm in arm, watching the fallow deer. On days when Kenny felt too weak to walk, they'd drive to Kensington High Street and find a pub where they could settle quietly into a corner. Their favourite was the Britannia on Allen Street, famous for being the home of some historical hellraising by the likes of Richard Burton and Peter O'Toole. It was there that the subject of Kenny's funeral was first raised, a conversation which Cate had been dreading. 'It was a strange day. Ev hadn't had a drink since Christmas and suddenly asked if he could have a whisky chaser. He had to take these little drops of morphine which had to be very carefully measured out and that was my job. So I gave him his drops and he started drinking his whisky chaser.' After taking a couple of sips Kenny began talking about a friend of his called Edward Duke. Duke was an actor famous for performing a one-man Jeeves and Wooster show, and had died the previous year from an AIDS-related illness. Kenny had attended his funeral, which had taken place at the Catholic church on Farm Street in Mayfair. Attending funerals was something he was sadly becoming used to, but this particular one had been different. 'It was a full Requiem Mass,' says Cate, 'and he'd found the whole thing quite beautiful and very moving. He was also very taken with the church and even mentioned how wonderful the choir was. Then he said what a pity it was that he wouldn't be able to have something similar. And I said, "Look, if that's what you really want, I'll arrange it. It's not a problem." And I promised him there and then that he'd have a full Requiem Mass at Farm Street Church, exactly the same as Edward had.' The church in question had a connection to the Cole family, as a cousin of Kenny and Cate's had been married there some years before. 'It's a stunning building,' says Cate. 'And I was so pleased he wanted to have his funeral there.'

The following Sunday Cate went to Farm Street Church for Mass and met up with the priest. 'He was very supportive and said it would be fine. After that I went back to Ev and told him what had occurred and he was really pleased. Ev also began talking a lot around this time about the afterlife and religion. During one such discussion, as he lay in bed, I felt he wanted me to ask him if he wanted to see a priest. He was obviously thinking about it so I asked, "Really?" not expecting him to want that path. But as soon as I asked him he nodded and said, "Yes please, I would."'

By this time Conor had also come over from Australia. 'I think Ev knew the end was coming,' recalls Cate, 'and he said to me, "It's unfair that you're here by yourself. Why don't you ask Conor to come and stay too?" And I thought, OK, he's preparing. He knows it's the end. So I asked Conor, who was retired, to come over and stay. It was great to see him, but the fact Ev had suggested it upset me. I knew what he was thinking.'

Asking Conor to come over was a timely move, however, as caring for Kenny had begun to take its toll on Cate. 'When I got to London, Cate was a shadow,' recalled Conor. 'She was skin and bones. There was a point where I thought we were going to have a second funeral.' To organize a priest, Conor called the nearest presbytery and eventually got through to a chap called Father William. Conor explained the situation as best he could, and the priest said he'd come over the following day. He obviously changed his mind though, as about eleven p.m. that evening, the doorbell rang. 'I thought surely it can't be the bloody *News of the World* at this hour,' remembers Cate. 'They were always ringing the doorbell, and I was always telling them to bugger off. When I answered, it was Father William. He said as opposed to leaving it to tomorrow he thought he'd come over now, and I thought there's service for you!' Because of the impromptu arrival, what could have been quite a nerve-racking first meeting turned into something quite the opposite. 'He took us all by surprise,' remembers Cate. 'He just breezed straight in, sat on the end of Ev's bed, said, "Hello, Kenny, how are you?" and started nattering. Chat chat chat! They got on like a house on fire. It was wonderful.'

It would be difficult to overestimate the positive effect Father William had on Kenny's preparation for death. Despite requesting a Requiem Mass at his funeral, he continued to wrestle with his conscience and beliefs. He quite naturally assumed that the Catholic Church continued to consider him morally evil. Father William did not subscribe to this one bit. Despite what he too had been taught, the God he believed in was full of love and forgiveness, not threats and purgatory. He was aware of Kenny's past experiences with the Church and sympathized. What he would endeavour to do for him was to restore his faith in the Church and realign it with his belief in God. Then there was the question of forgiveness, which had plagued Kenny since his childhood: 'The worst thing that ever happened to me was being a child,' he once revealed. 'Because I was in a constant state of neurosis about sinning and getting run over before I could confess. I was told that if it happened I would go to hell for ever.' As we know, this had snowballed throughout his adult life and had shown no signs of abating. 'He shouldn't have had to confess or seek forgiveness from the Church,' claims Jo Gurnett. 'It's the Church who should have been seeking his forgiveness. It makes me angry that he felt so guilty for so long. He carried it around with him most of his life.' Rightly or wrongly, confessing and believing himself to be forgiven by God was important to Kenny, and achieving it was something that helped allow him to die in peace.

Despite the underlying inevitability of what was to come, Cate, Conor and the family back in Australia all did their best to remain optimistic. 'Every day you'd read about some new drugs that were being developed and each article offered you a little bit of hope,' says Cate. 'So I'd ring Mum and Dad, and I'd say, "He might get better, you know. He might come through. There are loads of new drugs being trialled. You never know." All in all, we remained quite hopeful.'

Hope was now a valuable commodity in the Cole household and its value wasn't lost on Kenny. In his last interview, which had been conducted by the journalist Angela Levin, he was asked, although indirectly, if he would ever consider suicide as a way out of suffering the final stages of AIDS. 'I know various people have said that if they became terminally ill they would take a pill and end it all before it got too bad, but once you are in a situation like that, it's a different story. You keep thinking someone will invent something to make you better. I couldn't consider suicide to save my life.' What an extremely ironic choice of words! But to Kenny, the prospect of jumping into the unknown with, as he put it 'your own propeller' was far too horrifying. 'If someone ran up behind me and stabbed me between the shoulder blades, I would be quite happy – I wouldn't have done it. Otherwise, as long as I have the chance to survive, I'm going for that, whatever the conditions.'

As with keeping fit, hope on its own didn't stand a chance against an ever-failing immune system and it was only a matter of time before the inevitable happened. At the end of March 1995 Kenny came down with a dose of flu, something which would prevent him receiving treatment for the one disease he was desperately trying to avoid: pneumonia. Back then, pneumonia was responsible for the deaths of the majority of the patients with that particular strain of HIV – and, once contracted, all hope of recovery was gone. Every week Kenny had been receiving anti-pneumonia treatment at the AIDS Unit. 'He'd have to breathe in this kind of medicated oxygen for hours on end,' remembers Cate. 'He absolutely hated it and always said it tasted like the corners of old cupboards. But it was keeping him alive. One day, out of the blue, Kenny decided he no longer wanted treatment. 'He obviously wasn't well but he was well enough to travel to hospital. I was taken by surprise really. He just said, "I'm not well, I'm not going." We both knew that things would become a lot worse if he hung on. I think he must have had enough.'

A few days after missing his treatment, Kenny began displaying the symptoms of pneumonia. This was a devastating discovery for Cate, as she knew that within a matter of days Kenny would probably be dead. The realization came as a terrible shock. 'Kenny had only recently been told by his doctor that he could live for another six months, and I suppose we treated the prognosis almost as a kind of

promise. He'd have six months to live. That's what would happen.'
Cate's daughter, Joanna, to whom Kenny had become especially close
over the years, had brought the date of her wedding forward to June
so that Kenny could attend. 'We even ended up moving the location of
the ceremony from Australia to Italy,' explains Cate. 'Joanna had got
engaged in Italy and had originally wanted to get married there, but
as we were all based in Australia it seemed like madness. Then I
suddenly found myself in the UK and when we were told Ev only had
six months to live it became a really good idea. Ev so wanted to be at
the wedding and he was thrilled when I told him it was happening
well within the six months.'

Kenny knew better than anyone what was happening, but it was
never discussed and everyone carried on as best they could. 'I just
concentrated on trying to make him comfortable, and he carried on
trying to make us all laugh,' remembers Cate. 'We couldn't do anything else really.'

As the month progressed, the weather improved, and on seeing the
April sunshine through his bedroom window Kenny decided he'd like
to spend one last hour on his beloved balcony. 'He made such a
desperate effort to climb up the stairs,' remembers Cate. 'It was so
upsetting to watch. His bedroom was on the bottom floor and his
balcony was upstairs outside his living room. He had to crawl up the
stairs on all fours, just so he could feel the sun one last time. He was
very weak, yet he was so determined. You should have seen his face. It
was as if his life depended on it.' While Kenny was crawling up the
stairs Cate was at his side, helping where she could. 'I was trying to
help him and I went and stood on one of his bare toes. He let out this
scream – 'FUUUUUCK!!' I felt absolutely awful. I'll never forget it. He
laughed about it when we got on the balcony, but at the time I think
he wanted to wring my neck!'

Kenny and Cate talked a lot during their time together, and it was
usually Kenny who would set the pace. 'I didn't want to make him sad
or anything so I just kind of waited for his cues,' recalls Cate. 'I never
wanted to start deep conversations, not unless he initiated it. We
talked when he felt like it and about whatever was on his mind.' One

of the few conversations Cate did initiate took place just days before he passed away. 'It was very late at night and he'd got himself into an awful state. He was extremely agitated and had begun removing his morphine pump.' Cate asked what the hell he was doing. 'I'm going,' said Kenny. 'I want to go now, right now. I'm taking this bloody thing off and I'm going to die.'

'That won't help you to die,' said Cate. 'It'll just make the pain a lot worse.'

After calming Kenny down and re-attaching his morphine pump, Cate began asking him questions about the Beatles. Kenny happily began recalling some of his experiences. 'He was so enthused. Suddenly all these anecdotes started coming. I hadn't seen him like that for years.' When the conversation eventually broke off, Cate asked Kenny if he'd ever met Yoko Ono. 'There was suddenly this trans-formation,' says Cate. 'He sat up, and became Japanese. I'm not kidding you; he turned into Yoko Ono – mimicking her voice and expressions perfectly! It was honestly one of the most amazing things I've ever seen.' Kenny's impersonations normally involved things like huge teeth and chest wigs, or rapidly inflating bottoms, so this was a new one. 'I'd never seen him do anything like that before,' says Cate. 'It was the last time he ever "performed" though. His last show.'

Sleep was at a premium during this period. 'He couldn't sleep because he couldn't breathe,' says Cate. 'It was so uncomfortable for him and on the nights before he died I moved a camp bed into his bedroom. He actually tried to sleep in it on one of the nights. He loved it! His doctors were all due the following day but I think he knew that was it.' But by 3 a.m. Cate could stand it no more, and in a fit of des-peration asked Conor to call for a doctor. 'Even before the doctor arrived we knew there was nothing he could really do,' says Cate. 'He offered to have him taken to hospital, but there was no way that was going to happen. Ev wanted to die at home no matter what. He made me promise him. So the doctor just told us to try and keep him as comfortable as possible.' God knows how, but Kenny, Cate and Conor all managed to scrape a couple of hours' sleep and at 8 a.m. that morning a steady stream of visitors began arriving at 91 Lexham

Gardens. Kenny's doctors were first to ring the bell, followed by Father William. Shortly after they left, Eric Gear arrived, and finally Jo Gurnett. 'Something felt wrong when I walked into the flat,' says Jo. 'This might sound strange, but I could sense he was going to die. I think Cate could too.'

'I think he was ready,' says Cate. 'He'd suffered enough.'

Cate and Jo weren't the only people having premonitions that morning, as Eric Gear had been scheduled to visit Kenny in the afternoon. 'I don't know why I came earlier that day. I just suddenly thought I should. I'm so glad I did though, otherwise I'd never have seen Kenny alive again. I got to see him one last time. I was also there for Cate too, which I was glad about.'

When Eric arrived at about 9.30 a.m., Cate was trying to persuade Kenny to eat some breakfast. 'He was horribly frail by this time,' remembers Eric. 'Anyway, we were chatting away and I'd told him to eat all his breakfast so he'd be strong enough for us to go walking again. Then Cate came down, so I said I'd nip upstairs to get a coffee.' Cate sat down, took Kenny's hand and began chatting quietly to him. 'I was just soothing him really. It was very quiet and he looked very peaceful, and he wasn't in any pain. I remember the nurse came up and dropped some water into his mouth from a sponge, and he patted her on the head and said "Thank you." That made us smile. A few minutes later I was looking at him and he just slipped away. I could feel he'd gone. I squeezed his hand and talked to him for a bit, I suppose I was trying to send him on his way. But he wasn't there any more. I'd been in denial about it all for so long, and the realization of him actually going hit me very quickly. I was beyond crying though.'

Kenny Everett passed away at 10.30 a.m. on Wednesday, 4 April 1995. He was fifty years old. Not once had he complained about what he had been going through. He'd cried once or twice, the last time being when he'd been told by his doctor he had six months to live, but just quietly. There were no histrionics and he never moaned or felt sorry for himself. Since going public about the disease exactly two years before, Kenny had done much to promote awareness and understanding about both HIV/AIDS and its sufferers. He hadn't always done this intentionally, of course, but that was one of the most delightful things about Kenny Everett. Much of what he achieved in his life was done without any intention whatsoever. It just happened. It had been exactly the same when he was diagnosed as being HIV positive. He never intended to catch HIV, just as he never intended to revolutionize music radio or get sacked from Big L for slagging off Garner Ted Armstrong. But his reaction to the three had been the same. 'It had happened. So what? Get on with it.' His final words in his last ever interview sum up his attitude perfectly:

'I've done a lot of heavy-duty living and laughing with a lot of jolly people, so even though I'm not looking forward to the end, the only way to approach it is to just get on with it. The worst crime I could be guilty of now is being miserable about my condition. Please don't make me appear too miserable. I want to be as jolly as possible, for myself and other people. If I stop trying, I'll feel I'm letting them and myself down.'

It didn't matter what was happening to him inside, emotionally or physically. In those final months Kenny never stopped trying and he didn't let anybody down, least of all himself. In fact he did everybody proud. He had died with dignity, courage, and, most importantly of all, with humour. He hadn't had them rolling in the aisles as he was slipping away, but his gentle, waspish asides and saucy quips had kept everybody smiling through the most difficult of times.

Although not a religious person, Cate is adamant that Kenny was still around after he died. 'I certainly felt he was still in the apartment. The house alarm, which he never used and that wasn't even switched on, suddenly started ringing at three in the morning. And then there was this picture. He absolutely hated it for some reason and I'd stood it up on a chair in his bedroom. I swear to God every time I went in there it was face down. He was everywhere, but especially in his studio. That's where you could really feel him. It had the most amazing atmosphere.'

After the initial shock began to subside, Cate, Jo, Conor and Eric went into stoic and responsible mode. 'Cate and I began picking out some clothes to dress him in,' remembers Jo. 'We chose a nice pair of jeans, his favourite shirt and ubiquitous trainers. It was good to keep busy.'

Picking up the phone and informing close friends was always going to be one of the more difficult tasks, something Cate remembers only too well. 'I wasn't looking forward to doing it, but it was important that people who knew and loved Ev didn't just find out from watching TV.' One of the first people Cate spoke to was Lee. 'She was devastated. That was a very difficult call. Despite Kenny falling out with Lee many years before, they were together a long time and had been through so much.'

Also keen to keep busy, Eric decided to walk to the Town Hall and register the death. 'I was glad I could do something. But when I came back the whole place was surrounded by reporters. The street was full of them.'

Somebody had seen Kenny's body being removed from the flat and had informed the press, who were round in a matter of minutes. On their arrival they began ringing the doorbell almost constantly. Somebody was going to have to speak to them. 'In the end I said to Cate that I'd go down and give a statement,' says Jo. 'I went downstairs, opened the door and there was this sea of people. When they saw me there was complete quiet. Everybody stopped talking and looked straight at me. I took a deep breath and thought, how do I do this? I honestly didn't think I could. I read out the statement we had prepared, but I had no idea what I was saying. I was just numb, really. I remember telling myself to try and remain as dignified as possible. When I finished they started shouting questions at me, which I answered as best I could. Who was there when he died, what were his last words, that kind of thing.'

When news of Kenny's death began to spread, so did a cloud of sadness which would descend wherever his radio or TV shows had brought pleasure, and by the end of the day the entire country was engulfed. Some of the first to hear the news were Kenny's colleagues and friends at Euston Tower. 'When he died, the whole of Capital and Capital Gold was in mourning for a very long time,' recalls Paul Burnett. 'Everybody was in tears.' Chris Tarrant had been at lunch with his producer when the news broke and on returning knew immediately that something was wrong. 'We came back in about three o'clock, and everybody, the girls at reception, the security guards; everybody had tears pouring down their faces. I remember thinking, Oh my God, what's happened? Then Annie, my producer, turned to me and said, "Kenny's died." I went up into the office and of course the world was on the phone, and TV crews were coming round. Everybody at Capital loved the guy. He was totally anarchic and irreverent and funny. The superlatives were all true. But most of all he was a very kind, gentle guy.'

As soon as they felt ready, Cate and Jo set about organizing the funeral. It would take place, at Farm Street of course, at 2 p.m. on Monday, 10 April. Father William would take the service, together with the parish priest Cate and Conor had known from their days living in Wimbledon. As expected, Kenny's parents would not be able to attend the service, and instead sent a wreath of flowers with the message: 'Goodbye, son, love you, Mum and Dad.'

When the day of the funeral arrived, Cate woke up feeling dreadful. She was having trouble breathing and felt very unwell. 'I'd caught Ev's bronchial pneumonia. It was just the start of it but by the end of the day I felt awful and had to get a doctor round. That really was so upsetting. It wasn't a good time.'

To make matters worse, Cate was also painfully nervous about who would, or, more importantly, who would not turn up for the funeral. 'I remember saying to Jo Gurnett that I didn't think there'd be many there. You see, he wouldn't see anybody or take any calls for the last few months, and in the end people stopped ringing. I just assumed that people would stay away.'

Stay away they did not. People knew Kenny had had his reasons for not maintaining contact and they respected his privacy. They certainly hadn't stopped loving him and were all going to miss him terribly.

What Cate initially feared might be twenty people, and a stray journalist or two, turned out to be radio's equivalent of a State Funeral. 'The entire profession turned out,' remembers Paul Gambaccini. 'All of the leading DJs, from Wogan to Tarrant, all his old

Radio 1 colleagues, Capital people, they were all there.' And so they were: Noel Edmonds, Alan Freeman, Paul Burnett, Dave Cash, Paul McKenna, David Hamilton, David Jensen, Tony Blackburn – all gathered together in groups, swapping stories and memories of the one person who was widely considered to have perfected the art which the majority of them still practised. This was such a relief for Cate, and, as she took her seat in the church beside Conor, she felt almost overcome with pride.

'So many people turned up for the funeral,' remembers Jo Gurnett. 'Even I was a bit worried about whether people would come, but they did. My God they did. It was a real who's who of the industry.' Jo also remembers the service itself being an extremely dignified affair. 'It was beautiful, and I know Ev would have adored it. Cate had asked me to read the lesson, and I was so nervous when I walked to the pulpit. Then, as I was reading, I remember I kept looking down at the coffin thinking, He's going to jump out. The lid's going to come up and he's going to jump out. It was the only thing that stopped me from breaking down.'

Barry Cryer also delivered a reading, while Kenny's niece, Joanna, recited bidding prayers. The final address was made by Father William, who stated, 'All of you asking, Where is Kenny now? I'm going to tell you. Kenny is with God, because that is where I sent him. I rely on the fact God has the most wonderful sense of humour. Anyone who gets given the gift of laughter and humour will be a very welcome guest in heaven.' The significance of Father William's words would be lost on the majority present, but those who could appreciate their poignancy could not help but be moved.

As the service came to an end and the congregation spilled out on to the road, Farm Street was suddenly awash with tears symbolizing innumerable emotions. 'It's a happy ending,' said a visibly moved Terry Wogan. 'I just give thanks for his life and I'm sure he will be happy in the next life.'

Kenny's old buddy Alan Freeman said, 'It was one of the most beautiful services I have ever been to. I am sure that Kenny, from afar, appreciated it greatly.'

While the full Requiem Mass had been at Kenny's behest, he rather surprisingly decided not to involve himself in selecting the music for the ceremony. 'Father William and I chose Fauré's Requiem for the church, and Jo Gurnett and I chose the music for the crematorium,' reveals Cate. 'After he died, I asked Father William what they'd chosen and he said that Ev hadn't been too bothered about the music and so left it up to us.' At a loss as to what to choose for the crematorium, Cate suddenly remembered Kenny's appearance on *Desert Island Discs* which had taken place a year or so before. 'That was obviously full of his favourite music, so Jo Gurnett and I picked out three tracks: "Children of the Sky" from *The Hunting of the Snark*, "Strawberry Fields" and Puccini's "Symphonic Prelude".' The latter meant more to Kenny than any other piece of music and was in fact requested by him (although perhaps unintentionally) to be played at his funeral on *Desert Island Discs*. He said: 'If I ever do die, I think that as I'm hoiked aloft in a ray of God's lovely sunbeam, I'd like this to be on the gramophone as I go.'

The only regret Cate has about the funeral is that she didn't have the chance to organize a wake for the full congregation. 'Had I had my wits about me and not been so ill, I would have hosted a wake for everyone, just to say thank you for coming. I would have had to hire the Albert Hall though!' The undertaker, who was obviously unnerved by the melee outside the church, had tried his best to hurry things along so as not to be late for the crematorium. 'There was hardly any time to speak to anyone or even say hello or goodbye,' recalls Cate. 'I was ushered away and that was that. It was a shame. As it was, we just had a quiet wake at the flat for a very select group.'

Kenny had requested that half his ashes be interned in his old garden in the Cotswolds, and half on a hill in Dovedale, where he and the Gears had some of their favourite walking holidays.

But before this took place, Jo Gurnett asked Cate if she could take Kenny to one other destination; one which he'd always intended to visit, but sadly never got around to. 'I wanted to take some of Ev's ashes out to the Greek island of Mykonos. I used to go there all the time with friends and Ev always said that one day he'd come with me.

Unfortunately that never happened, so after he died I asked Cate if I could take some of his ashes over there. She very kindly agreed so I put some in a box and arranged to go out.'

A day or two after arriving in Mykonos, Jo and her friends took a walk out towards the harbour. On the way she stopped suddenly. 'I'd just like to be alone for a bit. Do you mind?' As her friends walked away, Jo took out the little box and wandered along the harbour towards some rocks. 'When I got there I stopped and had a look around. He really would have loved it there. Then I climbed up on to a rock and opened the box and said, 'There you are, love, you always wanted to come here. Take care,' and scattered his ashes into a wave as it crashed into the rocks.'

Those assuming Kenny Everett died a rich man would be sadly mistaken, as on death his estate was valued at just £357,438, which also took into account his flat and his car. As we now know, in Kenny's eyes, cash was not king, but many still argue that he should over the years have become one of the richest men in the entertainment industry. Our argument is that any acumen or interest in business would only have kept him away from his studio, and his lack of it is therefore a blessing! Kenny's only financial laments were that his private pension matured when he was fifty, and that his private health insurance scheme didn't cover HIV. The former upset him as it reminded him of all the holidays it was supposed to have paid for, but the latter angered him, and perhaps for good reason. 'I've been with private medical insurers for over twenty years and now they've written to me saying they won't pay for anything that arises from my being HIV. I signed up with them for the purpose of being taken care of for the whole of my life and well before AIDS was known about.' The extent of his lamentation was four or five lines in a newspaper interview though. He didn't go on.

So a businessman he was not, but an archivist he most certainly was. As we mentioned earlier in the book, Kenny left behind over two hundred cartridges and reel-to-reel tapes when he died, which comprise mainly jingles, sound effects (his Kremmen-aids), interviews and shows. Cate donated the entire collection to the National Sound

Archive, which now forms part of the British Library, and it's hoped that one day the compendium will be digitized, so that anybody with a spare few hours will be able to walk in, sit down and be amazed – either for the very first time, or perhaps all over again.

Even Kenny's fabled studio remains in working order, and was for many years situated at the Liverpool Institute of the Performing Arts where it was used as a teaching studio. Long since superseded by digital technology, it now sits in storage at the British Library where it awaits a new home.

By far the most eclectic part of Kenny's archive was his collection of vinyl. Andy Simons works for the British Library and was the man responsible for sorting through it all. 'I spent a long time going through his stuff and was surprised at the lack of vinyl. He hadn't even kept his old 45s!' Some DJs have vinyl collections which run into the tens of thousands, and Kenny must have been given a similar number over the years, but he kept only a couple of hundred. When Cate had given the majority of these away to family members and friends of Kenny's, only four records remained, all of which were catalogued by Andy and remain at the British Library. The four are: *Tony Blackburn Sings*, *Can't Stop Yodelling* by Mary Schneider, *Some of Me Poems and Songs* by Pam Ayres, and, best of all, *Barbara Cartland's Favourite Love Songs*. Kenny had once impersonated Dame Barbara on his television show. In actual fact he appeared as a Scottish Barbara Cartland, complete with a tartan kilt and beret. 'Hello, I'm Barbara Cartland, and you're all under arrest,' was the opening line. 'I'd like to read you an extract from my latest romantic novel: When Lady Penelope swoons, her bosoms pop out like balloons. The butler stands by with a gleam in his eye, and pops them back in with warm spoons.' Maybe the LP was part of his research, or perhaps a reject from one of his *World's Worst Wireless Shows*?

While writing and researching this book, we have often asked ourselves what Kenny might be doing if he were alive today, a question which first arose after an interview with Paul Burnett, during which he recalled a conversation he'd had shortly after Kenny's death. 'I remember somebody coming up to me and saying, "Do you know the biggest shame of all, Paul? Kenny would have made such a wonderful senior citizen; a cheeky, irascible old curmudgeon, but lots of fun." And I thought yes, you're right. I think he'd have slipped into old age very nicely, going on his walks and making the odd jingle.'

After posing the same question to many other interviewees, we were left with an assortment of thought-provoking answers. The general consensus is that Kenny would have presented only occasionally, and would instead have been more involved in the development of technology. 'Imagine Kenny Everett with a Mac!' was one reply. Yet by far the most detailed, personal and heartfelt response came from Cate, who witnessed first-hand his burgeoning fascination with technology, not to mention his genius for presentation. She saw the birth of Kenny Everett, and a good ten years before he was given the name:

'If Ev were alive today he would be the Grand Dame of radio and television, and I for one would be campaigning for him to receive a Knighthood. Ev's misdemeanours were nothing compared to many who've been awarded them. He had four long-term boyfriends, so what? He was impetuous and would tell the press whatever they wanted to hear, so what? He went to Maggie Thatcher's rally, so what? He was scrupulously honest and brave. He did a lot for charity and a lot for the entertainment industry, but especially radio. In the sixties and seventies he was the benchmark to aspire to in terms of being a radio entertainer, and I think he still is. He was the George Martin of the wireless. George Martin helped the Beatles turn their songs into brilliant records, just as Kenny changed the radio format of the time, injecting far more lustre, fun and humour so it could be better enjoyed by a generation of British listeners. George Martin produced the music, but Kenny produced the environment. That makes me very proud.'

37

A Great Legacy

KENNY EVERETT COULD create pictures with sound in a way that had never before been heard on the radio. What he put between the records was as interesting and entertaining as the songs he played, and there aren't many DJs you can say that about. 'Kenny was one of the few DJs where you wanted the records to end to hear what he was going to do next,' says Johnnie Walker. 'He was just so entertaining.'

Sometimes his shows seemed like organized mayhem, like those of his heroes, the Goons. 'He was so funny on the radio,' says Sir Cliff Richard. 'Completely zany, like a one-man *Goon Show*, and I was a great fan of the Goons, too. Just talking into a record, he'd find something to say that was a hoot. I guess that's why he was so popular, because he changed it from just being somebody who said, "And this is . . . and that was the song title," he actually made it fun to listen to his show.'

Words like 'genius', 'one-off' and 'unique' are bandied around so readily today that they have lost all meaning, but leaving aside everything else, what Everett did technically, just the sheer wizardry of what he did with the equipment that was available then, is frankly astonishing. 'What he did technically is probably beyond what any DJ has ever done technically,' believes Paul Gambaccini. What he couldn't do with a reel-to-reel tape recorder wasn't worth doing. 'To be able to record all those amazing harmonies,' says Nicky Horne, 'when you only had a quarter-inch machine and bouncing backwards and forwards from one to the other, and masking the loss of quality – because it's not like digital; every time you bounce something across it's second generation, third generation, fourth generation. The quality was reduced so you had to be very technically adept at knowing how far you could push this antediluvian technology, and he pushed it to its absolute limit.'

His presentation seemed to sum up the spirit of the age, and it was a changing age. It was a spirit of a future age as well as a spirit of itself. Kenny didn't simply play or introduce records, he didn't just read out news, he turned the whole thing into a quick-fire pantomime, and that in many ways is what the best kind of radio presenting has become, in a much more staid and formulaic way. 'Kenny paved the way for all those Chris Evans and Chris Moyles types,' believes Leo Sayer. 'And he opened the door for all radio DJs who wished to self-engineer and produce their own programmes.'

He was a genius on so many levels: the jingles, the voices, the Captain Kremmen stuff. Analyse the technical side of a Captain Kremmen episode, and the attention to detail is gobsmacking. He was a genius on that level. He was a genius on the writing level. He was a genius on the simple, presentation level. He was a genius when it came to creating characters. On so many different levels, he excelled. 'Kenny was the one person that used radio creatively,' says Annie Nightingale. 'His approach to radio was different to anybody else anywhere.'

One early trick he mastered, and before anyone else, was the art of being able to remove the vocal track from a record. Because of the ping-pong stereo of early Beatles albums and the like, where instruments are on one side and vocals on the other, Kenny could uncover the instrumental backing in order then to add his own harmonies. In essence, he was an early pioneer of karaoke.

Now is perhaps the time to reassess Kenny's incredible contribution to popular culture. 'I would say there's nobody around to touch him today,' says Tony Blackburn. 'There isn't another Kenny Everett anywhere. He was quite unique.' People need to begin to sift through it all. Not just to pick out the good bits, but to appreciate the consistency and the genius. He produced an extraordinarily high standard of broadcasting, consistently, for the best part of thirty years. Who else has done that? And when it came to the radio stuff, it was just him.

There were no writers. Even the producers were more often than not there to help choose the records and assist. The creativity though, was him and him alone. It's almost too vast, really. 'I think of him as one of the geniuses of British radio,' says journalist Matthew Parris. 'If any DJs are ever remembered in the future, I really think he'll be right up there with the best who ever existed. He was absolutely brilliant. Day after day, year after year, he was just so funny and so quick. I don't know how spontaneous it all was but it always seemed like it was. There was nothing routine about his shows.'

Perhaps the most remarkable thing about Kenny isn't the admiration that he elicits, but how much he was genuinely loved by those who worked with and knew him. 'There are only three DJs who I've known over the years where I have never, ever heard a bad word said about them: Kenny, Gambaccini and Fluff,' reveals Nicky Horne. 'Kenny, he was just a very lovable character, and not the madcap, zany one that everyone knows. When he was off duty, if you will, he was just as lovable and actually really quite vulnerable, and it was that vulnerability that was part of his charm.'

Yet he opened up to very few people. Many of his contemporaries have spoken about an inability to get past the façade that he put up and to interact with the 'real' Kenny. 'He was a very troubled person,' believed his old Capital Radio boss, Michael Bukht. 'And he used broadcasting as a means of relating to the world in a way that nobody else ever did. He was on the edge a lot of the time and he used broadcasting as a means of staying sane, because he could put the various bits of himself forward without risking them.'

There was a childlike quality to Kenny, too. There was never any malice in what he did. 'He was well loved by all types of people,' says Sir Cliff Richard. 'And he appealed to all types of people. And I'm sure it's because of this lack of malice. They felt comfortable watching him and certainly as an artist I felt comfortable working with him and I trusted him completely.'

He could be petulant, though. Barry Cryer tells a great story about dining with Kenny in a restaurant with a group of people. One of the guests was extremely overbearing. He kept on talking over everybody and trying to dominate the table. 'After a while I looked over at Ev, who was staring at this idiot with a marvellous glint in his eye. The kind that said, "I really don't like you." He finished his meal and said, "Oooh, is that the time? I'm off, Baah. Goodnight," and got up to leave. He then walked over to this man and said, "And goodnight to yooou," before picking up this man's plate and pouring its contents very slowly and very deliberately over his head. This man was lost for words. There's pasta coming down his face and he just sat there with his mouth open.'

Kenny could be impatient and frustrating, too, but that was his creativity. He was a child and almost constantly in need of love, affection and attention. And he could and would play up sometimes. 'That's the element that made him a genius, in a way,' believes John Alkin. 'Because even when he was in his thirties and forties, he never lost the child inside him, it was part of his sense of humour, what inspired him. There was a childlike quality about him. He was always looking for the next laugh, the next high – not necessarily chemical – the next technical gizmo.'

Imagination was another secret to Kenny's success and when he moved seemingly effortlessly into television it showed that his imagination recognized no boundary between mediums, becoming, in the estimation of critic Clive James, 'The most original mind on TV.' But Everett did not truly enjoy his status as a television star, and one wonders how much of his overall success he could truly sit back and take pride in. Wilfred De'Ath, the man who first brought the young and callow Maurice Cole to London, remembers an enlightening conversation he had with Kenny in the early seventies. 'Kenny had to be nice to me,' says De'Ath, 'because he said to me once, "I owe it all to you." He actually said that to me. And he said a very interesting thing: "You took the little fish out of the pond and sometimes I wish you hadn't, sometimes I wish you'd thrown me back in." He'd obviously gone through some difficult times and wondered whether all this success was worth it. You see, I don't think he expected to become a famous disc jockey – but he did.'

The world is a much sadder place without Kenny. He brought the radio alive and was a 'must' to listen to. 'No other DJ has come up to his high standard of creativity,' states fellow Radio 1 jock Keith Skues. 'Fifty is far too young to die. I attended his funeral, and even then we all half expected him to pop out of his coffin and say, "It's all done in the best possible taste!"'

And what of Kenny's legacy? In the context of everything he accomplished, it's a simple one at the end of the day, believes Chris Tarrant: 'I still can be driving along in London in a traffic jam, frustrated, bad tempered, and I will suddenly think about something daft that Kenny Everett said on the radio twenty-five years ago and I look in the mirror and I'm smiling. I think that's a great legacy.'

Acknowledgements

First and foremost, we would like to thank Kenny's family for granting us permission to write this book, but especially his sister Cate, who has worked tirelessly with us these past two years, despite having several other mountains to climb.

We are also indebted to the all of the following, who spoke to us on numerous occasions and between them offered us all manner of Kenny-related bits – not all of them naughty: John Alkin, Lee Everett Alkin, Johnny Beerling, Paul Burnett, Barry Cryer, Eric Gear, Jo Gurnett, Simon Hirst, Kevin Howlett, Geoff Mullin and Andy Simons.

Every interview for this book has been enjoyable and we're extremely grateful to all who've taken part: Rod Argent, Mike Batt, Wayne Bickerton, Philip Birch, Lord Birt, Kevin Bishop, Tim Blackmore, Noel Blanc, Sue Blyth, Simon Booker, David Briggs, Mike Brown, Peter Brown, Dave Cash, Jess Conrad, Brian Cosgrove, Wilfred De'Ath, Pete Drummond, Russ Evans, David Essex, Paul Gambaccini, Bruce Gowers, Germaine Greer, David Hamilton, Jenny Hanley, David Hawkins, Peter Hince, Rupert Hine, Nicky Horne, David Jensen, Duncan Johnson, Bob Kerr, Jonathan King, Oliver Lansley, Neil McDonald, David Mallet, Royston Mayoh, Jim Moir, Jon Myer, Laurence Myers, Kara Noble, Annie O'Neill, Ron O'Quinn, Matthew Parris, Andy Peebles, Chris Peers, Mitch Philistin, Arlene Phillips, Mike Quinn, Emperor Rosko, Sir Cliff Richard, Leo Sayer, Maurice Sellar, Keith Skues, David Smith, Sheila Steafel, Dave Symonds, Chris Tarrant, Richard Taylor, Ben Tony, Mike Vickers, Johnnie Walker, Paul

Walker, Clive Warner, Julian Lloyd Webber, Mike Webster, Bill Wilson, Mark Wirtz and Peter Young.

We are also grateful to the following for their time and assistance: Louie Barfe, John Dredge, Georgy Jamieson, Tony Kennedy, Spencer Leigh, Mark Lewishon, Marc Morris at Nucleus Films, David Noades, Scott Owen, Chris and Mary Payne from the indispensable www.radiolondon.co.uk, Richard Porter, Mark Robinson, Cleo Rocos, Paul Rowley, Ian Watkins and Andy Walmsley.

Special thanks to our friend and supporter Joe Henderson, our agent Tim Bates, our editor Michelle Signore and absolutely everyone at Transworld Books.

Photo Acknowledgements

All images have been supplied courtesy of the parties listed below. Every effort has been made to contact the copyright holders. We apologize for any ommisions in this respect and will be pleased to make the appropriate acknowledgements in any future edition.

Pages 8, 3 (top), 7 (bottom), 16 (top), 17 (bottom), 19, 20, 21, 24: photos reproduced courtesy of Cate Horgan.

Page 2: photos reproduced courtesy of Tony Kennedy.

Pages 3 (bottom), 4, 5, 6, 8, 9, 10, 11, 12, 13, 14, 15, 16 (bottom): photos reproduced courtesy of Lee Everett Alkin.

Pages 7 (top) and 17 (top) © Rex Feaures.

Pages 18 (top), 22, 23: reproduced courtesy of Eric Gear.

Page 18 (middle and bottom): reproduced courtesy of Geoff Mullin.

Bibliography

The Custard Stops at Hatfield by Kenny Everett, Willow Books, 1982.

In The Best Possible Taste by David Lister, Bloomsbury Publishing, 1996.

Fun at One: The story of comedy at Radio 1 by Tim Worthington, www.lulu.com, 2012.

Radio 1: The Inside Scene by Johnny Beerling, Trafford Publishing, 2008.

He Sounds Much Taller – Memoirs of a Pirate by Dave Cash, www.davecashwebsite.com, 2012.

Matt Monro: The Singer's Singer by Michele Monro, Titan Books, 2010.

The Reporter's Tale by Tom Davies, Berwyn Mountain Press, 2009.

Index

Having researched comedy since his mid-teens, **James Hogg** started writing in 2005. His first book, the biography of James Robertson Justice, *What's the Bleeding Time?* was published in 2008. He also collaborated with Robert Sellers on *Little Ern! The Authorized Biography of Ernie Wise*. After a fifteen-year stint in sales, James now devotes his time purely to writing and researching.

Robert Sellers is the author of more than ten books on popular culture, including the bestselling *Hellraisers* series, as well as the definitive book on the genesis of the Bond franchise, *The Battle for Bond*, and the true history of Handmade Films, *Very Naughty Boys*. His latest book is the authorized biography of Oliver Reed.

James Hogg and Robert Sellers have unrivalled access to exclusive Kenny Everett content, including audio, interviews and photographs. To access their exclusive content archive visit www.kennyeverettcomedy.com